Stories of the Holocaust

"Clearly, we haven't done enough. If over a quarter of our youth believe the Holocaust is a myth, we need to both admit our shortcomings, and reconfigure our approach. The Holocaust needs to no longer be stories from the grave, nor talking heads who preach, but rather to be imbued with life and creativity. Our answer may lie in these pages. Stories of the Holocaust may just very well be our new playbook."

–Rabbi Shmuel Lynn, Executive Director,
Olami Manhattan, Theatrical Writer and Producer

STORIES OF THE HOLOCAUST:

Art for Healing and Renewal

VOLUME I

Onstage and in Concert

Edited by Karen Berman, Ph.D., and Gail Humphries, Ph.D.

International Psychoanalytic Books (IPBooks)
New York • http://www.IPBooks.net

Stories of the Holocaust: Art for Healing and Renewal–Volume I

Published by IPBooks, Queens, NY

Online at: www.IPBooks.net

Copyright © 2024 Karen Berman, Ph.D., and Gail Humphries, Ph.D. (Editors)

All rights reserved. This book may not be reproduced, transmitted, or stored, in whole or in part by any means, including graphic, electronic, or mechanical without the express permission of the author and/or publisher, except in the case of brief quotations embodied in critical articles and reviews.

Cover design by Kathy Kovacic.

Cover photo by Tom Caravaglia of *Cat's Cradle*, Carolyn Dorfman Dance.

Music on cover is from *Sonata for Cello and Piano—Mir zaynen do!* composed by Dr. Laurence Sherr.

ISBN: 978-1-969031-04-5

Table of Contents

Foreword:	Can Art Heal Trauma? Joshua Sobol	ix
Acknowledgments		xiii
Preface:	Art As An Imperative for Healing: Stand Up Against Hate Karen Berman, Ph.D. and Gail Humphries, Ph.D.	xvii
Introduction:	The Purpose in Memorializing Stories of the Holocaust Karen Berman, Ph.D. and Gail Humphries, Ph.D.	1
Part I	A Call to Action: Never Again	11
	Reflection The Complexity of Context: Voices of Hatred and Heroism Lori Weintrob, Ph.D.	11

Stories Onstage

Chapter 1	The Visionary Art of Čapek: A Call to Action Karen Berman, Ph.D. and Paul G. Accettura, Esq.	17
Chapter 2	The Staged Process for *The Diary of Anne Frank:* A Universal Voice Miřenka Čechová, Ph.D.	43
Chapter 3	*Signs of Life*: Finding These Signs Within You Through Theatre Virginia S. Criste, Esq. and Joan Liman, M.D., M.P.H.	67
Chapter 4	Healing Through Talkbacks and Difficult Dialogues: Creating a Safe Space for Empathic Understanding Sara Herrnstadt Crosby, M.S.W., CSW-PIP	89

Stories in Concert

Chapter 5   Music of Resistance and Survival: Composition, Performances, and Education for Understanding and Healing   109
Laurence Sherr, D.M.A.

Chapter 6   Silent Echoes: Dancing to Rise   131
Carolyn Dorfman

Part II   Healing Through the Pain: The Arts as Provocateur and Lifeline   143

Reflection Holocaust Stories: Resistance, Renewal, Recognition   143
David Crespy, Ph.D.

Stories Onstage

Chapter 7   Children's Stories from Terezín: I Leave You These   149
Gail Humphries, Ph.D.

Chapter 8   Holocaust Impact Theater: Utilizing Theater as a Catalyst for Acceptance and Respect   161
Ruth Gordon

Chapter 9   This is What I've Scene: Teaching the Holocaust Through Theatre   183
Mira Hirsch

Chapter 10   *The Eichmann Trial*: A Theatrical Interpretation   197
Motti Lerner
English translation by Shoshana Olidort, Ph.D.

Stories in Concert

Chapter 11   Music in Terezín: Creativity in Chaos   217
Wendy A. Mullen, D.M.A.

Chapter 12   Small Dances About Big Ideas: Moving Past the Limits of Dancing About Genocide   239
Liz Lerman

TABLE OF CONTENTS

Part III	Embedding Remembrance	259
	Reflection The Importance of Witnessing the Unbearable Nancy R. Goodman, Ph.D.	259

Stories Onstage

Chapter 13	"They Escape": Paula Vogel's *Indecent*, LGBTQIA+ Issues, and Genocide Bess Rowen, Ph.D.	265
Chapter 14	A Mosaic of Hope: Haunting Echoes of the Holocaust on Stage Gail Humphries, Ph.D.	285
Chapter 15	Nazi Whores, Kapos, and Collaborators: The Women of *Pankrác '45* Karin Rosnizeck	297
Chapter 16	Hine Ma Tov: A Devised Theatre Project with Holocaust Survivors and Adolescents Valérie Issembert and Tim Reagan, Ph.D.	321

Stories in Concert

Chapter 17	Performing *Defiant Requiem*: The Journey of a Messenger Not a Scholar Murry Sidlin with Karen Berman, Ph.D.	339
Chapter 18	The Piano: How We Survived Manuela Mendels Bornstein as told to Karen Berman, Ph.D.	363
Appendix 1	Holocaust Theater: Representation or Misrepresentation speech by Arnold Mittelman	387
Appendix 2	Study Guide for Voices of Terezín Gail Humphries, Ph.D.	397
Editors		**441**
Volume 1 Contributors		**443**

Foreword

Can Art Heal Trauma?

Joshua Sobol

To say that the Jewish people are traumatized, traumatized by the irreversible event that was the Shoah and traumatized still by the ever recurring monster of antisemitism, is to say a truism.

What are the characteristics of a traumatized society?

People in a post-traumatic condition tend to remember the sensations and emotions they experienced at the moment the trauma was inflicted upon them, but they tend not to remember the chain of events that sparked and caused the trauma.

People tend to remember the anxiety, the feeling of fear, the shock they experienced at the time the trauma took place. They will scarcely remember what has really happened at the most difficult moments.

Later, they will invent a story with a whole set of details to explain their terror and shock. Those imagined details and the story they will make up will have a psychological logic. Their story will be logical, and therefore not really true to the authentic facts. At the same time, their story will not necessarily be wholly false. True data will be brought forth alongside imaginary facts. It will all be finally arranged to form a convincing, trustworthy narrative that can be transmitted as a legacy from generation to generation. It is the trustworthiness and reasonability that will prevail more and more as the made-up narrative, and not the true plain memory, will be related time and again.

The more the story is recapitulated, the more elegant the narrative becomes, and the farther it is withdrawn from the true course of events that caused the trauma. If this description is true to the nature of post-traumatic storytelling and plotting, there are a few pertinent questions that impose themselves.

1. Can the concocted narrative be repeated time and again without creating a so-called imaginary, made-up memory?
2. Does a legendary memory help people to overcome and to outgrow the post-traumatic condition?
3. Is it in the interest of the community to cherish figmental memories?

The spinning of imaginary yarns is one degree of separation from the post-traumatic condition, yet it is not a full denial of the trauma. Fanciful or imprecise as it may be, it is still an attempt to deal with the trauma.

My play *Ghetto*, written in 1983, which tells the story of the Vilnius ghetto theatre during the occupation of Lithuania by the Nazis, was inspired by documents written in the Vilna ghetto between 1941 and 1943. Yet the play that seeks to capture a tragic moment in history is no less appealing to the imagination since a major role is held by a dummy.

It is, at first glance, a distortion of "realism;" however, the ventriloquist's doll, free of any angst, including the human fear of death, can act in a way that human beings cannot and would not dare to do in the face of the "Angel of Death" represented by a ruthless Nazi brute. "The puppet embodies a perfection inaccessible to man," says Heinrich von Kleist. The play ends with the massacre of the comedians followed by the murder of the puppet, which may be understood as the ultimate realization of the Nazi project: the terminal and absolute destruction of humanity and its soul.

FOREWORD

When I was writing the play, at the moment I invented the Dummy, I was aware that it was a figment of my imagination, but, from its first appearance, the fearless Dummy imposed itself and established its status in the realm of the drama with an imperious presence that made it impossible to continue composing the drama without it. I did not know, and I did not ask myself, what it was that the Dummy stood for. As a dramatist I trusted the figure that emerged from some dark precinct of the imagination. At the same time, I knew that the killing of the Dummy would mark the end of the drama. It was only after the play made the tour of the world, and after I directed performances of *Ghetto* in Germany, Austria, Israel, and China, that I realized what the Dummy embodied. It incarnated the pertinence of the human spiritual courage that discovered its expression in the founding of a theatre in the Vilna ghetto and, in its unbelievable audacious functioning under the most horrendous circumstances. Yet, in actual reality, there has been no Dummy in the Vilna ghetto theatre.

The second degree of separation is the plain and simple rejection of any narrative that may remind the members of a community of their post-traumatic condition. This phenomenon of denial is characterized by indulging in stories and developing narratives that have nothing to do with the trauma or the post-traumatic experience. It goes together with an escapist policy of the culture and art institutions. The theatres will play the most irrelevant comedies or melodramas, and audiences will flock to fill up the halls that offer them that anesthetic stuff. At the same time, the artistic directors of those institutions will reject any play that may try to come to grips with the traumatic subjects.

Conclusion

The playwright working in a traumatized society has got to make a choice: whether to offer his audience a theatre that will anesthetize it and let it go gently into the good night of unawareness of fallacious narratives, or to rage against the dying of the light, and not let society continue to adopt the false arguments that engender a self-justifying indulgence in bad faith. To rage against the dying of the light involves being stigmatized as an "enemy of the people" and paying the full price for being an enemy of the established ruling power structure. Sometimes Art must first heal itself of self-imposed mutism and censorship before it can start to heal the traumas of society.

Acknowledgments

Karen Berman, Ph.D. and Gail Humphries, Ph.D.

We thank each and every contributor to these books for their dedication to the importance of standing up against hatred, bigotry and antisemitism and for their courage to facilitate profound understanding of the Holocaust through the arts.

Our deep appreciation is extended to IP Books and Tamar Schwartz and Larry Schwartz, as well as Arnold Richards for their vision, tenacity and guidance throughout the process of creating the two volumes. Thank you to typesetter Noel Morado and cover artist Kathy Kovacic.

We wish to thank Paul Accettura for his proofreading and organizational contributions without which the editing of these books could not have been completed.

DR. KAREN BERMAN

My work is dedicated to my parents, the late Dr. Jerome Berman and Mrs. Betty Green Berman, Esq. who nurtured my creativity, empathy and the ethics of Judaism.

My grandparents, Samuel and Zelda Berman and Max and Mary Green, immigrants from Eastern Europe, are present in the heart and spirit of these books.

I extend deep gratitude to my dear husband Paul Accettura whose understanding, support and wise counsel guided me each step of the way through the process.

These volumes are in honor of my sisters, Ellen Berman and Sally Berman.

Special thanks to Cindy Homel Stoerchle, MS, LMFT whose wisdom undergirded all my efforts.

Thank you to Guy Ben-Aharon for his help in acting as a resource in connecting us with Joshua Sobol for his foreword. Gratitude is also extended to Mike Weinroth for connecting me with survivor Manuela Mendels Bornstein whose story is told in these books.

These books are a tribute to all the students, faculty, and staff at Georgetown University and Georgia College & State University, including Dr. Wendy Mullen and Dr. Dwight Call, as well as Dr. Standa Bohadlo of the University of Hradec Králové, who delved into the arts of the Holocaust with me and inspired me to write these books.

Dr. Gail Humphries

My work is dedicated to my father, the late William Carroll Humphries, who first introduced me to the Holocaust as a young girl growing up in Pennsylvania through his dear friend Max Tailor, who survived Auschwitz.

I applaud each artist and every student that I worked with on substantive and difficult dialogue through the theatre—at American University, Stephens College and professionals in Prague, Czech Republic and at the Academy of Performing Arts also in Prague.

I am grateful to Dr. Nancy Goodman who introduced me to the possibilities of witnessing when viewing the Holocaust through the arts.

My gratitude to the late Dr. Felix Kolmer who survived three camps and still imbued me with hope and inspiration with his wisdom and insight.

ACKNOWLEDGMENTS

Thank you to Charles Mallory Dean for your uplifting spirit.

Special gratitude is extended to my dear friends and colleagues Cheryl Black and Dorothy Chansky for sharing their special gifts and talents in the final stages of preparation for publication.

This work would not have happened without the support of my daughter, Maria Breeskin McLain, and the joyful times I spent with my grandchildren, Declan and Lennox, whose spirits always lifted me up and also grounded me with joy throughout the process of generating these books.

PREFACE

Art As An Imperative for Healing: Stand Up Against Hate

Karen Berman, Ph.D.
Gail Humphries, Ph.D.

The Point of Departure: Personal Context and Conviction

The contemporary world begs pertinent questions about the relationship of the Holocaust to our times. In these two volumes, we challenge our audiences to consider the significance of the events of the Holocaust relevant to our time through the unique power of telling stories through the arts. Each of the co-editors experienced pivotal moments in their lives that provided seminal events for the generation of this work.

The crosses burned on co-editor Berman's mother's lawn by the Ku Klux Klan in the mountains of Toccoa, Georgia are small flames in comparison with the contemporary signs signaling unrest in our nation, including violence by domestic terrorists against synagogues. Yet this violence has incendiary antecedents in the quota system that restricted entrance to medical school to only a handful of Jews in each class (Halperin, 2019), of which Berman's father was one of the lucky few. This systematic discrimination against Jews in U. S. medical and dental schools, which was later acknowledged by the universities, stifled many Jews from achieving their aspirations to help society.

ART FOR HEALING AND RENEWAL

Dr. Karen Berman remembers her first introduction to the Shoah as a 13-year-old seeing a devastating documentary film on the Holocaust at summer camp, away from home, after Berman's history teacher declared there had been no Holocaust. As a Hillel advisor for 13 years, Berman viewed, and continues to view, antisemitic acts against students in the climate of antisemitism nationally and internationally. Antisemitic political rhetoric and hate crimes are escalating. K-12 schools, of which only 23 states require Holocaust education (Kornbluh, J. (2022), have done a poor job at educating about World War II. Globally, there is an expansion of authoritarian leaders. Co-editor Dr. Gail Humphries remembers that imprint and lasting impact made on her life as a young girl growing up in Pennsylvania upon seeing a number tattooed on a survivor's arm while sitting in a kitchen, and his sorrow describing his wife's and children's deaths at Auschwitz.

The authors have been creating art nationally and internationally about the Holocaust for more than 50 cumulative years, Dr. Humphries as a Fulbright Scholar and Dean of a School of Creative and Performing Arts, and Dr. Berman as a Theatre and Dance Chair. Thus, these co-editors were compelled to redress these historical and contemporary attacks on human rights by embarking on this book. Friends for thirty years, the co-editors with converging interests in the Holocaust in both educational and professional settings, united on this challenging storytelling journey.

National Medal of Arts winner Joan Didion wrote in the first line of her book *The White Album*, "We tell ourselves stories in order to live" (Didion, 1979, p. 11). So, too, did the victims of Nazi persecution generate visual and performing arts to tell stories in order to live. Through our work, we honor their stories. Their artistic accomplishments were used to reckon, heal and renew, to assert individuality and to give meaning to lives lived in inhumane circumstances. Modern and contemporary arts onstage, in concert, on the screen, and in the gallery keep their stories alive through new artistic creations which revitalize their pertinent messages for future generations. In these two volumes composed of integrative studies, we have addressed the ways arts can re-represent the Holocaust. In Volume I, we present the arts onstage and in concert. In Volume II, we present the Holocaust on screen and in the gallery. However, these chapters investigate artistic expression as more than just a reminder of the past, but as a herald of ways the arts respond to current political hate messages, antisemitism, and violence. These messages constitute a vigorous call to action.

Artists/scholars in our work converge with creative voices and insight for stories that cultivate empathy and understanding through the arts. Like psychologist Dr. Gilbert Rose (1999), the editors believe that art created out of trauma engenders not only the ability to understand, but the capacity to feel. It is with this perspective on empathy and change that we honor and commemorate the victims of the Holocaust. Opening one's mind to the possibility of empathy affords personal choice and healing. Survivor Dr. Victor E. Frankel, neurologist and psychiatrist and survivor, poignantly discusses the importance of taking responsibility for the right answer, right action and right conduct in our lives (Frankel, 2006). Let the lessons of the Holocaust be remembered forever through the art, dance, film, museum exhibitions, music, and theatre that continue to trumpet the resounding message: *Never Again.*

The Arts as a Force for Change

For all of our contributors, these two volumes are a responsibility and a privilege that compel personal and community change. Thus, a prestigious cadre of scholars, practitioners, survivors, and artists have assembled in a unique collaborative sharing to catalyze a journey and educate the next generations.

Contributors provide tangible examples of artwork, lesson plans, playscripts, study guides, and approach methodologies to educate and to empower learners. The chapters present an array of approaches including memoirs, interviews, traditional scholarship, visual essays, and case studies. These examples facilitate action which we define as: learn, teach, advocate. We contend that the arts provide an empathetic pathway to these goals for impactful results.

Passionate contemporary authors from eight countries embrace themes of healing and metamorphosis to revisit the Holocaust using contemporary methodologies to re-represent history in these chapters. The contributors consist of survivors, second and third generation survivors, Jewish and non-Jewish artists, practitioners, museum curators, and scholars—all of whom act as witnesses to the unbearable and who utilize the arts as a catalyst for change. Topics range from powerful visual essays on art and dance representing the Shoah, and filmic and stage productions of music and drama that promote transformation and justice, to innovative art gallery installations that provide unique opportunities to hear and see survivor stories. Authors reveal the leaps of defiance and faith of the victims. The scope and breadth of themes, discussing both victims and perpetrators, present art to promote paths to restoration.

Both the trauma of silence for some survivors and the echoing voices of many enable a solemn remembrance and intervention to impact bodies, minds and hearts. In their introduction to *The Power of Witnessing: Reflections, Reverberations, and Traces of the Holocaust*, psychologists Dr. Nancy Goodman and Dr. Marilyn B. Meyers note that "the power of witnessing creates space in which courage, resilience and connection are discovered" (Goodman & Meyers, 2012, p. xi). It is our intention that this power generate analyses and initiatives to sustain equality and respect for all individuals in the generation of a world that will not tolerate injustices such as the Holocaust.

Arts for Healing and Social Justice: Influences and Theoretical Foundation

These stories bring echoes from the past into our contemporary lives for healing and allow our society to witness, encounter, and understand the unthinkable to which readers may, or may not, have been present. As a leading scholar in the field of arts and wellness, Past President of the American Arts Therapy Association Shaun McNiff in his book, *Art-Based Research* (1998), has conducted abundant experimental research to prove that the arts heal. McNiff asserts that:

> Emotional difficulties are problems of the soul. It thus seems logical to relate to these problems through the language of the soul—the arts, which express the many nuances of emotional life through symbols, movements, and sounds corresponding to a person's inner feelings. The arts place a value on deepening the mysteries of life and opening ourselves to them with a conviction that the process of creatively engaging problems and tensions is healing. (2004, p. 291)

We provide significant practical and diverse examples of the ways in which art leads to healing and revival of the soul. Noted psychologist Dr. Batya Monder speaks to the power of art for the incarcerated in concentration camps "to facilitate survival and transform the external world, a world that threatened to become devoid of meaning ... with art helping survival widening one's vision and offering alternative perspectives and ways of seeing things" (Monder, 2013, p. 5). This outlook seems all too applicable for our contemporary world.

In the Jewish religion, the choice to embrace moral responsibility, repentance, peace and renewal is possible every year during the High Holy Days. For the authors, this process of self-reflection and change aligns with performance storyteller and educator Noa Baum's assertions in *A Land Twice Promised: An Israeli Woman's Quest for Peace* (Baum, 2016). As a creative change-maker, Baum espouses the transformative power of storytelling and art to confront hatred and to discover peace.

Judy Daniels and Michael D'Andrea (2007) highlight the work of multicultural mental health and genocide expert Eduardo Duran, who notes that victims seeking solace often experience "a failure to heal the soul wound that was transmitted intergenerationally as a result of the historic trauma that their ancestors experienced" (p. 2). In response to this trauma, Rabbi Edward Feld of the Jewish Theological Seminary asserts in *The Spirit of Renewal: Finding Faith after the Holocaust* "the overwhelming events we have seen demand speech; our inner being clamors for it" (Feld, 1995, p. xvi). Thus, this book gives voice to these imperative stories.

We also look to astonishing leaders who have inspired us to consider standing up against hatred, bigotry, racism and all forms of social injustice. In particular, we have been ignited by two artist-leaders, Vaclav Havel and Augusto Boal, who fought authoritarianism through a unity of both politics and the arts. While they are from very different regions of the world, their outlook as leaders converge as each of them applies their artistry to move us forward in the struggle for societal reform. In particular, playwright and first President of the Czech Republic Havel, imprisoned for his dissident plays, cautions us to take courage against totalitarianism (Havel, 2018). American historian Timothy Snyder notes in his introduction to and analysis of Havel's essay *The Power of the Powerless* that it is an indictment of apathy (Havel, 2018).

With the same deep conviction, nominee for the 2008 Nobel Peace Prize Brazilian theatre theorist and former city council member Augusto Boal utilizes the arts for restorative justice. Mady Schutzman and Jan Cohen-Cruz (1994) define the work of Boal's protest theatre for social change as "more likely the collusion of politics, art, and therapy ... testimony to their inseparability when dealing with issues of change" (p. 1).

Thus, this book serves as a humanitarian signpost for advocacy against hate, terrorism and genocide, with unique dimensions that converge with the arts, arts therapy, diplomacy, social work, and psychoanalytic theory. These approaches interweave to create a singular voicing—an exhortation encompassing artistic, social and political redress, for contemporary society, of all generations and all nations. As the great conductor and composer Leonard Bernstein said, "it is the artists of this world, the feelers and thinkers, who will ultimately save us, who can articulate, educate, defy, insist, sing, and shout the big dreams" (Bernstein, 1970, p. A-22). The hope is that the arts will educate—teaching history, inclusiveness, and empathy in the void left by bans on both books, such as *The Diary of Anne Frank* (Paul, 2022), and bans on teaching critical race theory (CBS News Miami, 2022).

Dr. Savneet K. Talwar, in her book *Art Therapy for Social Justice: Radical Intersections* (2019) believes, like the co-editors, that through creative and critical inquiry, the wounds of the Holocaust can become the foundation of expression, leading to growth. Dr. Talwar (2019) contends that:

> Artists, activists and cultural workers have used arts-based methodologies to demonstrate the link between critical inquiry and praxis when critiquing the social and personal consequences of violence, trauma, shame, and stigma ... when affect, memory, and feelings become the subject and method of analysis, feelings can be something useful in creating spaces for expression, creativity and hope. (p. 38)

We explore a wide range of artistry from the memories of children's poetry and drawings to adult symphonies reasserting humanity and uniqueness. The voices of the victims sing loudly throughout the universe. With the goal of

Tikkun Olam, to heal the world, we witness the resilience of Holocaust survivors despite pain, trauma, and violence through the mechanism of the arts. We summon future generations: beware and be aware; it is in your hands. Never again.

The Time is Now: The Importance of Re-Representing and Witnessing

We challenge our readers of these stories presented on stage, screen, and in the gallery, to consider how they can generate progress against antisemitism and violence. We envision this readership to include academics, students of history and the arts, survivors of trauma, psychologists, politicians, arts therapists, arts educators, curators, social scientists, and inquisitive readers.

It is that time when obligation propels us to act. Data from the Anti-Defamation League's Center on Extremism shows a 38 percent increase in white supremacist propaganda incidents in the United States from 2021 to 2022 with "a total of 6,751 cases reported in 2022, compared to 4,876 in 2021" (Center on Extremism, 2023, para. 1). Americans for the Arts research studies published in the National Arts Administration and Policy Publications Data Base on "The Value of the Arts" demonstrate that the arts are a prime mechanism for communication, understanding, and empathy (Americans for the Arts, 2022). The arts embody a people's heritage and history, as well as rouse emotion and inspire (Americans for the Arts, 2022). With a prospectus of the future and embracing a lens of insight to the past, this book is a signal and an attempt to generate a world that values respect, equity, and diversity.

In this era when hate groups (and even some politicians throughout the world) are marginalizing people and fanning the flames of hatred, it is time to sound the alarm. We must use our creative voices to fight. The notion of diversity is under siege, voting rights are imperiled, synagogues are attacked, swastikas appear in college dorms, and hate messages appear on the exteriors of synagogues and Holocaust museums. Politicians have been using hyperbole to compare minor events to the Holocaust, or twist legitimate legal procedures into calls against the Gestapo. The Anti-Defamation League has declared that racism, antisemitism and anti-immigrant views are fueling violent acts in the United States and throughout the world. The Anti-Defamation League states that in 2020, statistics demonstrate that there was a six percent increase in reported hate crimes from 2019 and it was the highest level in 12 years (ADL, 2021). While hate crimes increased against African Americans and Asian Americans, 60 percent of the religion-based hate crimes were against Jews (ADL, 2021). For example, Covid conspiracy theories in social media claimed that Jews caused Covid (Gerstenfeld, 2020). We can and should use the arts to combat this hate, to encourage introspection and social responsibility, to heal the nation and the world.

We must preserve the stories told in the arts and continue to tell them with intention and purpose. Elie Wiesel, Holocaust survivor, Nobel Peace Prize winner, and author of 57 books, including *Night*, in his 1986 Nobel Peace Prize Lecture, noted, "There may be times when we are powerless to prevent injustice, but there must never be a time when we fail to protest" (Wiesel, 1986, paragraph 29). Action is demonstrated in these chapters through personal change and growth as documented in journals, audience response, media reviews and assessment by each contributing author. Wiesel said "People become the stories they hear and the stories they tell" (Brown, 2022, p. 1).

Ongoing tragic events must be addressed, and the power of the arts is a significant force to address other genocides and large-scale violations of human rights. As the International Holocaust Remembrance Alliance (2022) states, "A clear and well-informed understanding of the Holocaust, the paradigmatic genocide, may help educators and students understand other genocides, mass atrocities, and human rights violations" (p. 1).

We turn to documentary filmmaker Ken Burns to bring Holocaust history to our present-day reality:

> So, like an amputated limb that you feel long after it's gone—it itches, it hurts, you feel like it's still there, a phantom ghost—those six million, I hope, will always continue to haunt us. And then finally it's about resonance. We are in this refugee crisis right now, and it speaks to the present day. (Rothman, 2016, p. 4)

The refugee crisis that Burns was speaking of resulted primarily from the Syria Civil War. However, according to Refugees International (2016), "in 2016, the world witnessed a global refugee crisis of historic proportions, with the number of refugees and displaced people reaching 65 million world-wide—the largest number since World War II" (p. 1). This crisis has continued, including instances of human rights persecutions of distinct populations such as the Rohingya community in Myanmar. The long-standing plight of Ethiopian Jews, the discrimination against ethnic Darfuri people in Sudan, and Russia's 2022 war on Ukraine are other examples of the long list of mass human rights violations. As Dr. Linda Woolf of Webster University stated, "Mass violence, torture, violations of fundamental human rights, and the mistreatment of human beings is not a new aspect of humanity; documentation of such events spans the historical record" (International Holocaust Remembrance Alliance, 2022, p. 1).

We hope that our work stirs the conscience and provides readers with the tools, wisdom and historical precedence to address genocides and human rights violations through the telling of stories through the arts. As Vaclav Havel so aptly reminds us, "For this reason, the salvation of this human world lies nowhere else than in the human heart, in the human power to reflect, in human meekness and in human responsibility" (Havel, 1990, para. 61). We challenge our readers to make a difference in combatting bigotry, hatred and genocide in our world.

References

ADL deeply alarmed by 2020 FBI hate crimes data; Reiterates calls for increased reporting (2021, August 30). https:www.adl.org/news/press-releases/adl-deeply-alarmed-by-2020-fbi-hate-crimes-data-reiterates-calls-for-increased.

Americans for the Arts, The Value of the Arts (n.d., retrieved February 4, 2022). https://www.americansforthearts.org/by-program/reports-and-data/legislation-policy/naappd/the-value-of-the-arts.

Baum, N. (2016). *A land twice promised: An Israeli woman's quest for speech.* Familius.

Bernstein, L. (1970, July 5). *Bernstein's message: Hope: Tanglewood address stresses artist's role in chaotic world. Boston Globe,* p p. A-19, 22.

Brown, B. (n.d., retrieved February 8, 2022). *Stories are just data with a soul.* Livingartscorp.org/what-we-do/story-telling.

CBS News Miami. (2022, March 10, 2022). Florida Senate passes bill banning teaching of critical race theory in schools, private businesses. https://www.cbsnews.com/miami/news/florida-senate-passes-critical-race-theory-ban-bill-schools/

Center on Extremism (2023, March 8). *White supremacist propaganda soars to all-time high in 2022.* ADL Center on Extremism. https://www.adl.org/resources/report/white-supremacist-propaganda-soars-all-time-high-2022

Daniels, J. & D'Andrea, M. (2007, June 18). *Trauma and the soul wound: A multicultural social justice perspective.* Counseling Today: A Publication of the American Counseling Association.
https://ct.counseling.org/2007/06/dignity-development-diversity-6.

Didion, J. (1979). *The white album.* Farrar, Straus and Giroux.

Feld, E. (1995). *The spirit of renewal: Finding faith after the Holocaust.* Jewish Lights.

Frankel, V. (2006). *Man's search for meaning.* Beacon Press.

Gerstenfeld, M. (2020). *Anti-Jewish coronavirus conspiracy theories in historical context.* Ramat Gan, Israel: Begin-Sadat Center for Strategic Studies.

Goodman, N. R. & Meyers, M. B. (2012). Preface: An Invitation. In N. R. Goodman & M. B. Meyers (Eds.), *The power of witnessing: Reflections, reverberations, and traces of the Holocaust* (pp. xi-xxiii). Routledge.

Halperin, E. C. (2019). Why did the United States medical school admission's quota for Jews end. *American Journal of the Medical Sciences,* 2019 Nov; 358(5), 317–325, doi: 10.1016/j.amjms.2019.08.005.

Havel, V. (1990, February 22). *Text of Havel's speech to Congress.* The Washington Post.
https://www.washingtonpost.com/archive/politics/1990/02/22/text-of-havels-speech-to-congress/df98e177-778e-4c26-bd96-980089c4fcb2/

Havel, V. (2018). *The power of the powerless.* Los Angeles: Random House.

International Holocaust Remembrance Alliance (2022). *The Holocaust and other genocides.*
https://www.holocaustremembrance.com/resources/educational-materials/holocaust-and-other-genocides

Kornbluh, J. (2022, August 10). *NY governor signs Holocaust education bill, citing spike in antisemitism.* Forward. forward.com/fast-forward/514007/new-york-gov-signs-holocaust-education-bill-citing-spike-in-antisemitism/.

McNiff, S. (1998). *Art-based research.* Jessica Kingsley Publisher.

McNiff, S. (2004). *Art heals: How creativity cures the soul.* Shambhala.

Monder, B. (2013). *Signs of Life.* International Psychoanalytical Association Congress. Prague, Cz.

Paul, M. L. (2022, August 18). *Anne Frank adaptation, 40 more books pulled from Texas school district.* The Washington Post. https://www.washingtonpost.com/nation/2022/08/18/anne-frank-book-school-texas/

Refugees International (2016, December 22). *The 2016 Global Refugee and displacement Crisis.* https://www.refugeesinternational.org/reports/2016/successes

Rose, G. J. (1999). *Necessary illusion: Art as "witness."* International Universities Press, Inc.

Rothman, L. (2016, September 20). *Ken Burns: Individual can change history.* Time Magazine. https://time.com/4496048/ken-burns-defying-nazis-interview/

Schutzman, M. & Cohen-Cruz, J. (1994). Introduction. In M. Schutzman & J. Cohen-Cruz (Eds.), *Playing Boal: Theatre, therapy, activism* (pp, 1–16). Routledge.

Talwar, S. K. (2019). Identity matters: Questioning trauma and violence through art, performance, and social practice. In S. K. Talwar (Ed.), *Art therapy for social justice: Radical intersections* (pp. 38- 65). Routledge.

Wiesel, E. (1986, December 11). *Elie Wiesel Nobel Lecture.* htpps://www.nobelprize.org/prizes/peace/1986/wiesel/lecture/

INTRODUCTION

The Purpose in Memorializing Stories of the Holocaust

Karen Berman, Ph.D.
Gail Humphries, Ph.D.

As two friends whose decades-long work in presenting Holocaust plays in the United States and abroad converged, our mission to disseminate the momentous value of the arts in Holocaust Studies ignited us in this endeavor. We are publishing these two volumes simultaneously to serve the wide range and scope of the performing and visual arts that we believe make a comprehensive and profound statement. Contemporary circumstances remind us to continue the crucial and critical fight against hatred and bigotry The cumulative voices within these volumes of such extraordinary scholars, teachers and artists resoundingly do just that. As such, the content of the two volumes is inextricably linked as an integrative study converging to generate a resonating call to action.

Representation and Misrepresentation

We are guided in this two-volume work by inspiration from one of our essayists, Arnold Mittelman, President of the National Jewish Theatre Foundation and long-time Producing Artistic Director of Coconut Grove Playhouse in Miami Florida, with whom we spoke as we embarked on our book journey. Mittelman (2012) states that the essential ethical responsibility of artists is to depict the Holocaust truthfully, accurately, and with accountability. In his January 10, 2012 speech titled "Holocaust Theater: Representation or Misrepresentation" (included as Appendix 1 in this book) to the Association of Holocaust Organizations, Mittelman (2012) addresses this challenge:

> How do we make certain that the power of artistic creation will always triumph over the powers of destruction? ... that will inspire future generations to understand this atrocity and create, in its memory, with their own unique voices? In part, we must define, ever vigilantly, what Holocaust Theater represents, and what it must never misrepresent. We must enlist professionals from many disciplines to reinforce this goal. And, finally, we must challenge ourselves to open our minds and provide to all of our audiences the great gift of theater [and the arts] as a unique tool in Holocaust education and awareness. (p. 6)

The co-editors agree and are inspired by Mittelman's wisdom. Our storytellers and artists in these books interpret events from their own creative viewpoints and from their own histories, bringing their own unique and sometimes divergent visions to the work.

Historical Ramifications and Memory

We acknowledge the historical ramifications of memory and authenticity, again utilizing Mittelman's (2012) insights when he says that:

> The other great dilemma that we all face is that the primary reporters of the Holocaust, the eyewitness survivors, have now reached an age where inevitably in the near future, their voices will not be heard except through recordings, manuscripts, and their portrayals within the framework of movies and theater. (p. 2)

Who will tell their stories when the authentic storytellers are no longer with us? The chapter authors who are eyewitness reporters or second and third generation family members bring singular authenticity to their work. However, the authors, whose souls have been touched by these primary reporters of the dreadful events of the Shoah, bring equal power and urgency to the performance of the Holocaust stories. The expressive arts embody the trauma of the events and attempt to turn them into lessons of resistance, hope, and renewal.

The chapters weave a tapestry of poetic personal reflections and artistry, practitioners' sharing of process and product, and scholarly research. The book is composed of case studies, memoirs, interviews, visual essays and grounded research. There is a unity of visionary reflection and personal dedication with the contributing authors as they tell the stories of the Holocaust to a world that should hear and view the stories. We say "no" to expressions of hatred and acts of antisemitism. We view our book as a tangible rallying cry by "upstanders" (Power, 2002) of "Never again."

The Storytellers and Their Stories: Intertextuality

We agree with survivor and artist Alice Koubova (Koubova, Urban, Russell & MacLean, 2021) that art intensifies facts and we present the intensified voicings of seasoned artists, teachers and scholars to that end. The intertextuality of art—the overlap of the literary and visual text, the texts of performers and the texts of the audiences—provide an impetus for reflection and action (Yordon, 2002 & Humphries, 2017).

Remembrance is a sacred responsibility in Judaism. Our wish is that the stories of the Shoah within these pages inspire positive action for diversity, understanding, empathy, healing and renewal. These authors bear witness to the ways in which art can educate future generations for allyship, empathy, and moral courage. These books commemorate artists who in extreme adversity had the courage to make art, which we re-represent in these pages.

Our focus of interrogation connects the Holocaust to the present times and considers the significance of the unique delineation of stories through the arts. Each of these books demonstrate the arts as stimulation for deep understanding and the generation of insight about the horrific circumstances of the Holocaust. They create a mosaic for understanding, empathy and provocative thinking to compel action in our contemporary world. These works also provide tangible examples of how theatre, art, dance, music, film, literature and galleries provide penetrating lenses for healing and renewal.

These two volumes include an international cadre of writers from countries that include the Czech Republic, France, Germany, Israel, Poland, Slovakia, the United Kingdom and multiple regions of the United States. These arts scholars and practitioners range from Holocaust survivors to prestigious members of academia, to notables in film, literature, museum studies, as well as the performing and visual arts. We acknowledge each member in the cadre of nationally and internationally acclaimed artists and scholars in performing, visual and creative arts who have contributed to the books. We anticipate that you will carefully examine the table of contents to discern the wide swath of contributors.

Structure of the Book and the Journey

Within these two volumes, we have divided the book into five parts. In Volume I, we explore stories onstage and in concert through theatre, dance, and music. In Volume II, we explore stories on screen and in the gallery encompassing film, visual arts and museum exhibitions. Each of the five sections contained within the two volumes is introduced by a Reflection, authored by notables within the disciplines, commenting on the individual and collective content of the designated section.

Foreword

The journey of this book begins with our central thesis question: Can Art Heal Trauma? Award-winning Israeli playwright Joshua Sobol and author of the play and film *Ghetto*, one of the most widely produced Holocaust plays in history, addresses this significant question in the Foreword.

Part I—A Call to Action: Never Again

In Part I of our book, "A Call to Action: Never Again," the contributors reveal the book's primary purpose to create social awareness and social change to prevent future human rights tragedies. While the authors considered making this section the climax of our thesis, we determined to examine this comprehensive goal first. Dr. Lori Weintrob, founding director of the Wagner College Holocaust Center, writes the Reflection, "The Complexity of Context: Voices of Hatred and Heroism," contextualizing our viewing of the Holocaust for newcomers to this history while embracing nuances and challenges for historians and seasoned readers.

Part II—Healing Through the Pain: The Arts as Provocateur and Lifeline

In Part II of our book, "Healing Through the Pain: The Arts as Provocateur and Lifeline," we assembled chapters that address the utilization of the arts as both a lifeline for victims and as a provocateur in addressing tragic events. We are humbled by art that emerged from the circumstances of oppression and which was employed as both protection and resistance.

Dr. David Crespy, University of Missouri professor, playwright, director, and Fulbright Senior Scholar, provides the Reflection titled "Holocaust Stories: Resistance, Renewal, Recognition." We stand on the shoulders of many scholars and theorists from multiple fields. Their outlooks and research provide a scaffolding and throughline for our work. Dori Laub and Daniel Podell (1995) wrote about work related to the Holocaust as "the art of trauma" (pp. 991–1005), a special kind of art that can imaginatively recreate traumatic events that defy representation. Dr. Crespy examines this perspective with exceptional insight gleaned from his personal history.

Part III—Embedding Remembrance

In Part III of our book, "Embedding Remembrance," we honor and remember the six million who perished to remind the world of the continuing threats to humanity that intolerance brings. These volumes bear witness in order to defy efforts of annihilation of memory. Noted psychoanalyst Dr. Nancy R. Goodman addresses "The Importance of Witnessing the Unbearable" in her Reflection. Her work with survivors and witnessing offers a learned and insightful perspective.

Part IV—Lessons for Change

Part IV of our book, "Lessons for Change," addresses how the arts and artists provide a template for action and, in so doing, challenges our readers to utilize these educational resources in the classroom, museum, and in creative arts spaces. Screenwriter, executive director, and author Dr. Rosanne Welch connects stories on film and in the gallery that manifest significant messages. In her Reflection "Art as Transcendence" she explores the ways the arts contain universal and enduring messages of hope. The physical experience and psychological ramifications lead to insight and action.

When the internationally renowned psychoanalyst Batya Monder (2013) responded to one of co-editor Dr. Humphries' productions of *Signs of Life* in Prague, she noted the power of art "to facilitate survival and transform the external world, a world that threatened to become devoid of meaning ... with art helping survival by widening one's vision and offering alternative perspectives and ways of seeing things." This transformation provides lessons for change.

Part V—Generating Empathy and Inspiration

Part V is titled "Generating Empathy and Inspiration." Reflection writer and award-winning playwright, philosopher, and professor dedicated to reckoning, connecting, and healing through the arts Caleen Sinnette Jennings speaks to "Leaps of Defiance and Faith: Reckon, Heal, and Renew."

The arts generate a compelling empathy and a means of speaking out that brings resonance for the heart, mind and even the soul. While these books focus on the lens of the Holocaust, the collective voicing of the authors provides a magnetic mechanism for empathy, generating a "space in which courage, resilience and connection are discovered" (Goodman & Meyers,

2012, p. xi). It is our intention that this power engender action and analysis to sustain equality and respect for all individuals in a world that will not tolerate injustices such as the Holocaust.

Afterword—Beyond Pain

The afterword of the book, titled "Beyond Pain," by Rabbi Joseph Prass, Director of the Weinberg Center for Holocaust Education at the Breman Jewish Heritage Museum in Atlanta, Georgia, reminds all of us of a mandate for tolerance, empathy and compassion. Mittelman (2012) said in his speech that the arts have the:

> unique power of telling these stories and individualizing the personas and their biographies, which is the exact opposite of what the Nazis attempted to do by depersonalizing, through numbers and mass deaths, the victims of the Holocaust. Therefore, every play [every art work] that is created, that has integrity, honesty, quality, and truth proves that the attempt to annihilate individuality did not succeed. (p. 2)

Glorious works of art, music, literature, poetry, music, theatre, and film have emerged to capture and generate memory. As Jewish people say when someone dies, may their memories be a blessing.

THE PURPOSE IN MEMORIALIZING STORIES OF THE HOLOCAUST

Our Resolve

Through our 33 chapters in these volumes we are guided by the principles in the Hebrew meaning of the number 33 (in Hebrew שלושים ושלוש). In Hebrew numerology, known as gematria, 33 refers to the resilience of the human spirit. The 33rd time Noah's name is repeated in the Bible represents God's promise after the flood, and a rainbow. 33 is the numeric equivalent of the word "Amen" uttered at the end of a prayer, and the representation of the star of David. These two volumes of our book, *Stories of the Holocaust: Art for Healing and Renewal Volume I. Onstage and in Concert* and *Stories of the Holocaust: Art for Healing and Renewal Volume II. On Screen and in the Gallery* are our response to the resilience generated by the arts for the survivors, hopefully providing inspiration for future generations.

References

Goodman, N. R. & Meyers, M. B. (2012). *The power of witnessing: Reflections, reverberations, and traces of the Holocaust.* Routledge.

Jewish Women's Archive (2010, October 19).

Humphries Mardirosian, G. (2017). A staged reading for remembrance, reminder, and inspiration: Traces in the wind. In P. L. Ellman & N. R. Goodman (Eds.) *The courage to fight violence against women: Psychoanalytic and multidisciplinary perspectives* (pp. 233–251). Routledge.

Koubova, A., Urban, P., Russell, W. & MacLean, M. (Eds.). (2021). *Play and democracy: Philosophical perspectives.* Routledge.

Laub, D. & Podell, D. (1995). *Art and trauma.* International Journal of Psychoanalysis, Oct. 76: Part 5 (pp. 991–1005). PMID 8926145.

Mittelman, A. (2012). (2012, January 10). *Holocaust theater: Representation or misrepresentation.* Speech to Association of Holocaust Organization. (Text is included as Appendix 1)

Monder, B. (2013). *Signs of life.* International Psychological Association Congress. Prague, Cz.

Power, S. (2002). *A Problem from hell: America and the age of genocide*, Basic Books.

Rovit, R. & Goldfarb, A. (Eds.). (1999). *Theatrical performance during the Holocaust: Texts, documents, Memoirs.* The Johns Hopkins University Press.

Yordon, E. (2002). *Role in interpretation.* McGraw Hill.

Part I—A Call to Action: Never Again

Reflection

The Complexity of Context: Voices of Hatred and Heroism

Lori Weintrob, Ph.D.

Artistic performances in ghettos and in concentration camps were acts of heroism which challenged Nazi efforts at dehumanization. Part I focuses on individuals defying Nazi oppression and why remembrance of their voices, and their courage and resilience, matters. The spectrum of educational, cultural, spiritual and armed resistance is explored in these chapters. Offering new interpretations of Nazi brutality and Jewish survival on stage, we recall the wartime suffering and defiance of men, women and children in perpetuity—and speak to the contemporary world. The profound and impactful nature of theatre, music and dance can contribute to a deeper sense of our shared humanity. Empowered with empathy, our generation and the next can say "Never Again."

As founding director of the Wagner College Holocaust Center, a significant focus of my teaching in recent years has been using the narratives of resilience of survivors from my own community. "Ordinary Jews," as so many contemporary authors have defined them, from Krakow, Warsaw and other sites in Nazi-occupied Europe made courageous choices. Our college students of all faiths select and study in context an impactful excerpt of eyewitness testimony. Learning under the guidance of my colleague theatre professor Theresa McCarthy, students emulate an acting technique developed by Anna Deavere Smith, learned dramatist and author of significant plays of the 21st century. This theatre project led us to co-author a Holocaust play with Obie-winning playwright Martin Moran centering on testimony from six survivors, *Rise Up: Young Holocaust Heroes*. Students are thus guided to critical reflection on how the Nazis rose to power, how persecution escalated and why it matters today. We pay particular attention to those who did not stand silent, exploring the spectrum of Jewish spiritual, cultural and armed resistance and heroic voices—as in this moving volume. Thus, the arts become a call to action, a moral imperative, the significant content of each chapter contained in Part I.

In their chapter "The Visionary Art of Čapek: A Call to Action," Dr. Karen Berman and Paul Accettura are cautionary about the warning signs of democracy's fragility in the past and in contemporary American society through their new play. They introduce audiences, including their own students, to the Czech writer Karel Čapek and the first President of Czechoslovakia Tomas Masaryk, enemies of bigotry and antisemitism. Despite their cries of alarm against fascism and dehumanization, international institutions that had pledged to protect the new, fragile nation broke their promises. Instead, Adolf Hitler's expansionist policies and war spelled doom for families there and across Europe, cutting short the dreams of millions.

In Chapter 2, *The Diary of Anne Frank: A Universal Voice*, choreographer, director and author Mirenka Čechová reflects on how to capture the disruption, destruction and genocide of a young generation of adults and children. She created a physical theatre production to speak to this issue. Intimate portraits of the vivaciousness of youth and other scenes from Anne's diary (first staged in 1955) come to life in sharp contrast to the inhumanity of life under the Nazi occupation of the Netherlands in this production staged in Prague, the United States, and South Africa. *The Voice of Anne Frank* abruptly and poignantly ends in a dark theatre, in which we might imagine her arrest, deportation to Auschwitz and her death in Bergen-Belsen on the eve of her 16th birthday.

In Chapter 3, "*Signs of Life*: Finding These Signs Within You Through Theatre," Virginia Criste and Joan Liman describe the development of a play they hope speaks to a multicultural audience about the Holocaust. They narrate how individuals trapped behind the walls of the Terezín ghetto and transit camp outside of Prague used the power of the arts to undermine Nazi efforts and provide sustenance. By focusing on the 1944 visit by Adolf Eichmann and the Red Cross to Terezín, they demonstrate the terrible and tragic consequences of subterfuge.

REFLECTION

To sustain the fight against hate and indifference, theatre and reflection on performances can be used to create trust and hope and to rebuild lives—the focus of Chapter 4. For example, in the wake of the genocide against the Tutsi in Rwanda, theatre has been a tool for constructing new relationships and community dynamics between perpetrators and survivors. Sara Herrnstadt Crosby, a clinical social worker and actor, discusses how theatre can help to address institutionalized racism in America as well as trauma, suicide, depression, misogyny and domestic violence. She speaks to the power of "Healing Through Talkbacks and Difficult Dialogues: Creating a Safe Space for Empathetic Understanding" in her chapter. In teaching the play *Traces in the Wind* developed by Gail Humphries, Crosby explains how talkbacks enabled audience empathy through the shared stories of three extraordinary female survivors who utilized the arts as a mechanism of survival.

In Chapter 5, "Music of Resistance and Survival: Composition, Performances and Education for Understanding and Healing," Dr. Laurence Sherr introduces Vilna poet Hirsh Glik's partisan song *Zog nit Keyn mol* (Never Say), the most famous Jewish anthem of resistance. In the defiant concluding refrain: *Mir zaynen do!* (We are here!) gives inspiration to Sherr's original *Sonata for Cello and Piano–Mir zaynen do!*. This music of resistance reminds us that over 30,000 Jewish men and women fought back as partisans against the Nazis and their collaborators. In fact, Glik also wrote an anthem to heroic female resistance fighters, "*Stil, di Nakht,*" (Quiet is the Night). Sherr weaves in Yiddish music, prayer and other powerful elements, including the unforgettable lullaby of Ilse (Herlinger) Weber, a German-Jewish children's author and radio producer. Weber's quiet heroism endures in defiance of the genocidal Nazi regime.

For those who survived, post-war life was marked by both trauma and the triumph over tragedies that were difficult to discuss and share. Carolyn Dorfman uses dance as an embodiment of the complexity of the struggles to vanquish oppression. In Chapter 6, "Silent Echoes: Dancing to Rise," Dorfman translates the universal message of overcoming trauma into movement. Her chapter enhances our understanding of the difficult journey encountered by refugees, immigrants and other displaced persons as they heroically attempt to rise above.

To understand how the Holocaust happened and why it matters, we need to discuss the complexity of the context that allowed hatred, as well as the heroism, to flourish. While the arts are often used to heal and resist, the Nazis chose to pervert culture for evil purposes. We must be wary of the power of music, the arts, and theatrical spectacle to promote anti-democratic values, as the Nazis widely implemented. Using the music of Richard Wagner, the *Horst-Wessel-Lied* and other folk tunes, the Nazis promoted nationalism, the *völkgemeinshaft* ("national community"), antisemitism [sometimes called anti-Jewish racism], and other forms of intolerance. German university students who sought to define "un-German" theatre and literature initiated nationwide book burnings. Joseph Goebbels' Ministry for Public Enlightenment and Propaganda, along with the Reich Culture Chamber (*Reichskulturkammer–RKK)*, excluded and attacked Jews, while offering prestige and power to artists who turned a blind eye to prejudice, discrimination and brutality. Our call to action is to speak up against oppression and indifference, past and present, and to become upstanders rather than bystanders.

The arts can offer resistance and resilience to those who seek to divide us with words and actions of hate. Art can convey emotions, of joy or despair, across geographical and cultural boundaries. The visual and performing arts can promote critical reflection that offers an antidote to anti-democratic forces and can elevate those who fought heroically with pistol and pen for human dignity and freedom. An examination of genocide is amplified by music, dance and theatre performances that promoted empathy, courage and shared values of humanity and morality.

CHAPTER 1

The Visionary Art of Čapek: A Call to Action

Karen Berman, Ph.D.
Paul G. Accettura, Esq.

Development and Process

Introduction

The creative work of the famous Czech brothers Karel Čapek and Josef Čapek is significant because it presages the impending occupation of the Nazis in Czechoslovakia. The playwriting, novels, and book illustrations of the Čapek brothers inspired the authors of this chapter to construct and tour an original play titled *The Vision of Čapek* (*Čapkovy Vize* in Czech). Playwright, novelist and journalist Karel Čapek used his visionary and prescient allegorical art, from his 1921 play *R.U.R. (Rossum's Universal Robots* or *Rossumovi Univerzální Roboti* in Czech) (Čapek & Čapek, 1923) to his last play in 1938, *The Mother* (or *Matka* in Czech) as calls to action, making impassioned warnings against the rise of Hitler and fascism (Čapek & Čapek, 1923; Kussi, 1990). His brother Josef, who illustrated many of his brother's books and co-wrote several, was arrested by the Nazis early in World War II and died in the Bergen-Belsen concentration camp in 1945, just before the concentration camp was liberated (Bradbrook, 1998, p. 20; Kussi, 1990, p. 24). This chapter's authors co-wrote

The Vision of Čapek to celebrate the Čapeks' social justice work and their prophetic efforts to try to guard Czech independence.

With the resurgence of authoritarianism in contemporary society, the authors of this chapter—mirroring the Čapek brothers' works—wrote the original play *The Vision of Čapek* as a current day call to action against looming xenophobia and rising dictatorships. *The Vision of Čapek* play was performed by invitation from the European Region International Theatre Festival (now called the REGIONS International Theatre Festival Hradec Králové) in the Czech Republic by Georgia College & State University (GC) undergraduate students (where the author chaired the Theatre and Dance Department). Performances were held at the Festival in Hradec Králové, at Karel Čapek's birthplace in Malé Svatoňovice, and in Prague at Trmal Villa. The production utilized Polish theatre theorist Jerzy Grotowski's physical movement technique (Grotowski, 1968; Richards, 1995) in rehearsals and performance. This chapter details the powerful impact of the play on the performers and audiences in both the Czech Republic and in Milledgeville, Georgia. As proof of its impact, one participating student actor noted that theatre transcends all language barriers.

This chapter begins with the developmental process of the new play *The Vision of Čapek*, the dramaturgical background of the history and context of the play, followed by the audience and performers' reactions to the play. *The Vision of Čapek* mirrored the Čapek brothers' art form by using theatre as a rallying cry against the rising threat of similar populist authoritarian leaders of today. The Čapek brothers and the authors of this chapter aspired to bring attention to the enduring ways that the arts can be used to further social justice and resist authoritarianism.

Developing *The Vision of Čapek*

In the process of researching and writing the new play *The Vision of Čapek*, the authors were intrigued with the famed Čapek brothers, writer Karel and painter/illustrator Josef who, as children, grew up in the area of Bohemia which was part of the Austro-Hungarian Empire. They lived to see Bohemia become part of the newly independent democratic country of Czechoslovakia in 1918 at the end of World War I. Conscious of the precarious state of geopolitical affairs, the Čapek brothers envisioned and addressed a perilous future. Their prescience is evident even in their nomenclature, as they are inventors of the word "robot" ("robota" or "drudge laborer" in Czech) in the 1921 play *R.U.R.* (Robertson, 2018, p. 4). They warned of the dangers of the looming fascism that provoked a world war and the Holocaust.

The Vision of Čapek begins in their childhood and takes the audience through Karel Čapek's death and Josef Čapek's arrest by the Nazis, using their lives to caution against authoritarian extremism arising in the 21st century in the United States and in much of the world. Using the Čapek brothers as a model of artistic creativity and heroism in their new play, the authors referred back to the robots in *R.U.R.* who were created as slaves and inferiors. Like the Čapek brothers in their 1921 play *R.U.R.* and in their later plays and novels, the authors of this chapter used their 2016 play to mirror the Čapeks' call for democracy and freedom. In 2016, the impetus emerged from the rise of antisemitism, xenophobia, and the upcoming United States presidential election in which candidate Donald Trump was calling for "America First," a phrase used by the Ku Klux Klan in the 1920s to denote their racism and, again, during World War II to denote a movement of antisemitic, pro-fascist doctrine (Churchwell, 2018 and Rothman, 2016).

As Adam Roberts writes, *R.U.R.* addresses new technologies that create "alarming new potentials for exploitation and destruction" (Čapek, 2011, p. vi). It is clear from the works following *R.U.R.* by the Čapek brothers that their growing awareness of the dangers of fascism and the need for justice were at the forefront. Their mission to protect democracy and human rights derived from a profound understanding of history and special insight gained through their friendship with the leader of Czechoslovakia, Tomáš G. Masaryk. Additional works by the Čapeks, including the plays *The White Disease* and *The Mother* and the novel *War with the Newts*, manifest a deep understanding of the precarious nature of freedom and a rising fear of oppression from autocratic leaders. The Čapeks, thus, used art to precipitate social change through the widespread performances of their plays, the popularity of their novels, journalism and artworks. The authors of this chapter chose these Czech heroes as biographical precedents upon which to model a new play with a contemporary admonition.

Like the Čapeks in their response to the dangerous political landscape of their time, the authors of this new play reacted to the concerns in the 2016 political landscape. As the Presidential election of 2016 began to heat up between Hillary Rodham Clinton and Donald J. Trump, white supremacist leaders in the United States began to see Donald Trump's campaign as an ally of their beliefs (Berger, 2016). Right-wing authoritarians from numerous countries, such as Hungary, Poland, Turkey, and the Philippines began to rule after winning elections that overthrew more moderate incumbents and rivals.

To respond to rising white supremacy and authoritarianism, the playwrights focused on how the Čapek brothers' writings and influence helped shape political events in the history of the Czech people with application to contemporary political challenges in the world. A primary emphasis of the research was on the threat to the new democratic state of Czechoslovakia from the rise of the Nazis in Germany. *The Vision of Čapek* dramatizes how the arts were used by the Čapek brothers, aligned with their good friend Czechoslovakia's President Tomáš G. Masaryk, in their long fight against oppression. Masaryk, as the founder of Czechoslovakia, was comparable to

George Washington for the Czech people and is a character in *The Vision of Čapek*. *The Vision of Čapek* also portrays the early family life of the Čapek brothers, and Karel Čapek's important contributions in journalism, children's stories, and plays. The play includes a dramatization of the premiere use of the word, "robot" in *R.U.R.* a science fiction play about technology and fascism (Čapek, 2011).

The Vision of Čapek honors the Čapek brothers' artistic, and also somewhat eccentric mother Božena, who influenced her family of three children, including the Čapeks' sister and writer Helena, to became creative artists. The Čapek brothers' father, Antonin, was a medical doctor who worked long hours and served as a stern taskmaster to his children (Bradbrook, 1998). The playwrights used this biographical background to begin dramaturgy, otherwise known as background research. As part of their background research the authors delved into Czech history and peoples in relation to the surrounding nations, the coming war, militarism, fascism, and antisemitism. In addition, the authors did extensive research into the artistic works of the Čapek brothers and the critical and popular reaction to their works.

The Rehearsal and Dramaturgical Process

For one year prior to the arrival in the Czech Republic of the director and actors in June 2016, the research on biography and history led to the evolution of the script that formed the basic structure and dialogue of the play, titled *The Vision of Čapek* (*Čapkovy Vize* in Czech). The Čapek brothers' art provided the guideposts for *The Vision of Čapek* utilized in creating its own social justice art that contains a modern-day warning of the renewed dangers of fascism. Karel's plays and novels utilized powerful allegories about these coming dangers of fascism. His brother Josef's visual art amplified his brother's words through his illustrations that helped popularize the works. Both artists' works inspired the playwrights of *The Vision of Čapek* throughout the creative process.

The Vision of Čapek was a joint production of the GC Department of Theatre and Dance in Milledgeville, Georgia and Washington Women in Theatre, a Washington, D.C. professional theatre company of which the co-author of this chapter, Dr. Karen Berman, is the co-founder and artistic director. Professor Stanislav Bohadlo of the University of Hradec Králové was the host and tour manager in the Czech Republic. *The Vision of Čapek* is the fourth new play of the authors' Czech Quartet chronicling Czech heroes and taking GC students on a summer study abroad experience to perform the plays (Berman, 2017). The production of *The Vision of Čapek* was written by Berman and collaborator Paul Accettura, and directed by Berman who was the chair and artistic director of the GC Department of Theatre and Dance at the time of the production.

During the rehearsal process of *The Vision of Čapek* in the Czech Republic, the author and the racially diverse cast of 15 student actors, six males and nine females, continued to develop the play. The student actors studied the historical figures, visiting key sites in the Czech Republic connected to the people and events in the play. These major historical, political, and cultural sites in the Czech Republic grounded the students in authentic experiences to inform their characters. A visit to the Terezín Ghetto/Concentration Camp was especially moving for the student actors as they absorbed the tragedy of the Holocaust that played an important role in Czech history and the story portrayed in *The Vision of Čapek*.

The student actors' immersion in the dramaturgy created deep and honest portrayals in performance. As Kindelin (2012) notes, "students see the play's humanistic or social implications through preproduction dramaturgical integrative explorations" (p. 82). The student actors (two of whom doubled as stage manager and sound designer) and the authors worked through the rehearsal process to modify parts of the play, especially through the creation of important ideographs, or symbolic stage pictures that stylized the movement.

Ideographs proved essential in bridging the language barriers of an international audience by facilitating a vivid visual storytelling for audience members who might not speak English. A powerful series of mimetic actions was created throughout the play based on the work of Jerzy Grotowski (Grotowski, 1968; Richards, 1995). These ideographs were stage movements developed through improvisation to create wordless picturizations.

One example of the use of ideographs in *The Vision of Čapek* is demonstrated in the representation of the servant/robot characters in *R.U.R.* whose subservience is clarified through staccato bowing and serving gestures that evolved into intense and intimidating movements by the actors in their futuristic silver robot costumes. Another example is the swirling, dance-like movements of Karel and Josef's mother, Božena, as a representation of possessiveness and artistic influence over her children. Ideographs were also crucial at the end of the play. In a nod to Karel's play *The Mother*, in which the Mother tries to prevent her sons from going to war, the actors portraying the sons are dragged into the spiderlike movements of their mother in her fight to wrap them in her web of protection rather than allowing them to confront the oppressors. Actors in militaristic Nazi salutes are presented directly behind her.

Historical Perspective

The Čapek Brothers

In addition to Karel's authorship of his most famous play *R.U.R.*, he wrote novels, influential journal articles, and fairy tales that became famous worldwide. A number of England's notable writers of the time, including playwright

George Bernard Shaw and science fiction writer H. G. Wells, were good friends of Karel who was the founder and President of the Prague chapter of the International PEN Club promoting literature and freedom of expression. Karel's presence as a person of stature was noted "as a symbol of a free beleaguered country, as a model of a literate democratic man" (Kussi, 1990, p. 11). While he was a strong competitor for the mid-1930's Nobel Prize for Literature given his six novels and six plays performed worldwide, he did not receive the award. There was speculation that the Swedish committee may have feared "offending Nazi Germany by honoring an outspoken anti-fascist" (Kussi, 1990, p. 11).

The family heritage that grounds this work begins with Karel's brother and collaborator, Josef Čapek, who illustrated a number of Karel's books and was the most famous Czech cubist artist between World War I and World War II. The Čapek brothers' sister Helena became a writer as well, penning a popular memoir about her two brothers. Their father, Antonin Čapek, was a physician who was viewed by his children as "a man fully dedicated to his work, who almost never had a free moment" (Klima, 2001, p. 24). Their mother was, in the words of Josef's wife, "immensely gifted and perceptive, and I heard a doctor say that 'women like her often have sons who are geniuses'" (Klima, 2001, p. 28).

Olga Scheinpflagova, another character in the play, was a famous Czech theatre actress who married Karel in 1935, and remained a famed Czech actress after his death, living until 1968 (Kussi, 1990, p. 21). Karel's final play, inspired by his wife, favors devotion to the nation state in the troubled times when he wrote the play in 1938 (Holy, 1996, p. 65; Čapek, 1990, p. 338).

Karel's work was admired by many of the greatest writers of his time, including Arthur Miller and Thomas Mann, among others (Kussi, 1990; Klima 2001). It is also important to note that, in addition to Karel's overt political work, he was beloved in his time for the whimsical nature of much of his work, and the equally whimsical illustrations by his brother Josef. These works included popular fairy tales (Čapek, 1932) memorably illustrated by his brother, as well as a series of charming travel books titled "Letters from" several countries that he visited including Spain, Italy, England, and Holland (Čapek, 1933), and *The Gardener's Year*, his 1929 account of the life of a gardener, illustrated by his brother (Čapek, 2002).

Historical and Political Background

When Karel was born in 1890 in Malé Svatoňovice, Bohemia was part of the Austro-Hungarian Empire. After World War I ended in 1918, the democratic country of Czechoslovakia was created on October 28, 1918 and prominently included Bohemia as its core and Prague as its capital. The majestic Prague Castle built in the ninth century was the seat of government. The first elected President, Tomáš Masaryk, is considered the founder of a democratic Czechoslovakia, as he spent many years lobbying for the creation of a free democratic Czechoslovakia before and during World War I. Karel was a fervent Czech nationalist and friend and advisor to Masaryk. Karel was "a passionate democrat and pluralist" (Kussi, 1990, p. 13).

Several interviews by Karel of President Masaryk were published as books promoting peace and democratic principles for the preservation of small democratic countries. In one interview, Masaryk told Karel that "whether we want to or not, we live politically in the world, and with the whole world" (Masaryk & Čapek, 1938, p. 164). For smaller or less powerful countries, a more powerful expansionist nation always poses a threat. Masaryk told Karel, "Democracy is a guarantee of peace, for us and the world" (Masaryk & Čapek, 1938, p. 199).

The setting of the play *The Vision of Čapek* is in Bohemia as it emerges as part of the small democratic state of Czechoslovakia until just prior to the end of World War II. The rise of the Nazis and fascism was a direct threat to

Czechoslovakia as it borders on Germany and became an initial subject of expansionism by the Nazis. During the 1930's, fascism and the Nazi government of Adolf Hitler in neighboring Nazi Germany began to threaten the rest of Europe.

Karel continued to write against fascism and utilize his plays and novels in his fight. By 1938 as Karel "was expressing the feelings of his nation through art; he was now seen as one of the greatest contemporary writers who have fully responded to the expectations to speak on behalf of the nation" (Bradbrook, 1998, p. 18). Karel was shocked by the September 29, 1938 Munich Agreement. In the Munich Agreement, the British and French agreed to allow Hitler to take over the Sudetenland part of Czechoslovakia and make it part of Germany over the objection of Czechoslovakia (Evans, 2005, pp. 672–678). Soon after, Nazi Germany began World War II by invading what remained of Czechoslovakia and then the rest of Europe. Tobrmanová-Kühnová (2010) wrote of Karel that, "the Munich Agreement broke him ... After the tragic event the fascist ... press launched a slanderous campaign against him" (p. xxii). Bradbrook (1998) states that "the Munich Agreement had a devastating effect on Čapek ... He lost heart and, moreover, realized that his prominent position in the cultural and political areas made him vulnerable and exposed to the ever-growing fascist threat" (p. 19). Then with his spirit broken by the rising danger and his awareness of what the betrayal at Munich really meant, not just for Czechoslovakia, but the world, he caught double pneumonia and died on Christmas Day in 1938. As a leader against fascism through his art and journalism, he had become a prominent target of the fascists. "He was threatened in the street, and his house and office were flooded with abusive anonymous letters, warning him that he would die in a concentration camp" (Tobrmanová-Kühnová, 2010, p. xxii). That very scenario, in fact, happened to Josef who was arrested in 1939 immediately after the Nazis invasion of Czechoslovakia. After spending the war in various concentration camps, Josef died in Bergen-Belsen in 1945 (Bradbrook, 1998,

p. 20; Kussi, 1990, p. 24). At the same time, Karel was also receiving "many letters of sympathy and support from both Czechs and local Germans and foreigners" (Tobrmanová-Kühnová, 2010, p. xxii).

With the looming threat of fascism immediately before and after the Munich Agreement, prominent artists were beginning to leave the country. According to Klima (2001), Karel's friends "tried to convince him that he could be more useful abroad" (p. 234) as a provocateur and spokesperson. Karel's wife Olga, as an actress, faced many challenges performing in theatre abroad "because of the substantial role played by one's native language" (Klima, 2001, p. 234). Thomas Mann, the famous German novelist and 1929 winner of the Nobel Prize in Literature had fled to Switzerland, and was soon to head permanently to the United States. He joined the people encouraging Karel to leave. As Tobrmanová-Kühnová (2010) notes "His friends had pressed him to go into exile, but even when Thomas Mann sent his daughter for him, Čapek, a believer in personal responsibility, refused" (p. xxiii).

Performance History of Karel Čapek's Plays

Karel's plays were widely read or seen, especially in Czechoslovakia, but also in much of Europe. His early play *R.U.R.*, had its world premiere at the National Theatre in Prague, Czechoslovakia in January 1921 and has remained lasting in its influence because of its widespread performances all over the world and its first use of the now ubiquitous term "robot." The robots in *R.U.R.* were a servant class treated as inferior, possibly a forewarning of the Nazis treatment of the Jews as an inferior race. The robots in *R.U.R.* rebel against their "masters." Klima stated, about *R.U.R.*, that "it was a single play that gained world attention for Čapek almost overnight" (Čapek, 2004, p. xi). Bradbrook (1998) states that "After the premiere" of *R.U.R.* "the theatre world was taken by storm ... " and that in Prague, "one had to book tickets two months in advance and that children played 'robots' for months afterwards" (p. 49). *R.U.R.* was translated into thirty languages (Bradbrook, 1998, p. 49). The play was even performed on Broadway for four months beginning in October 1922. The Broadway performances were presented by The Theatre Guild at the Frazee Theatre on 42nd Street (Playbill for R.U.R., 1922; Broadway World, 2022) (Figure 1.1).

Figure 1.1
Playbill from 1922 Broadway Production of R.U.R.
Photo by Paul G. Accettura

Karel's reach was also extensive as a novelist. His novel *War with the Newts* was published in 1936. According to Klima (2001) *War with the Newts* was "intended to warn against the dangers of Nazism, and therefore it is a very direct response to the political situation in Europe at the time" (p. 199). *War with the Newts* is a witty and humorous novel in its first half, with a provocative and compelling blow against racism and fascism in the second half. The "newts" are large salamander-like creatures that reproduce easily and are very docile and susceptible to use as servants to humans and to human industry. The basic plot of the novel is about "how a species of giant intelligent newts—docile by nature—are ruthlessly exploited, and finally turn on their human oppressors" (Radio Prague International (2020, April 1, para. 1).

Radio Prague International (2020, April 1) notes that "despite the all-pervasive humour," Čapek's core message in *War with the Newts* "was deadly serious" (Radio Prague International (2020, April 1), para. 1). Racial discrimination against the newts, fascism, and even climate change with an "approaching deluge" involving a "sort of greenhouse effect as beaches and coasts disappear" (Bradbrook, 1998, p. 108) were the futuristic themes. The impending disasters end the book with overwhelming pessimism with the final words of the book: "I don't know what comes next" (Čapek, 2011, p. 349). As Adam Roberts writes, "the total destruction of humanity" is the conclusion of both *R.U.R.* and *War with the Newts* (Čapek (2011), p. vii). Two other Čapek plays, *The White Disease* (also translated as *The White Scourge*) and *The Mother*, were anti-war, anti-authoritarianism triumphs during the immediate years before World War II.

The White Disease was first performed in 1937 when it premiered at the National Theatre in Prague. The production occurred just under two years before the Munich Agreement and Karel Čapek's death in December 1938 (Radio Prague International, 2020, December 9). *The White Disease* focuses on a disease similar to leprosy that first appears as a white mark that, in a short time, kills its victims. The lead character finds a cure. Zdenek Vacek, director of the Karel Čapek Memorial, said that "Čapek chose leprosy as an embodiment of the moral rot eating away at European democracies and humanist ideals" (Radio Prague International, 2020, December 9, para. 5). The play was performed at a time of great political tension in Europe as the rise of the Nazis and the increase in their military capability began to trouble democracies in Europe. As Zdenek Vacek states, "It was quite a provocative play, a powerful play, and moreover, from today's perspective, the atmosphere in society was unimaginably tense. The fear of war was overwhelming" (Radio Prague International, 2020, December 9, para. 19). Through the allegory of a dreaded disease and the divisions in attempts to deal with it, Karel raised the enormous dangers of fascism itself. Karel was aware that even among Germans living in his democratic Czechoslovakia "more and more people were impressed with Hitler's method of governing," and some of them openly denigrated democracy and believed it had "no hope of resisting the dynamic totalitarian regimes" (Klima, 2001, p. 215). Karel continued to vividly express his concerns and his exhortation in this troubling atmosphere.

According to Vacek, "*The White Disease* was positively received by those who saw clear parallels with the authoritarian regimes of Hitler, Mussolini and other dictators. At the same time, the play showed how many people will tolerate fascism" (Radio Prague International, 2020, December 9, para. 20).

The Mother was written and premiered in 1938 during the civil war in Spain and the beginning of Hitler's aggressive acts against his neighbors to expand his Nazi ideology. As Klima (2001) notes, "two main ideologies dominated the political situation in 1938, both ... highly aggressive and dangerous: Hitler's nationalism, with its racist and nationalistic hatreds, and communism, with its ... class hatred" (Klima, 2001, p. 223). The fundamental point of *The Mother* is the "senselessness of fanaticism" as her sons become radicalized, one as a fanatic reactionary and the other as a fanatic revolutionary (Klima, 2001, p. 223). As one of Karel's friends noted in a memoir after World War II,

"His *White Plague, Newts,* and *The Mother*—they shout: People pay attention, defend yourselves!" (Klima, 2001, p. 226).

Performances of *The Vision of Čapek*

The rehearsals of *The Vision of Čapek* in the Czech Republic took place in the historic town of Kutna Hora, the rural town of Kuks, and the university town of Hradec Králové, as well as the capital of Prague. The various types of rehearsal spaces prepared the actors for the flexibility necessary to perform later at the disparate venues.

The Vision of Čapek was performed in three different venues in the Czech Republic in the summer of 2016. The first performance venue that hosted the opening performance of *The Vision of Čapek* had special meaning, as it was the birthplace of Karel Čapek in Malé Svatoňovice. Karel Čapek's original home is now a museum dedicated to the lives of Karel and Josef Čapek. The play was performed in the museum in the very building where Karel was born.

Other performances encompassed varied venues ranging from an international festival and a historic house museum, to a university campus. The second and principal performance venue for *The Vision of Čapek* was in the main tent at the Open Air Festival of the European Regions International Theatre Festival in Hradec Králové (now called the REGIONS International Theatre Festival Hradec Králové). The performances of *The Vision of Čapek* were the sole offerings by a theatre company from the United States. Other countries represented at the international festival included theatre companies from the Czech Republic, Slovakia, Poland, Hungary, Russia, and Great Britain.

The Vision of Čapek was also performed in the outdoor garden at the Trmal Villa in Prague. The Trmal Villa is a historic house museum designed by famed Czech architect Jan Kotera in 1903. The final performance of *The Vision of*

Čapek took place late that summer in the Campus Black Box Theatre at GC in Milledgeville, Georgia. GC is the public liberal arts university of Georgia and this project was the epitome of its mission to promote the liberal arts.

Impact and Assessment

Reaction of Czech Audiences to the Play

The audience members at the performance of the play *The Vision of Čapek* at Karel's birthplace in Malé Svatoňovice were very moved by the play. The curator of the museum stood onstage in front of the actors and the audience at the end of the show to exclaim that it was the first time that the Čapek brothers truly came to life for her after many years at the museum. There were a number of Czech high school students in the audience who stayed afterwards to discuss the play with the actors. They had studied the Čapek brothers, but were amazed to see them come to life in performance. Several Czech adults in the audience surrounded the authors after the performance declaring that it had moved them immensely. They were adamant in their recommendation that the play be performed in the United States to show America what could happen if authoritarians took control. They were especially concerned about what they had read and seen on television about the upcoming Presidential election in the United States. The Czech adult audience members noted their concern with the rise of white supremacy in the United States. One gentleman expressed concern that "Trump reminds me of one of the European dictators."

The second performance venue was at the Open Air Festival of the European Regions International Theatre Festival in Hradec Králové (Figure 1.2). Before the performance at the festival, the students rehearsed at the University of Hradec Králové where they received several guest lectures by political science and theatre professors. Of particular note was the lecture by the Provost who spoke of the harsh rule under which his country had suffered, first under the Austro-Hungarian Empire, then under the Nazi occupation by Germany, and later under Communist rule orchestrated by Russia. He commented that, unlike America, the Czech people have always been surrounded by larger, powerful, and, often, dictatorial countries such as Germany and Hungary. The student actors absorbed this outlook as they continued their character development.

FIGURE 1.2
Georgia College Students Rehearsing The Vision of Čapek at the European Region Theatre Festival in Hradec Králové. Photo by Paul G. Accettura

It is important to note that, unlike America, democracy for the Czech people has only occurred for brief periods between the end of World War I and the Nazi invasion, and, later, after the Velvet Revolution, a non-violent revolution in 1989 that overthrew the communist dictatorship. The authors were very surprised with the casual attitude that some in the Czech Republic had toward democracy. Perhaps this outlook is best exemplified in a comment from one political science professor from the University of Hradec Králové who told the authors it made no difference to him whether the government was democratic or a dictatorship, as long as they ran the country well.

A newspaper review of *The Vision of Čapek* performance at the festival was published on June 24, 2016 in the Czech newspaper *Open News* in Hradec Králové, Czech Republic (Hen, 2016). The review, titled "Americký Čapek," was published in Czech (Hen, 2016) and bestowed appreciation on the American perspective of the work of the Čapeks. The reviewer stated that, "for us Czechs, I would say Karel Čapek is our genius, who had an incredible intuition" (Hen, 2016, p. 2). The review then debated the play's contention that the Čapeks' family upbringing informed their talent versus the general Czech view that the Čapeks were simply born geniuses concluding that "the most interesting thing ... [was] the difference of perspective" (Hen, 2016, p. 2). The reviewer noted that the performance was "very clear," was "an interesting study" and that the "performance works" (Hen, 2016, p. 2).

The performance in Prague was outdoors on a beautiful summer day in the yard of the Trmal Villa. Once again, after the performance, members of the Czech audience were inspired to discuss current politics and the upcoming Presidential election. The Czech people, after suffering for many years under totalitarian dictators during the Communist era and the Nazi occupation, clearly made the connections that contemporary society must also heed the warnings against populist dictatorial movements. The art of *The Vision of Čapek* was, through this story about the art of the Čapek brothers, heralding a call to action.

Reaction of Student Actors: Student Learning

As part of their experience, the 15 student performers from Georgia were required to keep journals, an essential component of the students' work. The students were allowed to prepare a free-flowing journal inspired by daily questions from the authors and six specific prompts that included:

1. What did you experience and discover? What was your reaction?;
2. How are the Czech people like you and different from you? In lifestyle, culture, politics, humor?; and
3. What characteristics do you associate with your nationality and what characteristics of your nationality might your host country be suspicious of? And alternatively appreciate?

Formative assessment (Trumbull & Lach, 2013) showed that the students had an unfamiliarity with the Czech people, the Holocaust, World War II, and the Čapek brothers prior to this experience. This may be due, in part, to the fact that Georgia does not require Holocaust education in its schools. The students responded as actors and as students of Czech culture. The journals indicate, through summative assessment (Table 1.1), what a major impact these authentic and creative learning experiences had on them. Excerpts of this assessment from student journal entries are detailed in the chart on the next page.

TABLE 1.1

Sample Assessment from the Journals of Student Performers 2016

Student	Enlightenment from Authentic Experience
A	"The girls we met after the performance made me sure that we had done this work justice. Learning what Karel Čapek meant to them was truly inspiring."
G	"We had most of the audience in tears and the curator of the museum … she said … this was the first time she felt truly connected to Karel Čapek as a person."
B	"Performing at Čapek's birthplace was incredibly moving and almost spiritual."
K	"There was something magical about performing in the room that he was born in."
Student	**Reflections on Terezín Ghetto/Concentration Camp**
G	"There are certain moments in life when history stops being part of a book and becomes very real and present. I felt sick and extraordinarily sad."
A	"We saw things in the camp that I will never forget."
H	"I think it is so important that we as a species don't forget about the Holocaust … I don't want anyone to forget. I don't want history to repeat itself."
C	"I was left speechless. I know I must learn history in order to not repeat it."
Student	**Student Reaction to Audience Response**
B	"I fully grasped how very strong and influential the story-telling we were doing could be to the people of the Czech Republic."
E	"The response was amazing. They said the most heart-warming things that by the time we got back to the dressing room everyone was crying their eyes out from joy."
D	"I love theater so much and I'm so grateful to have the opportunity to be here! It is beautiful and amazing to see an appreciation for theater in another country."
A	"Even though language divides us, theater transcends all."
F	"It was amazing that American students could relate to the soul of a Czech person."
Student	**Learning Beyond the Immediate Experience**
K	"Teaching tolerance and art through art is something I would like to pursue."
H	"It is beautiful how art transcends language barriers and can be appreciated by all."
I	"Theatre and art as a whole is really valued by the Czech people which is beautiful to me … It was truly a gift to be able to do what I love … grow as an actor."
L	"It's an experience I'll treasure for the rest of my life."
F, M, A, C	"The experience was life-changing."

As shown in Table 1.1, the overall experience was life-changing for the students and provides significant messages for our current world. According to Kindelan (2012) "Democratic values develop when students identify a play's overarching ideas, ask important questions, and strive to learn more about the play's humanity through collaborative research, discussion, and performance" (p. 92). This is the process that all of these student actors absorbed in developing and performing *The Vision of Čapek* in the Czech Republic.

A number of the students commented in their journals about the impact of their first performance in the country at the house museum in Malé Svatoňovice. The students' journal comments are detailed in Table 1.1. In one example, Student F quoted the curator: "It was amazing that American students could relate to the soul of a Czech person." The power of theatre was a revelation to these students. Several students commented on the unique and moving experience of performing in the building in which Karel was born.

The students also noted in their journals the power of performing the story of the heroic Čapek brothers before a Czech audience. As detailed in Table 1.1, Student G wrote that "we had most of the audience in tears" and Student B wrote that she had not "fully grasped how very strong and influential the story-telling we were doing could be to the people of the Czech Republic." The students were awed by the atmosphere at the international theatre festival. After multiple curtain calls, Student A wrote that, "Even though language divides us, theater transcends all."

There was a great value to these experiences for the students. During their visit to the Terezín Ghetto/Concentration Camp (also known as Theresienstadt) the actors learned about the horrors committed there and saw for themselves the conditions in which the prisoners lived. In research for *The Vision of Čapek* they had learned about the Nazi camps during the Holocaust, including the death in the Bergen-Belsen concentration camp of Josef Čapek. As noted in Table 1.1, Student H wrote that "I think it is so important that we as a species don't forget about the Holocaust ... I don't want anyone to forget. I don't want history to repeat itself."

After the United States debut of the play on campus, the GC student newspaper *The Colonnade* published an article, titled "Czech It Out" (Conner, 2016) that focused on the students' experience being part of this play and the performances in the Czech Republic. In one interesting quote from the article, the stage manager of *The Vision of Čapek* said, "while we were over there, people who would find out we were American would always ask us who we were voting for, because people over there are more interested in our election than we were" (Conner, 2016, p. 13).

Conclusion

The lives of the Čapek brothers were spent using art as a cautionary tale, as a prescient warning of the results of oppression, as a way to awaken the souls of their contemporaries to the forthcoming dangers of the Holocaust. They were indeed visionaries, whose social justice art continues to serve as a touchstone for the protection of freedom for all nations.

The reverberations and repetitions of their lives revealed in *The Vision of Čapek* resonated with new contemporary audiences and student performers. Both audience and performer reactions testify to the transformational power of theatre to council, to educate, and to communicate across eras and cultures.

References

Berger, J.M. (2016, October 25). *How white nationalists learned to love Donald Trump.* Politico Magazine. https://www.politico.com/magazine/story/2016/10/donald-trump-2016-white-nationalists-alt-right-214388/

Berman, K. (2017). Transformative cross-cultural dialogue in Prague: Americans creating Czech history plays. *Theatre Symposium.* 25, 82–92.

Bradbrook, B.R. (1998). *Karel Čapek: In pursuit of truth, tolerance, and trust.* Sussex Academic Press.

Broadway World (2022). https://www.broadwayworld.com/theatre/Frazee-Theatre.

Čapek, K. (1932). *Nine fairy tales and one thrown in for good measure.* Northwestern University Press.

Čapek, K. (1933). *Letters from Holland.* Faber and Faber.

Čapek, K. (1990). *Nine Fairy Tales by Karel Capek and one more thrown in for good measure.* Northwestern University Press.

Čapek, K. (1990). *Toward the radical center: A Karel Čapek reader.* Catbird Press.

Čapek, K. (2002). *The gardener's year.* Modern Library.

Čapek, K. (2004). *R.U.R. (Rossum's Universal Robots).* Penguin Books.

Čapek, K. (2010). *Believe in people: The essential Karel Čapek.* Faber and Faber, Ltd.

Čapek, K. (2011). *R.U.R. (Rossum's Universal Robots) and war with the newts.* Orion Publishing Group.

Čapek, K. & Čapek, J.. (1923). *R.U.R. and the insect play.* Oxford University Press.

Churchwell, S. (2018, April 21). *End of the American dream? The dark history of "America First"*. The Guardian. https://www.theguardian.com/books/2018/apr/21/end-of-the-american-dream-the-dark-history-of-america-first

Conner, M. K. (2016, August 31). *Czech it out: Students of Georgia College take the original play the vision of Capek, abroad*. The Colonnade: The Official Student Newspaper of Georgia College.

Evans, R. J. (2005). *The Third Reich in power*. Penguin Books.

Grotowski, J. (1968). *Towards a poor theatre*. Simon & Schuster.

Hen (2016, June 6). Americký Čapek. Open News 8. Open Air Programu Mezinarodniho Festivalu Divadlo Europských Regionu: Hradec Králové,

Holy, L. (1996). *The little Czech nation and the great Czech nation: National identity and the post-communist transformation of society*. Cambridge University Press.

Kindelan, N. (2012). *Artistic literacy: Theatre studies and a contemporary liberal education*. Palgrave Macmillan.

Klíma, I. (2001). *Karel Čapek: Life and work*. Catbird Press.

Kussi, P. (1990). Introduction. In Čapek, K. (1990). *Toward the radical center: A Karel Čapek reader*. Catbird Press.

Masaryk, T. & Čapek, K. (1938). *Masaryk on thoughts and life: Conversations with Karel Čapek*. George Allen and Unwin Ltd.

Playbill for R.U.R. (1922). Frazee Theatre.

Radio Prague International. (2020, April 1). *War with the newts: Karel Čapek's prescient, Dystopian magnum opus*. https://english.radio.cz/czech-books-you-must-read-8506310/6.

Radio Prague International. (2020, December 9). *Karel Čapek's "The White Disease": A pandemic of fascism*. `https://english.radio.cz/czech-books-you-must-read-8506310/20

Richards, T. (1995). *At work with Grotowski on physical actions*. New York: Routledge.

Robertson, J. (2018). *Robo sapiens japanicus: Robots, gender, family, and the Japanese nation.* University of California Press.

Rothman, L. (2016, March 28). *The long history behind Donald Trump's "America first" foreign policy.* Time. https://time.com/4273812/america-first-donald-trump-history/

Tobrmanová-Kühnová, Š. (2010). Introduction to Čapek, K. (2010). *Believe in people: The essential Karel Čapek.* Faber and Faber, Ltd.

Trumbull, E. & Lash, A. (2013). *Understanding formative assessment: Insights from learning theory and measurement theory.* WestEd. https://www2.wested.org/www-static/online_pubs/resource1307.pdf.

CHAPTER 2

The Staged Process for *The Diary of Anne Frank*: A Universal Voice

Miřenka Čechová, Ph.D.

The Genesis

I have great faith in the power and strength of theatre as well as its transformative possibility. Theatre has the potential to turn human suffering into a healing process for those who expose themselves to it in a raw, vulnerable, and open way. This outlook applies to the audience who have the opportunity through emotional experience, identification, and empathy, to experience a catharsis of their own. This catharsis can be admitted, latent or as experienced as an individual or a group. However, this healing process also works reciprocally, for the creators themselves as they recognize and channel subliminal personal experiences and pain to an aesthetic level. This process of re-apprehending and elevating personal experience to a universally valid level of meaning generates liberation from the state of exclusive tragedy. Everyone is alone in a crisis. And we need to follow the examples of those whose courage and faith enabled them to face liminal situations with dignity and humanity.

The theatre enabled me to recognize the crisis, process and attempt to offer a certain healing dimension of art to the public. However, none of this would have happened without a meeting with Anne Frank through her writing which I encountered at the crucial age of my young adulthood. Her intimate confession of the liminal situation taught me never to give up and never to be silent when facing an injustice and to always aspire for the right to live in a respectful environment, the right for happiness and love, as well as for conscious meaningful existence. Thanks to the meeting with Anne Frank's diary, I began to process the stories of women who at a certain point in their lives were forced to disappear, be forgotten, become nameless or invisible. (Invisible, 2018, 2020, 2022). Thanks to Anne Frank, something inside of me snapped, shattering that indifference and defenselessness towards the world in which I live now. And something was born: the responsibility and the awareness that each of us has the potential to influence the world, even in the smallest gesture, which, like circles on water, can grow. All this triggered the little girl whose incredible testimony of the darkest era of European history has such an important relevance even today and, thus, must be passed on.

In this chapter, I would like to try to depict the way in which I decided to carry on the testimony of Anne Frank through theatre art, the magical act of sharing, in all its psychosomatic width. Theatre for me is the place of sharing where empathy and sensitivity can transform the human potential.

I would like to demonstrate this magical act through the description of the creation of *The Voice of Anne Frank* performance, inspired by the world-famous *Diary of Anne Frank* (Frank, 1997).

As a director, choreographer, performer and an author, I am concerned with the discipline of physical theatre, for which an essential feature is an emphasis on original work in the form of devised theatre. This approach primarily entails sensitive physicality and the bodily expression of emotional and imaginative experiences. In this chapter, I will explore the context of the creative process and the rehearsals of *The Voice of Anne Frank*, around which a theatre group and lifelong friendship were formed. The performance emerged from a small school rehearsal room in the Czech Republic to the Terrace Theatre in the John F. Kennedy Center for the Performing Arts in Washington, DC and the famous dissident Market Theatre in Johannesburg,

South Africa. This production was seen by thousands of children in many different parts of the world.

At the beginning of the creation of *The Voice of Anne Frank*, several personal long-standing desires, aspirations, and passions came together in a rare symbiosis. It was intended to be my final authorial performance for my master's degree at the Non-Verbal Theater at the Music Faculty of the Academy of Performing Arts in Prague, but the whole course of its creation, the circumstances and the subsequent premiere, showed the exceptionality of this act, completely outside the framework of a mere graduate school performance. At that time, I, a former ballerina and future theatre author, met Petr Boháč, a student of the Faculty of Philosophy of the Charles University, and together we wanted to test whether our worlds could meet in the language of theatre.

When we searched for the character that would be close to me, Petr Boháč named several characters that would fit my own character, and Anne Frank was among them. I first read her diary in my youth, but reading it from my young adult perspective, it appeared as a completely extraordinary document. It combined not only the personified testimony of a fundamental historical tragedy, but also the testimony of a very specific human life (that of a young teenage girl in an extreme situation), as well as an appealing message for the contemporary reader of not only historical relevance, but an extreme contemporary relevance, with ever increasing urgency in today's world.

The idea of our play grew from the context in which the Diary was written; from the terrifying and hard-to-grasp contrast between the phenomenon of life and something that we can hardly relate to life, that is beyond life, that forced humanity to experience hell on earth, that forcibly turned humans into a number. At the beginning, we therefore asked: What are the possibilities of theatrical expression in the confrontation with the liminal situation represented by the topic of the Holocaust and hiding? What does the Holocaust and its consequences mean to us today? What do specific memories, published memoirs mean to us? How do we theatrically depict diary literature, specifically the phenomenon of writing by a thirteen-year-old girl (the phenomenon of searching for meaning), her daily life, sorrows and small joys? We knew that we did not want to classically dramatize Frank's diary, nor to use words as the primary means of expression. The only way to understand the incomprehensible was to find our personal point of entry, through sensitivity, empathy, and experimentation on ourselves.

At the very beginning of the working process, we read various testimonies of survivors, including Jakub Wiernik, Halina Birenbaum, Primo Levi, Eli Wiesel, Viktor E. Frankl and many others. We read the *Diary of Anne Frank* repeatedly in different ways, chronologically, through specific leitmotivs (hope, anger, awareness of the outside world, desire for closeness, memories of a normal life, etc.), with a focus on individuals or through abstract images.

Anne's diary, full of details of the daily life of two families living together in hiding from the Nazis, as well as her thoughts, emotions, aspirations and dreams brought me intimately closer and closer to everything that Anne Frank was deprived of in life, and conversely, what I am now enriched with—thanks to her writing.

The fate of Anne Frank does not end with the last diary entry, even if what follows it is difficult for today's readers to imagine. We can hardly feel or even understand this terrible non-life of the concentration camp that followed, but we cannot abdicate our responsibility to share her message. Anne Frank was murdered but her voice is still alive and poignant.

The Capturing of Anne Frank's Voice

It is one thing to grasp, understand and rationalize, and another to portray, and to perform. How does one portray the life and non-life (that I call an existence in a concentration camp) of a real person? We definitely did not intend to imitate and create a realistic illusion by external means (narrative plot, deep psychology, realistic scene and costumes, etc.); this kind of theatre was never my own. On the stage, I have always wanted to create space for highly intimate dialogue and co-experiencing emotionally challenging moments with the audience, space for imagination and co-interpretation of the situation. I come from the field of the European contemporary dance, Etienne Decroux's physical mime technique, Japanese butoh dance, Jerzy Grotowski's idea of the naked man on the naked stage and theatre as a ritual, combining expressive physicality and bodily voice using different voice registers (speaking through various resonators) or from Peter Brook.

I did not want to explain the situation, be literal or educate audiences by one single correct interpretation of the work. In the beginning, there was no script, no set, no music and no other performers—just me, an empty space and my first spectator (in this case, as well in the role of co-author and co-director Petr Boháč). Those are three basic elements without which the theatre could not be created and which are the only ones necessary for a theatrical experience (Brook, 1968).

During the first months of rehearsals, I didn't have the courage to speak, to use my voice. I was afraid that I wouldn't hear Anne's voice, but my own. The visualization became our method of searching for depiction of the character of Anne. We started by visualizing a specific environment. I walked around the space and behind my closed eyes drew every detail of her hiding place, a secret annex of the Opekta factory building. I imagined where her little room was, which she shared with Mr. Dussel (real name Fritz Pfeffer), where the room of the van Daans (real name van Pels) was, what she could see from the small crack of the dormer under the roof, how everyone huddled in the kitchen while shelling peas, what kind of eyes does Peter van Daan (real name Peter van Pels) have, and what does the upset mother look like when Anne talks. I learned to hear the kind voice of her beloved Pim (Otto Frank—father) and the scolding chicken cluck of Mrs. van Daan, tried on Margot's (sister) bra and dreamed of a career as a writer.

We rehearsed intensively for eight hours a day, with several breaks, for nine months (half a year just two of us, the other months with five more actors), using movement improvisations to provoke imaginative and emotional responses and insight (Figure 2.1). As the director, Petr Boháč observed me from the outside and read excerpts from the diary aloud while I generated the images in movement. I tried to deepen my awareness and feelings, to sharpen all my senses, especially my inner sight and inner hearing. Significant inner life, a psychosomatic background, was building up inside of me. From that I could later draw her image at any time. To use the voice for the first time was a strong experience, I felt as if I lent my body to Anne's voice. As Anne, I talked back to mother, was curious to meet a new member of the annex or complained bitterly to father about my sister Margot. At one point, Kitty, an imaginary friend, was also born. We decided that it would be the cello voice that would best suit Kitty.

It was clear from the beginning that just as the diary is a purely subjective matter, burdened by the writer's own point of view, and also often unfair to other characters (see Mother), our performance will not be an objective interpretation of Anne Frank's life either, but a kind of intimate dialogue between her diary and me, aspiring to embody her thoughts.

THE STAGED PROCESS FOR THE DIARY OF ANNE FRANK: A UNIVERSAL VOICE

FIGURE 2.1
Miřenka Čechová assumes the persona of Anne Frank.
Photo by Martin Mark

Symbol of a Bird

The movement vocabulary of the Anne character was born from an essential line from the diary: "I wander from one room to another ... and I feel like a songbird after somebody has broken its wings, that keeps bumping into the bars of its cramped cage in total darkness ... " (Frank, 1997, October 29, 1943 entry). The symbolic leitmotif that runs through the entire performance, therefore, became a bird. Not only in the first act, when Anne feels like a bird trying to break through the prison of its cage, but also in the second and third acts as developed initially, the bird has become a hidden symbol.

In the second act of the performance, together we transformed the symbol of the bird: into the bodies of the prisoners; dead birds as the piled up bodies of murdered, emaciated people; birds as the constant presence of ravens circling over the Auschwitz camp, twisted bird bodies, pecking beaks as a physical struggle with death; but also birds as freedom and the desire to transcend the barbed wire fortifications. The third act became the allegorical fairy tale about the pearly bird, an obvious metaphor for the symbolic outcome of the performance, performed by the characters of prisoners led by a historical figure Janusz Korczak, for children from the Warsaw Ghetto (Holocaust Encyclopedia, n.d.). The character of Anne, who was at that moment no longer alive, appears in the role of a pearl bird emerging from the back space behind the stage, where all the prisoners were gradually disappearing.

Transformation of the Diary Literature into Uplifting Play Within a Play (Act I)

The entire form of the first act of the performance arose from a few sentences of *The Diary*. "A bit of air and some laughter, it's crying out inside me, Kitty!" (Frank, 1997, October 1943 entry) directed us to think about the temperament of a girl who desperately wants to live a normal, happy, girlish life and tries at all costs to steal a piece of this joy and carefreeness despite the circumstances. But she feels terribly alone: "besides me, who else is going to read these letters, Kitty? ... who is going to comfort me besides me myself, Kitty?" (Frank, 1997, October 29, 1943 entry).

We created a fifty-minute solo performance representing a prolonged solitary moment of a young girl, who talks to herself in order to overcome the feelings of loneliness among the others as an Act I. In order to fill the silence, she puts down her feelings in writing letters, all of them to one non-existing imaginary friend Kitty, who is the only one to understand. Some moments were intimate confessions, others represented the ordinary desires of a young girl (longing, for example, for clothes to buy in the scene called Dresses). Other letters were specific situations from common daily existence in the shelter with undisguised delight in a parody of individual members who annoyed her. This allowed me as a performer, to develop a whole range of acting and dancing skills, where I could play all the other characters from Anne's life. However, this was not a realistic grasp of the characters, but rather a certain stylized shortcut, an ironic mockery, when my character of Anne complains to her non-existing friend about situations in which she was confronted by others, just as Anne Frank did in her own writing.

The full development of the play-within-a-play principle, the moment of re-enacting a specific situation for the imaginary Kitty, was used across the whole show but mainly in the scene later called Dinner. In that scene, both families together with Mr. Dussel sit at the table and Anne describes each of them. Under the fun and imitation, there is latent anxiety and fear, and obvious misunderstanding. The tension arose between all the members and often results in the injustice towards the youngest one. Anne caricatures her roommates in order to find a way to cope with them, how to get closer to them. She uses the moment of acting and her imaginative re-enacting of the situation in order to elevate the burden of her inner self and conflicts with others into the aesthetical level; therefore she is re-writing the situation.

Anne Frank once heard a radio announcement that after the war the government would be collecting written materials as testimony. This probably influenced her such that she handles the diary in a way one might write a novel (that she wished to do in the future), with a knowledge of the future reader. She also mentioned that she was entertaining her roommates by reading some parts of her diary aloud. In the process of writing itself, the young girl was aware of the spectator, the diary was already becoming an art work. With a knowledge of a potential audience, the pain can be justified as a person's way to bring the important internal information from the subconscious into awareness, to give to one's own suffering the raison d'etre. Thanks to this perspective, it is also possible to experience oppressive situations with a lighter touch. This is mature thinking of the future artist, who withdraws from an experienced event as an object of one's own investigation, reshapes and elevates it through her lens, thereby changing her own coping with that, too. This action, I consider to be artistic as well as therapeutic.

The Deeply Impactful Existence of Anne in My Life

Anne Frank's way of dealing with an oppressive situation, and her approach to it (looking through the lens of a potential viewer), influenced my relationship to art. It is quite possible that the way of elevating my own traumas to an aesthetic level that I use in my work since then is a legacy of my intimate encounter with the writing of Anne Frank. Thanks to this experience I process liminal experiences of my life later on the stage by reshaping them into a work of art as a way of understanding them. It is definitely not an emotional recall or an affective memory method used by Stanislavsky or Lee Strasberg, it is rather the opposite. It is reframing the situation, presenting the situation with my personal/authorial opinion about that, playing it for the viewer's perspective with my new emotional curating of it, using stylized physicality, changing the moods and theatre forms in a way as post-modern theatre does.

Staged Improvisation as a Way to Touch the Present Moment

Some parts of the first solo act were open for improvisation, so that liveliness and spontaneity would not be lost and I could have a chance to authentically react to the viewers' perceptions. The play-within-a-play scene mentioned earlier called Dinner, where Anne's character plays all the other characters, was always different. Sometimes there was an emphasis on the playfulness and irony, other times on painful misunderstanding among roommates, or

THE STAGED PROCESS FOR THE DIARY OF ANNE FRANK: A UNIVERSAL VOICE

fear from an air raid that became the highlight of the scene, always based on the encounter with the present audience.

We used this playful, intuitive procedure in other parts as well, especially in the INTERplay with material that contained aspects of puppetry and object theatre so that the body of an actor disappears.

The very skeleton and order of scenes was also created intuitively in the process, that gradually appeared as I began to name the main thematic lines (the topic of hiding, growing up, desire for life and love, internal and external conflicts, fear from uncertain future and an unimaginable situation if found by Nazis, etc.) more thoroughly. One of the situations was the need to depict the moment when Anne stops being a child and feels her first love, her first desire and recognizes her upcoming womanhood that she described initially in her dream. As a product of the unconscious, I did not want to create the dream scene in any rational way. With that, I locked myself in the rehearsal room one night, put on music that had a dreamy character and "played." I let myself be guided by feelings AND by an awakened imagination. I improvised. I played Anne in the same way that children play different characters. I incorporated the material into the game, the fabric we used as the tablecloth in the Dinner scene. Thanks to the material, various metaphors began to emerge—fabric became an ice rink, bird wings, a boat, a bed. I remembered a line from the Diary where Anne describes how she stayed overnight at her friend Jacques' (Jacqueline Yvonne Meta van Maarsen) and had a desire to touch her breasts (this moment is in the last uncensored published version of the diary). In the improvisation, there was a moment when Jacques rejects this idea of Anne's and Anne does not understand the reason for her rejection—after all, it is natural—"out of pure friendship," (quote from the performance). Then I remembered her other dream, which she describes in the diary, when she asked an unknown boy on skates what his name was, and he answered her that it was Peter. Peter was the son of the other family that shared the shelter with them. I connected Peter on skates with the real Peter who lived with her in a secret part of the house. My hands embodied his hands while the rest of the body played Anne. In the next improv, I put these "his hands" through the sleeves, which in another part of the performance that would symbolize the forgotten hands of the gassed victims of the concentration camps. With this gesture, the imaginary Peter found his theatrical form.

When expressing moments of intimacy in which Anne speaks about her imaginative desire for closeness as well as a moment of curiosity about her own body, it brings the spectator to another level of identification with the character. This is because the spectator is connecting with the protagonist on a very sublime level. This connection is to the inner space that exclusively belongs to the spectator's own intimate life. Recalling this feeling brings back a memory of the spectator's own childhood in the moment of realizing the transformation of their own body. These feelings, which appear as new, are a crucial moment in the development of a person. It is a formative moment when a defenseless childhood acquires a new awareness of itself as a future self-confident personality, when powerlessness transforms into the power to act. Being aware of one's own feelings is the first step to becoming independent of the will of others. In the closed space in the annex, these feelings can be the more intense and also come earlier than in an unlimited space. External limitation allows a closer insight into oneself. In the production a spectator is allowed to witness this essential moment of Anne's transformation into a self-confident personality that is happening in spite, but also because of, the extreme situation in which she resides.

Creating Act I and Weaving for the Entire Play

The entire first act was constructed together with Petr Boháč, in the form of a so-called small and large diary. The small diary was a fifteen-minute Prologue which in chronological order represented the written short notes directed to

THE STAGED PROCESS FOR THE DIARY OF ANNE FRANK: A UNIVERSAL VOICE

Kitty, a brief recording of feelings and events over the course of two years, from 1942 to 1944, from the establishment of the diary to the last entry. The whole small diary was built on imaginary writing on walls through dance and words; the wall represented individual pages of diary created by sharp lighting and the whole prologue was performed with my back to the audience. The audience could read meaning through exposed moving muscles, arms, shoulders and shoulder blades resembling bird wings. The face of the character was revealed for the first time only at the moment of the last entry, which was a painful appeal to the audience in the sentence: "If there were no other people in the world!" The content of the prologue consisted of selected motifs that proved to be essential during rehearsals and that were intended to act as sentences plucked at random from a diary. The awareness of the chronological development of situations is indicated by the date before the designated diary entries on the screen.

This small diary became a summary of Anne Frank's whole life in hiding according to her notes. The big diary was then its development and performance of key scenes, including the aforementioned play-within-a-play in the Dinner scene and the metaphorical Dream. However, the performance display often differed from the small diary; it was either the completion of the mentioned fragment of the scene, a new outcome of the scene, a transformation into a metaphor, or a new interpretation connecting to the final sentence in the small diary. "If there were no other people in the world" thereby closes the circle. Anne's life is presented twice, at first as traces left over by the random reading of her diary, a second with the insightful microscopical look at significant events sifted by re-telling it for the viewer. The possibility of repetition meant for us the possibility of re-telling her story over and over and sharing it endlessly.

The amount of text used in the final form of the performance was approximately twenty-five percent, since the second and third acts were completely non-verbal. The words as the logos (coming from logical meaning) were silenced and the gap after them was filled with allegory. We rehearsed the first act of the show for six months at the residency because of the unlimited rehearsal space. To create a dialogue with Kitty, I approached a cellist Hana Suchanová, a member of the Czech Radio Symphony Orchestra who looked forward to an innovation beyond classical repertoire. Hana responded to fragments directed at Kitty through spontaneous musical improvisation, with some melodies fixed, and others changing every performance. The presence of Hana Suchanová in the role of Kitty as Anne's imaginary friend had two important reasons. Anne Frank invented her in order to psychologically support herself with a dialogical space in which she could reflect on the events. The second reason was to support my physical presence on stage, to strengthen my performance with sound and music bringing emotional interpretation of movements, gestures and words, adding particular atmosphere.

As the performance and events progressed towards the tragic end, the words became less and less, and music and movement took over the dominant role. Last entry: "Dear Kitty. Life here is much easier for me now. Much easier. God has not left me alone here, and he is not going to leave me alone … (music stops) If there were no other people living in the world … Kitty … Pim … Peter … mom … je viens, tu viens, il vient …" (Frank, 1997, August 1, 1944 entry). It was violently interrupted by a pounding on the door, just like in Anne Frank's real life, when the Franks' hideout was revealed and the Gestapo burst in and connected with the sound of a train passing played on cello, accompanied by recorded music. The French inflection is a leitmotif that was repeated in moments of fear. Anne Frank mentioned that when she was unbearably afraid, she either was falling down the stairs to distract herself from the physical pain of fear, or she was repeating French verb conjugation to herself.

At the end of our working process of the first act there were eight main scenes named: Prologue (small diary), Quarrel with Mother, Dresses, Dinner,

Bombs, Dream, Love and the Epilogue—repeating the crucial sentence "If there were no other people living in the world."

The Iterative Creation of Act II and Act III: The Performance Unfolds

After this period, we began working on the second and third acts. We invited friends and classmates from Academy of Performing Arts which I attended who were as keen to experiment as we were. They were Jindřiška Křivánková, Petr Reif, Radim Vizváry and Václav Jelínek.

The first group improvisations were pure, without any assignments (Figure 2.2). We decided to search in our collective unconscious or subconscious memory and to let instinctive bodily experience speak in place of rational objectives. We were to open all our senses to put us into the possibility to discover what is the initial impulse to move, being as in a state of hypersensitive anticipation. Perhaps, in one moment, everyone breathes together, and this becomes the stimulus that develops the subsequent improvisation. At this still and silent presence, the characters of the individual actors sharpened as well. The anticipation of the initial impulse created a kind of subconscious level of communication among us, filled by the suppressed emotions. We felt as a kind of medium that lent their bodies and thoughts to the certain archetypical dramatic situation. To give an example of that, there was a moment around an initial sound created by one actor that triggered the dramatic situation. The other reacted to it by bodily twitch. The sound continued and small twitches increased and changed the meaning to imaginary punches. The third actor suddenly grasped the moving actor with the motivation of saving him: the sound, the movement and the embrace progressed. At the end there was a dead body in the arms of a saver and an oppressor standing on the other side of a space. The obvious violence had happened without any touch, just through the physical implication.

Figure 2.2
Miřenka Čechová as Anne Frank.
Photo by Martin Mark

Sometimes the improvisations were successful and looked like pre-rehearsed parts of the performance, sometimes we failed. It always depended on how much the actors were sensitively aware and connected to each other, how much they asserted their acting egos, or let themselves be guided by true emerging impulses.

The other two parts, the second act, which dealt with non-life, in which the identity of Anne dissolved among nameless numbers, and the third act, allegorical part—the fairy tale about the pearl bird, told by Janusz Korczak to the children of the Warsaw Ghetto, disappeared from the following English version and we have not even returned them to the Czech version. The first act proved to be sufficiently supporting, and its non-literalism and sudden ending with a knock on the door, followed by darkness, in which music with the rhythmic motif of a passing train fades away for several minutes, were the audience's emotional catharsis, referring to the violently interrupted life of Anne Frank.

The music was composed by Varhan Orchestrovič Bauer and recorded with the Instant Music Orchestra. The composer was using hidden musical references and quotations and left the space for free improvisation to the cello player who sometimes connected with the prerecorded music. Among important musical motifs was the traditional Jewish lullaby *Raisins and Almonds*, that was played live on cello, recorded by the orchestra and in Yiddish by a singer Alice Bauer which I accompanied without words, like an echo of Anne's voice that we can search in every eager young girl.

The Premiere and Unfolding of the Performances: From Prague to Washington, DC

We finished the entire show after a year of intensive rehearsals and premiered it on April 4 and 5, 2007 in the Roxy/Nod Experimental Space in Prague. At the second premiere of the performance, we announced the founding of the theatre group Spitfire Company, of which Petr Boháč, some original members, and I are still a part. A year of intensive testing and searching for a distinctive voice and an intimate answer to *The Diary of Anne Frank* created an exceptional project according to critical and audience responses, which far exceeded the dimensions of a graduate school performance.

In 2009, I met Dr. Gail Humphries, who came for her Fulbright appointment and sabbatical year to Prague's DAMU (Theatre Faculty of the Academy of Performing Arts) when I was immersed in my Ph.D. studies. She saw a performance of *The Voice of Anne Frank* at Roxy/Nod in English. The following year, I received a Fulbright scholarship for Artistic Research and the Study of Creative Approach at American University in Washington under her mentorship. As part of my scholarship, I received an offer to perform *The Voice of Anne Frank* but I had to find a cello artist. Gail introduced me to cellist Nancy Jo Snider, director of music at American University, and a life-long creative dialogue began. Playing together with the "new Kitty"—the cello as the external voicing of Anne—was a defining moment for me. Nancy did not use a music score (because there was none), but created her own music in dialogue with me from scratch. As a result, my movement also changed, breathing a new life into the production with a new performer. We rehearsed for several weeks, and our onstage connection became key, as did Nancy's emotional input into the performance. Due to the ability to actively react at a given moment and immediately improvise emotionally and physically, it was not difficult for me later to perform alternately with both cello players, in the Czech Republic with Hana Suchanová and in the U.S. and abroad with Nancy J. Snider.

The United States premiere took place at the Black Box Theater at the Katzen Art Center in 2011. We also performed the show at the Atlas Performing Arts Center's Lang Theatre in Washington, DC in November 2015. Critic Lisa Traiger in *Washington Jewish Week* reviewed the production with the following comments:

> With few props — a valise, a swath of white fabric — and her agile hands and fingers, Cechova invents character and conversation, imitating the shrill voice of Mrs. van Daan and the husky one of Mr. van Daan. With a single sleeved arm, she captures an intimate moment with Peter — a caress and a kiss. And then there's a little ballet sequence, danced against the back wall. Cechova's arms undulate. Then, they erupt in a tremor, hummingbird-like, before they fold away like a

> butterfly expanding and then contracting its wings. But her silences were equally effective, adding depth of character to the physical approach Cechova emits on stage. (Trailer, 2015, para. 6)

Dance critic George Jackson (2015) from the website Danceviewtimes, had these comments:

> Cechova spends considerable time establishing the vitality of Anne's activity, even though confined, hidden away as it is within walls, in secret rooms, in order to shield her from the Nazi gaze ... Cechova also speaks what are presumably some of Anne's lines, but their impact is that of a voice easier to understand as tone — just like that of Snider's cello — than as text. (Jackson, 2015, para. 2)

Eliza Anna Falk (2015) for DC Theater Arts wrote:

> It was a privilege to see the artist showcasing all her talents and skills, combining narration with dance, movement, and live cello music brilliantly played by Nancy Jo Snider, transforming herself into Anne Frank, a young Jewish girl hiding from the Nazis, and telling Anne's extraordinary story in her own distinctive way—original, powerful, humorous, and moving. ... As a spectator last night, I not only 'met' Anne Frank, but also my once young self, bursting with energy and budding emotions, full of dreams and secret longings. Čechová, using words from Anne's diary and her own body as props, takes us inside the world of an average teenage girl. ... Not paying attention to the words I find myself glued to the sight of the danc-

er's bare back, telling a painful story while using its intricate muscles, moving dramatically in the light which is dancing on the white skin. Mesmerizing! I quickly embrace dance, narration, music, light and sound effects interplaying, and I sit back and become a fly on the wall of Anne's family's hiding quarters. (Falk, 2015, para. 1, 3, 5, 7 and 8)

The Expansion of the Performances from a High School in Pennsylvania to South Africa

Since the American premiere at American University and thanks to the kind permission of the Anne Frank Foundation in Basel, Switzerland, I have performed *The Voice of Anne Frank* for young audiences at various universities and theatres and made wonderful friendships through it. Just to name a few, I repeatedly performed at Mercersburg Academy in Pennsylvania, thanks to Laurie Mufson, did a lecture-performance at Stephens College thanks to Dr. Gail Humphries and at Tampa University in Florida thanks to Susan Lennon. In Europe, the performance has achieved several awards, including Outstanding Performance Award (Prague Fringe) or Best of Fringe (at Amsterdam's Fringe festival). The most important were at the Acco festival in Israel and at the National Arts festival in Grahamstown in South Africa, where the performances won the Top of the overseas production.

Market Theatre's Artistic Director James Ngcobo saw the performance there and invited the show to Johannesburg for a longer run. The Market Theatre is considered a visionary theatre, one of the places where the history of the resistance against apartheid was literally made. It received the prestigious "American Jujamcyn Award," which was also given to the Shakespeare Globe and the Yale School of Drama. The South African premiere took place on August 20, 2014. Critic Sharmini Brookes wrote about the animated voice of Anne Frank: "Cechova beautifully conveys the untamed spirit of a thirteen-year-old girl ... This performance is a must see." Robyn Sassen begins her review with the words: "It's heartbreaking, dramatic and spectacular" (Sassen, 2014, para. 5).

For me, the social, cultural and political context of every country in which we performed the show was extremely important. Whether for the young Americans, Eastern Europeans or South Africans, I always tried to bring more than just a great performance. In Johannesburg, we felt that we had a lot in common with the people at the Market Theatre. Dramaturgy of our Spitfire Company, born thanks to *The Voice of Anne Frank* performance, was constructed on the phenomenon of "a person in a liminal situation" coinciding with the everyday situation in Johannesburg. This city has kept many traumas in itself. Petr Boháč and I were paralyzed when we visited the Hector Pieterson Museum dedicated to the protest of school children in Soweto, which ended completely tragically. Over five hundred children were killed, literally shot, in a few days in June 1976.

In Johannesburg, more than anywhere else, I felt that theatre, which has a social and political dimension, also has a healing possibility. This outlook had a deep influence on my future artistic direction (especially in my following solo performances *S/He is Nancy Joe*, *FAiTH*, *Miss AmeriKa* and *Balerinas*, as well as in my directing of a documentary series *Invisible*). In Johannesburg, I felt that the performances were speaking about the similar struggle that many of them were experiencing on an everyday level. In addition to the scheduled performances, we received a call one morning saying that a group of children from Soweto wanted to come and had raised money for a bus ticket to take them to the center of Johannesburg. Completely unplanned and unexpected, the whole team got organized and met everyone in the Market Theatre within an hour. Most of the children either saw a theatre performance or experienced theatre for the first time in their lives. The performance was like a football match as the children outwardly and expressively showed emotions; fear, crying, joy, enthusiasm, and, at the end, they did not want to let us out of the theatre. It was one of the strongest theatre experiences I've had in my entire life. The phenomenon of identifying with a character and co-experiencing trauma, struggle and emotional upheaval is universal across continents, cultures and social backgrounds.

The Continuum: The Complexity of Creating and Honoring the Seminal Voice

I am convinced that what the artist consciously or unconsciously puts into her work in the process of creation remains present in the result itself. For us, the meeting with *The Diary of Anne Frank* became a matter of consecration. It affected me personally, as it affected everyone else involved. Nancy Jo Snider wrote me this beautiful note about the encounter with the work and the heritage of Anne Frank:

> I consider my work with Mirenka Cechova and The Voice of Anne Frank as one of the most important and life-changing moments of my life. Not just my creative professional life, but in my life as it relates to my personal development. Indeed, the creative life and the personal life are very much the same for me and this work on "Anne" helped me to accept that in a culture where such a position is not readily understood or accepted ... The set has the cellist perched high above the stage. This gave me a vantage point that was unique and allowed me to see things in Mirenka's performance no one else could which gave us a special intimacy and feeling of trust. I share Mirenka's feelings about that performance for the school children in Johannesburg and could not describe it better. It

represented the reason we do what we do and what we aspire to achieve. Those sublime moments when we were beyond our selves and inhabiting Anne's world, in all its facets, were among the most magically incredible moments I have ever experienced.

Lastly, one of the most important lessons I learned concerns the Holocaust itself and the very pronounced differences there are culturally between Europeans and people in the United States in terms of how we experience this history. My sensitivity and awareness have been greatly enhanced through living with Mirenka, Petr, and Anne, and having this most personal meaning revealed to me through The Voice of Anne Frank. (Personal email correspondence to Mirenka Cechova on December 28th, 2022)

For over a decade, we felt an obligation to carry Anne Frank's voice further, to the corners of the world and to the children for whom her story became an opportunity to take action, to be heard. For me and for many viewers who saw the performance, Anne Frank became a symbol of immeasurable positive power, as if showing us that despite all the tragic moments that a person goes through in life, it is possible to maintain hope, kindness and enthusiasm until the last moment; the ability to embrace life despite the knowledge of a possible end. Through the depiction of the thirteen-year-old girl's tremendous desire for life, the viewer co-experienced the terrifying context of her tragic death and the death of millions of other innocent victims on a physical level. However, Anne Frank did not disappear, her tragic victimhood did not remain anonymous. Thanks to Otto Frank who published her diary at a friend's insistence, Anne was able to testify and leave a significant mark in history. Anne Frank not only influenced millions but continues to do so even after her death. Her diary teaches young people (and people of all ages) never to give up, never to be silent and never to resign themselves even in circumstances that are limiting or extremely difficult in various ways.

References

Brook, P. (1968). *The empty space.*

Falk, E. A. (2015, November 8). *The voice of Anne Frank by Miřenka Čechová* at Atlas Performing Arts Center. D.C. Theater Arts. https://dctheaterarts.org/2015/11/08/the-voice-of-anne-frank-by-mirenka-cechova-at-atlas/

Frank, A. (1997). *The diary of a young girl.* Bantam.

Holocaust Encyclopedia. (n.d.). *Janusz Korczak.* United States Holocaust Memorial Museum. https://encyclopedia.ushmm.org/content/en/article/janusz-korczak-1

Invisible. (2018, 2020, 2022). *Invisible—Series of autobiographical performances of living women telling their stories of the oppression.* Tantehorse, Palac Akropolis, Prague, 2018, 2020, 2022

Jackson, G. (2015, November 7). *Unhidden: Mirenka Cechova's "The Voice of Anne Frank."* Dancereviewtimes. https://www.danceviewtimes.com/2015/11/unhidden.html

Sassen, R. (2014, August 23). *Anne Frank's voice: Raw but ruptured.* My View. https://robynsassenmyview.com/2014/08/23/anne-franks-voice-raw-but-ruptured/

Traiger, L. (2015, November 10). *Voice of Anne Frank speaks through mime and dance, words. And movement,* Washington Jewish Week. https://www.washingtonjewishweek.com/voice-of-anne-frank-speaks-through-mime-and-dance-words-and-movements/

CHAPTER 3

Signs of Life: Finding These Signs Within You Through Theatre

Virginia S. Criste, Esq.
Joan Liman, M.D., M.P.H.

One of the ten most memorable shows of 2010 you won't want to miss. (Broadway World, 2010, para. 10)

How a Play About Terezín Was Formed

Based on the true story of the Czech ghetto, Terezín (Theresienstadt in German), the musical drama *Terezín* (and later renamed *Signs of Life*), tells one of the most fascinating and least known stories of World War II. Originally a military town on the outskirts of Prague, Hitler transformed it into a hybrid ghetto/camp that served as a transit station to Auschwitz and other concentration camps "in the East." Many of its inhabitants were among the academic and cultural elite of Europe—poets, philosophers, cabaret performers, musicians, artists. Aware of the problem of explaining the disappearance of vast numbers of Jewish intellectuals and celebrities, the Nazis co-opted their talents to convey the ruse that Hitler had created a so-called "model city for the Jews."

Towards the end of the war, Hitler invaded Denmark and many Danish Jews were transported to Terezín. The Danish king, concerned about the kinds of conditions his subjects faced there, arranged for a delegation from the International Red Cross to get a firsthand look. In an attempt to deceive the group's members in advance of their June 1944 visit, the Nazis created an elaborate propaganda scheme forcing the inmates to "beautify" the ghetto.

Signs of Life portrays the struggles of the inmates as they grapple with the question: When survival depends on hiding the truth, how does the truth survive? Librettist Peter Ullian, composer Joel Derfner and lyricist Len Schiff were commissioned by Virginia S. Criste, Esq. to answer this question. In creating the production, characters were based on composites of the prisoners and their experiences. The artistic team used the conceit of hiding and smuggling inmates' photos and drawings, some of which were created in classrooms, as in the case of children who were taught clandestinely by Bauhaus-trained painter and designer Friedl Dicker-Brandeis (1898–1944). Others were drawn by inmates wherever they happened to find themselves in the ghetto at any given moment, helping them to endure the harsh reality of ghetto life.

Criste's account of how an idea in the lobby of a theatre bloomed into a full-fledged musical telling the tale of Terezín is equally moving. She knew her father's parents were dead at the end of WW II and that he got government checks. He seldom spoke of his parents and had no siblings. She knew he had religion and philosophy books all over his desk trying to find the best vehicle for spirituality. However, it was not until around the age of 50 and experiencing divorce that Criste considered exploring her father's past. What she did know was that Terezín was the last place her grandparents had been. So when the Berlin wall came down, she saw it as an opportunity to go there. Once there, she was allowed into the vaults where numerous artifacts had been stored during Communist rule and she was amazed at what she found. In addition to the detailed demographic records kept by the Nazis there were announcements of upcoming poetry readings and concerts, playbills, hand-drawn show posters, diagrams of soccer fields. Criste became more and more emotionally absorbed by the items she was picking up.

The idea for a musical illuminating the cultural life at Terezín did not crystallize until after she left Prague and went to London. There she saw one of the early versions of *Miss Saigon* where pictures of the Bui-Doi were displayed throughout the lobby. Criste imagined in that moment what a poignant display the prisoners' paintings would make on the lobby walls.

New York Development and Workshops

The following narrative of the show's development was shaped by a questionnaire sent out on July 18, 2022 and phone interviews conducted during July and August, 2022. We contacted the people hereafter mentioned who were involved in the production for knowledgeable discussions of the impact of their work on the production. The initial discussion focused on some of the members of the creative team and producers that developed the play. The first person on board was award-winning playwright Peter Ullian, known for *Flight of the Lawn Chair Man, Black Fire, White Fire* as well as screenplays. "I had distant family members on my mother's side who were inmates in Terezín. So, I knew a fair amount about the subject going into the writing of this show" (P. Ullian, personal interview, August 18, 2022). He embraced the idea of doing *Signs of Life* as a musical while acknowledging its challenges:

> There's a bias among people who don't have a deep and thorough knowledge of musicals that musical theatre means light comedy. But American Musical Theater has always tackled serious subjects and done so powerfully because it allows for greater scope as well as powerfully evocative emotion, e.g.,

> *Showboat, Oklahoma, West Side Story.* If you look at a show like *Hamilton*, produced years after our show, you could not create a show with that kind of scale and emotional depth as a straight play. Only musical theatre could capture it. (P. Ullian, personal interview, August 18, 2022)

He admits that there is always a danger that tackling a subject as awesome and terrible as the Holocaust in any artistic form will trivialize the subject. "Works based on history are not a substitute for scholarly study of history, but they can serve as a gateway to scholarly study by creating a compelling, emotionally resonant connection with the historic setting" (P. Ullian, personal interview, August 18, 2022). Cross-cultural casting could amplify this effect.

> *Signs of Life*'s depiction of the cruelty of family detention could have a powerful impact on members of the LatinX community with regard to the current day border crisis, and strike a chord with Japanese Americans whose collective history includes confinement in internment camps during WWII. Casting the inmates as LatinX or Asian or including actors from those communities could create a power and resonance beyond what's on the page. Also, while most of the inmates of Terezín were white, 40% of Jews world-wide today are non-white, so cross-cultural casting can serve to better represent that group. (P. Ullian, personal interview, August 18, 2022)

When Ullian finished the libretto, the next part of the creative team that was brought on was Joel Derfner, a teacher in the musical theatre master's degree program at NYU's Tisch School of the Arts, through the recommendation of Lucy Simon (best known for composing the score for *The Secret Garden*). Derfner then recommended Len Schiff, a graduate of NYU's program. Their collaboration resulted in a full-length book musical titled *Terezín*, with a cast of nine, accompanied by a four-piece orchestra (cello, piano, drums and reeds).

The show's developmental history unfolded over the next 20 plus years. Initial readings featured New York University students. These initial readings were followed by audience-attended readings in Manhattan's Zipper Theater and Melting Pot Theater's reading series, "Preludes to New Musicals." The next producer to become involved was Robb Hunt, Executive Director of the Village Theatre in Issaquah, Washington, who saw it at Melting Pot Theater and agreed to develop it in Issaquah with a cadre of locally experienced actors.

Issaquah, Washington Staged Development

The show wound up being done in Issaquah, Washington over two summers in a row, first as a reading in 2006 and followed by a fully staged production in 2007 (Figure 3.1). The latter was accompanied by a lobby exhibit of reproductions of some of the original artwork by inmates from Terezín.

ART FOR HEALING AND RENEWAL

FIGURE 3.1
A Scene from the 2007 Issaquah, Washington Production of Terezín.
Photo Courtesy of Village Theatre in Issaquah, Washington

This two-year development was rewarding to many, and on many levels. Hunt said it gave him a "new reality" of the Jewish camps. "I got to see them from an artist's perspective, not just as victims, and I wound up with a new and unique empathy, not just sympathy" (R. Hunt, personal interview, July 13, 2022). He felt it was relatable and good storytelling. He saw his audiences moved (R. Hunt, personal interview, July 13, 2022).

A number of actors in those two summers of productions in Issaquah, Washington provided great insights into the process as they developed these powerful characters based on real people. Jason Collins, long active with Issaquah productions, played the role of "Kurt" which was based on the life of Kurt Gerron. A Berlin actor and cabaret impresario, Gerron was banned from the German stage in 1933 but believed his talent and charm would save him in the end (Tugend, 2011). As an actor himself, Collins found the experience gave him new perspective on life and death. He found the sounds unique and the lyrics, poetry. "This show was not work to do" (J. Collins, personal interview, July 25, 2022).

Sarah Rose Davis was 17 and 18 years old when she played the lead role of "Lorelei" in the two Issaquah productions and 20 when she did a reading in New York City. She has since appeared in about thirty shows at Seattle's Fifth Avenue Theatre. "Lorelei" was a big role that resonated for her but challenged her as well. "Playing a part of a group of artists in those most trying of times gave me insight and placed a lot of thought and experience into my tool belt" (S. R. Davis, personal interview, August 17, 2022). Davis recalls the discomfort she felt in the scene "where I held a gun in my hand and considered killing myself, but it made me contemplate what kinds of actual situations could bring that on" (S. R. Davis, personal interview, August 17, 2022). She remembers the important connections she felt with the writers and actors, and cites meeting survivors in New York City as "an astounding experience" (S. R. Davis, personal interview, August 17, 2022).

Kai Daly played Lorelei's pre-teen brother "Wolfie," in Issaquah. Kai remembers:

> I was thirteen years old ... I feel so fortunate that this was my first professional job, because I was surrounded by adults who were prepared to take on the material ... *Terezín* required respect in a way I had never experienced before ... it was so humbling. It has stuck with me in how I approach my work today ... I had access to art that so honestly and viscerally told the experiences of people going through tragedy and loss, but also deep love and connection. (K. Daly, personal interview, August 19, 2022)

Daly also talked about the bonding between actors, describing it as a group that made him feel safe, and ready to approach the material with vulnerability.

He hopes university students producing the show will feel the same sense of safety from classmates and professors in order to facilitate the space to reflect, to verbalize feelings, and to ask questions about such a pivotal and tragic event in our shared history.

Daly shared that the script was challenging at such a young age. One of his most impactful learnings was the Nazis' use of Terezín as subterfuge against the Red Cross. During the show, Terezín's internees were forced to hide the brutality of the concentration camp during a Red Cross investigation. In the scene, a cast member leaned against the set and the streamers put up to cover the drab walls tumbled to the ground. "It was this beautiful, totally accidental snapshot into the reality of those people trapped in Terezín; surrounded by a veneer of normalcy meant to deceive the world" (K. Daly, personal interview, August 19, 2022). Daly has never forgotten that moment.

Joan Liman's involvement with *Signs of Life* began more serendipitously, as this excerpt from her forthcoming memoir, *A LimanAde Life*, reveals:

> "You remind me of a friend. I think you should meet her. Her name is Virginia Criste." Those three sentences were uttered in the spring of 2007 by a theater colleague at a brunch I hosted. I had no idea they would lead to my debut as an off-Broadway producer and change my life in the process. Here's the back story ...
>
> In the aftermath of 9/11, I began volunteering in the NYC not-for-profit theater community. It was a way to deal with the gut-wrenching tragedy of the attack but it also helped fill the void in my life created by the loss of my job as the associate dean for student affairs at New Jersey Medical School three months earlier. That job WAS my life and I had hoped to remain in my position until I retired. Especially since I had traveled a long and often challenging route to obtain it (two

bouts with cancer and episodic depressions). I loved my job and was dedicated to my students.

Fast forward six years, by which time I was at the helm of the board of directors of Amas Musical Theatre (AMT), a NYC not-for-profit organization devoted to the development of quality musical theater presenting different cultural points of view. When my brunch guest, Robb Hunt, suggested I contact his friend Virginia Criste, he didn't know I was associated with AMT; he just thought we would hit it off because our personalities were so alike. Imagine my surprise when I phoned Virginia and learned she had commissioned a musical currently playing at the Village Theater. I asked if she'd ever heard of AMT and suggested she submit it there for consideration. Her response? "I did but never heard back." I blithely replied, "Well I happen to be the president of its board; maybe I can help you." And so began our journey—literally—to bring the show to life in NYC. (Liman, memoir, in progress)

At Criste's invitation, Liman and AMT's producing artistic director, Donna Trinkoff, flew from NY to Issaquah to catch a Wednesday evening performance in June 2007. By the time they left the next morning, Trinkoff had agreed to collaborate with Criste in an off-Broadway production.

Production History of the Newly Titled Play

New York Production: Retitled *Signs of Life*

The next step for Liman was to learn more about the Holocaust by becoming a gallery educator at the Museum of Jewish Heritage in lower Manhattan.

ART FOR HEALING AND RENEWAL

There, she was privileged to meet many Terezín survivors and invited them to several AMT readings preceding the show's off-Broadway opening at the YMCA's Marjorie S. Dean Little Theater on February 16, 2010 (Figure 3.2). As in Issaquah, a photo exhibition of the artwork from Terezín was on display in the YMCA's main passageway leading to the theatre. Since the corridor had heavy foot traffic from morning until night, it was accessible for viewing by hundreds of individuals who frequented the YMCA on a daily basis, enabling the show to make a brief impression on people who never even stepped into the theatre. But it left a long lasting one on the people working inside the theatre, both on and off the stage.

Figure 3.2
A Scene from the 2010 New York Production of Signs of Life.
Photo Courtesy of Amas Musical Theatre.

The next producer involved in the production of the show was Donna Trinkoff. She felt an obligation to produce it to combat the increasingly prevalent "revisionist approach to history" as well as convey the stories of Holocaust survivors before we lose them. She believed she did a "mitzvah" in that she contributed a "beautiful piece of theatre to the canon" and was able to educate people about a chapter of the Holocaust who otherwise would not have known about it.

Trinkoff admits the show took an emotional toll on her both personally and professionally. Given the difficult subject matter, her goal was to present it in the most creative, artistic and sensitive way possible. Rather than use a realistic set, she opted for a more stylistic one to metaphorically clue the audience into the world the characters inhabited. The use of period suitcases scattered across the stage conveyed how they were uprooted from their homes and forced to leave in a hurry.

The actors in the New York production provided additional important insight into their development of the characters in the production. Patricia Noonan, just a few years out of college when she auditioned for "Lorelei," was non-Jewish as were all but two of the New York City cast. Her hauntingly beautiful performance was singled out for praise in the *New York Times* review. She found the work a great responsibility, especially since the heritage depicted was not her own. "I felt very honored" (P. Noonan, personal interview, July 28, 2022). To prepare, she started researching extensively, reading books and going to Jewish museums. She found the arc of her character as written "a catharsis that left me with hope" (P. Noonan, personal interview, July 28, 2022). It deepened her purpose in acting and inspired her to continue writing which she has gone on to do. She felt the story required the cast to really trust each other as all of them were working viscerally and on new material. These many years later, the cast remains bonded, and many members continue to contact each other.

Stuart Zagnit, a veteran of stage, screen, and television, portrayed Lorelei's grandfather "Jacob," the owner of an art gallery prior to deportation to Terezín. Zagnit felt *Signs of Life* was, "an artful portrayal of sending people who had vibrant lives similar to our own off to camps. It demonstrates autocracy spares no one—even those well off." Zagnit goes on to say, "That situation is beginning to resemble what's happening in the world today with the rise of figures like Hungary's Victor Orban and Russia's Vladimir Putin" (S. Zagnit, personal interview, July 26, 2022.). Performing it was eye-opening for him: "It showed me how far the Nazis were willing to go in their propaganda efforts. Their elaborate deception campaign really made an impression on me, as did the resolve and determination of the inmates." Zagnit says, "Everyone has something to learn from a show like this. For Jews, it's especially inspirational to learn how strong our ancestors were and take pride in this part of our heritage" (S. Zagnit, personal interview, July 26, 2022.).

Erica Amato performed with a rock band in California before moving east to concentrate on her acting career. Though raised a Catholic, her mother was very interested in the subject of the Holocaust so Amato had already read a lot of books on it. This background helped inform her performance as "Berta," a role that challenged her as an actor and singer. "To me, Berta was like a raw angry wound because of her life circumstances." Born Jewish, she converts to Christianity at the behest of her Nazi-officer husband, only to be abandoned by him when he realizes her ancestry will hinder his chances of promotion. At the end of the war, she learns he has fled to Switzerland, taking their only child with him and invites her to come join them. Despite his treachery, she is willing to accept his offer, a choice revealed in the penultimate song, *I Will Forget*. Amato was afraid audience members would be unsympathetic to Berta's decision and by extension, her character. Yet, Schiff's artful lyrics had the opposite effect. "At the end of the song, you could hear a pin drop in the theater," according to Amato.

Jason Collins reprised his role as "Kurt" in the New York production, embracing even more the excellent story, unique sound and lyrics. He remained overwhelmed by the history, but by this time, the show had begun to take on more of a contemporary relevance, "allowing me to further identify with the conflicting emotions experienced by my character" (J. Collins, personal interview, July 25, 2022). This is made clear in the show-stopping song, "To Make a Man" where Kurt weighs the considerable personal risk at stake should he make what he knows to be "the moral choice."

American University, Washington, DC

After the New York run, Liman met Laurie Levy Issembert, director of a Bethesda, MD teen musical theatre, at a reading of *The Women's Minyan*, which marked the directorial debut of her sister-in-law, Tovah Feldshuh. Levy Issembert introduced Liman and Criste to Gail Humphries, Ph.D. then a professor of Theatre at American University (A.U.) in Washington, DC in the musical theater division at A.U. During Dr. Humphries' time as a Fulbright scholar in Prague, she directed a production onsite at the Nazi transit camp, a play written at Terezín by two inmates. She was taken by the power of the arts in the camp and this particular musical. Together with Levy Issembert, Dr. Humphries cast an all-student reading of *Signs of Life* on the A.U. campus in the spring of 2013. Again, inclusion of art from Terezín was on display in the halls. Though it was a staged reading, the students' efforts were intense, and they were privileged to have acclaimed New York musical supervisor, Paul Bogaev, on site to help them master Derfner's intricate score. It was an educational experience for him as much, if not more so, than the students. Bogaev noted:

> I knew nothing about Theresienstadt when I started ... and I came away with a lasting respect and, frankly, awe of what those artists went through in trying to tell the world the truth of the horror that they were living through. It has furthered my desire to not let the memory and impact of the Holocaust die out as the years go by. (P. Bogaev, personal interview, September 7, 2022)

Lisa Wiener, the A.U. student cast as "Lorelei," had previously done another Holocaust play *I Never Saw Another Butterfly* at A.U. but still felt very vulnerable in a play with such dark and difficult subject matter as *Signs of Life*. Knowing many of the other cast members made it easier to relax and open up, allowing them to plunge into their roles earlier in the rehearsal process. Wiener felt it was important that productions like *Signs of Life* be performed for wide audiences of different backgrounds but at the same time, realized such works often face the dilemma of "preaching to the choir" (L. Wiener, personal interview, July 15, 2022). Nevertheless, she felt the show was quite successful in answering the show's thematic conundrum about the survival of truth in difficult times.

Working with Dr. Humphries, A.U. graduate and honors students developed educational material to be used in conjunction with the show. The University still allows this material to be used with the show today.

Prague

As Liman and Criste started to develop a production for a Fall 2013 commercial run in Chicago, Dr. Humphries received an invitation from the International Psychoanalytical Association (IPA) to speak at its July 2013 annual conference in Prague. Dr. Humphries suggested the incorporation of that year's theme, the use of theatre as a healing tool for Holocaust survivors, so she decided to incorporate a one-night performance of a staged reading of *Signs of Life* as part of her presentation, using her previous A.U. students. She made arrangements with The Academy of Performing Arts to house everyone and Liman sponsored a fundraising campaign to help subsidize the travel costs. Since Bogaev had made a commitment to work on the Chicago show, he agreed to go to Prague to work on the production.

He felt doing the show in Prague was very moving and meaningful for several reasons: the location, so close to Theresienstadt; performing for an international audience of psychoanalysts at their conference on trauma and the guided tour given to the entire entourage which included a stop at the Attic Theater in the Hamburg Barracks on site at Terezín, the location of many inmate performances during the time the camp was in operation. While there, the cast gave an impromptu performance of a song from the show, leaving an indelible impression on him and everyone else, especially Criste. An equally memorable experience for her was the very favorable post-performance response from IPA members. Criste noted that being acknowledged with applause from an audience of psychoanalysts as having taken action to heal by doing this show as their profession advocates made her very proud.

Chicago

In September 2013, *Signs of Life* opened at Chicago's Victory Gardens Theater with a new director and, except for Jason Collins, an entirely new cast. In addition, the musical director, arranger, general manager and set designer were all new. The set designer made a precise replica of the Terezín theatre by measurement. The authors made adjustments to the book, including a new opening scene and song, which introduced Jason's character much earlier in the show. Jason noted, "The changes in the opening caused me to change the evolution of my character, which I was proud of having been able to accomplish" (J. Collins, personal interview, July 25, 2022). Jason admitted he had some concern that he would not feel the same bonding with the cast as he had experienced in New York but was amazed when he did. "It was obvious from the cast's off-stage communication how the show felt important, impacted their feelings and taught them new history" (J. Collins, personal interview, July 25, 2022).

Of the new members of the Victory Gardens Theater cast, Megan Long, who played "Lorelei," was in her late 20's at the time, but still vividly remembers the show nine years later. Megan described doing the show as "existentially tough" (M. Long, personal interview, July 30, 2022). She worked hard to stay in touch with the humanity and not let her prior knowledge of the history interfere with her character. She found the story of Terezín special, noting the power of theatre to tell these types of stories. Like, Jason, she also commented on the special bonding of the cast.

Liman and Criste were able to work more closely on this production as they were its sole producers. Because the show features characters inspired by real people and stories, they recall that at the start of this run, as in New York, there was always a certain amount of push-pull regarding audience resistance to a musical about the Holocaust. Both acknowledge that since then they have seen a big change.

But there is still a certain amount of resistance to pairing this type of challenging material with a particular kind of art form. They did not want the musical format to be perceived as too trivial. They maintain that despite any initial resistance, most people were won over by the end and there were significant standing ovations at almost all performances in both cities.

Florida Holocaust Museum in St. Petersburg

After the Chicago production, Dr. Humphries introduced Liman and Criste to Elizabeth Gelman, who had recently left Chicago's Skirball Institute of Jewish Learning to become executive director of the Florida Holocaust Museum in St. Petersburg. Gelman was already familiar with the Chicago production, as she knew a few of its cast members. She agreed to showcase American University students in a concert version for a meeting of the International Association of Holocaust Organizations to be hosted by the Museum in August, 2014, subsidized by a grant from the Florida Department of Education. The success of this production, again as a staged reading in a small professional theatre space, gave rise to the insight that *Signs of Life* need not be confined to traditional stage settings; it could be reprised in non-theatrical venues, albeit reconfigured in length, casting choices, even format.

Virtual Presentation

Ironically, the opportunity to test out the hypothesis that the musical could be produced in non-theatrical settings arose one year before the pandemic began. Liman, by then living in Boca Raton, Florida, had re-connected with Avi Hoffman, the co-founder and president of Yiddishkayt Initiative (YI), a not-for profit South Florida organization dedicated to promoting Jewish arts and culture. She helped him secure grant funding from Miami-Dade County for a Spring 2020 week-long series of live events in and around Miami Beach, to include a performance of *Signs of Life*. The day the audition notice was to be announced, news of potential lockdowns began circulating. Hoffman and Liman made the difficult decision to postpone auditions and pivot to a virtual format. Fortunately, plans had already been put in place to hire Caryl and Roy Fantel, a husband-and-wife creative team, to cast, produce and record the show. Both acknowledged the obstacles inherent in digitally producing musicals where characters break into song throughout the narrative when dialogue alone is insufficient to convey the intensity of their feelings (a technique aptly summed up in an observation made by Hans Christian Andersen: "Where words fail, music speaks") (n.d.).

Trying to make this transition seamless while complying with social distancing requirements was difficult. As the music director, Caryl had to rehearse each performer separately so cast members were never in the same room together; in addition, she had to instruct them in mastering self-recording techniques. For Roy, the biggest challenge was editing the music and video together. On the plus side, a virtual production allowed for maximizing the number of audience members who could view it together at one time.

Caryl did double duty as a dramaturge (researcher). With the director's approval, she cast the show without auditions and had a particular person in mind for "Kurt." While he was excited about doing it, he had some concerns as to how he would be received in the role because he was biracial. Since Caryl knew the use of cross-cultural casting would need to resonate with reality, she thoroughly researched Black history in Germany. She found that due to the influx of Africans after Germany's defeat in WWI, there were many of mixed race (the pejorative Nazi term was *mischlinges*) (Mischlinge, n.d.). After the virtual performance aired in April 2020, Liman and Criste were thrilled to learn that Peter Ullian was nominated for a Young-Howze Theatre Award, recognizing excellence in digital theatre, for Best Dramatic writing of the year, which validated their efforts.

Testimony from Holocaust Survivors

What has been especially rewarding for Liman and Criste has been the response from Holocaust survivors who saw the show. Liman recalls that as thrilling as hearing the poignant words and music of *Signs of Life* spoken and sung by amazingly talented casts, the most inspirational moment for her came during intermission at a Sunday performance in NYC. She was seated next to one of the survivors who had been invited to speak during the post-performance talkback. They had never met before so Liman was understandably quite nervous about what her reaction would be. When the lights came up, the survivor turned to her with tears in her eyes, placed her hand on Liman's arm and quietly said, "Thank you, Joan. You've put my life on that stage." She then revealed she came from a comfortable family near Prague who often took ski vacations at nearby resorts. Then well into her eighties, she was still very active. She had a pool and a tennis court in her Stamford, Connecticut backyard and used both on a regular basis. A considerable amount of her time was spent giving talks to Connecticut school children about her experiences at Terezín, Bergen-Belsen and Auschwitz. Her encounter with a sixth grader during one such visit illustrates the value-added component of experiential learning in teaching about the Holocaust. At the end of her talk, a student approached and asked if he could feel the numbers on her arm. After he respectfully brushed his fingers over her tattoo, he reverentially proclaimed he had touched history.

Post-performance testimonies from other survivors and their families proved to be very enlightening. One was a woman whose daughter and granddaughter were actively involved at The Museum of Jewish Heritage. A photo the family had donated depicting the survivor as a young woman at work on a sewing machine was one of the artifacts Liman regularly pointed out on her tours. The daughter disclosed to the audience that although she had been born in a displaced persons (DP) camp, her mother had never spoken about her Holocaust experiences while she was growing up. Asked by the moderator if she had ever shared them with people outside her family during the postwar years, the woman ruefully shook her head and replied, "No—not because I didn't want to but because I was told no one would believe me if I did."

Another recounted his personal history in a spellbinding manner, stunning the audience with tales of outwitting the Nazis early in the war when they invaded his hometown in Poland. He eventually wound up in Terezín where he was put to work painting the facades of buildings as part of the Nazi's "beautification" efforts. After liberation, he made his way to the United States where he became a well-known painter of contemporary art, and, today, some of his work hangs in the Smithsonian Institute.

His take on whether or not to give testimony had a somewhat similar slant. He felt the most effective conduit for imparting what had transpired in the camps was to "stick to the facts"—i.e., the objective data of archival documents and statistical records of the deportations and deaths—rather than the subjective memories of the survivors, as no two of them were likely to remember identical events in the exact same manner. "What's more," he said, "my memories of that time are hard to even recapture because I struggled mightily to repress all the horrible things I saw and experienced in order to get through each day."

Like Liman, Criste was exceptionally moved by the survivors' feedback as well as the audience reaction to it. She would find it especially interesting if audiences of any ethnic background could come away empathizing with the plight of Terezín's inhabitants and hopefully ponder some of the agonizing choices one has to make in the face of difficult circumstances.

Going Forward

Because *Signs of Life* is a theatrical event which also educates, Liman and Criste believe it is a uniquely effective storytelling tool. Criste adds that performances provide empathy and understanding for those people in the world right now who are suffering similar circumstances—a most valuable lesson. Towards this end, they plan to take it on an educational road tour to universities, community organizations and specialized venues both here and abroad. In addition, the success of Yiddishkayt Initiative's digital performance paves the way for on-demand streaming of future productions, providing a cost-effective alternative to the traditional bricks-and-mortar method of theatre production.

Both women hope by doing so, they will not only be making an important contribution to keeping the history of Terezín and the plight of its victims intact for future generations but allow them to continue seeking professional and personal fulfillment, a journey that began when each faced a significant crossroad in their respective lives. As Liman sums it up, thanks in part to a stroke of fate that introduced her to Hunt and Criste at a low point in her career, her search to find a meaningful life as a "recovering academic" has exceeded her expectations, culminating with the honor of being invited to contribute to this book.

In Criste's case, she discovered a profoundly meaningful way to honor the memory of her father. And though his search for the best vehicle for spirituality may never have come to fruition in his lifetime, her quest to add meaning to her life has been more than fulfilled by bringing *Signs of Life* from the page to the stage.

Liman and Criste are both enormously proud of the impact their producing efforts have had on the hearts and minds of the many talented theatre professionals who embraced their passion in bringing the tale of Terezín to life—a place where so many lives were lost. By the time Soviet troops arrived on May 9, 1945 to liberate Terezín, approximately 150,000 Jews, including some 15,000 children, had passed through its gates. The majority were deported to other camps to be murdered; over 35,000 perished in the ghetto (Jewish Virtual Library, 2022). They hope that their efforts on this production honor their memories.

References

Andersen, H. C. (n. d.). https://nortoncenter.com/2020/05/09/music-speaks-where-words-cannot/

Broadway World (2010). *2010's ten memorable theater moments you might have missed.* https://www.broadwayworld.com/article/2010s-Ten-Memorable-Theater-Moments-You-Might-Have-Missed-20010101-page2#ixzz1A5yw-2P3d

Jewish Virtual Library (2022). *Terezín concentration camp: History & overview.* Jewish Virtual Library is a Project of American-Israeli Cooperative Enterprise. https://jewishvirtuallibrary.org/history-and-overview-of-Terezín

Liman, J. (2022). *A LimanAde Life.* (Unpublished manuscript)

Mischlinge (n. d.). Yad Vashem, Shoah Resource Center. https://www.yadvashem.org/odot_pdf/Microsoft%20Word%20-%206504.pdf

Tugend, T. (2011, April 28). Rare Nazi film shows Terezín camp as paradise. *Jerusalem Post,* 17:29. https://www.jpost.com/jewish-world/jewish-news /r Home page.

Yad Vashem Coping Through Art—Friedl Dicker-Brandeis and the children of Theresienstadt https://www.yadvashem.org/articles/general/coping-through-art-brandeis-theresienstadt.html

CHAPTER 4

Healing Through Talkbacks and Difficult Dialogues: Creating a Safe Space for Empathic Understanding

Sara Herrnstadt Crosby, M.S.W., CSW-PIP

A Personal Story of Healing

It is 9:00 AM on a cold winter morning in the Northern Plains. The sun has only been above the horizon for a little over an hour as the 7th and 8th grade students file into the auditorium for a performance by Dakota Academy of Performing Arts (DAPA) Plays for Living Theatre Company. The high school actors will present *The Survivors,* a 30-minute play on suicide prevention, by Leslie Glass. Post-performance, I facilitate a talkback with the audience. Quickly I am able to gain their trust, as I am neither teacher nor parent, and they openly begin to process their own stories, feelings and questions. Afterwards one boy comes forward to speak privately and confesses that he has a plan in place to end his own life. The school is able to contact parents, and a sheriff from this smalltown escorts him to the Behavioral Health Hospital some nine miles away, where he is made comfortable and safe as he begins his journey toward healing.

Similar scenarios have occurred at each and every performance of not only this play but of all the plays where I have facilitated post-performance discussion. Performances followed by talkbacks are a powerful way to bring the unspoken out into the open and to create an empathic understanding of difficult subject matter. In 1990, I was a relatively new psychotherapist working at a family service agency in Madison, WI. I had left NYC and acting behind six years previously when one day my supervisor asked me about implementing a program utilizing theatre as a way to educate people about advanced directives. Recognizing this opportunity as a way to blend my theatre background with my work as a psychotherapist, I created my first Plays for Living Theatre Company.

My evolution as a facilitator has been enlightened by so many brilliant and courageous people who have informed my growth in the utilization of theatre to teach empathic understanding through post-performance talkbacks. Dr. Gabor Maté, whose work on trauma and addiction is shared in his books, *In The Realm of Hungry Ghosts: Close Encounters with Addiction* (2010) and *The Myth of Normal* (2022) has played a large role in my understanding of how trauma informs our beliefs. *The White Privilege Conference*, a yearly event sponsored by The Privilege Institute and led by Dr. Eddie Moore Jr., has broadened my lens around all issues pertaining to social justice. My mission as a facilitator is to illustrate the lived experiences of characters in a play, following up with thoughtful and intentional talkbacks. I am able to challenge the audience to explore their own perspectives, beliefs and biases through the story the actors have told. Our own beliefs are among those things we, as individuals, have the power to change.

This chapter will explore, through examples, the purpose for talkbacks, the process for preparation and implementation, as well as the desired results and outcomes.

Antisemitism on a Personal Level

"Nazi," the boy whispered as he passed the young girl in the crowded hallway of the middle school. As the only Jewish student in the school, the girl began to dread the change of classes. When time came to celebrate her Bat Mitzvah, the coming-of-age ritual for Jewish girls, this same girl wanted to include her classmates in her service project, often done as a meaningful way to celebrate adulthood. She was careful in her presentation to the school administration explaining her desire to create some ancestral healing between two groups who were victims of genocide, the Native American population on the Pine Ridge Indian Reservation and the Jewish people. The principal gave his full approval and she presented her request for a collection of new blankets for the Elders on Pine Ridge that would be given out at the senior center in Wanblee, SD. The new blankets were to represent the genocide of small pox passed to this great indigenous nation through infested blankets sent by the U.S. government. The girl was thrilled that so many of her 7th grade classmates were enthused to help. But as was often the case when this child attempted to include and educate her classmates about her Jewish traditions, she was shut down by a parent who complained about "Judaism being shoved down her child's throat." But in this instance, the principal overrode the objecting parent and, in the end, over 200 brand new blankets were distributed to the elders on Pine Ridge along with a large homemade meal.

This girl is my daughter, who navigated growing up, one of five Jewish people her age, in the largest city in South Dakota. Unfortunately, this is not an isolated story. Often those who are not exposed to diversity or issues that are outside their lived experience rely on stereotypes and myths that create biases and fear. Although diversity has grown in the 11 years since my daughter graduated and moved beyond the bubble of this small city, the work being done is often met with resistance. This reality makes it important to find less threatening ways to help people expand their empathic understanding of issues beyond their own lived experiences.

Using Empathy Techniques in Talkbacks

As a clinical social worker, I have been teaching empathic understanding through the use of post-performance talkbacks for over 30 years, and the lack of education and understanding by those in the dominant culture around diverse groups, particularly regarding the Holocaust, as well as stigmatized issues, such as depression, suicide prevention, prejudice, discrimination, and addiction, to name several, continues to surprise me. Just the other day, for example, a white well-educated woman working in healthcare sat in a book club discussion of *Caste: The Origins of Our Discontents* by Isabel Wilkerson (2020), and was surprised to find out that Black people in America have been victims of lynchings. How can it be possible that there are people in our country who, even before the current move toward banning critical race theory, have not been taught the history of the many evils that have been perpetrated on human beings throughout time?

The reality is these issues are things that people find difficult to talk about openly, or even acknowledge. Whether the resistance to discussing complicated and painful issues is pre-embedded in societal stigma, a sense of guilt, fear or unearned privilege, talking directly with people can and often does elicit defensive responses.

While empathic understanding is the goal of productive conversation, even this can prove difficult. Humanistic psychologist Dr. Carl Rogers describes empathic understanding as follows:

> If I am truly open to the way life is experienced by another person ... if I can take his or her world into mine, then I risk

> seeing life in his or her way ... and of being changed myself, and we all resist change. (Feldman, 2022, p. 1)

This authentic interaction between myself and the audience is, thus, delicate. Relinquishing old patterns of thinking, accepted stereotypes, and beliefs is challenging as it is more comfortable to maintain denial of those things which might trigger discomfort.

Live theatre is a less threatening way to bring the unspoken out into the open. "Attending a play can increase empathy, according to brain scientists" (Bengs, 2022, p. 1). Connection to the characters on the stage has been shown to increase an audience member's empathy.

Post-performance discussion centers around the people and groups portrayed and a growing understanding of the experience and issues outside the audience's own lived experience.

Of particular note is the impact talkbacks have on audience members experiencing performances centering on the Holocaust, such as Gail Humphries' (2017) *Traces in the Wind, A Tone Poem of Remembrance* (Figure 4.1). I was fortunate to facilitate a post-performance talkback of this brilliant piece at Theater Works, in Peoria, AZ where audience members explored the real lives of three female survivors, Rosalina Glaser, Charlotte Delbo, and Eva Kavanova, who embraced the arts as a strategy for survival. Each character has a unique story and Humphries uses their words and music (an original score by Tom Andes) to connect these experiences in a way that reaches a new understanding of the Holocaust and those individuals who found themselves caught in the web of atrocities woven by Hitler and the Third Reich. It is easy to dehumanize these stories and to detach ourselves from these realities as happening elsewhere to someone else. Humphries weaves together the lived experiences of these women in such a way that the audience is able to experience their stories on a universal human level. After all, the need to survive is innate in all that lives.

ART FOR HEALING AND RENEWAL

Figure 4.1
Sara Crosby facilitating a talkback with audience and cast, music director and director of Traces in the Wind.
Photo Credit: Marketing Team of Theater Works in Peoria, Arizona

Traces in the Wind, like many other stories told in play form, is a powerful way to bring the unspoken out into the open. Post-performance discussion gives the audience an outlet to explore what they have just witnessed and leave with a deepened empathic understanding of difficult subject matter.

It is unbelievable in this day and age to realize the extent of the broad lack of knowledge and understanding of this dark time in our history. Harriet Sherwood (2020) of *The Guardian* states:

> Almost two-thirds of young American adults do not know that 6 million Jews were killed during the Holocaust, and more than one in 10 believe Jews caused the Holocaust, a new survey has found, revealing shocking levels of ignorance about the greatest crime of the 20th century. (para. 1)

To emphasize the dearth of knowledge, young adults have regarding the Holocaust, Sherwood (2020) further reports:

> According to a study of millennial and Gen Z adults aged between 18 and 39, almost half (48%) could not name a single concentration camp or ghetto established during the second world war. Almost a quarter of respondents (23%) said they believed the Holocaust was a myth, or had been exaggerated, or they weren't sure and 12% said they had definitely not heard, or didn't think they had heard, about the Holocaust. (para. 2–3)

Several years ago, I directed a short reader's theatre production that combined writings of Holocaust Survivors' lived experiences for a local high school forensics team. In preparation, I shared with the students a documentary about the Holocaust featuring life inside the concentration camps. One 17-year-old student was astounded to find out, that upon entrance into the camps, the prisoners were often forced to have their heads shaved. I do not fault this student for their ignorance, as their capacity for empathy was well beyond that of many of their peers. It was frustrating, but understandable, that deeper exploration is not accomplished, considering the broad-brush strokes used in covering WWII in World History classes, limiting discussions that help students process information. With Texas House Bill 3979 signed into law, which aims to "prohibit teachers from discussing some of the most important and relevant matters that concern us all," (Prose, 2021, para. 9) teachers have become hesitant to spend time discussing controversial historical issues. For many non-Jewish students the horror of this genocide is a story that happened to the "other" long ago, in a different time and place, and has little, if any, relevance to their lives. It is easy to remove oneself from the realities of such atrocities when those moments in history are presented simply and briefly as words on a page.

"Nineteen U.S. states require Holocaust education ... 31 do not," said Andy Hollinger, a spokesperson for the United States Holocaust Memorial Museum in Washington (Karimi, 2021, para. 7).

Mental Health

It is no secret that mental health and addiction are stigmatized in our societies. Those struggling with these brain diseases and their families are often judged and avoided. Accessibility to appropriate care is lacking as our country deals with an epidemic of anxiety and depression amongst our adolescent population (Caron, 2021). Current drug education and prevention in our schools is cerebral at best and has proven not to work as we can clearly see by the epidemic of addiction and overdoses plaguing our country (Provini, 2011). Gabor Maté, MD (2010), in his book, *In the Realm of the Hungry Ghost: Close Encounters with Addiction*, explains that, "Addictions always originate in pain, whether felt openly or hidden in the unconscious" (p. 36). Addiction is a symptom of a larger problem.

Underlying trauma, and/or a mental health diagnosis, often feed drug and alcohol use as a means of self-treatment. Merely addressing the consequences of addiction without understanding a person's underlying pain only deals with the symptom of the larger issue. The characters in a play can reveal the underlying problems with which a person might be living. The drug/alcohol use is then understood as a means of coping, and becomes a springboard into a deeper conversation post-performance. By first identifying with the characters in the play, followed by exploration and validation of emotions and situations, students, as well as adults, gain an understanding of how to put words to feelings. This, in turn, helps to reduce a stigma which has often kept people from seeking help. By giving permission to talk, facilitators are able to encourage dialogue about our common shared humanity. This is the beginning of building an empathic understanding and compassion around the suffering and behavior of others.

I have produced plays and led hundreds of discussions around suicide, depression, prejudice/discrimination around race, religion, gender identification, as well as drug and alcohol prevention for middle schools. Oftentimes these plays on important human issues have been met with resistance from administrators. Schools cite fears that performances followed by talkbacks will leave them vulnerable to a rise of suicides, addiction and a promotion of LGBTQ+. It is true that a performance of another's lived experience can illustrate painfully the messiness of the human condition. It can hurt to watch when many of us wish not to feel. Unfortunately, we do not often grow without pain, for it is in discomfort that we are motivated to rethink what we previously held as our beliefs (Rodriguez-Fischer, 2015). The fact is, there is greater danger in not addressing these human issues, in not talking, and most importantly in not listening. When people feel alone, misunderstood or not heard, mental health issues are often exacerbated as people feel shut down and not able to openly express their own lived experiences, their thoughts and emotions. Intolerance and misunderstanding, ignorance and prejudice happen when we stay in our bubbles of certainty and never expand our knowledge base beyond what we feel we can control. We have to speak the unspoken so change and healing are able to occur, so our lens of understanding might broaden.

Currently university and college campuses are either faced with intentionally creating Diverse, Equitable and Inclusive (DEI) environments in response to the increasing awareness of systemic racism and other injustices experienced by underrepresented students, faculty and staff or faced with mandates against teaching Critical Race Theory (Alfonseca, 2022). According to Southern Nazarene University's Professional and Graduate

Studies program (SNU, 2021), "Those who don't fully support diversity and inclusion measures may express skepticism, asserting that the only reason to support diversity is to avoid legal trouble" (para. 5). But, according to this same SNU Professional and Graduate Studies program statement, it is important, in preparing students for the real world, that they "understand how cultural norms influence communication" and "recognize that their experiences are not everyone's experiences" (SNU, 2021, para. 6). The SNU Professional and Graduate Studies program statement also emphasizes that it is important to understand "that certain words and ways of speaking can be profoundly harmful ... even when their intentions are good, they can still say and do things that may harm people who are not like them" (SNU, 2021, para. 6). Finding ways to infuse DEI into all areas of a higher education campus can be threatening. Here theatre can be useful in bringing a deeper awareness and exploration of the importance of DEI.

In recent years, resistance around teaching disturbing aspects of history has become more common. Slavery and the Holocaust are two examples in which the dominant culture feel that teaching the truth and depth of these injustices will only make their children feel badly for being white and non-Jewish. "White fragility" is well defined in Robin DiAngelo's book, *White Fragility: Why it's So Hard For White People to Talk About Racism* (2018). In a CNN interview, DiAngelo (La Motte, 2020) explains:

> The term "fragility" speaks to how little it takes to throw us out of our racial comfort zones, but our reaction is not fragile at all in its impact. We lash back in ways that actually end up being punitive to whoever challenged us, but highly effective to repel the challenge. The impact is a weaponized defensiveness, hurt feelings and umbrage because it marshals behind it the weight of history and institutional power. (para. 24–25)

Utilizing live theatre has proven itself to be a less threatening way to open people up to a deeper understanding, and a change of beliefs that previously held them captive to false narratives and stereotypes.

According to Elizabeth Heaney, "Theater is unparalleled in terms of its potential for learning. Theater engages the audience in ways that other forms of communication cannot. Besides the power of emotional engagement, there's full sensory engagement" (Pasier, 2019, para. 17–18). Laura Bengs (2022), in her article, *Research Links Increased Empathy with Live Theater Experience* (2022) cites a 2021 study published in the Journal of Experimental Social Psychology that captured theatre's power to increase empathy. The data revealed that, "live theater experiences increased audience members' empathy for the people and groups portrayed. The increase in empathy correlated with how transported the audience members felt" (p. 2). In this same article, child mental health counselor and registered drama therapist Katie Lear says, "Elements inherent in theater as an art form can increase the emotional investment in understanding and connecting with characters that are very different from us, which is a critical part of how our minds engage in empathy" (Bengs, 2022, p. 3).

During a post-performance talkback of a Dakota Academy of Performing Arts (DAPA) Plays for Living production of a play on diversity, fourth graders are deep in discussion as to the definition of diversity (Figure 4.2). One boy admits that perhaps he hadn't been very nice to another boy earlier that same day on the playground and he needed to apologize. According to the team at Brainstorm Productions, an educational theatre company in Australia, (Brainstorm, 2016):

> Theater is a safe space to develop empathy. Theater is an opportunity for children to explore and mirror difficult and challenging emotions. A person can safely watch an actor bully

another actor, and can learn how both parties experience and respond to this situation. (para.14)

Figure 4.2
Dakota Academy of Performing Arts Plays for Living Theatre Company Performing What's the Difference, a Play on Diversity Issues by William Baldwin Young.
Photo credit: Washington Pavilion of Arts and Science

Strategies for Implementation

By creating a safe space and carefully developed questions to prompt discussion, audience members are able to discuss, ask questions and explore what they have just experienced. In this feedback process, the feeling of empathy, opened up while watching the performance, is moved into a deeper intellectual understanding of the story told.

Undoubtedly, there is a challenge for facilitators to negotiate the varied unconscious biases that come from learned perspectives based on an individual's lived experience. A few years ago, I facilitated a post-performance talkback around *Where Does it End?*—a play by William Baldwin Young, on prejudice and discrimination for teens, to a small rural middle school of all white Christian students. The play centers around a Jewish mother and her son who own and run a pizza parlor and a young man who acts out his prejudice in increasingly violent ways. We explored each of the characters and the choices they made and I asked the audience, "By show of hands, how many of you would think differently of me if I told you I was Jewish?" Every hand went up in the air. I then asked, "How many of you, to your knowledge, have ever met a Jewish person?" All hands went down. This opened up a discussion around how our lived experiences inform our perspectives and how exposure to new experiences helps break stereotypes.

The performance becomes the springboard for facilitation prompt questions. For example, to begin a post-performance talkback of *Traces in the Wind* (Humphries, 2017), I might use this prompt referred to as the "Epic Question" by The Citizen Artist (Wallert, 2022, p. 128):

> Imagine that two weeks from now, you will wake up one morning and you find yourself thinking about the production you saw here today. What is it that you'll be thinking about? It could be a word, a line, a phrase, an image, or a moment. What do you think will resonate with you over time?

It is a good idea, then, to base your next questions on some of the audience's responses. From there we could ask more specific questions that might prompt deeper discussion. How did you see the theme of the use of arts for survival played out in each woman's story? Why is this story relevant today? What are some social actions that you could address that are at the center of the play? At the end you might ask, now that you have had the opportunity to explore the play further, what will you take away from today's performance (Table 4.1)?

TABLE 4.1

Facilitated Talk-Back

> ***When We Were Young and Unafraid*, by Sarah Treems**
> **Produced and Performed at Stephens College**
> **Directed by Gail Humphries**
>
> **Facilitated Talk-Back**
>
> **Sample Audience Prompts:**
>
> 1. Do any of these characters end with a sense of resolve and or hope? Which ones? Why or why not?
> 2. The play takes place in 1972 the year before Roe vs. Wade. How were things different after 1972? How do you feel the overturning of Roe will effect issues around violence against women?
> 3. How does the play speak to us through the ME TOO movement of 2018?
> 4. Penny, the daughter, is initially dismissive of sex and relationships. How do we see sexual desire as a compelling force that may lead women away from a sense of independence and purpose? In Penny? And in Mary Ann?
> 5. Viktor Frankl says, "Between stimulus and response there is a space. In that space is our power to choose our response. In our response lies our growth and our freedom." What drives the choices that Mary Ann makes? Is she finding growth and freedom at any level through her choices?
> 6. What is gaslighting? What are some examples in the play of gaslighting? What tendencies do we see in Mary Ann that make her vulnerable to gaslighting?

HEALING THROUGH TALKBACKS AND DIFFICULT DIALOGUES

In facilitating post-performance discussion, regardless of subject matter, it is important to remember the following pointers for leading an effective discussion.

1. *Be very familiar with the discussion guide that you will be using.*
2. *Don't pretend to be an expert, even if you are. There is nothing wrong with admitting that you don't have the answer.*
3. *Listen and respond to the audience's needs. Remember, you are a discussion leader not a lecturer. Do not monopolize the discussion. Your role is to guide the audience with questions and comments that encourage audience discussion, leading the group to make their own discoveries and arrive at their own conclusions. Often this can be done by saying, "That is a good question. How would someone else respond to that?"*
4. *Remain as neutral as possible throughout the discussion. This may be difficult, particularly when the audience does not share your point of view. However, for the discussion to be effective, it is essential that the audience is not swayed by your values and judgements.*
5. *Expect the discussion to be slow in the beginning. In order to create a safe and trusting environment you may have to draw out your audience by starting with non-personal, non-threatening questions that focus on specific moments in the play.*
6. *Keep the atmosphere friendly. You may have to shift the discussion if one topic becomes too controversial.*
7. *Encourage broad participation. No one should monopolize the discussion.*
8. *Restate good points made by audience members.*
9. *Save a few minutes at the end of the discussion to summarize the main points.*
10. *Try closing the discussion while the audience is still enthusiastic. This is more effective than wrapping things up after the discussion has lost momentum.*
(PLAYS for LIVING, 1995)

Facilitators are advised (PLAYS for LIVING, 1995):

> Remember that your job as facilitator is to remain sensitive to the needs of the audience. You will help them better understand the story's issues and how they relate to real life by leading a well-focused discussion. Post-performance discussion when done well will help audiences to begin to find their own answers, learning more about the subject and its meaning in their own lives. (p. 30)

The 2021 study, in collaboration with two prominent theatre companies on opposite coasts, and published in the *Journal of Experimental Social Psychology* (Bengs, 2022) on theatre's power to increase empathy used a synthesis of surveys conducted before and after participants witnessed the plays to prove that theatre performance increases empathy. I have used this model in schools with consistent success. The repeat scheduling of our DAPA PFL performances over the past 21 years has also been an indicator of the positive effect our plays and talkbacks have on our young audiences. Teacher and administration feedback through surveys also provides us with valuable outcomes.

Development of empathic understanding is needed to change previously held beliefs that can be a hindrance to the dismantling of racism, antisemitism, and myths surrounding addiction and mental illness. After all, systems are made up of people, so in creating opportunities for people to develop empathic understanding, we then might begin to create a world that is no longer afraid to accept the truth of what is. "When you learn the history of the Holocaust, you are not simply learning about the past," said Deborah Lipstadt, a professor of modern Jewish history and Holocaust studies at Emory University (Ramgopal, 2020, para. 14). "These lessons remain relevant today in order to understand not only antisemitism, but also all the other 'isms' of society. There is real danger to letting them fade" (Ramgopal, 2020, para. 14). Through live theatre coupled with post-performance talkbacks we are able to take action to raise awareness, empathy and understanding so the words "NEVER AGAIN" will become a true reality.

References

Alfonseca, K. (2022, March 24). *Map: Where anti-critical race theory efforts have reached.*
https://abcnews.go.com/Politics/map-anti-critical-race-theory-efforts-reached/story?id=83619715

Bengs, L. (2022, July 8). Research Links Increased Empathy with Live Theater Experience. *Discover Magazine*, 3.

BrainStorm Productions. (2016, November 24). *How Theatre In Education Helps with Student Empathy.* Brainstorm Productions: Award-Winning In-School Theatre.
http://www.brainstormproductions.edu.au

Caron, C. (2021, February 17). *Nobody has openings: Mental health providers struggle to meet demand.*
http://nytimes.com/2021/02/17/well/mind/therapy-appointments-shortages-pandemic.html

DiAngelo, R. (2018). *White fragility, why it's so hard for white people to talk about racism.* Beacon Press.

Feldman, B. (2022). *Humanistic therapy.* http://boazfeldman.com/mindfulnesstherapygeneva/humanistic-therapy/

Humphries, G. *(2017) Traces in the Wind.* National Jewish Theater Foundation, Holocaust Theater Catalog.

Karimi, F. (2021, May 29). *31 states don't require schools to teach about the Holocaust. Some laws are changing that.* cnn.com
https://www.cnn.com/2021/05/29/us/holocaust-marjorie-taylor-greene-states-trnd/index.html

La Motte, S. (2020, June 7). *Robin DiAngelo: How 'white fragility' supports racism and how whites can stop it.*
https://www.cnn.com/2020/06/07/health/white-fragility-robin-diangelo-wellness/index.html

Maté, G. (2010, January 5). *In the Realm of the Hungry Ghosts: Close Encounters with Addiction.* North Atlantic Books.

Maté, G. (2022). *The Myth of Normal.* Penguin Random House.

Pasier, J. (2019, October 14). *Study finds live theater enhances student learning and empathy.*
https://www.purdueexponent.org/campus/article.html

Prose, F. (2021, October 19). *Texas schools are being told to teach 'opposing views' of the Holocaust Why?*
https://www.theguardian.com/commentisfree/2021/oct/19/Texas-holocaust-curriculum-schools-hb-3979

Provini, C. (2011). *Is your drug prevention working?*
https://www.educationworld.com/a_curr/school_climate/drug_prevention_program_isnt_workind.shtml

PLAYS for LIVING. (1995). *Guide to Facilitation.* PLAYS for LIVING.

Ramgopal, K. (2020, September 16). *Survey finds 'shocking' lack of Holocaust knowledge among millennials and GenZ.* h
ttps://www.nbcnews.com/news/world/survey-finds-shocking-lack-holocaust-knowledge-among-millennials-gen-z-n1240031

Rodriguez-Fischer, M. (2015, July 13). *What motivates people to change?*
http://newpathwayscounselingndcoaching.com

Rogers, C. (1975). Empathy: An unappreciated way of being. *The counseling psychologist*, 5(2), 2–10.
https://journals.sagepub.com/home/tcp

Sherwood, H. (2020, September 16). *Nearly two-thirds of U.S. young adults unaware 6m Jews killed in the Holocaust.* The Guardian.
https://www.theguardian.com/world/2020/sep/16/holocaust-us-adults-study

SNU (2021, February 4). *The importance of diversity and inclusion in higher education.* Southern Nazarene University Professional and Graduate Programs.
https://degrees.snu.edu/blog/the-importance-of-diversity-and-inclusion-in-higher-education

Treem, S. (2015). *When we were young and unafraid.* Dramatist Play Service.

Wallert, J. (2022). *Citizen artists: A guide to helping young people make plays that change the world.* Routledge.

Wilkerson, I. (2020). *Caste: The origins of our discontents.* Random House.

CHAPTER 5

Music of Resistance and Survival: Composition, Performances, and Education for Understanding and Healing

Laurence Sherr, D.M.A.

The *Music of Resistance and Survival Project* was developed to expand the outreach, educational potential, and impact of my *Sonata for Cello and Piano: Mir zaynen do!*, a work that integrates newly composed music with Holocaust-era songs of resistance and survival. The project evolved to include multiple modular, adaptable, and complimentary components. These components comprise the sonata, source songs presented in live or recorded performances, my media presentation and historical commentary about the source songs and their creators, and online educational material and pedagogical resources. This modular design enables productions that can be effectively adapted to various venues, circumstances, and audiences. Links to music and information are listed at the end of the chapter for those who wish to listen to the music described.

The primary focus of this chapter is the genesis of the *Music of Resistance and Survival Project*. The genesis is tracked through two successive multi-year stages. At the conclusion of the chapter, the realization of the *Music of Resistance and Survival Project*'s artistic and educational goals is demonstrated though consideration of its dissemination and audience impact.

ART FOR HEALING AND RENEWAL

Project Genesis: Stage 1

The *Music of Resistance and Survival Project* (*MoRaSP*) evolved from my initial idea to compose a cello sonata whose purpose, in addition to being a standard concert work, would extend to exposing audiences to the artistic work of creators oppressed under Nazi rule. Following in the line of my two previous vocal compositions that set poems of Holocaust survivor and Nobel laureate Nelly Sachs, I intended in this case to create an instrumental composition that would draw on the work of Holocaust-era creators, and that would educate audiences about them. Based on my previous experience, I foresaw that this could engender appreciation for the lives and stories of the creators I featured, and more broadly, achieve a degree of remembrance and Holocaust education through music.

This first stage of the project's genesis, comprising continued general research on music related to the Holocaust, specific research on possible musical sources for reference or quotation, and the composition of my *Sonata for Cello and Piano–Mir zaynen do!* (generically referred to as "cello sonata"), spanned 2011–2014. My research then, an inquiry into music wrought by members of groups who experienced persecution and genocide during the Nazi era, was pursued for the ongoing preparation of information and teaching materials for the Music and the Holocaust course I developed and had been teaching at Kennesaw State University since 2010, as well as for potential material for my compositional work. I had pursued this research at archives and onsite locations in Terezín, Czech Republic (the Theresienstadt ghetto/camp) and Oświęcim, Poland (the Auschwitz concentration camp), at various museums and archives in the U.S., Europe, and Israel, and through survivor interviews and a literature review.

With support from a 2012 Kennesaw State University Faculty Incentive Grant, I began to look more deeply at folk-song creation during the Holocaust and further referenced song collections I had encountered at various libraries and archives. I became interested in several song collections published in the years immediately following World War II, particularly those collected and edited by Vilna (now Vilnius, Lithuania) ghetto survivor Shmerke Kaczerginski (1908–1954), himself a lyricist and song creator. The most comprehensive of these collections, which contains 235 song lyrics and a separate section with 100 of the song melodies, is the Yiddish-language *Lider fun di getos un lagern* (Songs of the ghettos and camps) (Kaczerginski, 1948). As I played through these melodies in *Songs Never Silenced*, a contemporary songbook also including English translations of lyrics and song information from *Lider fun di getos un lagern* (Pasternak, 2003), I became particularly intrigued not only by the melodies and lyrics of a number of these songs, but also by what I consequently learned about the stories and life circumstances of the song creators. These creators were active not only in the ghettos and camps, as indicated by the collection's title, but also as partisans actively resisting Nazi aggression and occupation. Such partisan songs were among those in the collection that I found most relevant and appealing, and I chose to draw on three of these for the cello sonata.

Composition of the cello sonata began in 2013. The sonata-form first movement uses Shmerke Kaczerginski's *Yid, du partizaner* (Jew, you partisan) as source material (Kaczerginski, 1948, pp. 351, 428). Kaczerginski, active as an archivist and partisan, wrote the emboldening Yiddish lyrics to an existing melody while serving with a partisan unit in the forests (Werb, 2014, p. 22). The lyrics speak of survival and revenge, and indeed, Kaczerginski participated in the liberation of Vilna in 1944. The melody of *Yid, du partizaner* appears at the beginning of the movement, is fragmented in the development section, and returns in the recapitulation (Figure 5.1).

ART FOR HEALING AND RENEWAL

FIGURE 5.1
Sonata for Cello and Piano–Mir zaynen do!, movement I: Return of the Yid, du partizaner *melody in the recapitulation with added double-stops in the cello line*

The second movement draws upon the work of two Jewish musicians–as with the other movements, these sources are integrated with newly composed material. The first source is *Kel (El) mole rachamim*, a Jewish prayer for the souls of the deceased as sung by Cantor Sholom Katz (1915–1982) (Various, 2000). Katz recounted that his life was spared when he sang this prayer just before a mass execution during the Holocaust (Unidentified, 1982). He continued singing the prayer after the war with newly added text that laments the murder of European Jews and names the extermination camps of Auschwitz, Majdanek, and Treblinka. When I encountered his 1946 recording of this prayer, his musical expression, enhanced by the prayer text and his life experiences, moved me deeply and led me to choose this source for inclusion (Various, 2000). As the second movement unfolds, the cello "intones" several essential excerpts that I transcribed from his recording. The second source, which gradually emerges near the end of the movement, is the lullaby *Wiegala* by Czech children's author and musician Ilse Weber (1903–1944) (Weberova, 1943–1944). This lullaby, one of many songs she created while she was a prisoner in the Theresienstadt concentration camp, provided solace and comfort in lieu of the medicine that was not available in the children's infirmary where she worked. I was led to choose *Wiegala* by the compelling combination of the song's melody and lyrics, the circumstances under which she wrote it, and her life story (Migdal, 2008).

For the third movement, I decided on a theme and variations structure whose theme would be one of the most well-known partisan songs–*Zog nit keynmol az du geyst dem letstn veg* (Never say you are walking the last road) by Vilna ghetto partisan and poet Hirsh Glik (1922–1944) (Kaczerginski, 1948, pp. 3, 361). I envisioned a typical structure used in variation movements, where it is common for the theme to become progressively more embellished or otherwise changed in successive variations. After such a gamut, I planned to have the theme return intact in the final variation, only to be simultaneously layered with *Yugnt-Himn* (Youth-Hymn) (Kaczerginski, 1948, pp. 325, 427), a song that Glik's colleague Shmerke Kaczerginski created for Vilna ghetto youths (such a layering is referred to as a quodlibet). Because I envisioned this quodlibet as a significant arrival point at the end of the final movement, it was in fact the first music I composed for the sonata (Figure 5.2).

What Glik was able to capture in his uplifting Yiddish lyrics for *Zog nit keynmol az du geyst dem letstn veg* (abbreviated as *Zog nit keynmol*) is a sense of defiant optimism despite adversity. This 1943 song was soon adopted as the hymn of the Jewish underground resistance organization in Vilna and had spread across much of Yiddish-speaking Europe by the end of World War II. Kaczerginski's *Yugnt-Himn*, also from 1943, was dedicated to the Vilna ghetto youth club, where singing was a crucial activity for stimulating group identity, zeal, and courage.

FIGURE 5.2
Sonata for Cello and Piano–Mir zaynen do!, movement III, Variation 8 quodlibet: the piano continues Glik's Zog nit keynmol *in e minor while the cello enters with Kaczerginski's Yugnt-Himn in G major*

The composition was completed in December 2014, and titled *Sonata for Cello and Piano–Mir zaynen do!*. The subtitle, *Mir zaynen do!* (We are here), is a refrain in *Zog nit keynmol*. In the song's lyrics, this emblematic Yiddish phrase signified identity, resistance, and survival, and it has been used similarly in numerous titles and initiatives since then. In addition to music, the cello sonata score contains content aimed at engaging and educating audiences. An appendix provides short biographical sketches for the four Holocaust-era creators along with their song lyrics/prayer text in the original language and English translation. Program notes in the score, prepared for inclusion in printed program booklets, refer to each of the featured creators and the integration of their work in the sonata. I concluded the program notes with this observation:

Each of the creators of the songs used in the sonata has a compelling story. Their songs provide illumination of their lives and circumstances, allow us to gain perspective on lost and forbidden voices, and help us to understand the unprecedented tragedy of the Holocaust. By creating a new composition drawing on the work of these creators, it is my hope that performers and audiences will connect with their stories, and that the legacy of their cultural contributions will be strengthened and remembered. (Sherr, 2015)

Project Genesis: Stage 2

The second stage, spanning 2015–2017, saw the gradual development and evolution of presentation and audience engagement materials, creation and dissemination of additional educational information, assessment of varying concert and lecture formats, and titling of the project. Following completion of the cello sonata, this stage began with plans for a series of premieres and other performances in 2015, to be followed by further performances in subsequent years. It was through these opportunities for audience interaction that the *Music of Resistance and Survival Project (MoRaSP)* was gradually developed, as a primary goal for the cello sonata was to expand the impact I had achieved in my Music and the Holocaust course to a wider audience, not only to concertgoers, but also to potential radio, TV, and internet audiences.

As another means to help realize this goal, the cello sonata score has performance notes recommending that the source songs be performed directly before the sonata. For the initial public performances, I also proposed speaking to audiences—I envisioned that verbally sharing the stories of the creators of my source material could enhance audience experience, engagement, and education. While this approach contained the germinal seeds for the *MoRaSP*, ideas were not yet fully realized, and the project was not yet named.

The world premiere of the cello sonata was given on January 15, 2015, by Karen Becker, cello, and Jay Mauchley, piano, at the University of Nebraska–Lincoln, where Dr. Becker is on faculty. Becker and I arranged for three of my cello sonata's source songs to be performed before my sonata, and for me to address the audience during the recital. Because the other work on the program was the cello sonata by German composer Richard Strauss, whose work was predominantly supported but on occasion suppressed by the Nazi regime, we titled her program *Favored and Forbidden*. My remarks drew a contrast between Strauss and the creators of the source songs for my sonata, whose music, along with that of other Jewish and modernist creators, was banned by the Nazis. Following this first event, I deemed that several components were effective: my in-concert commentary about the group of source songs before their live performance; the inclusion of the song lyrics in the printed program; and, immediately preceding my sonata, to help the audience apprehend the quodlibet at the beginning of the last movement's final variation, a brief demonstration teasing apart the two layered songs. As they evolved, all of these were to become important components of the *MoRaSP*.

The six 2015 events following the premiere provided further opportunities for designing and refining new approaches, and for adapting components and formats to fit each venue. The second event was the January 26, 2015 cello recital of my Kennesaw State University faculty colleague Charae Krueger at our university concert hall in metropolitan Atlanta. For this U.S. east coast premiere, I once again gave in-concert comments about the source songs and narrated the performer demo of the quodlibet. Since a live performance of the source songs was not feasible for this event, newly added to my commentary were audio excerpts from historical recordings of two source songs, including a 1948 recording of Kaczerginski himself singing a verse of his *Yugnt-Himn*

(YIVO Institute for Jewish Research: The Ruth Rubin Legacy: Archive of Yiddish Folksongs, 2023).

Concluding a year of planning, the next two events, titled "Music of Resistance and Survival: A Holocaust Remembrance Concert," were staged on March 23, 2015, in the splendid sanctuary of The Temple, an historic synagogue in Atlanta, GA. The first was a morning event for students ages 11–18 and the second was an evening concert for the public, both events leading to the development of a range of novel approaches, components, and formats. For the morning event, which included comments by the congregation's rabbi, theatrical scenes performed by a youth troupe, and a Mendelssohn piano trio movement, I designed a program appropriate in length (45 minutes), variety, and content for the age group. To help prepare students for the concert, and to provide additional educational material, I collaborated with the Kennesaw State University Museum of History and Holocaust Education to produce the *Teacher's Guide: Music in the Holocaust, Grade 6–12*, an online resource with lesson plans, information for teachers and students, photos, and links (a link to this guide is included in the Links section). For the cello sonata section of the program, only selected verses of three source songs were sung, and these were tied directly to corresponding excerpts from the second and third movements of my sonata. My abridged comments, tailored for this audience, included interaction with the students. The successful adaptation of these components provided models for their future use in project events with young learners.

The first half of the evening program was a new version of the project. Novel project developments were manifold. This was the first event where all four source songs were performed live. I had organized the event in partnership with several organizations –The Temple, the Kennesaw State University Museum of History and Holocaust Education, the William Breman Jewish Heritage Museum, and the Georgia Commission on the Holocaust—so information I prepared about the source song creators was included in the comments those organizations' representatives gave before the source song performances. My remarks included two observations particularly relevant to the project's identity. First, noting that my cello sonata's outer movements are based on songs of Jewish partisans, I said:

> Rather than only remembering Jews and other persecuted groups as victims, this framing tells a different story of the Jewish experience during the Holocaust, a story of fortitude and resilience, of courage and boldness, of the active struggle against persecution and genocide. (L. Sherr, personal communication, March 23, 2015)

Second, the demonstration of my sonata's quodlibet was developed so that it was not only an explanation of musical technique, but also, as I told the audience in reference to the morning concert, because:

> ... we know that Vilna partisans like Kaczerginski were involved in educational efforts at the Vilna youth club ... Like the Vilna partisans, we realize that it is essential to include the next generation if we are to address prejudice, intolerance, and hate in our time. It is our youth who can carry these stories of resistance and survival to the next generation, and who can help us strive for a better world. (L. Sherr, personal communication, March 23, 2015)

These observations, the performance of all four source songs, the complementary Holocaust educational exhibits in the lobby for both events, and the involvement of community organizations would all prove important for future project versions. Finally, while this was the first event to use my suggestion of *Music of Resistance and Survival* as part of its title, the naming was for this pair of events only, and not yet the identifiable name of my project.

The fifth 2015 event, on October 28, 2015, at the International Summit on Civil and Human Rights at Kennesaw State University, was especially significant. As the initial event in which the live performance of the four source songs and my cello sonata comprised the entirety of the music, there was now time available for more extensive in-concert commentary. I accordingly developed further historical information about the lives and work of the source material creators, and the contemporary relevance of remembering their contributions. Original to this production was the media slide presentation I created to support my comments. Enhancing the presentation media were two recorded examples: a 1946 audio recording of Cantor Sholom Katz's prayer lamentation and video excerpts from my 2014 interview with Vilna ghetto survivor Ann Klug. In the video clip, Klug recounts knowing Hirsh Glik and the occasions in which she and other Vilna youth sang his *Zog nit keynmol* in the ghetto. I chose an interstitial format for my presentation, covering each of the source material creators immediately prior to the performance or recording of their contribution. All these developments proved to be successful and became the core model for a public concert version of the project.

The sixth and seventh 2015 events brought the project to the international stage. For both these concerts, I developed condensed in-concert remarks to allow time for a translator to deliver them in the national language. The November 3, 2015, European premiere, given in the Chapel of the Evangelical Church of Czech Brethren in Prague, Czech Republic, was an adapted version of the project, without projections. In a development that would occasionally be used for future productions, I presented a stand-alone project lecture in English, with projections, the day prior at the august Charles University (founded 1348): *Remembering the Silenced Voices of Holocaust Song Creators: Weaving Songs of Resistance and Survival into a New Cello Sonata*. On November 5, 2015, a slightly different project version was featured at the Days of Mutual Respect festival in Wrocław, Poland. Titled *Songs of Identity and Survival: A Kristallnacht Remembrance*, this event at the Karol Lipinski Academy of Music featured two of the four source songs along with other Holocaust-era songs chosen by the festival organizer. This concert, as the second event for my media slide show, and the second for translated remarks, enabled the refinement of each of these, to the benefit of future productions.

In 2016, the international reach of the project was expanded to a half-dozen events in New Zealand, Australia, and Israel. These saw the continued development of project materials and components. The Australasian premiere occurred on May 1, 2016, as part of the series Wellington Chamber Music: Sunday Concerts 2016, taking place at St Andrew's on The Terrace in Wellington, New Zealand. Because this concert, and the one following, were recitals featuring cellist Inbal Megiddo performing repertory that included my cello sonata, I prepared a shortened version of my media presentation that would be appropriate for such cello recitals, and that could serve as an embedded version of the project for similar future events. I presented this during the concert, in a segment comprising my media presentation about the source music, the quodlibet demo, and the cello sonata performance. I presented an updated version of my project lecture–*Remembering the Silenced Voices of Holocaust Song Creators: Weaving Songs of Resistance and Survival into a New Cello Sonata*–at the Holocaust Centre of New Zealand in Wellington on April 27, 2016.

On May 4, 2016 (Yom Hashoah in 2016), I had two project events in a single day–events in different cities, with different performers, and at different types of venues. The first was Inbal Megiddo's Guest Artist Recital at the Conservatorium of Music of the University of Waikato in Hamilton, New Zealand. In connection with this matinee performance, I gave a presentation about my compositional work at a university music class, where I spoke about the cello sonata and its sources. At Megiddo's recital, we presented the in-concert media presentation and cello sonata performance segment.

On the evening of May 4, 2016, a concert version of the project, titled *Holocaust Memorial Concert: Music of Resistance and Survival*, was produced as a community event at the Auckland Hebrew Congregation. This was only the second event combining the project's core components: my interstitial media presentation about each of the source song creators, including the historical recording of the prayer and the Vilna survivor interview clip; live performance of the four source songs; the quodlibet demonstration with observations about the relevance to youth; and my cello sonata. The observable effectiveness and success of this event, as measured by my assessment and audience feedback, and considering that each of these components had been refined through previous productions, led me to consider this combination as my preferred full *MoRaSP* event type and format. It also led me to conclude that *Music of Resistance and Survival* was an appropriate way to name and identify my project.

Several other international *MoRaSP* and cello sonata events took place in 2016. On May 9, I presented two Auckland educational events, each allowing the further development of presentations adapted to the educational setting and age-range of the students. The first, for high-school-age students from the Dilworth School and Diocesan School for Girls, featured my verbal commentary and the live performance of cello sonata excerpts. Speaking about the relation of source material to my ancestry initiated a student discussion about their ancestry and how it might inform their lives (identification with ancestry is an important aspect of many Australasian and Pacific Island cultures). For the second, at the Kadima School, I used an abridged and modified version of my media presentation adapted for the primary students. On May 11, 2016, I gave my project lecture for the Creative Collaboratorium and RHD Seminar Series at the University of Queensland in Brisbane, Australia. The lecture was followed the next day by Inbal Megiddo's performance of my cello sonata for her University of Queensland Artist Series Concert, during which I provided verbal comments about the cello sonata and source material. Megiddo performed the cello sonata three more times that year, at a November 9 *Kristallnacht* Holocaust Commemoration Concert in Wellington, a December 10 cello recital at the Eden-Tamir Music Center in Jerusalem, Israel, and at my December 13 English-language *MoRaSP* presentation at the Jerusalem Academy of Music and Dance.

Although further adjustments, adaptations, and refinements of the *MoRaSP* have continued to the present, by 2017 the project was established and identified by name and core content. This provided a project description and identity that could be more readily communicated to prospective venues, several of whom chose the *MoRaSP* for remembrance events. These included a *Kristallnacht* commemoration at the Florida Holocaust Museum in St. Petersburg, Florida, on November 9, 2017; a March 10, 2018, *Commemoration Event for the Establishment and Liquidation of the Krakow Ghetto* at the Galicia Jewish Museum in Krakow, Poland; and the January 26, 2019, San Marino National Day of Remembrance (marking International Holocaust Remembrance Day) in San Marino City, Republic of San Marino.

Further Project Dissemination

Dissemination of the historical, cultural, educational, and artistic components of the project is its *raison d'être*, and even during the 2016–2017 development of the project, it was reaching beyond event audiences. Broadcast opportunities started with the January 2015 cello sonata premiere for which I was interviewed by National Public Radio Nebraska affiliate NET (the broadcast is no longer available online). Coverage continued through the pair of March 2015 concerts in Atlanta, when three Atlanta radio stations broadcast interviews with me prior to the event, including "KSU Composer Pens Music in Remembrance of Holocaust Victims" on an Atlanta National Public Radio affiliate and "The Haunting Music of the Holocaust" on Georgia Public Broadcasting (neither of these broadcasts are still available online). Later broadcast on aib-tv (Atlanta Interfaith Broadcasters) were *A Conversation With—Laurence Sherr*, a 30-minute interview recorded between the morning and evening concerts, and the morning concert (AIB, 2015). My 2016 interview on Radio New Zealand, for the Australasian premiere, was broadcast nationally, as was a 2019 spot on San Marino TV (both items are available on my *Media Interviews and Broadcasts* web page included in the Links section).

A highlight of media coverage is the series of five 2017–2019 *Performance Today* broadcasts of my cello sonata (Your Classical, 2017), each with the host commenting about my work remembering the Holocaust (*Performance Today* is the most widely heard classical radio program in the U.S.). A recording of the July 7, 2017 broadcast is archived at my *Media Interviews and Broadcasts* web page, which is in the Links section. Performances of the cello sonata have also been broadcast on Radio New Zealand and have been archived on YouTube and Vimeo (embedded videos and links to these recordings can be found at these pages at my web site: *Videos: Compositions*; *Videos: Concerts with Commentary, Lectures with Performances*; *Media Interviews and Broadcasts*; and *Sonata for Cello and Piano–Mir zaynen do!*. All are included in the Links section). Additional online coverage includes a New Zealand concert review, San Marino event previews, several articles in Kennesaw State University magazines, and numerous other project event articles (the Links section points to two pages on my website where many of these items can be found: *Publications and Studies*, and *Reviews and Previews: Online Articles*).

My remembrance work, including the cello sonata with source material information, was included in the 2021 Kennesaw State University Museum of History and Holocaust Education exhibition *Words, Music, Memory: (Re)presenting Voices of the Holocaust* and featured in the accompanying *Gallery Guide* (Kennesaw State University: Museum of History and Holocaust Education, 2021). My cello sonata, with information about the source material creators and the *MoRaSP*, is included on my album *Fugitive Footsteps: Remembrance Music*. The album was released internationally in 2023 (Navona Records, 2023) and won a Gold Medal in the Global Music Awards competition.

Crucial to the dissemination of the *MoRaSP*, and a gauge of others' belief in the project's significance, has been the international grant, award, and production support for project events. Financial and in-kind support have been provided by a range of individuals and public, private, and corporate entities, especially SNCF America, Inc. and Kennesaw State University.

Audience Response

Following *MoRaSP* events and broadcasts, written and verbal responses have come from general audience members, educators, project performers, Holocaust survivors, and children of survivors. There is a convergence among these responses, regardless of nationality, cultural background, age, religion, or other identifying considerations: many respondents noted that the music's expressive content touched them deeply, often in an emotional way, providing a complementary heightening of the historical information, and increasing the impact of the *MoRaSP* event.

A brief selection of responses from the 2015–2016 events described above will serve to illustrate. For example, a middle school teacher wrote, "Today's experience showed ... the importance of the arts in human expression, especially during dark times in humanity," and a Jerusalem Academy of Music and Dance faculty member noted, "Your wonderful lecture and your music which was so beautifully performed, left a deep impact on our students!" Comments on the emotional impact included "the second movement ... brought tears to my eyes," and "you directed the cello to pluck the heartstrings of remembrance. I was very close to my [deceased] mother in the 'lamenting' part of your sonata ... you share loving memories and hopefulness to so many people." New Zealand audience comments included, "You have created an inspiring tribute to those murdered by the Nazis," and "your work and concert touched the hearts of many!" A particularly effective realization of *MoRaSP* goals can be seen in the reflections of a university history professor:

> I loved your comments about remembering the past to inform the present and building a bridge to the past to preserve the legacy of the voices that were suppressed. How much more fruitful it is to see the European Jewish composers and performers of that era not as victims but as people of fortitude whose work became a testimony to the human spirit! ... your cello sonata was a powerful tribute to those who were sacrificed in the Holocaust as well as to the survivors ... emotionally it was often stirring and in places very sad–but a sadness that can't help but make us better, more tolerant, and more loving, people. (T. Scott, personal communication, March 24, 2015)

Future Plans

Following a 2020–2022 hiatus during the Covid pandemic, planning for future *MoRaSP* events resumed. I hope to stage productions in additional U.S. and international locations, and to continue refining the event content and production. For example, for the 2023 *Yom HaShoah: Holocaust Remembrance Program* in Augusta, GA, I adapted the *MoRaSP* production to allow more time for the community program segment. I plan to pursue further research on the source material, and to continue adapting the production in collaboration with the communities where it is staged.

Summary

By integrating the creative work of Shmerke Kaczerginski, Cantor Sholom Katz, Ilse Weber, and Hirsh Glik with newly composed music in my *Sonata for Cello and Piano—Mir zaynen do!*, I sought to remember and pay tribute to these Holocaust victims and survivors. My desire to share the stories of their lives and cultural contributions with audiences, through the combination of their music in its original form, my cello sonata, and the associated educational initiatives I developed, and to thus provide a counter to intolerance, bigotry, and hate, led to the development of the multiple modular and adaptable components of my *Music of Resistance and Survival Project*. Since its 2015 launch, the project has been produced on four continents. It has received international grant and production support, media coverage, and audience accolades attesting to its impact. The project continues to achieve its overarching objectives: to engender remembrance relevant to our current world, to promote healing, and to increase intercultural understanding, tolerance, and mutual respect.

References

AIB. (2015, June 26). *A Conversation With—Laurence Sherr* [Video]. YouTube. https://www.youtube.com/watch?v=F280TOf6Vq0&list=PLEP-CZg0x5gPwCNG2Jc2aSxCXjNHbF3TqU

Kaczerginski, S. (1948). *Lider fun di getos un lagern* [Songs of the ghettos and camps]. Cyco.

Migdal, U. (2008). *Wann wohl das leid ein ende hat: Briefe und gedichte aus Theresienstadt / Ilse Weber* [When will the suffering end: letters and poems from Theresienstadt / Ilse Weber]. Carl Hanser.

Kennesaw State University: Museum of History and Holocaust Education. (2021). *Words, Music, Memory: (Re)presenting Voices of the Holocaust.* https://historymuseum.kennesaw.edu/exhibitions/traveling/words_music_memory.php

Navona Records. (2023, March 10). *Fugitive Footsteps: Remembrance Music* [album]. https://www.navonarecords.com/catalog/nv6492/

Pasternak, V. (2003). *Songs Never Silenced.* Tara Publications.

Sherr, L. (2015). *Sonata for Cello and Piano—Mir zaynen do!* [Musical score]. Laurence Sherr Music.

Unidentified. (1982, February 26). *Cantor Sholom Katz Dead at 67.* JTA Daily News Bulletin. http://pdfs.jta.org/1982/1982-02-26_039.pdf?

Various. (2000). *Legendary cantors* [Album]. Nimbus Records.

Weberova, I. (1943–1944). *Wiegala* [Music manuscript]. Jewish Museum in Prague, Archives Department (Box 319a). Jewish Museum in Prague, Prague, Czech Republic.

Werb, B. (2014). *Yiddish Songs of the Shoah: A Source Study Based on the Collections of Shmerke Kaczerginski.* [Doctoral dissertation, University of California, Los Angeles]. UCLA Electronic Theses and Dissertations. https://escholarship.org/uc/item/6x72f9t5

YIVO Institute for Jewish Research: The Ruth Rubin Legacy: Archive of Yiddish Folksongs. (2023, January 6.) *UNDZER LID IZ FUL MIT TROYER—YUGNT HIMEN.* https://ruthrubin.yivo.org/items/show/1882

Your Classical. (2017, July 7). *Performance Today: Laurence Sherr.* https://www.yourclassical.org/episode/2017/07/07/laurence-sherr

Performer List

I would like to acknowledge the many talented musicians who collaborated with me to share *Music of Resistance and Survival Project* events with the public. Those musicians performing in events mentioned in the chapter are listed here.

January 15, 2015, Lincoln, NE, U.S.
    Karen Becker, cello
    Jay Mauchley, piano
    Kate Butler, mezzo-soprano

June 6, 2015, Red Lodge, MT, U.S.
    Karen Becker, cello
    Jay Mauchley, piano

January 26, 2015, Kennesaw, GA, U.S.
    Charae Krueger, cello
    Robert Henry, piano

March 23, 2015, Atlanta, GA, U.S.
October 28, 2015, Kennesaw, GA, U.S.
    Charae Krueger, cello
    Robert Henry, piano
    Deborah Hartman, soprano
    Nancy Kassel, mezzo-soprano
    Judith Cole, piano

November 3, 2015, Prague, Czech Republic
    Petr Nouzovsky, cello
    Yukie Ichimura, piano

November 5, 2015, Wrocław, Poland
    Petr Nouzovsky, cello
    Yukie Ichimura, piano
    Anna Blaut, vocals
    Tomasz Kaczmarek, piano

May 1, 2016, Wellington, New Zealand
May 4, 2016, Hamilton, New Zealand
November 9, 2016, Wellington, New Zealand
December 10, 2016, Jerusalem, Israel
December 13, 2016, Jerusalem, Israel
    Inbal Megiddo, cello
    Jian Liu, piano

May 4, 2016, Auckland, New Zealand
    Katherine Hebley, cello
    Penny Christiansen, piano
    Fay Hadden McNeil, soprano

May 9, 2016, Auckland, New Zealand
    Katherine Hebley, cello
    Penny Christiansen, piano

May 12, 2016, Brisbane, Australia
    Inbal Megiddo, cello
    Anna Grinberg, piano

November 9, 2017, St. Petersburg, FL, U.S.
    Theresa Villani, cello
    Colleen Schmitt, piano
    Gerald Arnold, tenor

March 10, 2018, Krakow, Poland
    Jan Kalinowski, cello
    Marek Szlezer, piano
    Urszula Makosz, singer

January 26, 2019, San Marino City, Republic of San Marino
    Nicola Baroni, cello
    Lorenzo Meo, piano
    Elena Tereshchenko, soprano

Links

Kennesaw State University Museum of History and Holocaust Education: Teacher's Guide: Music in the Holocaust, Grade 6–12
https://historymuseum.kennesaw.edu/docs/music-in-the-holocaust.pdf

Kennesaw State University Museum of History and Holocaust Education: Words, Music, Memory: (Re)presenting Voices of the Holocaust
https://historymuseum.kennesaw.edu/exhibitions/traveling/words_music_memory.php

Laurence Sherr: Events Archive 1: 2009–2015
https://ksuweb.kennesaw.edu/~lsherr/events-archive-1.html

Laurence Sherr: Events–Current and Recent Seasons
https://ksuweb.kennesaw.edu/~lsherr/events.html

Laurence Sherr: Holocaust Remembrance Compositions, Concerts, and Lectures
https://ksuweb.kennesaw.edu/~lsherr/Holocaust-music.html

Laurence Sherr: Media Interviews and Broadcasts
https://ksuweb.kennesaw.edu/~lsherr/media-interviews.html

Laurence Sherr: Music of Resistance and Survival Project
https://ksuweb.kennesaw.edu/~lsherr/ResistanceandSurvival.html

Laurence Sherr: Publications and Studies
https://ksuweb.kennesaw.edu/~lsherr/publications.html

Laurence Sherr: Research: Music and the Holocaust
https://ksuweb.kennesaw.edu/~lsherr/research.html

Laurence Sherr: Reviews and Previews: Online Articles
https://ksuweb.kennesaw.edu/~lsherr/reviews-online.html

Laurence Sherr: Sonata for Cello and Piano–Mir zaynen do!
https://ksuweb.kennesaw.edu/~lsherr/CelloSonata.html

Laurence Sherr: Videos: Compositions
https://ksuweb.kennesaw.edu/~lsherr/videos.html

Laurence Sherr: Videos: Concerts with Commentary, Lectures with Performances https://ksuweb.kennesaw.edu/~lsherr/videos-lectures.html

CHAPTER 6

Silent Echoes: Dancing to Rise

Carolyn Dorfman

A Search for Meaning

FIGURE 6.1
Interior Designs, Carolyn Dorfman Dance (2013).
Photo by Christopher Duggen

Silent Echoes. The juxtaposition of these words reveals the essence of my search for meaning in my family's history of life, loss, and renewal. The lives and stories of survivors of the Holocaust, told and observed, shaped my person and art. The silence of those left behind echo in the memories and actions of the survivors; their ability to fall, endure and rise again taught me about perseverance and the life-sustaining capacity of hope.

Through this chapter, I explore the extraordinary power of dance to create "worlds" that speak about family, memory, pain, survival, and resilience. I use the word "speak" because, as a choreographer, dance is my language and movement my words. Creating and speaking from the inside out has been my way of processing and healing. I am, after all, a "Witness of the Witness." Through my work I reveal the family history that shaped and inspired every aspect of my being. In both content and process, this legacy has shaped the evolution of my work. In the pages ahead, selections from the *Legacy Project* (1983–2009) are introduced through historical, cultural, and familial contexts, as well as artist statements, images, and video links to the works. These works include *Cries of the Children* (1983) (Figure 6.3), *Mayne Mentshn (My People)* (2001) (Figure 6.4 and Figure 6.5), and *Cat's Cradle* (2007) (Figure 6.2). These dances reveal the depth of my experiences and give voice to those who survived and, through them, to those who perished.

The impact of such work is also significant as explored here. It is through the trials and triumphs of each individual story that we find profound universal connections and our common humanness. The impact of this work on audiences of all ages is viscerally heartening, yet the relevance of this work to today's events is deeply troubling. These works were created to *remember* important historical events: pre-war Polish Jewish life; the horrors of the Holocaust; the trials of immigration to America; and the destructiveness of antisemitism, racism, and xenophobia. Yet, their unquestionable and heart-breaking relevance to today's realities make them more vital than ever. Each day we witness the rise of hateful speech and attacks in our streets and across all media. Antisemitism, racism, and xenophobia have become normalized and accepted. We are a society at a tipping point. Who are we? Who will we become, individually and collectively? The dance speaks and we must listen.

I am a choreographer, a maker of dances. It has been my life's work to create dances that speak about the human story. From the intimacy of the duet to the vastness of global issues; the joys of love to the pain of human failure. Amidst the making of such dances, I created a body of work exploring and celebrating my Eastern European Jewish roots and history called the *Legacy Project*. It is a body of work I never intended to make, yet each dance percolated at a different time of my life and each for a different reason. Each was an outgrowth of my lived experience surrounded by Holocaust survivors and their stories of life, loss, and the profound will to live.

The Beginnings

My parents, Mala Dorfman, née Weintraub, and Henry Dorfman, were raised in vibrant Jewish communities in Poland, my mother in the city of Łódź and my father in the village of Głowaczów. They were fifteen and sixteen years old, respectively, when the war broke out. They each survived the war, my mother working in labor camps and my father in hiding and working with the resistance. They met in Marburg, Germany after the war and were married in 1945. Both lost dozens of family members to the gas chambers of Auschwitz and Treblinka, but luckily my father's father Moshe and my mother's two sisters, Franka and Rosa, survived. My grandfather moved to Israel; my parents, aunts, and uncles came to the United States to build new lives in a new land. I grew up immersed in the joys, sorrows, and rich legacy of Eastern European life in suburban Detroit. Yiddish, klezmer music, family, and tradition were integral parts of our daily lives. It is through my work that I have tried to chronicle their joy, pain, lessons, and love. I was blessed, as my

ART FOR HEALING AND RENEWAL

parents chose LIFE; not all survivors could. They worked, laughed, loved, and most importantly ... remembered. "Never forget where you come from," my father would implore. "Why did you choose life?" I would ask. My mother would answer, "Because if we did not, Hitler would have won again!" She also told me that she "never lost hope." To know this is to understand that while my work digs deep into the pain and loss, it always celebrates life and rises with hope.

FIGURE 6.2
Cat's Cradle, Carolyn Dorfman Dance (2007).
Photo by Tom Caravaglia

Inspired by both my family's horrific past and survival, I confess, I started with the pain. Ironically, it was not their pain, but mine as a child of survivors. My parents and extended family of survivors spoke often and in detail of their excruciating experiences during the war. It was, as they say, a blessing and a curse. I was the youngest of my extended family. I listened carefully and in silence. I was very young when my nightmares about the war began.

Separation anxiety gripped me. I never told my parents. In fact, as a child of survivors, my mission was to hide my fears and feelings from them. They had suffered enough; I would cause them no more pain.

In 1983, I was moved to create a dance about the Holocaust. But how could I? I hadn't been there! It wasn't my story to tell; it was theirs. I did not feel worthy to speak for them. They shared their experiences often, with sadness, defiance, and gratitude. So, in the end, I decided to tell mine. With the backdrop of Roman Vishniac's photographs of pre-war Poland (Vishniac, 1972) and a hauntingly moving score by David Darling (1980), *Cries of the Children* (1983) (Figure 6.3) speaks not about the survivors, but about the questions and pain of their children. It asks: "Who were these people I did not know? Was I like them? How did my parents survive?" And ultimately, "Would I have survived?"

When my mother first saw *Cries*, she asked, "Why on earth would you make a piece about this?" This is what I told her: There isn't a day that goes by in my life that I don't think about the Holocaust and your experiences. It is the single most defining element of my life. It has shaped every facet of who I am as a woman, artist, mother, wife, daughter, friend, and member of the human race. It has shaped my commitment to justice, equality, and humanism. It taught me that we are individuals who exist in relation to one another and that we must care for and about each other … that we are all inextricably linked. These principals are the essence of my life and art.

ART FOR HEALING AND RENEWAL

FIGURE 6.3
Cries of the Children, Carolyn Dorfman Dance (2008)
Photo by Carolyn Dorfman Dance

As my career progressed so did my life as a mother. I realized that remembering the pain of the Holocaust was only part of the rich legacy of my people: that for my children and future generations to fully understand the profound agony and loss, they must experience and celebrate the life and traditions that were interrupted and almost obliterated. Sifting carefully through the rubble, I discovered a joyous legacy and a story that had to be told. If not, the pain would remain, and the lives and memories would be lost forever.

FIGURE 6.4
The Klezmer Sketch from Mayne Mentshn (My People) Carolyn Dorfman Dance (2015).
Photo by Daniel Hedden

The Klezmer Sketch (2000) (Figure 6.4 and Figure 6.5), set to a commissioned score and soundtrack by musician/composer Greg Wall, was my answer, my offering. Through this work I acknowledge the strengths, trials, humor, and joys that have sustained 'my people.' Through the exuberant, joyful, yet soulful, quality of klezmer music, I celebrate the uniqueness of the Eastern European Jewish journey and the extraordinary universal connections that it engenders. The opening, *My Father's Solo*, presents a larger than life image of the survivor as one who rises after every fall … one who perseveres: one of the many lessons of survivors. *The Three Sisters* depicts my mother and her two sisters, Rosa Schaumberg and Franka Charlupski, and their deep commitment to one another and to our family. Through *The Table and The Arrangement*, we learn about family gatherings, in this case the Passover meal (Seder) and the mixed emotions of an arranged marriage. *The Freylach* is a wedding celebration that ends with the searing sound of the Shofar (ram's horn) … a call to warning. My mother told me that it was amidst such life at its fullest that the Germans invaded Poland and, at the age of 15, her life turned upside down.

FIGURE 6.5
Mayne Mentshn Act I—The Klezmer Sketch. Carolyn Dorfman Dance (2013).
Photo by Andre Constantini

Cat's Cradle (2007) (Figure 6.6) and its adaptation, *Silent Echoes* (2009), take us to a darker place, a darker time. *Cat's Cradle* was inspired by the moving voice of Norwegian, Jewish actress/vocalist, Bente Kahan and her one-woman musical theatre production *Voice from Theresienstadt* (1995), created by Ellen Foyn Bruun and Bente Kahan. This work includes poetry and music written in Theresienstadt by Ilse Weber, a prisoner and nurse in the children's ward and music and performance by Bente Kahan and her klezmer band. In *Silent Echoes*, Bente Kahan performs with the dancers through her music, vocals, and text throughout the dance.

Theresienstadt, or Terezín, was a ghetto in Czechoslovakia. It was a city designed to house 5000 residents. Shockingly, it became a holding ground for

50,000 Jews and others destined for the gas chambers of Auschwitz. The irony? Art, too, was part of life in Theresienstadt. Operas, symphonies, visual art, poetry, and cabaret dance performances (forced and voluntary) were made. Their art depicted the horror, and it portrayed the hope. I was moved by this duality of life in Terezín. In the worst of times, there was the capacity of the human spirit to rise above horrific circumstances and create: another lesson of the survivors. My mother and her two sisters survived the war in part because they could knit. Balls and strings of yarn are used with reverence throughout the work. As young children, we sat at their feet as they wove their yarn, shared their stories, and knit our family together—past and present.

Fragile Threads: The Old Meets the New

While not in temporal order of creation, the *American Dream* (2001) shared the immigrant story and my life in two worlds. It premiered with the *Klezmer Sketch* creating a full evening work in two parts titled *Mayne Mentshn* (*My People*). It is a work in two parts because as a first generation American, I grew up in two worlds—the world of my parents' past and life in America. While the *Klezmer Sketch* celebrates the life before, *The American Dream,* continuing my collaboration with composer Greg Wall, addresses the complexities of living in and growing up in a European Jewish family in America. My family came to a purported land of freedom, yet they faced xenophobia, antisemitism, and loss of culture through assimilation, both by choice and in response to societal pressure. From chopped liver and white fish sandwiches at school to klezmer music at my family gatherings, I knew I was different. The problems my family faced are not unique; they represent the constant struggle of all immigrants to maintain their cultural identity and roots while becoming part of a larger whole. All who come to America arrive with histories, legacies, tragedies, and joys. They seek to build new lives yet struggle to maintain the fragile connections to their own families and cultures. These are the trials my family faced, and the trials faced by immigrants today.

The Call to Rise

In creating these works, I wanted to honor the past and, more importantly, to inspire all of us to remember. "Never Again" is the emphatic cry of the survivors and the words that we must echo and amplify. As Carolyn Dorfman Dance tours these works through live and virtual performances across the United States and the globe, the response is universally one of profound understanding, compassion, and connection. These dances are shared with audiences of all ages, presented with age-appropriate narration and content. After watching excerpts of the *Klezmer Sketch* and *Cat's Cradle* together, I asked a kindergartener what she would most remember about our performance today. She stood up boldly and replied, "Sometimes life is really happy and sometimes it is really sad!" After seeing *Cat's Cradle*, a high school student in Florida exclaimed, "We are reading *Night* by Eli Wiesel and watching the dance was like seeing the words come alive in front of me." An older woman in Sarajevo hugged me with tenderness after seeing *My Father's Solo*. It made her think of the father she lost in the war. She felt connected. She spoke no English, but she felt the dance. Student after student, audience member after audience member speaks about the power of the work to open their hearts and minds, inspire compassion and empathy, and most importantly, to *act* to create a more humane world.

I lost my mother on July 11, 2022, at the age of almost 99 years young. To her last breath, she lamented that yesterday's history has become today's grim and frightening reality. The hate and fear of "the other" permeates our country and the world, including by those with the loudest voices and platforms. At this distressing time, when the teaching of history is being censored and books banned, the lessons of the Holocaust are more critical than ever. These lessons inspire humanism, respect and the value of each individual life and community. They teach us that, in our uniqueness and strength, we as individuals and communities must exist in relation to one another. These critical lessons underscore that we are inextricably linked and that our survival depends upon our taking care of one other. They challenge us to stand up … be heard … to act.

Dance has the incredible power to present the world as it is and to reveal the world as it can be. The dance speaks and we must listen.

Figure 6.6
Cat's Cradle, Carolyn Dorfman Dance (2007).
Photo by Tom Caravaglia

This chapter is dedicated to my parents, survivors Mala Dorfman, née Weintraub, (1923–2022) and Henry Dorfman (1922–2001).

References

American Dream (2001). Choreography by Carolyn Dorfman. https://vimeo.com/manage/videos/785312935

Cat's Cradle (2007), Performance 2007. Choreography by Carolyn Dorfman. https://vimeo.com/manage/videos/39302776

Cries of the Children (1983), revised 1991, Performance 2009. Choreography by Carolyn Dorfman. https://vimeo.com/manage/videos/785289814

Darling, D. (1980). *Journal October Stuttgart*, Journal October: Solo Cello (CD). ECM Records.

Dorfman, H. (1989, August 11 and 25). Interview by Sidney M. Bolkosky. The Voice/Vision Holocaust Survivor Oral History Archive. the University of Michigan-Dearborn, Dearborn, MI, 1989. http://holocaust.umd.umich.edu/dorfman/ (Link to audio on youtube) https://youtu.be/30EesmOTj9o

Dorfman, M.W. (2005, September 15). Interview by Sidney M. Bolkosky, The Voice/Vision Holocaust Survivor Oral History Archive. the University of Michigan-Dearborn, Dearborn, MI, 2005. https://holocaust.umd.umich.edu/dorfmanm/ (Link to the video on You Tube) https://www.youtube.com/watch?v=T9EnKNbkJnM&list=PL9EE11A7BE19A36DE

Mayne Mentshn—Act I—*Klezmer Sketch* (2000), Performance 2015. Choreography by Carolyn Dorfman. https://vimeo.com/manage/videos/782686394

Silent Echoes (2009). Choreography by Carolyn Dorfman. https://vimeo.com/manage/videos/785306443

Voices of Theresienstadt (1995). Ellen Foyn Bruun and Bente Kahan. https://www.youtube.com/watch?v=afZfJQrgPcw

Vishniac, R. (1976). *Polish jews: A pictorial record.* Schocken Books.

Part II—Healing Through the Pain: The Arts as Provocateur and Lifeline

Reflection

Holocaust Stories: Resistance, Renewal, Recognition

David Crespy, Ph.D.

When I was first approached with the offer to reflect on the six excellent chapters that follow, I felt like I was the least likely theatre researcher to provide commentary on the Holocaust as, in fact, until relatively recently, it was a subject on which I resisted writing. As a Jewish child going to an orthodox synagogue in Freehold, New Jersey, I had been inundated with its horrors from a very young age. However, in more recent years, under the aegis of the Fulbright Scholar's Award, I have had the opportunity to examine my own roots in the Jewish community of Thessaloniki, first in 2018, writing a series of plays that I titled *Madre de Israel: Three Plays of Salonica*, documenting that community's history from 1897 to 1957, including the near total demise of this Sephardic community of Jews during the German occupation of Greece.

In 2022, I once again received a Fulbright to both Spain and Greece, and wrote six more plays digging deeper into the Spanish roots of the Jewish communities of Thessaloniki and Veria, from where my grandmother, Mary Massarano Crespy, and my grandfather, Isaac Morris Crespy, my dad's mom and dad, had immigrated. My grandparents lost their entire families to the Holocaust, and one of the driving forces for my writing these plays was to recover and resurrect these unique Sephardic communities.

I have avoided these stories much of my life because of the pain that they evoke not only in me, but in my family members. In 1943, the Jewish population of Thessaloniki was nearly 50,000 Jews, having been one of the glowing beacons of the Sephardic Jewish Diaspora—by its end, after the murder of nearly 95 percent of its community by the Nazis, perhaps only 1,500 survived. During my Fulbright residency in 2018, I was given the German deportation papers of my grandmother's brother, Saul Massarano, by Aliki Arouh, the archivist there who has been helping the families of Salonican Jews find their lost relatives for over a decade now. The papers, filled out by my great uncle Saul in the Baron Hirsch Ghetto to document his family's meager belongings, are the only evidence we have of the names of his wife and children, who were transported in cattle cars from Thessaloniki to Auschwitz where they perished.

Neither my grandparents nor my father discussed any of this, because it was not something anyone felt comfortable exploring—and so the idea of making theatre of it was, for years and years, the farthest thing from my mind. As such, imagine my amazement and admiration for the authors of these chapters who have risen to the challenge—artist educators who have not only made art, but opened minds to the whole history of the Holocaust through their inspiring initiatives of renewal to transform horror into hope, anguish into understanding, and loss into transformation. Using the arts to challenge their performers and their audiences to make sense of the terrible tragedy of the Holocaust.

Each chapter brings a different dimension of pedagogical technique, educational approach, and style to the theatricalizing and storytelling of the Holocaust. In Gail Humphries' "Children's Stories from Terezín: I Leave You These," we are introduced to the powerful musical *I Never Saw Another Butterfly*, based on the play by Celeste Raspanti; book and lyrics by Joseph Robinette; music by E. A. Alexander. With a title based on a poem by Pavel Friedmann, one of the children in Terezín, and a story tied to the extraordinary vision provided by their gifted teacher Friedl Dicker-Brandeis who encouraged these potentially doomed children to write and draw about their lives in the past, present, and into projected future, the chapter documents Dr. Humphries' remarkable journey working on the play in production across the U.S. and Europe.

Ruth Gordon's chapter, "Holocaust Impact Theatre: Utilizing Theatre as a Catalyst for Acceptance and Respect" recognizes the ongoing legacy of the Holocaust Impact Theatre in the Alper Jewish Community Center (JCC) in Kendall, Florida. What struck me as one of the greatest personal ironies was how deeply committed the students become to this project, which was originally initiated as a one-time experience, and lasted eighteen years. Even as I have personally tried to move away from the Holocaust and all of its implications, Ruth Gordon and HIT have moved toward it and found real meaning and lasting relevance, engaging with Holocaust survivors to transform school bullies into caring young citizens.

In "This is What I've Scene: Teaching the Holocaust Through Theatre," the next chapter by Mira Hirsch, I found myself transported by the creative process of the "This is What I've Scene" dramatic enactment technique, and noted how challenging it can be to bring this history into the classroom in an ethical, engaging, and transformative way. The process challenges students to determine elements of a specific Holocaust survivor's story, and create scripts based on transcripts of an interview that involves storyboarding, conferencing, and collaboration.

In Motti Lerner's chapter, "The Eichmann Trial: A Theatrical Interpretation," I found myself taking a deep dive into playwriting technique and dramaturgy, as Lerner shared his process of dramatizing the challenges of prosecutor Gideon Hausner as he made his case against one of the most infamous Nazi perpetrators of the Holocaust, Adolf Eichmann. I was stunned by Hausner's harrowing experience of prosecuting a case against Eichman's smooth, slimy, and clever lies to evade what would be his inevitable prosecution. I was gripped by how close Eichmann came to slipping out of Hausner's grasp and was also mesmerized by the harsh realities of depicting history, despite one's desire to have some artistic license. Hausner's narrative reinforced for me how tricky that can be—and yet, how necessary!

What engaged me the most in the chapter "Music in Terezín: Creativity in Chaos" by Dr. Wendy Mullen about the near miraculous musical and theatre performances which took place in the Theresienstadt Ghetto, a waystation to the extermination camps, was the discussion of Ela Weissberger's performance of the Cat in the children's opera, *Brundibár* written by Hans Krasa. The sheer exuberance of the performances, and the love her students from Georgia College and Atlanta had for the opera was translated into an amazing learning experience for Dr. Mullen as they performed with Ms. Weissberger, with several survivors of Terezín present to witness the event and memorialize those who died in the camps.

Finally, after I read Liz Lerman's chapter, "Small Dances About Big Ideas: Moving Past the Limits of Dancing About Genocide," I felt compelled to actually watch the dance discussed in the chapter in an online video, which transforms the horrifying realities of the Holocaust into physical enactments, moving bodies through space and time, to distill an essence of the experience. What struck me as an impossible task was realized in the depiction of a single moment in the trial of Nazis at Nuremberg, with the image of the piles of paper evidence in the office of Supreme Court Justice Robert Jackson, who had taken a leave from his position to prosecute the case against the executors of the Holocaust.

As I ponder the composite impact of these chapters, tremendous admiration is elicited for the writers/practitioners as they reckon with the application of their craft to the thorny and ethically problematic challenge of depicting the Holocaust on the stage. It also demonstrated to me the embodiment of the tremendous determination required to create art that embodies the fundamental reason why we, as theatre artists, tell these stories on the stage. We aspire to prevent history from repeating itself, to dramatically insist that these kinds of events must never again happen, and to memorialize those who were lost in one of the most awful moments to ever confront not just the Jewish people, but all of humanity.

CHAPTER 7

Children's Stories from Terezín: I Leave You These

Gail Humphries, Ph.D.

Introduction: The Sustaining Power of Art

Aesthetics, as just another, thinner skin protecting against chaos ... last motor capable of creating production, while defending man from forces over which he has no control. (Friedl Dicker-Brandeis to Hildegard Kothany, September 12, 1940)

One is grateful when reading about the children who were able to escape before and during the Holocaust and grow into thriving adults, albeit carrying unfathomable scars. However, one must ask the pertinent question: what about those children who could only escape through the world of their imagination amidst horrific conditions? Anne Frank wrote to escape her bondage in Amsterdam, and both astutely and wistfully analyzed life in her extraordinary diary. Her voice has certainly reached a universal and timeless stature (Cooper, 2021). So, too, did the children of Terezín escape the confines and harsh world of Terezín—one of frigid temperatures, starvation, and disease—through their poetry, prose, and artwork, generating lasting remembrances of life as they recollected it before imprisonment, as well as life as they saw it in the tumultuous and tenuous life in the Nazi transit camp of Terezín. They wrestled with the beauty of life before Terezín, the somber world they lived in while there, the fear and hunger, and projected possibilities for a world beyond their confinement. Imagination can become a form of environmental adjustment, and, indeed, the imaginative outpouring of the children incarcerated at Terezín manifests that perspective.

I Never Saw Another Butterfly (based on the play by Celeste Raspanti; book and lyrics by Joseph Robinette; music by E. A. Alexander) (Robinette & Alexander, 2007) is an intense chronicle of the lives of children in Terezín and the exceptional guidance and hope provided by an extraordinary teacher who encouraged them to write and draw about their lives in the past, present, and projected future (Figure 7.1 and Figure 7.2). Directing this production was haunting for me. I was in awe of their teacher, an artist of enormous talent and integrity herself—Friedl Dicker-Brandeis, upon whom the character of the teacher was modeled. She inspired children at Terezín to channel their pain, suffering, and anguish through their art and poetry, offering them solace through their imagination. Their artistry survives because of her ingenuity and resonates to the contemporary world.

It is often said that play is the work of children. I see that in my own preschool grandchildren and remain in awe of Friedl's and the children's efforts. However, it is exceptionally difficult to fathom all of this occurring under the horrors of Terezín as children were removed from the presence of their parents and faced the ghastly confines and starvation of Terezín. Educational psychologist Dr. Lynn Fox (2016, p. 27) notes that a "learner actively constructs his/her own understandings of the world—the physical world and the world of language, ideas, and concepts. The teacher's role is to facilitate this construction of knowledge in a variety of ways." Friedl did this with the students through their imaginative drawing and writing, facilitating reflection about the world that they had lived in before Terezín, offered coping mechanisms with their lives in Terezín, and generated creative contemplation on lives beyond the confines of the walls that contained them. Clinical neuropsychologist Dr. William Stixrud provides us with insight into the process of education and the igniting of the imagination by Friedl. He notes that "activities that engage the brain flow, active participation, imagination, creativity, and self-expression have a better effect on brain functioning" (Stixrud & Markova, 2016, p. 82) and impact a reckoning with stress. It is hard to fathom the stress that these children experienced, removed from their parents, uprooted to a strange, barricaded environment, yet Friedl discerned channels for them to constructively confront the horrific circumstances, travesty, and loss. Friedl persevered, and the poetry, prose and drawings of the children remain for us to read, view, and ponder. This musical version chronicling selected journeys and the children's work remains inspiring for contemporary audiences. The "play" of these children was, indeed, their work and their lifeline.

It is also a sobering reminder of the loss of life and talent at Terezín during the Nazi occupation. The title of the play *I Never Saw Another Butterfly* originates from a poem by Pavel Friedman, a child interred at Terezín. He perished at Auschwitz in 1944. The artwork and poetry were compiled after World War II by Czech art historian Hana Volakova, a survivor and curator at the Jewish Museum in Prague (Makarova, 2001). In this musical, Celeste Raspanti presents the stories of the children and their inspirational work in a poignant dramatization that captured the spirit and the struggles of the children. The music composed by Joseph Robinette adds a striking component to the script. One of the closing moments of the production continues to penetrate my soul. As Irena Synkova (the Friedl character), is transported from Terezín to Auschwitz, she secretly passes the poetry and drawings of the children to her student, Raja Englanderova, and sings "If these poems and pictures will live on after us all, then on these days the sun will never set and the night shall never fall, the world will not forget the children's distant call" (Robinette and Alexander libretto). Through this chapter, I celebrate Franta, Hana,

ART FOR HEALING AND RENEWAL

Ruth, Petr, Josef, Helena, Soňa, Irena, Gertruda, Vilern, Jiri, Bedrich, Milena, Heinrich, Hanus, Dorit, Kurt, Zuzana, Marianna, Eva, Ernesta, Margit, Anna, Jitka, Emilie, Pavel and every child who breathed life into their existence within Terezín through their art.

Part One: For the Children and Their Teacher

Figure 7.1
Lisa Michelle Weiner as Raja Englanderova, a child at Terezín and a survivor in American University's production of I Never Saw Another Butterfly.
Photo by American University Marketing

> I am a Jew and will be forever. Even if I should die from hunger, never will I submit.
> I will always fight for my people,
> On my honor ... Even though I am suppressed,
> I will always come back to life.
> Franta Bass died in Auschwitz in 1944. (Published in *I Never Saw Another Butterfly*, H. Volakova, 1993)

Modern and contemporary research underscores the significance of teachers in the learning process. Noted scholar/researcher, Linda Darling-Hammond (2007) speaks to the teacher as the single most important influence in learning. Friedl is certainly the embodiment of that significance with both the artwork and the writings of the children as living testimony to her guiding influence. Yet, again, how do we fathom teaching, creating, guiding, and learning amidst oppression, starvation, and anguish? I cannot fully comprehend the magnitude of this challenge. One comment that seems pertinent and helpful here is that she "restored the shaken inner world of the child ... to compensate for the chaos of time and space" (Makarvova, 1991). Perhaps in doing so, she restored her own shaken inner world. One only needs to view the creations of the children, either in print, or authentically viewed at the Jewish Museum in Prague, to witness that restoration of a shaken inner world for the children.

As survivor Erna Furman stated,

> Friedl's teaching, the time spent with her, are among the fondest memories of my life. Terezín made it more poignant, but it would have been the same anywhere in the world. Friedl was the only one who taught without ever asking for anything in return. She just gave of herself. (Makarova, 1999)

ART FOR HEALING AND RENEWAL

One description of her approach is apt here: "Despite the application of a precise method, she managed to respect the individuality of each child and allow them the freedom to express themselves, unleash their fantasies and emotions" (Jewish Museum, Prague, CZ). "In the fall of 1944, she and the majority of students were deported and with her nearly all of the children perished in the gas chambers of Auschwitz" (Jewish Museum, Prague, CZ). However, their work of nearly five thousand drawings remains a telling legacy of Friedl's teaching and her students' outpouring of imagination and creativity.

Part Two: For the Artists—The Artistic Process and Performances

FIGURE 7.2
Elizabeth Bartolotto as Irena Synkova (right), the teacher (based on Friedl-Dicker Brandeis) with Jenny Christine as Renka, Irena's assistant (left).
Photo by American University Marketing

And the canons don't scream and the guns don't bark
And you don't see blood here. Nothing, only silent hunger.
Children steal the bread here and ask and ask.
And all wish to sleep and keep silent, and just to sleep again.
The heaviest wheel rolls across our foreheads
To bury itself somewhere inside our memories.
(MIF, *Terezín*, 1944) (Volakova, 1993, p. 17)

Preparation for the production with undergraduate students at American University, over a six-week period, entailed a great deal of research and collaborative sharing on the part of the cast and production team. Having spent much time at Terezín prior to the onset of rehearsal, I shared many photos, images, and research from my own work as a Fulbright Senior Scholar and director in Prague and on site at Terezín. I charged the students to carefully research Terezín with a suggested list of readings and films. They approached the research with vigor and infused their characterizations with as much authenticity as they could emotionally and physically channel. Our rehearsals included improvisations and exercises to engender emotional connections to the lives they were depicting. Through their poetry and drawings, the resilience of the children was evident. We focused on presenting their attitudes and outlooks with honesty, integrity, and objectivity. Our goal was to serve the humanity of the individuals that we were depicting and the integrity of their stories. We viewed our work as living history to be shared with our audiences of all ages. Many of the cast members were able to see the actual drawings and writings of the children on a subsequent trip to Prague. Experiencing the authentic work of the children was powerful and sobering.

As Lisa Michelle Weiner, cast member, noted in a personal interview with me:

As a Jewish woman, I grew up learning about the Holocaust. I was aware of Auschwitz and Dachau. However, until I went to American University and studied under Dr. Gail, I had never heard about Terezín. It all made a lasting impact on me. Studying all of this and then visiting Terezín reminded me of the importance, power, and impact of the arts ... for survival. Having the opportunity to visit Terezín was chilling. I could now touch the barracks and feel the walls that entrapped these children and adults. It was no longer a set in a black box theatre, but a very real place. I could fully envision the struggle the characters lived through day to day and how far they pushed themselves to survive. Future generations need to learn their history. (July 2022)

The production was presented in a 99-seat black box studio theatre, for varied audiences, ranging from Washington, DC inner city school children and their teachers to undergraduate/graduate students and on the American University campus and faculty of varied disciplines, to community members, and guests from the Embassy of the Czech Republic. Each production was followed by a talkback (which I facilitated), to afford the audience the possibility to ask questions and process the content of the production. With each talkback, we encountered consistently empathetic responses. One grade schooler poignantly remarked that she used her own drawing to escape as the children did at Terezín. Another student commented that her teacher "was just like the teacher in the play." The classroom teachers had been provided with a study guide prior to the production and this appeared to be helpful for them in preparing the students for the content of the performance.

During the talkbacks, college students and other adults commented on their lack of knowledge about Terezín, their respect for the children and teacher, and their sadness in witnessing the stories. Several audience members became quite emotional during the discussions. As a cast and production team, we also experienced the need for the decompression that the talkbacks provided. During both rehearsals and productions, I used a "step out" procedure for the actors because of the intensity of the content. I viewed the talkbacks as providing the audience with a "step out" process, as well, and providing them with an opportunity to dialogue through the difficult and emotionally charged content of this work. (See Chapter 4 of this volume) We all became witnesses to compelling and provocative stories with deep emotional impact.

Cast member John Fritz who played the character Honza, adroitly synthesized the audience response in a personal interview with me (June 2022):

> We were amazed that small production details would resonate with the casual viewer. This would be the case for the duration of the production run, as audiences of varied ages—children, college students and seniors—were able to engage in healthy dialogue about the performance itself and the importance of the historical events in question.
>
> The American University performances attended by students, faculty and community members, and their talkbacks, resulted in some intense discussion about historical accuracy and the play's degree of relevance to contemporary society. I can recall a very impassioned dialogue about current political structures, ethnic and religious identity, and humanity's ability to survive even the most traumatic and horrific of events. Overall, it was an emotionally difficult conversation, but extremely valuable and enlightening, particularly in retrospect, given the current state of the United States' political affairs. It resulted in some intense discussion about historical accuracy.

It was rewarding to note that the teachers had carefully prepared their students with the study guide that we provided. It is my belief that this type of thought-provoking performance is a core responsibility of the artistic community and brings history to life with deep relevancy.

Part Three: For Posterity—We Must Remember

> For seven weeks I've lived in here,
> Penned up inside this ghetto.
> But I have found what I love here.
> The dandelions call to me
> And the white chestnut branches in the court.
> Only I never saw another butterfly.
> That butterfly was the last one.
> Butterflies don't live in here,
> In this ghetto.
> (Pavel Friedman, June 4, 1942 in *I Never Saw Another Butterfly*, Volakova, 1993) Died Auschwitz, 1944.

This production represents a bittersweet lightning rod for thought with unfortunate contemporary relevance. As we try to fathom this cruelty, we must remain dedicated to the prevention of such horrific injustice. The manifestation of the experiences of the children of Terezín and the brilliance of their teacher, however, remains an exaltation of the transcending power of the arts. Jiri Weill in his epilogue to the book *I Never Saw Another Butterfly*, reminds us, "The drawings and poems—that is all that is left of these children, for their ashes have long since sifted across the fields around Auschwitz," where most of the children perished. He also poignantly notes that "their drawings and their poems speak to us; these are their voices that have been preserved, voices of reminder, of truth, of hope ... preserved for posterity" (1993, p. 103). Our actors, production team, and audiences attested to the strength of theatre to sustain that preservation with integrity. Vaclav Havel, (*I Never Saw Another Butterfly*,1993, p. 104) in his *Afterword* speaks to the sustenance of their work, "The gentle traces of the children in the Terezín concentration camp continue to be, by their scope and impact, an expressive testimony in our day."

Ironically, I have always been drawn to butterflies in my life, both literally and metaphorically. Working on this production, I recalled a backyard release I did with my daughter, who is now an adult, but was a third grader at the time. We raised butterflies from the pupae stage, then as caterpillars, and finally we witnessed them becoming butterflies. We released them in our backyard rose garden, with cheers from my daughter and a group of her young friends, shouting "fly, fly away." When directing this production, I was haunted by the juxtaposition of that moment in my daughter's life—a bright-eyed and joyful little girl, delighting in the release of the butterflies amidst a backyard of roses—juxtaposed to the oppressive, deadly environment of Terezín for the children whose work I honored with this production. I also honor the magnificent Friedl who helped them find any possibility of joy and release to create their own sense of flying away.

My work here is dedicated to my daughter, Maria, and my two beautiful grandchildren, Declan and Lennox, and to all children who have the right to enjoy and pursue beauty and the soaring power of imagination in their lives. I aspire to a world where all children can thrive in the realm of imagination with a reality that affords flights of fantasy. It is also importantly dedicated to and in honor of the children who generated the drawings and poems from 1942–1944 in Terezín. Their fate was horrific. However, their drawings and poetry from Terezín that Friedl-Dicker Brandeis collected after the classes and kept in two suitcases—which she hid in one of the children's dormitories before her transport to Auschwitz—remain a telling affirmation of the creativity of children inspired by the catalyst of a great and remarkable teacher. All children deserve the right to see butterflies.

References

Cooper, R. M. (2021). *We never* said *goodbye*: *Memories of Otto Frank.* \Ryan M. Cooper Publications.

Darling-Hammond, L (2007). *Preparing teachers for a changing world: What teachers should learn and be able to do.* Jossey-Bass.

Fox, L. (2016). Cognition, knowledge construction, and motivation to learn: Models and theories. In G. Humphries Mardirosian & Y. P. Lewis (Eds.). *Arts integration in Education: Teachers and teaching artists as agents of change.* (pp. 15–30). Intellect Books.

Humphries Mardirosian, G. & Lewis, Y. P. (2016). *Arts integration in education: Teachers and teaching artists as agents of change.* Intellect Books.

Marakova, E. *Friedl Dicker Brandeis, Vienna 1898-Auschwitz 1944.* (1999) TallfellowPress.

Robinette, J. & Alexander, E. A., (2007). *I Never Saw Another Butterfly, the musical.* Based on a play by Celeste Raspanti. Dramatic Publishing.

Stixrud, W. R. & Marlowe, B. A. (2016). School reform with a brain: The neuropsychological foundations for arts integration. In G. Humphries Mardirosian & Y. P. Lewis (Eds.). *Arts integration in Education: Teachers and teaching artists as agents of change.* (pp. 15–30). Intellect Books.

Volakova, H. (1993). *I Never Saw Another Butterfly.* Schocken.

CHAPTER 8

Holocaust Impact Theater: Utilizing Theater as a Catalyst for Acceptance and Respect

Ruth Gordon

Life-Changing Call That Catalyzed Action

Holocaust Impact Theater (HIT) is a unique theater project developed by Ruth Gordon, a career educator. Students are taught the process of writing, producing, performing, and directing their own script, while learning theater and writing skills that will remain with them. The atrocities of The Holocaust are used as a platform for students to better understand and teach their audiences lessons focusing on the infiltration of hatred in a society. Bridging historical events from the past with current social injustices, the goal of each production is to develop a clear understanding of the need to obliterate these injustices while creating and celebrating tolerance and diversity. The program unites the efforts and energy of approximately 70–80 students annually, from the beginning in 2004 to the present. These students from varying backgrounds create an important theatrical statement. HIT provides a stage for them to voice their fears, thoughts, concerns, and solutions to relevant issues that need to be discussed, understood, and/or eradicated. HIT is an arm of The Alper Jewish Community Center (JCC) in Kendall, Florida and has been a self-funding program including several grants and monetary awards that have been received over the years.

HIT began with a phone call that this author never expected to receive. This was a call that would change not only her life, but the lives of nearly a thousand teenagers over the span of eighteen years. The author's good friend Lisa Reichert was the assistant director of programming for the local B'nai B'rith Youth Organization (BBYO) chapters. BBYO is an international Jewish youth organization focusing on leadership, community service, religious activities, and commitment. At the time of this life-changing call in 2004, the youth chapters flourished and were sponsored by The B'nai B'rith Organization. Today, they are an independent organization but still operate under the BBYO call letters.

Lisa discovered a dormant grant that would afford financial sponsorship of a theater group and asked this author to develop a Holocaust Impact Theater (HIT) program for high school students. In 2004, the author was a full-time educator with Miami-Dade County Schools, overseeing the largest middle school gifted program in the country. Lisa was looking for someone with both a history and strong Holocaust background, as well as a theater background. The program would be unique because it would give students the opportunity to write and perform their own original play in the Robert Russell Theatre at the Alper JCC in Kendall, a suburb of Miami, Florida. The concept of the play would focus on current issues of social injustice and intolerance, while linking them to the atrocities of The Holocaust, and demonstrating the dangers of social and political hate. The challenge of this proposal was huge.

The author's background in secondary social studies (with an emphasis on The Holocaust) and theater was the appropriate background for heading this program. However, despite her extensive experience in theater, performing and directing, the creation of an original work created by students presented an entirely new challenge. The first year of Holocaust Impact Theater (HIT) started with seventeen Jewish high school students recruited from various BBYO chapters. The goal for this group of students would be to write and perform their own original play with a running time of sixty minutes.

The HIT Process

Year One of HIT: Developing the Program

The students met after school, twice a week, functioning as both writers and performers of this first play. A format for the play needed to be developed that would incorporate timely, relevant social issues important to this group of students. Simultaneously, the play content needed to remain sensitive to the messages, stories, and history of hate that The Holocaust teaches. It seemed like it would take a miracle to accomplish these goals in one play, but, amazingly, the mission was accomplished. The first production, titled *Stained*, started a tradition of single word titles for all future productions.

The writing team of HIT decided to use a series of monologues, spoken by different characters, who would each tell their story of bullying, intolerance, or injustice. The first script highlighted two main characters: one Latine and one Black. As these student writers attempted to develop stories for these characters, the author realized that minority representation in the group was needed to portray these minority struggles. With recommendations from fellow teachers, students of many races and ethnicities were invited into the group. What was imagined as a one-year program developed into an eighteen year (and still counting) second, volunteer career, because the students involved in HIT wanted the program to continue. As they graduated high school, they passed the leadership torch to the next generation of participants. The program developed a life of its own at a time when social media did not yet exist.

Year Two of HIT: Layering the Process

In year two, open auditions were held to broaden the diversity of the group, and over one hundred students showed up. The power of emailing the casting call to local students and teachers proved to be an overwhelming success. Other forms of social media did not yet exist. To include as many participants as possible, the students were divided into separate auditions: those who wanted to write; those who wanted to perform; and those who wanted to work on the set, costumes and backstage.

Local students who participated in school drama programs did not have the time to get involved in an independent production because of their obligations to their school plays. As a result, the HIT students had never been in a play, written a script or had any backstage technical knowledge of running a show. At that first meeting in August 2005, students who wanted to be writers answered a writing prompt. Students from the prior year read those answers and chose a large writing team of twenty students, assuming some would drop out of the program. Not one student left!

Creating a Script: The Writing Process

The group continued to meet three times a week, with homework assignments to research pieces of history, Survivor's stories, along with social issues that concerned them. It took about six weeks to narrow down the multitude of social issues before they agreed on their topics. Each writer was asked to create a biography of a character for the play. Once again, the student writers chose to use a monologue format where character stories were interwoven with one another.

The Technical Theater Process

By the third year, the monologue format was dismissed because the writers wanted to develop a full-fledged playscript. The writing meetings took on new challenges. The plot intertwined lessons of hate from The Holocaust into the story line. With a defined story line came a larger cast and room for "extras" on stage. This also meant more lighting and sound cues, and a real set with more props and costumes. This movement generated forward growth.

Given this author's dearth of technical expertise, it was fortunate that the JCC has a contract with Reflections Productions, which runs and maintains all of the sound and lighting for every event in their theater and campus. Mario Alvarez is the JCC technician and for these past 18 years of productions, Mario who is widely respected by the HIT students, volunteers to train HIT students to use the equipment. He sets lights and teaches the tech crew how to record all the sound bites and music needed for every production.

Challenging Situations

Rarely does HIT have issues amongst the cast, but these personnel situations have been tricky. The entire concept of this group is to teach tolerance and acceptance, so when there are personality issues that clash, the students are encouraged to work it out amongst themselves. But sometimes this director must be the umpire. It was determined that this project should be limited to only high school students as the topics of conversations were mature, and rehearsals often ran late.

Initiating Student Directors

As HIT continued to expand, it was appropriate for students to begin directing their productions. The author's goal was for every aspect of each final production to be student developed, created, designed, and performed. HIT was moving in the right direction. As the program began earning respect and support from local drama teachers, they began coordinating their high school show dates with HIT so their students could participate in both school plays and HIT. This concession was a huge nod of validation to the importance to what we were doing.

Symbiosis and Social Service

The program gained the respect of local educators, administrators, and school counselors. Drama teachers from local high schools began encouraging their students to get involved in HIT, and they, in turn, scheduled their spring shows around the HIT production and rehearsal dates. This partnership with local high school teachers became a symbiotic relationship!

Teachers and administrators began to give students extra credit to attend the show and write a follow-up reflection of the lessons of the play. The significant impact of the experience was reflected in these critical essays that ensured the learning outcomes of the plays. Administrators sent students who perpetrated school "hate" fights or acts of bullying to HIT's productions and required them to report back to that educator, sharing the lessons learned from the show. This was a new social service the program was providing! Now reflection was added as assessment of learning (American Association of Colleges and Universities, n.d.).

Finally, the program became successful at recruiting students to sign the plays for the hearing-impaired population of our community. A local high school sign language teacher helped train her students to learn our script, using sign language, so they were able provide this service.

Actor Training

Every year HIT was faced with new problems, concerns, and hurdles. Some years the concern was funding, and other years it was scheduling and working around other functions at the JCC. One of the biggest problems was, and is, the time demands of this production. The very first lesson of Russian theater theorist Constantin Stanislavski in *An Actor Prepares* is that the actor must be committed and on time to rehearsal (Stanislavski, 1989). In HIT's productions, every person is of equal importance. Rehearsals don't begin until everyone is present, establishing the groundwork that everyone must be on time.

While other commitments are understood, learning to make choices is an important part of growth and education. Making choices, time management, dedication, and responsibility to a team, are some of the many life skills that theater teaches. As in any walk of life, choices must be made. Realizing that students have to embrace the commitment they make to be part of HIT, this author laid down the law: If a student was on a team sport or held a part-time job that would interfere with the rehearsal schedule, the student, unfortunately, could not be in the show. This was a matter of respecting the authors' time and their peers' time.

Portraying Others

There were many daunting tasks as the facilitator and guide for these students that included determining the boundaries of topics, subject matter and dialogue that parents, the school board (which supports us) and the audiences would find appropriate. One year, the writers had written roles for two lesbians flying overseas to adopt a child in Asia. After three months of rehearsals and only one week before the show, the mother of one of these actresses wanted to pull her child from the show because she was not comfortable with her child playing that role. This situation echoed the very core of the piece which entailed acceptance of others. That situation created a protocol: immediately after casting, this author, via an email, informs the parents what role their child has been cast for and will be assuming in each production. This has eliminated problems like this from reoccurring.

Often during the writing process, a student would be self-reflective and grapple with their own sexual orientation. They would use the opportunity to come out to their friends. Once they had their support, they found it easier to approach their parents with their struggles. Meg Greene (2016) wrote in her essay in HowlRound.com on *Gender Responsive Casting*:

> As a theatre educator, I think this is vital to the heart of my (our) work—developing skilled, ensemble-minded, brave, adventurous, socially-responsible, and empathetic artists. Moving forward, I want to cultivate casting practices that value identities, create opportunities, and deeply care for the artists we wish to work with ... (p. 6)

During the course of rehearsals, LGBTQ+ students came out to each other; some spoke about wanting to transition but could not tell their parents in fear of being kicked out of their homes. The author brought a psychologist to one of the writing sessions to talk about these challenging and personal issues.

Meeting Holocaust Survivors

Each cast meets at least one Holocaust Survivor or a family member of a Survivor. These Survivors and their stories are the foundation of HIT's entire purpose of existence. Eventually, these firsthand testimonies will only be told via videos, written documentation or from their descendants. Renowned acting teacher Uta Hagen (1973) wrote, in *Respect for Acting:*

> As I have said before, biographies of personalities of a given time stimulate me most ... Go to the library and to museums and begin to look—look with your present-day eyes for what truly matters. (p. 136)

These experiences were life changing and these students finally understood why HIT existed and the importance of including stories and lessons of The Holocaust in every production. During every rehearsal and writing session, students were taught portions of the history of the Holocaust. Dramaturgy included a Holocaust movie, followed by an emotional discussion. Students learned about antisemitism and how to use theater as a catalyst for acceptance and respect.

Stories of the Holocaust are woven into the fabric of both of this author's and her husband's lives. This author was able to share her own family's Holocaust and WWII stories: Her husband lost an aunt at Auschwitz, who was only fifteen years old. This author's mother-in-law and her identical twin sister and husband's grandparents had been arrested fleeing France. His grandfather was sent to various concentration camps, and his grandmother, mother and aunt were separated and survived the Nazi regime hidden at various farms throughout France. The grandfather and uncle survived many camps, both ending at Buchenwald and liberated by this author's father, who was serving in the Third Army under General Patton, on April 11, 1945 (United States

Holocaust Memorial Museum, n.d, and History.com, n.d.). However, these family members never spoke about the war. It was not until Florida mandated that all students, K-12, must be taught The Holocaust that this author heard her dad speak of his war experiences. As a social studies teacher at an elementary school, this writer's father, Irving Whitman, offered to come and speak to the students. He had remained silent about his war stories for forty years. From that first classroom visit, he came every year to speak at whichever school his daughter was teaching. From third to twelfth graders, they never wanted to leave the assembly. He spoke without a note, and always with a tear in his eye. He spoke from his heart and told exactly what a day in the life of a soldier was like, and what happened the day his regiment came upon Buchenwald, quite by accident.

As soldiers, they had never heard of the camps. It was hard for Irving Whitman to explain his first impressions of Buchenwald: starving, emaciated prisoners; mounds of human remains; vermin-infested sleeping quarters.

He always told the students that a platoon of Black soldiers had stumbled upon the camp right before his platoon arrived. Together they liberated the camp. This was an unreported detail one rarely reads about, so the author made sure this fascinating story was incorporated into one of HIT's plays. Unfortunately, her father passed away that year, and never saw his story performed on stage.

The Challenge of Antisemitism/Anti-Racism Social Issue Play Topics

Because of her personal background, this author felt a private responsibility to continue HIT. There were shootings and hate crimes prevalent in the news. The students' timing, in choosing each year's topics, has been uncanny. One year, on opening night, there was a mass shooting on a college campus in

Virginia. The play that year centered around gun control. The February killings at Marjory Stoneman Douglas occurred three weeks before HIT's play that dealt with school shootings. Police brutality was the major topic of one year's show, the same year that George Floyd was killed by a police officer's brutal force. The killings at a synagogue in Pennsylvania mirrored that year's play about murders in what should be safe places of worship. This phenomenon happened repeatedly. The students chose their topics in August, but, coincidentally, the plays always seemed to mirror a newsworthy story that occurred about the time of their production. Was it that these bright students were so in tune with the society that they were growing up in? Or was it that these events happened so often that the odds were that the events would unfortunately align themselves, in a timely fashion, with our plays?

The biggest obstacle facing the writers was creating a story incorporating timely, relevant social issues linked to historical stories of The Holocaust and Survivors to show the dangers of social hate.

Brazilian theatre theorist Augusto Boal (1985) wrote on page 102 of his book *Theatre of the Oppressed* that:

> Empathy is the emotional relationship which is established between the character and spectator, and which provokes, fundamentally, a delegation of power on the part of the spectator, who becomes an object in relation to the character: whatever happened to the latter, happens vicariously to the spectator.

Empathy is a key component in each year's productions. One play focused on a foster care child finding a diary of the family's grandmother with whom he was staying. That diary told her story as a camp prisoner and survivor. Another storyline reunited a rabbi, at his granddaughter's bat mitzvah, with a family friend who was a righteous Christian who hid that rabbi as a child.

Every time it seemed the students could not devise a new fresh story, they miraculously have. They have kept this lucky author on her toes for 18 years, learning as much from them as they do from her!

The Impact

Combatting Hate

The purpose of HIT has always been to impact the student participants involved in the program as well as the audiences who attend. Unfortunately, the need to educate and awaken the community never ends. It is difficult to understand why people hate one another. Why does the color of a person's skin matter? Why do religious and ethnic differences spark hate? Who cares who loves who, as long as there is love and respect in the world? Why can't we all respect each other and embrace our differences? These are the goals of HIT's productions: to break down the walls and barriers that create separation. This author's mantra has always been "Hate is taught. It needs to be untaught ... NOW!"

A Student Performer's Response

The impact on the students in the productions could not be more powerfully captured than in the words of one of our former performers and directors, Emily Ann Garcia:

> The years I participated with HIT, we tackled subjects such as: feminism, police brutality, immigration, racial discrimination, drug abuse, the foster care system, and mental illness. We

worked diligently to contribute research to HIT that was 100% factually accurate. The audience understood that our goal was to spread awareness and to make an impact! I learned how powerful theatre can be. I am incredibly grateful for my time with Holocaust Impact Theater and with our wonderful leader and mentor, Ruth Gordon. This experience changed my life forever, and I am now a theatre major in college. (July, 2022)

HIT has established itself as a program that allows and encourages out of the box thinking. A production template has been created that lends itself to inclusion and diversity and replication. Our plays always conclude with a student developed video. These videos have become small visual masterpieces.

Audience Response

Audiences who attend a HIT production have always said that they appreciate the closing videos that show people in crises, highlighting racial and antisemitic issues, bullying, mass shootings, hate crimes, battles for gay rights, cross burnings, slavery, pictures of the Holocaust, etc. But the videos also show progress with people helping people, an important aspect of HIT. Topics include the legalization of gay marriages and adoptions, organizations that help people in need, Anti-Defamation League (ADL), successful immigration movements, laws passed to help those with special needs, Survivors' stories, biracial marriages, and, again, the list is endless.

From the beginning, HIT has performed to sold out houses. The success of our attendance can be attributed to educators, politicians and clergy who strongly support our program. Stories in our local newspapers and appearances on local television news and talk shows help expand our following.

Technical and Dress Rehearsals and Student Leadership Roles

Through the developmental process, the students created the roles of "student producers." These students are the leaders of the group, each overseeing a facet of the production. Student producers are role models and leaders to their peers making production decisions with the author's nod of approval. At the end of each year's production, a few students interview students for leadership roles for the following year. Students are chosen to oversee the writing and editing process of the script; to direct; to run the backstage area; to do props, costumes and set design; and to be on the technical crew. This formula allows for more students to have leadership involvement knowing exactly what their responsibilities are.

Technical and dress rehearsals are always very time consuming and fatiguing. Every student involved in the show must be at the theater by 4 p.m., every day, for two weeks.

Food is an important component throughout the process. Pizzas are brought in for dinner most nights. HIT students might tell you the author's infamous brownies are the only reason they join HIT!! This expense for food is covered by their annual car washes and by the author and her husband. It does not come out of our actual budget.

Costuming, for the most part, is easily accomplished by pulling from the students' own wardrobes, or borrowing from local theater groups, unless the play deals with an historical period scene. If necessary, the author takes the youth to secondhand stores to find specific clothing items or accessories, and, if necessary, costumes are rented.

By the third day of dress rehearsals, make-up is introduced. Many of the girls do their own make-up at home once we decide on their character's look. Most of our male actors, who are new to theater, are reluctant to wear make-up ... but, that is show biz!

Often, the show must utilize a set that has been constructed for a production by Miami Children's Theater, the other theater group at the JCC. Our rehearsals and production dates often coincide so their set is already built, which thankfully saves HIT much time and money. Actors quickly adapt staging to their set. It does not work when our play is about the Holocaust and their play is *The Little Mermaid*! This requires creativity and re-blocking of scenes and covering portions of their set with artwork, furniture, banners, etc. If there is not a preexisting set, then the tech crew must create their own set by creating/building their own set.

Funding from Arnold Mittelman and the Transformation of HIT

In 2019, a wonderful supporter of HIT, President of the National Jewish Theater Foundation Arnold Mittelman—theater producer, and friend of HIT– received the honor of being chosen by The Knight Foundation as a pillar of the arts in South Florida. Arnold, in turn, was able to gift a grant to any arts organization of his choice.

Arnold selected HIT, and the program was celebrated at an event receiving the funds desperately needed to finally purchase HIT's own headsets.

Repercussions of the Pandemic

The last live HIT production was held March 12–15, 2020. As Covid spread, schools in Florida were closed on March 12, which coincided with our opening night, but the JCC never cancelled the shows. Over one hundred people surprisingly attended the theater each of the three performances. Every seat in the house was disinfected before and after every performance.

Following the performance, this author had multiple conversations via phone and Zoom as to what direction, if any, HIT should take for the following year. Would Covid even be an issue a year later? The problem was that the writers had to be chosen that spring to start writing in August. They were optimistic and they were willing to write this script, even knowing it could sit dormant on our computers. HIT has always been the constant in the students' lives. When everything else in their lives are changing, HIT is there. So, the production moved forward via Zoom. The only thing missing were the brownies.

Staging During Covid

The 2020/2021 writers knew that with the restrictions of Covid, each scene had to be written with a maximum of four students, who would have to be socially distanced on stage. They wrote the script, via Zoom, never meeting each other in person. During that time, this author helped Suzy Breitner, a grant writer for the JCC, develop a grant that HIT received to cover the cost of having our 2021 production, *Fractured*, professionally videotaped (https://vimeo.com/543282880/716088dbe8).

This initiated an incredibly unique situation: rehearsals and blocking were all done by the adult and student directors via Zoom. We would have cast and student producer meetings the same way. Technology allowed students who lived far away from the JCC the ability to participate in HIT. Technology was linking students together who would probably have never met to work for the common good!

Now it was nearing time to record this production, titled *Fractured*, that would then be shared with the community at large and our Miami-Dade County school system.

Filming the Play as a Pivot During Covid

Using Zoom interviews, a videographer was hired. Lee Gladstone totally understood the importance of this project from the start. Lee came and set up in the theater all day on a Friday, along with Mario, our JCC sound and lighting professional. A filming schedule for the performers and stage crew was developed although we had no way of knowing if it would work or how long it would take to record each scene. It was important that students not be at the JCC until it was time to film their scene, to minimize personal contact amongst our students because of Covid-19. Starting at 8 a.m. in the morning, the only people allowed in the theater were the author and her husband, Lee, Mario, and HIT's five student producers, texting one another from isolated corners of the JCC. The students in each scene arrived at the theater but never saw any other cast members. They did their scene and left. It was organized disorganization, but the mission was completed and not one single person got Covid!

A Culmination During Covid

The hope was to be able to gather all of the cast and crew of *Fractured*, at the JCC, to watch the final video together. Unfortunately, Covid numbers continued to climb, so that experience never happened. The camaraderie for the cast, that the author so hoped for, never happened. What a feeling of accomplishment that HIT had not missed a beat due to Covid, but the participating students never embraced this same feeling that former groups had developed. They were happy to be a part of the big picture. Because each scene was so compartmentalized, until they saw the final entity, the author wondered if they really grasped what had been accomplished.

A Covid-Forced Hiatus and Possible Finale

For the following year, 2021, *Fractured* was distributed by the JCC to all JCC's nationally and selected school systems. Covid was just taking its toll, so, the end of HIT was announced. During this two-year hiatus, with the help of the JCC and the Jewish Federation, an attempt was made to find a new volunteer leader, albeit unsuccessfully.

This author wrote a job description that could be touted around by the JCC and Jewish Federation, but, without funding for a program director, it would be almost impossible to find a new volunteer to lead HIT. HIT could have just folded, but this author and program director, who had worked without pay for most of those 17 years, had been determined to keep it alive. HIT had become a legacy to the community. This program director missed working with the students and each year's challenges from start to finish.

A New Beginning

A Fresh Start

Flash forward to 2022. This author's husband Ira, impressed by the value of HIT, suggested that, together, as equal producers and partners, the program could be restarted. However, given the changing circumstances in the local schools, during the interlude, many challenges were faced. Opening that door meant starting from scratch. Students the author had worked with had graduated. Teachers had retired. A call to the JCC resulted immediately with a "YES!" to starting HIT again, with assurance of the necessary funding through a grant proposal for the first year, until HIT was financially on its feet again. Several past producers, who were now in college, but home for the summer, gathered a group of students to reignite HIT. Nina Guerra, a former HIT performer, director and producer, jumped at the chance. By the time of the second zoom meeting, she had already posted flyers on social media. She wrote:

> I have always had these lenses of privilege over my eyes. Impact taught me how normal social injustice is within our systems and within our society. I learned that the only way to put a stop to these unequal systems is to talk about it and make the issue known.—Nina Guerra, former HIT performer, Director, and Student Producer, 2019–2021.

Nina expressed well how theater can be utilized as a catalyst for acceptance and respect.

Five high school students immediately responded to Nina's postings and, after a Zoom meeting, they committed on the spot. A month later they met in the co-producers' home, along with their parents, so the commitment their children were making could be explained.

This is the kind of student dedication and enthusiasm, along with a strong desire to make an impact in their community, which has kept HIT alive all these 18 years. Thrilled about reigniting this program, the co-producer planned audition dates in August, a rehearsal schedule and performance dates. As of 2023, three new student producers/directors, who were anxious to start the program again and who had given assurances that they would get the students to participate, succeeded brilliantly with the play titled *Choices*.

Ella DeCastro, a high school student created a closing video from the production (Figure 8.1).

FIGURE 8.1
Ruth Gordan with the Writing Team for Holocaust Impact Theater's 2023/2024 Production. Photo by Ira Gordon

HIT achieved its 18th year with its highest accolades. Palmetto Bay's Mayor Karyn Cunningham delivered a proclamation. Medals and certificates were presented to each cast and crew member by the Past Chair of the School Board, Dr. Larry Feldman. Christian Mayo, a *Miami Herald* columnist stated that:

> The mission of engaging youth in history, and how it relates to present day issues, is what the production of *Choices* accomplishes so well. Holocaust Impact Theater has been

making a difference in all lives, making an impact on them, for almost two decades. HIT's stories, written by students, keep conversations going and eyes open. There are few things more important and essential in our fragile world than that.

Many of the HIT scripts are available through The National Jewish Theater Foundation (https://www.njtfoundation.org/holocaust_theater_catalog) for teachers, elsewhere, to take up the charge and use theater as an artistic teaching tool for future generations. HIT encourages others to use this approach to address significant issues (Figure 8.2). As it is often said in Yiddish, the project is Bashert, or "meant to be," so the show will go on!

Figure 8.2
Ruth Gordon with her published book, INSIDE OUT OUTSIDE IN, teaching diversity and tolerance for young children. Photo by Russ Gordon

References

American Association of Colleges and Universities (n.d.). *Valid Assessment of Learning in Undergraduate Education (VALUE) Rubrics.*
https://www.aacu.org/initiatives/value-initiative/value-rubrics

Boal. A. (1985). *Theatre of the oppressed.* Theatre Communications Group

Greene, M. (2016). *Gender responsive casting. HowlRound.com.*
https://howlround.com/gender-responsive-casting

Hagen, U. (1973). *Respect for acting.* Simon & Schuster Macmillan Company.

History.com (n.d.). *The U.S. army liberates Buchenwald concentration camp.*
https://www.history.com/this-day-in-history/the-u-s-army-liberates-buchenwald-concentration-camp

Holocaust Theater Catalog. https://www.njtfoundation.org/holocaust_theater_catalog

Mayo, C. M. (2023, March 10). *Student Show Focuses on Social Injustice, Neighbors, page 8SE,* Miami Herald.

Stanislavski, C. (1989). *An actor prepares.* Routledge.

United States Holocaust Memorial Museum (n.d). *U.S. forces liberate Buchenwald: April 11, 1945.*
https://www.ushmm.org/learn/timeline-of-events/1942-1945/us-forces-liberate-Buchenwald

CHAPTER 9

This is What I've Scene: Teaching the Holocaust Through Theatre

Mira Hirsch

Nurturing Empathy Through Theatre

It is often said that you cannot truly understand another person and their circumstances unless you "walk a mile in their shoes." President Barack Obama once said:

> The biggest deficit that we have in our society and in the world right now is an empathy deficit. We are in great need of people being able to stand in somebody else's shoes and see the world through their eyes. (Conroy, 2017, para. 1)

But how does one walk in someone else's shoes, particularly when that person lived in a different time period and their experiences were extraordinarily tragic? Theatre is a method which allows us to experience history—to witness—in a way that few other experiences can offer. In *This is What I've Scene*, an educational activity designed to teach young people about the Holocaust through theatre, students experience through empathy. This comprehensive theatre experience for high school students is offered as a means by which they can learn about, understand and experience dimensions of the Holocaust with meaning, substance and connection to their own lives.

The process begins with watching videos of Holocaust survivors and liberators as they share their stories. The students then generate their own interpretation with authentic theatre pieces using those verbatim testimonies. This activity has been practiced, with great success, throughout the United States and England. In the past five years, I have facilitated workshops and instructed classes in Atlanta, Miami, San Diego, London, Birmingham and Kent, England, involving over 250 middle and high school students of various ethnicities, religions, nationalities, and economic backgrounds. Students have "stepped into the shoes" of those who survived the worst atrocities in modern day history and are now positioned to keep alive the stories of those who may no longer be here to tell them. What follows is a step-by-step description of the process as implemented at a private International Baccalaureate (IB) school in Atlanta, Georgia, which has a global mindset and a diverse student population, where I serve as a full-time theatre educator.

The Pre-Assessment

> I believe the Holocaust was a conflict between the Jewish. I also think that Hitler played a big role in this. From what I recall, I think a bunch of Jewish were captured and put into bootcamps by Germans. Later, Hitler murdered a lot of Jewish. (Student 1)

This theatre journal entry was written by one of my 8th grade students in response to the prompt "What was the Holocaust?" given to assess my classes' knowledge prior to commencing the unit titled *Enacting History*.

Another pertinent response included:

> The Holocaust was an era during which Nazi leader Adolf Hitler declared and ordered for all Jews to be placed in concentration camps where they would have tests run on them and they would often also be led into a gas chamber where they would all die. (Student 2)

Before we began the theatre portion of the *Enacting History* unit, I wanted to see what my students knew—or thought they knew—about the Holocaust. Overall, there was a general understanding that it was a terrible event caused by a man named Adolph Hitler which led to the deaths of many Jewish people. I then gave them a second writing prompt, this one opinion-based: "Do you think that theatre is a good way to learn about history?" Students shared responses such as: "Yes, I think it is, because it gives people a good visual perspective. I feel like if someone is reading something or learning about it in class, they are less likely to be paying attention" (Student 3).

Another student captured the unique nature of theatre to provide an immersive experience for those who are performing it, writing:

> 100% yes. Theatre is a good way to really feel and think about how the person you are portraying really feels in order to improve your performance. This is kinda why I like theatre, because this is the closest that I can ever get to walking in other people's shoes. (Student 4)

The most insightful responses pointed out the inherent ethical concerns of such an activity, acknowledging that writers, directors and student actors could inadvertently (or intentionally) impose a skewed version of history through performances that either disregard or take license with historical fact:

> I think that theatre has been used to tell history before, such as the Hamilton musical about America's founding fathers. However, in order to make their plays more interesting, directors can often change the plot, ultimately changing how the audience learns about history. (Student 5)

And:

> I think theatre can be a good way to learn about history depending on the level of respect and maturity the actors have during the piece and while creating the piece. Many times history can be very serious topics and with the wrong cast it can be a catastrophe. (Student 6)

I found these to be two extremely perceptive conjectures. The writer of the first statement had most likely seen at least one theatrical presentation that did not match what they had been taught about history, and had found that experience to be disconcerting, or false in some way. The writer of the second statement clearly had had some negative experience(s) with peers who were not as mature as they were and who had not taken a theatre activity seriously in the past, leaving the writer with trepidations about embarking on such a project again.

The Challenges of This Approach

Teaching the Holocaust through theatre is fraught with many ethical considerations. I was happily surprised that, even prior to beginning our work, these students were able to foresee the potential for theatre performances based on history to go awry. There are many stories about educators who have fallen prey to mistakes while teaching the Holocaust. Jennifer Goss (2021), the curriculum and instruction specialist for Echoes & Reflections, recounted in an article for Chalkbeat titled *The Holocaust Lesson I Regret Teaching: I Look Back with a Mix of Shame and a Commitment to Doing Better*, that one of her first Holocaust lessons involved instructing students to simulate being in a boxcar by cramming themselves into the corner of her classroom while she read a piece about transports to the concentration camps. She later realized how misguided this lesson and other such simulations can be, introducing students to emotions and frightening situations that may not be developmentally appropriate for them, exposing them to feelings of lack of personal safety. Another (far more harmful) example took place in December of 2021, when an elementary school staff member in the Washington, DC public school system directed a group of third graders to "dig their classmates' mass graves and simulate shooting the victims" (Asbury, 2021, para. 1), as a library class activity. This staff member was later placed on leave and investigated, having violated ethical standards.

The Moral Imperative

So, how can those of us who teach the Holocaust through interactive lessons avoid these unseemly traps? The truth is that there are numerous first-person narratives, memoirs, documentaries, photographs, and historical documents—*so many primary sources*—that I assert that there is no need for invention when developing theatrical depictions of the Holocaust. The stories exist. They are there for our exploration and our study. And as we enter the period of time when we will no longer be able to hear directly from the survivors, liberators, rescuers and witnesses who lived through the darkest days in modern history, we will need to find other ways to transmit their stories; ways that will reach young people in a dynamic fashion, so that this history and its multitude of lessons are never lost. As a Jew and as an artist, I feel this responsibility heavily. And my "way" is through theatre (Figure 9.1 and Figure 9.2).

Several years ago, I joined forces with colleagues Arnold Mittelman, President of the National Jewish Theater Foundation, and theatre professor Janet E. Rubin to write a book on the subject: *Enacting History: A Practical Guide to Teaching the Holocaust through Theatre* (Hirsch, Rubin & Mittelman, 2020). The book is an instruction manual aimed at middle and high school educators, with guidelines and activities that utilize theatrical methods and materials to teach the Holocaust. Scripted scenes from published plays, most featuring school-age characters, are included, as are devised theatre activities.

Figure 9.1
Students at Atlanta International perform verbatim testimony scenes from Enacting History. Photo credit: Alex Tat, Atlanta International School

THIS IS WHAT I'VE SCENE: TEACHING THE HOLOCAUST THROUGH THEATRE

However, the method I have used most frequently is one referred to earlier that I call *This is What I've Scene*, a technique for scene creation combining first-person narrative testimonies with theatrical tableaus. Some of these workshops have included Jewish students; most have not. I have encountered students who are well-versed in Holocaust history, and others who learned the word "Holocaust" only days before my arrival. I have been met with enthusiasm, indifference and even occasional questions as to why they were being asked to explore this particular historical tragedy rather than others. And in one workshop, I even uncovered antisemitic graffiti on a classroom wall when I began rearranging the desks in order to make more space for scene work—a crudely drawn swastika alongside the (misspelled) word "Heil." The offending message was quickly scrubbed away by a school staffer, and after an important bonus lesson in antisemitism, the workshop went on, albeit with more immediacy. What was initially a very upsetting incident became a catalyst for explaining why the work we were embarking on was more than just a look at a historical event. Antisemitism is still alive. Hate speech still occurs. The danger is still with us.

Figure 9.2
Students at Atlanta International perform verbatim testimony scenes from Enacting History. Photo credit: Alex Tat, Atlanta International School

The "Why" of Teaching the Holocaust

An important question in Holocaust education is the why. *Why* teach the Holocaust? The most obvious answer is "so that it will never happen again." But is that even a possible outcome? Time and time again, history is learned and yet still repeated. It can be argued that teaching the Holocaust builds empathy and dissuades bullying and discrimination. But does it? Have young people actually become kinder since we've been teaching the Holocaust? Then, perhaps we teach the Holocaust to hasten the end of antisemitism. However, we know that is not occurring. There are more incidents of antisemitism in the United States than ever before (ADL, 2022). Is the goal then to keep the memories of the victims and survivors alive? Or to attempt to understand, philosophically and categorically, man's capacity for inhumanity to his fellow man? Not a day goes by that I don't ask myself this question: *Why* teach the Holocaust? And not a day goes by that I don't inevitably answer myself—all of the above. All of it.

While none of these reasons alone define my moral imperative, and none has been ultimately achieved, I believe each goal is worth striving for, and each goal is reason enough on its own. Every student will have their own individual experience with these lessons. Some will be shallow; others profound. As educators, we cannot always be sure who we will reach or how deeply. Sometimes, the results of our efforts are not even apparent until months or even years after we've made contact with a particular student. But we persist, sustained by the more immediate signs of our success, such as when a student writes a thoughtful critique, or impacts an audience with a moving performance, knowing that other successes will follow, even if we, personally, never get to witness them.

The Process and the Performance

In the spring of 2022, I led my 8th grade students in Atlanta through a 10-week unit of learning the Holocaust through theatre, beginning with the screening of several short Holocaust documentaries. These students were then divided into eight project groups and instructed to create Google Slides presentations summarizing the historical context sections of the first eight chapters of the book *Enacting History* (Hirsch, Mittelman, & Rubin, 2020), from the rise of antisemitism and anti-Jewish laws in Germany through the Nuremberg trials. The group slide presentations were then shared with the whole class, allowing the students to teach each other about a particular period in the chronology of the Holocaust.

Then the students were finally ready to begin the theatrical activity—*This is What I've Scene*. This process, which is one of the three theatre techniques outlined in *Enacting History*, begins with dividing the class into scene groups. Each group then watches a video testimony of a selected survivor or witness from the University of Southern California's Shoah Foundation's IWitness website (Visual History Archive, n.d.). Next, they are given a transcription of that interview, and are tasked with making decisions about which points of the survivor's story should be enhanced by theatrical tableaus. They then create storyboards for their scenes, and select props, costumes and small set pieces to enhance their storytelling. Roles are divided up, with one student in each group serving as the narrator.

The narrator's role is to sit off to the side of the scene and read the first-person account, while the other actors portray a myriad of characters in the narrative through a series of frozen pictures. Appropriate musical underscoring selections are made, and the scenes are rehearsed, critiqued and rehearsed some more. The activity culminates with a performance of all of the scenes in sequence—a crucial part of the process. Performing the work for an audience is, I believe, absolutely necessary, as without an audience, there is no communication, and without communication, there is no theatre.

Our audience for this particular performance included middle and high school students and faculty from the school. An invitation was extended to all of the upper school teachers. Approximately six different classes attended. No pre-show materials were provided, and it was up to individual teachers if they wanted to give their students an introduction to the Holocaust prior to their attendance. All of the audience members stayed for a post-show question and answer session. They saw eight scenes that day—eight scenes constructed from the verbatim narratives of the survivors and witnesses who had testified in the IWitness videos that the students had watched. Each scene was preceded by the slide presentation that each scene group had created to introduce that particular part of the Holocaust timeline. Not a word was added or deleted from these personal stories, which moved through the chronology of the Holocaust and its aftermath.

The performance began with Scene 1, in which a group of actors stood before a wall plastered with pages from the German propaganda newspaper *Der Stürmer*. Filled with hateful images and stories about Jews with "long noses and saliva running from their mouth," these newspaper pages haunted young Esther Clifford as she made her way to school in Frankfurt am Main, Germany in 1934. Scene 2 depicted survivor Rudolph Lahnstein cowering in a storage bin with his sister on Kristallnacht (the Night of Broken Glass), often considered to be the unofficial onset of the Holocaust.

As men who had once played cards with their father ransacked their home, Rudolph and his sister peered through the wooden slats of their hiding place and prayed for the safety of their father, who was forced to stand in the courtyard as their family's furniture and heirlooms were thrown down on him from their apartment above. In Scene 3, audiences followed 10-year-old Henry Greenblatt as he snuck out of the Warsaw ghetto through a rain gutter at the bottom of a fence to find bread for his family, while Scene 4 saw Itka

Zygmuntowicz surviving another day in Auschwitz, carrying stones "from one place to the other," as she was mocked and threatened by guards.

Scene 5 chronicled the hunger, loneliness and fear of Aaron Elster who hid in an empty apartment in Poland with his parents. Scene 6 transported our audience to the Lipiczany forest in Poland, where Mira Shelub and her fellow partisans conducted acts of sabotage, including attacking a local police station and living to tell about it. In Scene 7, they watched as Lasar Gotz celebrated the arrival of American soldiers at the Kaufering concentration camp, while his father, too weak to even stand, could only inquire if Lasar had brought him his daily ration of bread.

And lastly, in Scene 8, they observed the trial of a Nazi guard named Brigitte, who was finally brought to justice in the 1960's, with the help of testimony from camp survivor Dora Abend. Our audiences took this journey, as did our actors, who, in telling the stories of others through theatrical performance, came as close as one can come to "walking in another person's shoes."

The Assessment Outcomes

Qualitative Results

Six months after participating in *This is What I've Scene*, some of the actors looked back on the experience, and spoke about its impact. Student 7 remarked, "Now that I know how words and actions can affect someone, especially in such a terrible way like the Holocaust did, I think that is always staying in the back of my mind." Responding to the question "Do you think that theatre is a good way to learn about the Holocaust?" she emphatically replied,

> Yes, because to be a good actor you have to really get into the character, and to get into the character you have to do

research ... you have to get to know them basically. And I think getting to know survivors of the Holocaust, I think that helps more with learning. Whereas, if you were to write an essay, you don't really have to go into that depth to figure out who they are.

Student 8 said,

I was definitely surprised at how engaged the audience was because I thought that they wouldn't really be able to feel how we were feeling in the scene, but a lot of people told me how they felt they had learned so much, like they were witnessing it right there, and that definitely surprised me.

Quantitative Results

In addition to this anecdotal evidence of the program's success, a professional evaluation of *This is What I've Scene* was conducted by Dr. Sam Mitschke for the British Pilot Programme, which took place in London, Birmingham and Kent, England in November and December of 2021 (Mitschke, 2022). Ninety-seven students, ages 12 and 13, took part in the program. Fifty-three of them completed Dr. Mitschke's survey, yielding the following results:

- 91% of the 53 students either Strongly Agree or Agree in response to "The session was interesting and engaging."
- 98% of the 53 students chose either Strongly Agree or Agree in response to "The project helped make the Holocaust more of a human story."

- 91% of the 53 students chose either Strongly Agree or Agree in response to "The project has helped in making me want to learn more about the Holocaust."
- 96% of the 53 students chose either Strongly Agree or Agree in response to "I feel like I know more about the Holocaust than I did before doing this project.

It is clear from these findings that the methodology of teaching the Holocaust through theatre using the *This is What I've Scene* methodology is a success, and can be utilized by other teachers to disseminate Holocaust education around the world.

Conclusion

At the very beginning of the *Enacting History* unit, I tell my students that very soon, there will be no first-hand witnesses to relay these stories. "Who will carry these stories forward," I ask them, "so that the world will not forget?" "Their children," they initially respond. "And their children's children." "Who else?" I ask. There is a pause. They look down, or stare at each other. I say nothing, anxiously hoping that someone will say what I am waiting to hear. Finally, inevitably, someone does. "Us. We will tell their stories. It will be our responsibility." And in those moments, I know for certain that this work is not in vain.

References

ADL (2022, April 25). *ADL audit finds antisemitic incidents in United States reached all-time high in 2021.*
https://www.adl.org/news/press-releases/adl-audit-finds-antisemitic-incidents-in-united-states-reached-all-time-high-in

Asbury, N. (2021, December 19). *D.C. third-graders were made to reenact episodes from the Holocaust.* The Washington Post.
https://www.washingtonpost.com/education/2021/12/19/holocaust-re-enactment-watkins-school-dc/

Conroy, C. (2017, January 30). *As a society are we losing our empathy?* The Irish Times.
https://www.irishtimes.com/culture/books/as-a-society-are-we-losing-our-empathy-1.2947921

Goss, J. (2021, November 9). *The Holocaust lesson I regret teaching: I look back with a mixture of shame and commitment to doing better.* Chalkbeat.
https://www.chalkbeat.org/2021/11/9/22745966/holocaust-lesson-regret

Hirsch, M., Rubin, J. & Mittelman, A. (2020). *Enacting history: A practical guide to teaching the Holocaust through theatre.* Routledge.
https://www.routledge.com/Enacting-History-A-Practical-Guide-to-Teaching-the-Holocaust-through-Theater/Hirsch-Rubin-Mittelman/p/book/9781138608740

Mitschke, S. (2022, May). *What I've scene: Project report.* British Pilot. November 22–December 3, 2021. Unpublished Book.

Visual History Archive (n.d.). *USC Shoah Foundation Visual History Archive.* https://vha.usc.edu/home.

CHAPTER 10

The Eichmann Trial: A Theatrical Interpretation

Motti Lerner
English translation by Shoshana Olidort, Ph.D.

Introduction

My play *The Eichmann Trial* was written for Habima National Theater in Tel Aviv in 2020, but production was delayed due to the Coronavirus, and the theater has plans to stage the play in 2025. The play deals with the trial of the Nazi war criminal Adolf Eichmann (1906–1962), who fled to Argentina in the aftermath of the second world war, was captured there by the Mossad, smuggled into Israel and tried in the Jerusalem district court. The play opens at the beginning of the trial and ends with its conclusion. It includes 40 scenes, 13 of which are set in the courthouse, with the other 27 set in various locations outside the court. The scenes in the courthouse follow selected testimonies of survivors, focusing primarily on the interrogation of Eichmann by the prosecutor, Gideon Hausner. Other scenes follow deliberations in the offices of the prosecution and of the defense regarding their strategies in court, and the pressures the German government exerted on the Israeli government to prevent the trial from raising sweeping charges against the German nation, and against senior staff in the post-war German government administration.

As I have noted in an earlier article (Lerner, 2020), writing a play about historical events does not allow for historical fastidiousness, because a historical event does not unfold, in general, in the manner of a dramatic event. The creation of a play, which is a dramatic event, requires certain significant changes in the portrayal of a historic event in order to arrive at a play with clear dramatic plot and well-formed characters. For this reason, among others, in most cases the playwright is not interested in the historical event as it occurred according to scholarly research, but is focused, instead, on the internal layers at work in the characters, which don't find expression through historical research, and which playwrights construct from their imagination. While the playwrights have complete freedom to choose their purpose in writing the play, ethically they have no right to manipulate their audience, and they have to be prepared to justify any deviations from historical truth, and cannot excuse them simply by invoking "artistic license."

The purpose that the playwright chooses, which is bound, as I argue, by the ethical principles mentioned above, is what justifies any deviations from historical accuracy (Lerner, 2014). For this reason, in critiquing the deviations I implemented in my play *The Eichmann Trial*, I must first clarify my purpose in writing this play.

The Play's Purpose

The purpose of a dramatic play is to generate a catharsis in the viewer, which also produces a change in consciousness and in emotion, and it is for this reason that the playwright has written the play. The viewer's catharsis can be produced via the cathartic process the protagonist undergoes over the course of the play (Lerner, 2014). The process of catharsis that the protagonist experiences is the same five-step process that Aristotle describes in *Poetics*: the tragic flaw (Hamartia), the terrible deed (Deinos), the reversal

THE EICHMANN TRIAL: A THEATRICAL INTERPRETATION

(Peripeteia), recognition (Anagnorisis), and suffering (Pathos) (Aristotle, 2004). Again, without elaborating in great detail on these various stages, I will simply summarize by saying that the protagonist's catharsis is located in the struggle to carry out some lofty deed that is beyond his capacity, and that derives from his own hubris. By the story's end, he fails to actualize the deed, and pays a heavy price for this failure. And yet, paradoxically, because of the empathy that the viewer feels toward the protagonist, the protagonist's failure is what actually motivates the viewer to implement in his own world the very action that the protagonist failed to execute. This paradox is known as the dramatic paradox, on which I have written in greater detail in my book, *The Playwright's Purpose* (Lerner, 2014).

The protagonist of *The Eichmann Trial* is the prosecutor, Gideon Hausner, and his primary task in the story is to reveal the extermination system that Eichmann was a part of, to convict Eichmann, and, on the heels of that conviction, to also try other war criminals and punish them in order to prevent additional war crimes (Figure 10.1). Indeed, in the play, Hausner succeeds in convicting Eichmann, but he does not succeed at turning the trial into the harbinger of a universal process that will bring other war criminals to justice and deter future war criminals. In other words, Hausner does not succeed at turning the Eichmann trial into the "Tikkun Olam" project he was aiming for. And yet, as mentioned earlier, it is specifically this failure of Hausner that makes the viewer recognize "tikkun olam" (repairing the world) as a lofty goal that he ought to recognize and support, and this, of course, is the purpose of the play.

FIGURE 10.1
Historical Photo of Prosecutor Gideon Hausner at the Eichmann Trial 1961.
Public Domain Photo from Yad Vashem Archive

Is this, in fact, what motivated Hausner in the course of the trial? In his book *Justice in Jerusalem* (1968), Hausner emphasizes that his purpose was to advance awareness of the Holocaust through the trial, so that it would take its rightful place in the national consciousness for many years. In addition, he emphasized that, for humanity, his purpose was to place the Holocaust in the order of important events of history that the world must always remember and that the world must account for in political and humanitarian considerations of the present day as well as in the future. Due to the strong sense of empathy that I felt towards Hausner in the course of writing, I was able to access his internal world and to recognize within this drive toward "tikkun olam," for whose sake he mustered all his emotional strength, and on whose account he fought so hard both inside and outside of the court.

THE EICHMANN TRIAL: A THEATRICAL INTERPRETATION

The Plot

A play, even when based on a historical event, must have a well-constructed plot to allow the viewer to follow events as they unfold, and in the end to also experience the essential catharsis. During the historical Eichmann trial, as it was conducted in Jerusalem, there was not a well-constructed story in any dramatic sense. In order to create a plot I needed to create a plot structure, and the structure I chose was based on the idea that, despite the efforts of the prosecution over the better part of the trial, Hausner harbored serious doubts about his chances of convicting Eichmann. The prosecution presented many documents from the German archives, but Eichmann, with the help of his lawyer Robert Servatius, managed, for the most part, to provide explanations for these documents that cleared him of direct responsibility for the destruction. For example, in scene 21, the prosecution tries to prove that Eichmann was directly linked to the Zyklon B gas used to murder Jews in the gas chambers at Auschwitz.

> **Hausner:** I would like to read to the accused another paragraph from the autobiography of Rudolf Hess (commandant of the Auschwitz concentration and extermination camp) (Reading): After the establishment of the camp, Eichmann approached me and gave me an itemized list of the total number of Jews in the coming transports ... Eichmann explained to me that in the East, killings had been carried out with the gas emitted by the engines of trucks, but this method would not be efficient enough, and he would try to find a more efficient gas. (To Eichmann): Do you confirm or deny?
> **Eichmann:** Deny, sir. I had nothing to do with what has happening inside the camp.

> **Hausner:** This is a report from the S.S. leader who was responsible for creating the Zyklon B gas. According to this report, your deputy ordered 100 kg of this gas from him. Did you know about this?
>
> **Eichmann:** No, sir.
>
> **Hausner:** Your deputy puts in an order of gas for the murder of millions, and you do not know?
>
> **Eichmann:** No, sir.
>
> **Hausner:** Honorable court, the accused ran his department like a dictator. His deputy would not have dared to order deadly gas without his knowledge.
>
> **Servatius:** Honorable court, the accused is not a signatory on this document. At the time the order was placed he was in France.
>
> **Eichmann:** I was involved with the transportation. Only with the transportation.

Another example occurs in scene 26 during the court testimony of George Weller, a Paris doctor:

> **Weller:** The Germans sent the parents to Auschwitz, and the children to the Drancy camp, near Paris.
>
> **Hausner:** How many children arrived?
>
> **Weller:** Approximately 4,000. Because I was a doctor they let me approach them. Many of them did not yet know how to speak. We did not know their names … The cries were heart-rending. We promised them that they'd meet up with their mothers in a few days. When I arrived in Auschwitz, after a few months, not one of them was still alive.

THE EICHMANN TRIAL: A THEATRICAL INTERPRETATION

Hausner: Honorable court, this is a letter from the accused's representative in Paris, dated July 10, 1942. In the letter, the representative requests urgent approval for the deportation of these children to Auschwitz. Here is a second document, a transcript of a telephone call between the accused and that same representative in which the accused approved the deportation. These two documents testify that the accused was the one who decided to deport these 4,000 children to their deaths.

Servatius: Mr. Eichmann, did you in fact decide on the deportation of these 4,000 children to Auschwitz?

Eichmann: No, sir. In the ten days that elapsed between when I received the letter from Paris, I discussed it with Reichsführer Himmler several times.

Hausner: Can the accused offer any evidence for the interference of Reichsführer Himmler regarding the matter of these children?

Eichmann: Unfortunately, all my department's documents were destroyed by fire during the bombing of Berlin.

Only later will the prosecution succeed in proving that Eichmann lied in his testimony, and that during the period that he claimed he was in conversation with Himmler, Himmler was on tour on the Eastern front.

Such examples demonstrate the routine difficulties that the prosecution faced in proving Eichmann's guilt, whether by means of testimony or documents. As playwright, I chose to highlight this difficulty and to deploy it in creating the dramatic tension that is crucial for a plot. Thus, despite the fact that the viewer knows that Eichmann will be found guilty by the trial's end, over the course of the play the viewer feels a deep sense of empathy with Hausner, and identifies with Hausner's fear that he will fail to convict

Eichmann. This lack of certainty regarding Eichmann's conviction continues up until the interrogation regarding the extermination of the Jews of Hungary. Only in this interrogation does Hausner succeed in proving Eichmann's guilt beyond any doubt. Even though this interrogation of Eichmann took place in the middle of the trial, I chose to have it take place at the end, in order to prolong the dramatic tension to the end.

German Sanctions on the Israeli Government Over the Course of the Trial

After World War II, the government in West Germany went to great lengths to prove to the world that Nazism had been a temporary episode in the nation's history and that the new Germany was a different country. The capture of Eichmann and his highly publicized trial spurred well-founded fear in Germany that this would lead to a renewed public reckoning with Nazi war crimes. The German government was particularly concerned that the trial was likely to reveal the many officials serving in the German government who had previously served the Nazi regime and were party to its crimes. The most prominent among these officials was Dr. Hans Globke, the director general of German Chancellor Adenauer's office and former legal advisor for the Ministry of the Interior under the Third Reich. For this reason, the German government put pressure on the Israeli government, in order to minimize the damage the trial was likely to cause. The Germans exerted pressure on Israel through: the freezing of reparation payments to Holocaust survivors living in Israel; freezing all weapons dealings with Israel; and freezing of funds toward the construction of a nuclear reactor in Dimona, Israel. At the conclusion of the trial, and after Israel had met most of the German demands, the sanctions were completely removed. Nevertheless, two years after the trial, when Israel and Germany began to negotiate the terms for diplomatic relations between the two countries, the Germans added yet another demand, that the Israeli government cease its pursuit of Nazi war criminals around the world, and not put them on trial. The Israeli government, which sought to establish diplomatic relations with Germany, acquiesced to these demands (Herman, 2017).

The fifth stage that Aristotle identifies in the protagonist's catharsis is pathos–the protagonist's suffering after he fails to carry out his deed. The capitulation of the Israeli government to the German demand to cease its pursuit of Nazi war criminals, and not to bring them to justice, worsens Hausner's sense of complete and painful failure in the struggle to turn the trial into a process of universal reckoning via the trials of additional Nazi war criminals. Hausner's failure to generate an international reckoning with the Nazi crimes is what propels the viewer to support, and perhaps even to act, in order to bring about such an international reckoning, and this, of course, is the playwright's goal.

The Character of Hausner

The figure of Hausner was etched into world consciousness thanks to his riveting words, delivered during the prosecution's opening remarks.

> **Hausner:** In this place where I stand before you, judges of Israel, to convict Adolf Eichmann, I do not stand alone. Along with me, there stand here six million prosecutors. Only they are unable to point a damning finger toward the glass box and to call out to the one who sits there: I accuse! Because their ashes were piled up high in the hills of Auschwitz and in the fields of Treblinka, and washed away in the rivers of Poland. Their blood cries out, but their voice cannot be heard. I will

therefore be for them a mouth, and in their name I will tell of this horrific indictment ... (Hausner, 1968, p. 323)

The astonishing power of these words (the only words in the play that are taken directly from the trial transcript) lay not only in the mighty evocation of six million prosecutors standing alongside Hausner, but also because they give expression to the fact that Hausner appointed himself the emissary of these six million. What, then, was his mission? He did, of course, accuse Eichmann in their name, but he also raises their memory, and mourns their deaths, elevates their legacy, and asserts that their last will and testament is the ongoing existence of the State of Israel. But as important as these components of this national mission are, in the play, Hausner broadens the scope of his mission beyond the boundaries of the Jewish nation and the State of Israel, and acts in the name of these six million to repair the world at large. This impressive impulse suggests the hubris of Hausner who, like the protagonist in a classic tragedy, takes on a mission that is beyond the capacity of a mere mortal. In the final confrontation between Hausner and Teddy Kolek, director general of the Israeli Prime Minister's office, in scene 39, Kolek threatens to fire Hausner on account of his refusal to comply with the orders of the Israeli government:

Hausner: I will fulfill my duties as a legal advisor to the best of my ability. But I will also fulfill my obligation as a person, and as a Jew, even if it deviates from my duty. And even if it contradicts the orders of the government. Specifically because we were the sacrifices of the most evil monstrosity in human history, we have the greatest responsibility to repair it.

The Eichmann trial was the pinnacle of Hausner's career. Though he did continue to serve as legal advisor to the government until 1963, that very year he resigned following a serious dispute with the minister of justice. He was later elected to the Knesset, and later yet appointed Minister without Portfolio under Prime Minster Golda Meir. After leaving government, Hausner served as chair of the international council of Yad Vashem for twenty years. But despite his far-reaching public service, he never again reached a level of accomplishment that came close to his performance at the Eichmann trial. This diminution in his public standing is also what justified the freedom I took to demonstrate, via his failure to bring other Nazi war criminals to justice, the Aristotelian phase of pathos, the phase that brings about the punishment for his arrogance in attempting to repair the world. This choice brought to completion the formation of the Hausner character as a tragic figure who undergoes catharsis, and in so doing generates a catharsis in the viewer.

The Character of Eichmann

The visual appearance of Eichmann throughout the trial created an impression of a dull commander, without charisma, docile and obedient (Figure 10.2). The cunning Eichmann knew well that in order to convince the court that he was just an obedient clerk fulfilling the orders of his supervisors, and that, therefore, his supervisors were the ones responsible for the war crimes that had been carried out — he needed to act the role of an obedient clerk over the course of the investigation and throughout the trial.

Figure 10.2
Historical Photo of Defendant Adolf Eichmann at the Eichmann Trial 1961, Public Domain Photo from Hebrew Wikipedia

The few witnesses who met Eichmann during the war made it clear that the person they met was of an altogether different sort: decisive, resolute, and an initiator. The most remarkable evidence that Eichmann was, in fact, a senior partner in carrying out the "Final Solution," appears in the play in scenes that deal with the extermination of the Jews of Hungary in 1944. For example, in scene 30, this dialogue occurs:

> **Servatius:** Mr. Eichmann, what was your job in Budapest?
> **Eichmann:** To coordinate the schedules of the transports going East with the Hungarian train companies.
> **Servatius:** Did you have any connection with the decision to deport the Jews to Auschwitz?
> **Eichmann:** No, Sir. The Reichsführer transmitted the orders directly to the Hungarian government.
> **Hausner:** Did you always comply with the Reichsführer's orders?

THE EICHMANN TRIAL: A THEATRICAL INTERPRETATION

Eichmann: Absolutely, sir.

Hausner: And also the orders of the Führer?

Eichmann: Absolutely.

Hausner: A lie, honorable court! After the American bombing of Budapest on July 2, the Hungarian ruler decided to stop the transports. Hitler was furious and demanded that they continue, but agreed to release 8,700 Jewish families with visas to foreign countries. (*Shows the memo to the judges*). But Eichmann refused to fulfill Hitler's orders.

Hausner: This telegram is proof that the accused's lust for murder was so great, that he was not able to spare the lives of this small number of Jews whose fate had taken a turn for the better, and who had managed to obtain foreign visas. And despite Hitler's orders to free them, he sent them, too, to their deaths. Only someone lacking a conscience altogether could carry out such a crime with such dedication.

Eichmann's true character is revealed most clearly in scenes of him with his lawyer, Dr. Servatius, and with his assistant Liesel Grude. In these scenes we observe a resolute and decisive Eichmann who is well aware of his standing, as in scene 3 during a prison meeting of Eichmann and his defense lawyers:

Eichmann: The prosecutor does not begin to understand how the extermination machine of the Reich operated. He read the protocols of the Nuremberg trials and he was carried away by the testimony of the S.S. officers who had planned it.

Servatius: The judges won't accept the Nuremberg testimony. Testimony that can't be challenged and interrogated is weak testimony.

Eichmann: But if all the heads of the S.S. say that I was responsible for the extermination, the judges will be convinced that it was so.

Grude: These are expert and experienced judges ...

Eichmann: They are Jews who fled Germany before the war. I saw how they were swept up in the pathos of the prosecutor. They've already sentenced me to hanging.

Servatius: Our line of defense could save you. If you reiterate the claim that you were just a mediocre clerk fulfilling orders, that you didn't take initiative, and that you never raised your own ideas, they will be convinced that your responsibility for the extermination was minimal.

Eichmann: They know I was not a mediocre clerk. They have the notes from meetings in which I participated with those of the highest rank.

Grude: We reviewed the notes from those meetings. In most of them you hardly speak up at all. You don't argue. You don't demand.

Servatius: You have no choice. Nobody is put to death for being mediocre. Don't let your pride send you the gallows.

Eichmann: (*Angrily*) I am a German citizen. I have acted all my life for the sake of Germany. If I must be put on trial, let Germany judge me. Not these accursed Jews.

The decision to portray Eichmann as an actor who plays nice in the court and reveals his true colors in secret creates a more compelling theatrical character, of course, but as I have mentioned, this decision was not something I came upon on my own, but was, as noted earlier, based on the testimony of witnesses who had encountered Eichmann during the war.

THE EICHMANN TRIAL: A THEATRICAL INTERPRETATION

The Extermination of Hungarian Jewry

As noted earlier, the decisive proof that Eichmann was not just an officer who merely obeyed orders, but an ideologue permeated with a hatred of Jews, was his responsibility for the extermination of Hungary's Jews, which took place in 1944. Testifying against Eichmann at the trial were several survivors who had met him and had witnessed the initiatives he implemented in order to accelerate the extermination and to sabotage the rescue efforts of the Zionist Rescue Commission which operated in Budapest. In fact, I did not take too much liberty in describing these developments with Eichmann, because the evidence against him was extremely compelling. In addition, regarding the episode known as "Blood for Goods," I chose to rely on historical research of recent years–primarily the scholarship of Professor Yehuda Bauer (1994), that was not available to the prosecution or the defense in 1960–61, in order to reflect on the episode with greater historical precision, which also correlates with my personal interpretation of these events, which I dealt with in earlier works including my play *Kastner* (1996), and the serial television drama *The Kastner Trial* (1994). The episode unfolds in scene 30 during the testimony of Joel Brand, a member of the Zionist Rescue Committee in Budapest:

> **Brand:** The members of the S.S. in Budapest knew of our rescue committee. They knew that we hid Jews who escaped from Poland and Slovakia and that we smuggled them into Romania. They also knew that most of our funds came from American Jews, and that's why they turned to us, so that we could connect them with the Americans because the Americans refused to conduct negotiations with Germany until its surrender. Himmler, who had gone behind Hitler's back to try and negotiate a ceasefire, decided to go through us to start

negotiating about the rescue of Jews, and from there to move on to political negotiations.

Hausner: Mr. Brand, what deal did the accused propose to you in the name of Himmler?

Brand: When I entered his office, he stood up and said: "You know me, Brand. I solved the Jewish problem in Germany, Austria, Poland, Czechoslovakia, Greece. Now it's your turn. I'm willing to sell you one million Jews. From Hungary, Poland, Austria, Theresienstadt, Auschwitz. From wherever you'd like. Take fertile women. Take fertile men. The elderly. Children. Blood for goods. Goods for blood."

I asked, "What kind of goods are you looking for?"

"Ten thousand trucks," he said.

"Where can I get ten thousand trucks?"

"Americans are controlled by international Jewry. If we burn 20,000 Jews a day, the Americans will give. Tomorrow, you fly to Istanbul. The Jewish agency will arrange a meeting with the American ambassador to Ankara."

Hausner: And what happened when you arrived in Istanbul?

Brand: Representatives from the Jewish Agency were waiting for me in the airport. The following day we set out to meet with the American ambassador to Ankara. The moment we got on the train I was stopped by the police ... The American ambassador made no effort to search for me ... I was taken to Cairo. After a week in jail I was visited by Lord Moyne, the British Secretary of the State for the Colonies and Minister Resident in the Middle East. I pleaded for a response to Eichmann's offer. He responded: "There are millions of refugees in Europe. If the Germans give me a million Jews, what will I do with them?

THE EICHMANN TRIAL: A THEATRICAL INTERPRETATION

Where will I put them?" When I was freed I hurried to Tel Aviv to meet with Sharet, Ben Gurion, Weizmann ...

Hausner: Thank you very much, Mr. Brand.

Brand: They rebuffed me, again and again. I sent letters. They did not answer ...

Hausner: Thank you very much, Mr. Brand. (*to Eichmann*) Can the accused explain where the idea to release one million Jews for 10,000 trucks came from?

Eichmann: It was my idea, sir. I was always in favor of a solution to the Jewish problem by means of migration. I thought that this would allow us to send new transports to the Eastern front, and I was glad that my proposal was accepted.

Hausner: (*holding a page*) Honorable court, the German ambassador to Budapest, who was present in the meeting between Himmler and the accused, testified: "The Reichsführer rebuked Eichmann for violating his orders: Until now you've killed Jews, now I need them alive." This testimony proves yet again that the accused is lying. The one who initiated this deal was Himmler, who was willing to release one million Jews in order to save Germany from destruction. Eichmann wanted to sabotage this deal. That's why he continued to send the Jews of Hungary to Auschwitz, against the explicit orders of Himmler. Therefore they were killed.

Himmler made multiple attempts to begin talks with the Americans, and the mission of Joel Brand, who testified at trial, was one of these attempts. The deal that Himmler ordered Eichmann to offer the Americans through Brand failed.

Conclusion

I was driven to write a high quality dramatic play that would absorb the viewer, and allow them to experience the play on multiple, profound levels and reach the Aristotelian catharsis that could generate substantive change within. In this chapter I wanted to offer a unique interpretation of the trial that could shed light on questions facing us in the present. One of these questions relates to the position of the justice system when facing political processes that permit crimes against humanity. For this reason, I focused at length on Dr. Globke, on Servatius, on Liesel Grude, and, of course, on the Israeli lawyer, Gideon Hausner. Servatius says to Grude, his assistant, in scene 13:

> **Servatius:** Nazi propaganda overpowered the justice system, Ms. Grude. They lost the ability to judge according to the law and instead ruled according to the party orders.

In this way he implies that if the court system had not been taken in by Nazi propaganda and had continued to operate according to the laws of Germany, human rights in Germany would not have been trampled on, and the sanctions against Jews would not have been enacted. In scene 22, he explains:

> **Servatius:** The rounding up of Jews in the ghetto was approved by senior members in the Reich's department of justice. Among them, for example, Dr. Globke, whose interpretation of the Nuremberg laws convinced the accused that his actions were legal. I request that the court invite Dr. Globke as an expert witness.

THE EICHMANN TRIAL: A THEATRICAL INTERPRETATION

In this way he emphasizes that had the senior members of the justice department not approved the legality of the roundups of Jews in the ghettos, it is possible that the Jews would not have been sent to the ghettos. And Dr. Globke responds indirectly in scene 23:

> **Globke:** What do they think there in Jerusalem? That I didn't see the Nuremberg laws paving the road to Auschwitz? I saw very well. But the cruelty of the Nazi party was horrific. Anybody who expressed any opposition was immediately sent to a concentration camp, interrogated, answered, and murdered. An entire society dedicated itself to the propaganda about our racial superiority and obeyed the party. I did what I could. If not for my interpretation the legislation would have been even more monstrous. One day the Jews will need to thank me for what I did for them.

Hausner is aware of the importance of Gobke's role in the justice system, in protecting human rights, and in scene 25 he says:

> **Hausner:** We, of course, will not give up. If we do not interrogate Globke at this trial, we'll interrogate him at the next trial, or the one after that. Until one day he will be found guilty, and will be punished. Legal experts must know that their purpose is to protect human rights. Not to undermine them.

In scene 32 he goes into detail about the importance of protecting human rights for civilization:

> **Hausner:** From the day Hitler rose to power, the allies saw the persecution of the Jews as an internal German issue, and

that's why they did not get involved, and that's why persecution turned into extermination. The world must understand that a violation of human rights is not an internal matter. We must offer aid to any persecuted minority in any country. That is the most important outcome of this trial.

I hope that those watching the play will agree with him.

References

Aristotle. (2004). *Poetics*. Kessinger Publishing.

Bauer, Y. (2001). *Jews for sale?: Nazi-Jewish negotiations, 1933–1945*. Yale University Press.

Glass, S. (1995, August 7). *Adolf Eichmann is a historical figure to me: Ricardo Eichmann speaks to Suzanne Glass about growing up the fatherless son of the Nazi war criminal hanged in Israel*. The Independent.

Hausner, G. (1968). *Justice in Jerusalem*. Schocken Books, Inc.

Herman, O. (2017). *The furnace and the reactor: Behind the scenes at the Eichmann trial*. Hakibbutz Hameuchad.

Lerner, M. (1994). *The Kastner trial: 3 episodes drama*. Israeli Broadcasting Authority. Jerusalem, Israel.

Lerner, M. (1996). *Kastner in Israeli historical drama*. Syracuse University Press.

Lerner, M. (2014). *The playwright's purpose*. No Passport Press.

Lerner, M. (2020). The playwright and the historian: Contradicting and complimenting each other. International Journal of Applied Psychoanalytic Studies, 17:2, pp. 1–7.

CHAPTER 11

Music in Terezín: Creativity in Chaos

Wendy A. Mullen, D.M.A.

Introduction: "Survival of the Spirit"

In times of great hardship and uncertainty, music can heal, console, strengthen and unite. For those in the Nazi transit camp of Terezín (also known as Theresienstadt), music was a lifeline that allowed creativity amidst the chaos. As Terezín survivor Ela Weissberger recalled, "Music was part of our resistance against the Nazis. Music, art, good teachers, and friends meant survival" (Rubin, 2000, p. 35).

I was first introduced to the story of Terezín in the early 1990s and wrote my doctoral dissertation on composer Viktor Ullmann who declared, "Our endeavors with respect to arts was commensurate with our will to live" (Schiff, 2003, p. 3). Almost twenty years later, after years of reading stories about the survivors, studying the music of Terezín and visiting the town, I was deeply touched to meet survivor Ela Weissberger. It was a profound experience to hear her personal story, spend time with her and direct her in performance.

On January 26, 2014, Atlanta Georgia's Am Yisrael Chai! hosted a Holocaust Remembrance Event titled "Survival of The Spirit: Art, Culture and Music of the Holocaust." Memorializing International Holocaust Remembrance Day, this event featured Ela as the keynote speaker. Beginning the program was a ceremony that had been created by Terezín survivor Rabbi

Richard Feder, who was a close friend of Ela's. The lights were dimmed as his words were read: "We come tonight to remember the Holocaust, and to remember those who perished at the hand of an evil empire. Let us vow never to forget their lives, lives that are symbolized by these flames. We light the six candles in their memory" (Am Yisrael Chai!, 2014, 1:00). Ela and Terezín survivors Ilse Reiner and Robert Fischer, among many other survivors, were included in those who lit the candles that memorialized the babies and children, the fathers and mothers, the grandparents, the relatives, the friends, and the liberators and rescuers of the camps.

Later that evening, I had the honor of conducting Ela, with a choir consisting of students from Georgia College and Atlanta, singing excerpts from Hans Krasa's children's musical, *Brundibár*. During WWII, this musical was performed 55 times in Terezín, with Ela singing the role of the cat in every performance from age 11. Directing Ela with the students was one of the most moving and rewarding experiences of my life. The same unbridled joy on Ela's face was surely what those in Terezín had experienced as they watched productions of *Brundibár*. During our performance, Ela exuded hope for the future and a love of life as a witness for a new generation, singing in memory of the other children who did not survive.

In her keynote remarks, Ela spoke of how the artistic opportunities for children helped them survive the war. She explained that Jews were required to wear yellow stars at all times. "When we performed (*Brundibár*), we didn't have to have [our yellow stars] on. Those were moments we felt free" (Ramati, 2014, p. 1). She shared that the children in Terezín "survived, many of us, with the help of our caretakers. About music. Little *Brundibár*. Those poems that were written by young people in Terezín. Those wonderful, wonderful pictures that we drew with my teacher Friedl Dicker-Brandeis." She continued, "and you see, she still lives in my heart. I can't forget her. And I'm repeating many, many times, her stories, that they helped us survive" (Am Yisrael Chai!, 2014, 40:42). Ela also poignantly expressed her joy that

Brundibár is now being sung all over the world to children who are free. Commenting upon this opportunity to sing the choruses with Ela, Allie Bankston, a Georgia College history major shared, "It's an exciting experience … it also needs to be remembered. It's strange to sing such joyful songs about something that was so horrible" (Ramati, 2014, p. 3). The student performers and those in attendance at the 2014 memorial event were deeply touched by Ela's words and carried with them an experience that would not be forgotten.

At the close of the evening, Ela, Ilse Reiner and Robert Fischer were given bouquets of daffodils representing the Am Yisrael Chai! Daffodil Project. This project continues today, planting 1.5 million daffodils around the world in memory of the 1.5 million children who perished in the Holocaust (Am Israel Chai, 2021). At the time of this writing, 664,000 bulbs have been planted, including those that Georgia College students planted with Ela on their campus with the support of Dr. Karen Berman and Mike Weinroth.

It is vital to remember the stories from Terezín and how the arts provided the prisoners strength and courage to face daily hardships and uncertainty. Survivors of Terezín have shared their stories in print and media, yet firsthand accounts are now rare. Sadly, Ela died in 2018, but her story continues to echo in the hearts of all who were touched by her life. This chapter discusses the world in which Ela and the Jewish population found themselves in the late 1930s, the creation and population of the Terezín transit camp, and selective examples of the wealth of musical efforts that took place in Terezín during WWII despite the most horrific of conditions.

The Protectorate and Plans for Terezín

On March 15, 1939, Hitler invaded Czechoslovakia and established the Protectorate of Bohemia and Moravia. There were approximately 118,000 Jews in this area—a fourth of them were refugees from Germany (Berkley, 1993,

p. 17). Cultural life was greatly affected by numerous restrictions that were placed upon the Jewish population. Radios, phonographs and musical instruments were banned. Jews were not allowed to attend the theater, concerts or movies. By September 1941, all Jews age 6 or older in the Protectorate were ordered to wear the star of David marked *Jude* on all their clothing (Brenner, 2009, p. 26).

Despite great risk of being discovered, Jewish musicians such as pianist Gideon Klein and conductor Karel Berman performed for non-Jewish audiences under pseudonyms. For Jewish audiences in Prague, several secret concerts were performed in homes as well as in the Jewish orphanage. Audience members would enter venues individually or in shifts as to not arouse suspicion. The 8:00 p.m. Jewish curfew would often require participants to remain at the concert venues overnight (Karas, 1985, pp. 4–5).

Even though the underground cultural life of the Protectorate flourished, it would soon come to an end. The Nazis made plans to move the Jewish population to the nearby town of Terezín. Located about 37 miles northeast of Prague on the Elbe and Eger rivers, Terezín [Theresa's town or Theresienstadt] was named in honor of Empress Maria Theresa, the mother of its founder, Emperor Joseph II. Built in 1780, the town was to serve as a military station to protect Prague from attacks from the north.

Terezín would be utilized differently than the extermination camps. As George E. Berkley says in his book, *Hitler's Gift* (1993), at the secret Nazi leader gathering known as the Wannsee Conference on January 20, 1942, "Reinhardt Heydrich, in disclosing the government's scheme to systematically exterminate the Jews, also stated that Theresienstadt would serve to house those Jews whose prominence might occasion anxious inquiries ... should they suddenly disappear" (p. 58).

Terezín would be publicized as a town "given" to the Jews by the Führer. However, all of the Jew's freedoms, jobs, and culture were banned in the

Protectorate. Thus, the Jews were deceived by the illusion that moving to this isolated town would allow them to return to a normal life.

Many of the elderly and war veterans signed contracts ensuring that they could safely stay in the "privileged resettlement" of Terezín. Residents were encouraged to take their dress clothes and spa necessities and were offered rooms on the lake or with a view of the square (Berkley, 1993, p. 8). Karel Fleischmann wrote in his memoirs concerning some of these mislead Jews upon their arrival to Terezín:

> I see them, the first people from Cologne, leaning against the wall, dead tired, with tormented faces ... [with] elegant suitcases as if they [had] come to a spa ... But everything was horribly crippled, deformed, dirty, and stank of human filth ... (Berkley, 1993, p. 55)

On November 24, 1941, 342 handpicked Jewish tradespeople known as the *Aufbaukommando* (building detail) arrived at Terezín to prepare the town for incoming prisoners. These men who possessed the needed skills to transform the town had been summoned by the Nazis (Ludwig, 2021, p. 19). They were promised that their families would not be deported to the east, and they would be able to write loved ones as they wished and to leave Terezín for weekend visits. In the evenings, they would gather to sing folksongs—a strong reminder of their homeland and heritage.

Early Musical Offerings in Terezín

Karel Švenk and Rafael Schächter are attributed with the earliest musical offerings. Karel Švenk was a cabaret actor from Prague who displayed his talent for biting satire and comedy in camp productions. Rafael Schächter was a Romanian-born pianist and conductor who was raised in Bruno and Prague. In these early days of the camp, he organized singing evenings of Czech songs for the *Aufbaukommando*. As Edward Krasa recalled, "Singing the songs brought our minds back home, where we lived a cultural life, and lifted our spirits and morale." (Davidson, Grajower, & Krasa, 2012, p. 22). Fellow prisoner Alexandr Singer provides further insight:

> [Rafael] pounced on me, a stranger to him until now, and confessed that his passion was music. He immediately invited those interested to perform ("let's say Czech folk songs") as a choir. He did not ask [if] there were any obstacles. ... The audience's reaction, in the courtyard of the Cavalier Barracks, indicated the power of art, especially music, for people who had been driven from their homes and stripped of their basic human rights. (Friesová, 2002, pp. 142–143)

The second *Aufbaukommando* of one thousand men arrived on December 4. Even though musical instruments were banned, members of the second *Aufbaukommando*, in an act of defiance and risking discovery, included instruments in their allotted 50 kilograms of luggage. One cellist dismantled a cello and smuggled in the parts, reassembling it in the camp. Karel Fröhlich brought a violin and a viola, and Kurt Maier smuggled in an accordion (Karas, 1985, p. 13).

By the end of December, 7,350 Czech Jews had been deported to Terezín. In the first half of 1942, over 50,000 more Jews would arrive (Berkley, 1993, p. 27). There were immense challenges caused by this massive over-population of a town meant for only about 7,000 inhabitants. Basic necessities such as food, clean water, toilets, showers, and laundry had to be shared with the masses. Families were parted into separate quarters. Diseases were rampant, and so many were dying that a crematorium had to be built (Adler, 2021, p. 81).

Ela Weissberger (Rubin & Weissberger, 2006), in her book *The Cat with the Yellow Star*, recalled that when packing their luggage for Terezín, her mother told her, "Wear as many dresses and sweaters as you can. They probably won't weigh us" (p. 9).

The Transports and Life in Terezín

Less than a month after the initial Jewish families had arrived in Theresienstadt, the first transport to the east was announced. Now that transports were leaving, anyone could be taken and separated from their loved ones (Berkley, 1993, p. 63).

The Nazis chose a Jewish Council of Elders to manage the town and its activities. This group had to do the unthinkable and choose who would go on the transports to the east. This created a life-or-death situation that depended on "who knows who" or if a bribe was possible. The problem was, another challenge emerged—members of the council often shifted because they, too, were transported from Terezín. Tragically, at the end of the war, approximately 88,323 prisoners had been deported from Terezín with approximately only 3,500 surviving (United States Holocaust Memorial Museum, 2022).

In the Little Fortress within Terezín, Jewish prisoners would be crammed into a cell that allowed them only a three-foot space. One survivor recalled seeing the SS order several prisoners to fight for their lives with pitchforks against each other. The SS watched the scene with laughter from the bridge above (Berkley, 1993, p. 63).

Life in the town of Terezín did not contain the horrors of the Little Fortress, but it was still remarkably difficult. Freezing or stifling hot, the rooms that once housed three or four people now were filled with 60 (Berkley, 1993, pp. 46–47).

The Early Organized Musical Events

Despite the living conditions and fear of transports, arts and culture thrived in Terezín. In the early days of the camp, men and women were placed into separate barracks. Although instruments were scarce, one could always sing, resulting in the formation of several impromptu all-male and all-female choirs (Friesová, 2002, p. 141).

One of the first documented musical programs in Terezín was a variety show presented on December 6, 1941 in the Sudenten Barracks. The performance included: violinists Karel Fröhlich and Heini Taussig; Viktor Kohn, flutist; Wolfi Lederer and Kurt Meyer, accordionists; a jazz orchestra with Fritz Weiss, Hans Selig, Pavel Kohn, Fredy Mautner, Franta Goldschidt, Tedy Berger, and Wolfi Lederer; recitation by Dr. J Bēhal and Franta Kraus; and Lewin, a magician (Karas, 1985, p. 13).

In early 1942, Karel Švenk produced the first all-male cabaret titled *The Lost Food Card*. It ended with the *Terezín March*—which quickly became the camp's anthem and was incorporated into all of Švenk's cabarets:

> ... Surely life begins tomorrow,
> and the time approaches
> when we can pack our bundles and head for home.
> All is possible if you try. (Friesová, 2002, p. 153)

Tragically, Karel Švenk would not survive the war. In autumn 1944, he was summoned to be transported.

Men were not the only organizers of musical events. Singer and actress Hedda Grab-Kernmayr organized the first cultural program in the women's barracks on March 21, 1942. The program included readings and recitation, dance, Hedda performing two of Dvořák's *Biblical Songs*, and two Schubert Lieder performed by Emmy Zeckendorf. (Karas, p. 18). Several women also performed in the Terezín hospitals, providing comfort and encouragement to the patients. In an article about Hedda in November 1945, she mentions a lullaby, composed by Karel Švenk, that the women would sing for sick children that includes: "The fairies will soon come and bring you a dream" (Friesová, 2002, p. 151).

The Power of Music

Although entertainment was forbidden in the camp at first, the Nazis seemed not to mind these early musical efforts. By December 28, 1941 the prisoners received permission to hold *Kameradschaftsabende* (evenings of fellowship) that allowed artistic expression (Karas, 1985, p. 14). In addition to Karel Švenk and Rafael Schächter, the first transports to Terezín included several musicians such as pianist/composer Gideon Klein, composer Pavel Hass, Carlo and Erica Taube, singer Hedda Grabová, and Egon Ledeč (previously concertmaster of Czech Philharmonic). These talented musicians and many more inspired and built the early cultural life of Terezín (Friesová, 2002, p. 140).

The human spirit can triumph over the most horrific of circumstances. In Terezín, the musicians made the best of what they had and continued to maintain their culture and heritage. Violinist Karel Fröhlich recalled:

> For an artist, it was a tremendous opportunity .... it was only an effort to get through the war, to survive ... you never knew

if you would be sitting here tomorrow or if you would depart with one of those trains. (Karas, 1985, p. 195)

Mariánka Zadikow remembers her surprise at discovering a bevy of activity in the attic of her barrack after entering Terezín.

> I realized that there was a flight of stairs going up, and then from there, there was a narrow pathway to more steps … This attic was humming with intellectual activities. Somebody had a speech about Einstein's theory of relativity. Somebody else about the mythology of Greece … Somebody reciting poetry … In one corner, an old woman … with white hair, who sang some old German songs and also taught a group of women … first the melody and then the harmony to it … At which point, a heavy-set woman … looks at me and my enthusiasm … She gives me a tiny piece of paper … and says, "Don't show to anybody. Come there after working hours … Do you like to sing?" (May & Dwork, 2008, pp. 11–12)

To facilitate the development of artistic performances and lectures, in 1942, the Nazis officially sanctioned the *Freizeitgestaltung* (Administration of Free Time Activities), an organization consisting of artists and scientists who were prisoners of the camp. Members were exempted from manual labor and permitted to practice, study, compose, and perform. Cultural activities were permitted under the watchful eye of the Nazis, who often censored works and programs (Hájková, 2020, pp. 169–170). Although the Nazis sanctioned most of these activities at Terezín, they understood that ultimately the population would be sent to the extermination camps on transports, and the artistic efforts would ultimately be silenced.

For the prisoners, every performance was cherished. Ruth Elias recalled when she heard her first Terezín concert: "There was such a reverential quiet among the audience that one could hear a pin drop, while on many a cheek tears rolled down" (Berkley, 1993, p. 131).

Opera in Terezín

Eventually, Rafael Schächter decided to produce Czech composer Bedřich Smetana's opera *The Bartered Bride*. Rehearsals began using only a pitch-pipe. A broken-down pipe organ and half-broken accordion were added to aid in the rehearsal process, and, finally, an old baby-grand piano. The opera premiered on November 28, 1942. With its Czech nationalistic themes and a talented cast, the production was a huge success and was performed thirty-five times. These performances gave a much-needed respite from the daily horrors of the ghetto life. This is seen so clearly from a 13-year-old girl who wrote in her diary after hearing *The Bartered Bride*: "I felt like a person having beautiful dreams, who awakens suddenly, and everything is again trite" (Karas, 1985, pp. 23–25).

Chorister Mariánka Zadikow reminisces about the 28 times she performed and the one time she watched the opera: "I witnessed an unbelievable performance where there were actually people hanging from the rafters ... There was not a dry eye" (May & Dwork, 2008, p. 12).

Rafael Schächter thrived in this environment, despite the painful setback he experienced when his beloved singers were sent on transports to the east. Alexander Singer described Schächter:

> ... Behind his fiery bohemian artist's soul, a child's joyful sense of humour, gentleness and playfulness often lurked ... he had to keep finding new choristers—untrained singers—when choir

members (and soloists) left, never to return. In spite of this, his demands never diminished. (Friesová, 2002, p. 145)

More than a conductor and teacher, Schächter was a friend:

> Months of intensive work in such a bizarre environment were as valuable as years and fostered new, and until then unknown, kinships ... Music was a substitute for personal relationships, community culture and national tradition. It dispelled hunger and sadness, it embraced knowledge. Perhaps this was so because its practitioners danced on the edge of death. (Friesová, 2002, p. 146)

Renèe Friesová, a young singer who worked with Schächter, wrote an essay titled *My strongest and most positive experience in the Home*. The work survived the war, and is included in her book, *Fortress of My Youth*.

> We girls in the Mädchenheim [girl's home] are lucky. Our building, L410, was the former army headquarters and is very large with extensive cellars ... I discovered that I could just go down the stairs to the cellar and suddenly I would find myself part of an incredible fairy tale—a world of exceptional and inspired people in a world of the most beautiful sounds ... Much to my surprise, the most magnificent thing in the world happened. Rafík invited me to join the choir ... Karel Berman, Šany Singer and Franta Stránský are my friends ... When Karel Berman sings ... arias from Blodek's opera *In the Well* while playing the harmonium, I have the feeling that I am a queen and that I could experience nothing more beautiful. These are

the finest moments I have had in the Mädchenheim. (Friesová, 2002, pp. 147–148)

Rafael Schächter produced Smetana's *The Kiss*, Mozart's *The Marriage of Figaro* and *The Magic Flute*. Pergolesi's *La Serva Padrona* was the sole fully staged opera that Schächter conducted. Franz Klein conducted Verdi's *Rigoletto*, Puccini's *Tosca*, and Bizet's *Carmen*. Before entering the camp, Klein had held the position of second conductor for the Viennese State Opera. Terezín opera productions utilized singers from many backgrounds, so it was not unusual to hear multiple languages within a performance. *Carmen* was fully staged and accompanied by two pianos played by Edith Steiner-Kraus and Franz Klein (Karas, 1993, pp. 27–29).

Additional productions in Terezín included *Cavalleria Rusticana* by Pietro Mascagni, Verdi's *Aida*, and Johan Strauss' *Die Fledermaus*. A one-act Czech opera, *In the Well* (*V studni*), by Vilém Blodek, was performed only once, by heroic efforts. When the SS required all future musical performances to be presented in the German language, the cast rehearsed all night to re-learn the entire opera in German, providing yet another testament to the strength of human will (Karas, 1993, p. 32).

It is impossible to know how many new compositions that were written in Terezín have been lost. However, Victor Ullmann's *Der Kaiser von Atlantis oder der Tod dankt ab* (*The Emperor of Atlantis, or Death Abdicates*) not only survived, but has become a staple of modern operatic repertoire. The libretto for the opera was written by Peter Kien, a young poet and painter who came to Terezín in 1941. Ullmann wrote the opera in 1943 in Terezín and scored it for seven singers and thirteen instruments including banjo, alto saxophone, and harpsichord. Ullmann brazenly includes in his opera the Nazi anthem, *Deutschland, Deutschland, über alles* (Germany Above All Others), but presented in a minor key. Finally, the opera ends with the well-known

Ein' feste Burg ist unser Gott (A Mighty Fortress Is Our God) (Kennedy, 1993, pp. 9–10).

The allegorical opera tells the story of Emperor Überall, a cruel ruler of the Empire of Atlantis. The Emperor orders Death to lead unnecessary wars, which promises to bring the Emperor fame and glory. Death refuses, going on strike. Chaos ensues, and the Emperor realizes his mistake. Death agrees to return to duty, but only if the Emperor becomes his first victim.

Rehearsals were held over the summer of 1944 and the work was almost ready for performance when the SS came in to watch and decided the Emperor was too much like Hitler. The opera was banned. In October 1944, Ullmann and most of the involved performers were sent to Auschwitz. Remarkably, the score survived and was finally premiered in Amsterdam in 1975 (Kennedy, 1993, p. 9).

Brundibár and Ela Weissberger

One of the most beloved musical events in Terezín was the children's opera *Brundibár* written by Hans Krasa. The first performance of this opera took place on September 23, 1943, and was performed at least 55 times in Terezín (Berkley, 1993, p. 138). Krasa had written the opera before the war, but only had one copy of the piano reduction when he entered Terezín. He re-scored it, using instruments that were available—flute, clarinet, trumpet, guitar, accordion, piano, percussion, four violins, cello and bass (Karas, 1985, p. 100).

The story of the opera tells of a brother and sister who have a sick mother. The doctor prescribes milk for her, but the children have no money to buy it. Brundibár, an organ grinder, is playing on the street corner. The children begin singing, and Brundibár is annoyed and chases them away. A dog, a cat, and a sparrow, come to their help. Together with the children from the neighborhood, they sing a charming lullaby and people give them money. However, Brundibár steals it from them. All the children and animals chase Brundibár and recover the money. The opera ends with a song of victory over the evil organ grinder.

Of all the musical activities in the camp, *Brundibár* was the most popular. Tickets were in great demand and difficult to acquire (Brenner, 2009, p. 139). The music was charming and easy to understand, and the children represented the hope for the future. Brundibár represented Hitler's oppression and fanatic personality, and his evil was overcome.

Ela Weissberger played the part of the Cat in every performance of Brundibár (Figure 11.1). Ela notes that "when she was singing all of her troubles disappeared" (Cohen, 2019, p. 3). František Zelenka, the original stage designer of *Brundibár* in Prague, had also become a prisoner in Terezín. He re-created the scenery for the production. Gideon Klein accompanied on a piano without legs that was propped up on bricks. Ela was costumed in her sister's black ski pants and her mother's black sweater. Zelenka had a bit of shoe polish, which he used to paint whiskers on Ela's face along with other makeup (Rubin & Weissberger, 2006, p. 23).

In her book, *The Cat with the Yellow Star* (Rubin & Weissberger, 2006) Ela recalls the words of the Cat:

> Let's extend our helping hand ...
> Add your talent to our efforts,
> Voice to voice, and we'll be strong ...
> United we'll win our stand. (p. 24)

"As the opera drew to its close," said Ela, "and we sang the victory march, Brundibár is Defeated, there was—each time—thunderous applause." Everyone at Terezín knew that Brundibár, the organ-grinder, represented Hitler. This satirical attempt to make fun of Hitler, unbeknownst to the SS guards, was surely an example of arts as provocateur. Enthusiastically the whole audience joined in and sang:

> We've won a victory,
> Since we were not fearful, ...
> Bright, joyful, and cheerful. (Rubin & Weissberger, 2006, p. 24)

FIGURE 11.1
Ela Weissberger Indicates Herself in a Picture of the Brundibar Cast.
Photo credit: Paul Guy Accettura

Inge Auerbacher, who lived in Terezín when she was a child from 7 to 10 years old, recalls seeing *Brundibár* and reflects upon its effect as "Anything to enlarge hope. Something to look forward to" (Gorton, 2022). Tragically, most of the children who performed in *Brundibár*, who could have become happy and productive adults, were sent to Auschwitz and did not survive the war. The talented 14-year-old Honza Treichlinger was an audience favorite with his portrayal of the organ-grinder. But he was sent to Auschwitz and immediately to the gas chamber as he did not measure up high enough to the string the Nazis held above his head (Admin, 2019, p.5).

The Beautification Project to Deceive the Red Cross

The artistic life of Terezín was to play an important role in the Nazi's overall propaganda efforts. Shortly before the end of 1943, the Nazis began a beautification project in the ghetto. Parcels of food from abroad were allowed and chocolate, marmalade and condensed milk were received by some of the prisoners. The library moved into a larger building and thousands of books appeared from storage and were placed on the shelves. Musical instruments and costumes were suddenly available for performances and productions (Berkley, 1993, p. 168). Grass and flowers were planted and the facades of homes painted. Shop windows displayed useful goods and advertisements. A playground for the children and a new bandstand were built in the central square.

The beautification project was anticipating a visit from the International Red Cross accompanied by Danish representatives. Despite the positive changes for the prisoners, because it was impossible to hide that the camp was horribly overcrowded, the Nazis sent approximately 7,500 elderly and ill to the Auschwitz gas chambers (Berkley, 1993, p. 169). The Red Cross visit was carefully choreographed and the healthiest of prisoners were the "actors." The representatives were driven on a planned route, and even "chance" meetings were pre-planned. Among their many activities, they heard the finale of *Brundibár*, a concert in the park with the Ghetto Swingers, and a rehearsal of the Verdi *Requiem* (Brenner, 2009, p. 228).

In the latter part of 1944, the Nazis created a propaganda film entitled *Teresienstadt: A Documentary Film from a Jewish Settlement Area*. The Jews nicknamed the film *Der Führer schenkt den Juden eine Stadt* [The Führer gives the Jews a Town]. In the scenes of "everyday life" of the town, several musical events are included such as a scene from *Brundibár* and performances by the Ghetto Swingers conducted by Martin Roman. The string orchestra, under the baton of Karl Ančerl, performed Pavel Haas' *Study for Strings*. Although the players wore suits, not all of them had shoes. Therefore, flowerpots were placed along the podium edge to hide their bare feet! Unfortunately, once the film was made, the "model ghetto" was no longer necessary, and so on October 16, nearly all of the composers and artists, as well as many of the "actors" in the film, were sent to their death in Auschwitz in a transport of 18,500 prisoners (Karas, 1985, pp. 154–155).

Final Days

The last major musical effort in Terezín was *The Tales of Hoffman* by Jacques Offenbach. Hanuš Thien was ordered by the Nazis to produce a one-hour version of the opera. The work was premiered in April and, just few weeks later, Terezín would be liberated on May 8, 1945. (Karas, 1985, p.177).

Conclusion

Following the war, many of the stories and artistic efforts of Terezín were suppressed while Czechoslovakia was under communist rule. In 1989, the communist stronghold was lifted. As a result, many survivors' stories could finally be heard. There are several recordings and performances of music of the Holocaust, and scholars have feverishly documented first-person accounts before the generation is lost.

It was an honor to know Ela Weissberger and personally hear many of her recollections of her time in Terezín. As Ela said: "We were not supposed to use our names. They wanted us only to be numbers" (Benson, 2014, p. 2). Yet, Ela not only survived, but was willing to share her experience with others. Student singer Mitchell Moore reflected upon his 2014 Am Yisrael Chai! experience in Atlanta, "I remember sitting there and hearing her talk

MUSIC IN TEREZÍN: CREATIVITY IN CHAOS

and having a hard time putting into perspective that she went through so much yet was incredibly open and available to talk about it. I was in awe of how strong she was" (M. Moore, personal communication, November 13, 2022). I was also profoundly touched by Ela that evening. While Ela and I were alone on stage before one of the performances, Ela pulled a small bag out of her pocket and placed her prized possession in my hand—a small crest. She shared that, while in Terezín, she used a piece of glass to reflect the sun and burned an image of the crest into the scrap of wood to give her mother for Mother's Day (Figure 11.2).

The determination and ingenuity that it took for Ela to create her mother's gift is the same spirit that permeated Terezín's musical life. In stark contrast to the prisoners' surroundings and situations, no matter the circumstance, musicians composed, practiced, and performed. Concerts were anticipated and cherished events. Despite great pain and fear of death, disease, and the transports east, music soothed. Amidst chaos, creativity endured—giving hope and comfort. The arts healed, consoled, strengthened, and united. It is astounding that numerous scores of new music survived the war. Thankfully, many of these works have been recorded and are still being performed today.

During the evening in 2014 with Ela, she signed my copy of her book, *The Cat with the Yellow Star*. I will always treasure her poignant words, "Remember me and my friends." We must never forget.

Figure 11.2
Ela Weissberger, Wendy Mullen and the Crest That Ela Made in Terezín.
Photo credit: Lev Ryabinin and Tim Mullen

References

Adler, H. G. (2021). *Theresienstadt 1941–1945: The face of a coerced community* (B. G. Cooper, Trans.). Cambridge University Press.

Admin. (2019, December 6). *We do not forget: autumn transports from the Ghetto Terezín in 1944 and reminiscences of two human fates.* Terezín Memorial Newsletter. Retrieved from
https://newsletter.pamatnik-Terezín.cz/we-do-not-forget-autumn-transports-from-the-ghetto-Terezín-in-1944-and-reminiscences-of-two-human-fates/?lang=en

Am Yisrael Chai! (2014, January 26). *2014 Survival of the Spirit—Program* [Video]
https://vimeo.com/635386100

Am Yisrael Chai! (2021) "The Daffodil Project." Retrieved June 22, 2022. https://amyisraelchaiatlanta.org/miracles-and-memories/2021daffodil-project.html

Benson, M. (2014, March 20). *Holocaust survivor reprises a role, tells a story the world must hear.* The Seattle Times. Retrieved from https://www.seattletimes.com/entertainment/holocaust-survivor-reprises-a-role-tells-a-story-the-world-must-hear/

Berkley, G. E. (1993). *Hitler's Gift: the story of theresienstadt*. Branden Publishing Company.

Brenner, H. (2009). *the girls of room 28: friendship, hope, and survival in Theresienstadt*. Schocken Books.

Cohen, A. (2019, January 9). *In 1944, she performed in an opera at a concentration camp. 70 years later I got to meet her.* Cleveland Jewish News. Retrieved from https://www.clevelandjewishnews.com/news/world_news/in-1944-she-performed-an-opera-at-a-concentration-camp-70-years-later-i-got/article_128edd67-05c1-53a8-805d-3ed3b953d005.html

Davidson, S., Grajower, F., & Krasa, E. (2012). *The Music Man of Terezín: The story of Rafael Schaechter as remembered by Edgar Krasa*. Ibbetson Street Press.

Friesová, J. R. (2002). *Fortress of my youth: memoir of a Terezín survivor*. (E. R. Morrisby & L. R. Rosendorf, Trans.) The University of Wisconsin Press.

Gorton, T. (2022, April 26). *The Story of an Artistic Community That Formed in a Nazi Concentration Camp*. AnOther. Retrieved from https://www.anothermag.com/design-living/14056/story-of-an-artistic-community-that-formed-in-a-nazi-concentration-camp-Terezín

Hájková, A. (2020). The Last Ghetto: An Everyday History of Theresienstadt. Oxford University Press.

Karas, J. (1985). *Music In Terezín 1941–1945*. Beaufort Books Publishers.

Kennedy, P. (1993). [Liner notes]. In *Ullmann: Der Kaiser von Atlantis* [CD] London: London.

Ludwig, M. (2021). *Our Will to Live: The Terezín Music Critiques of Viktor Ullmann.* Terezín Music Foundation and Steidl Publishers.

May, M. Z., & Dwork, D. (2008). *The Terezín album of Mariánka Zadikow.* University of Chicago Press.

Müller, M., & Piechocki, R. (2006). *Alice's piano: The life of Alice Herz-Sommer.* St. Martin's Press.

Ramati, P. (2014, January 24). *Holocaust survivor shares experiences at Georgia College.* Macon Telegraph. Retrieved from https://www.macon.com/living/religion/article30127965.html

Rubin, S. G., & Weissberger, E. (2006). *The cat with the yellow star: Coming of age in Terezín.* Holiday House.

Schiff, D. (2003, March 23). *MUSIC; A musical postcard from the eye of the Nazi storm.* The New York Times. Retrieved from https://www.nytimes.com/2003/03/23/arts/music-a-musical-postcard-from-the-eye-of-the-nazi-storm.html

United States Holocaust Memorial Museum. "Theresienstadt: Concentration /Transit Camp for German and Austrian Jews." Holocaust Encyclopedia. Retrieved July 5, 2022, from https://encyclopedia.ushmm.org/content/en/article/theresienstadt-concentrationtransit-camp-for-german-and-austrian-jews

CHAPTER 12

Small Dances About Big Ideas: Moving Past the Limits of Dancing About Genocide

Liz Lerman

Overture

In her review of *Small Dances About Big Ideas* in *The Arts Fuse* Debra Cash (2005) wrote:

> The dance is structured like a play advancing through a number of vignettes. Bodies falling dead under searchlights as planes drone overhead. An apprehensive judge ... edging his desk as if afraid it will burn his robes ... a young forensic anthropologist ... falls as she plants flags on a mass grave. She cradles a Rwandan victim ... The dancers toss reams of testimony, documentation, and scientific evidence on the floor, where it becomes flotsam ... These compelling images do their shocking work ... The hard, burning core of "Small Dances" is a question about how bystanders made violence ... possible ... (para. 9–11)

The Journey

The journey of creating *Small Dances About Big Ideas* has been unique, challenging and illuminating for me. It encompasses many complexities about storytelling, about engagement, about history. It involves asking ourselves how to remain hopeful during a research process that was painfully sad. And it is the story of friends trusting each other with our very different approaches. Martha Minow (then Harvard Law School Dean) asked me to make a dance for an international symposium in honor of the 60th anniversary of the Nuremberg Trials (The Legacy of Nuremberg, n.d.). The following is an account of what happened after that call.

The Nuremberg Trials at the end of World War II proved that crimes against humanity would be charged against all perpetrators, including heads of state. In the trials from 1945 to 1946 evidence was gathered and 199 Nazi German leaders were tried of which 161 were convicted (Holocaust Encyclopedia, n.d.). Despite the difficulty of the subject matter, we were inspired by stories of strength, the evolution of change in the international criminal law (Kibler, 2019), and by how communities resumed life after genocide. We found a physical language by embodying the stance of contemporary activists and their stories of persistence. We also found a means of involving the audience in the performance.

It all began when I received the call from Martha Minow. I have known Martha for a long time, and even though we are friends, and frequently talk about art every chance we can, her call brought me up short. Martha uses all kinds of art in her pedagogy and relies on a creative understanding of the world as an engine in her inquiry. It was the subject matter that made me pause.

Up to that time, I had made dances about everything from the defense budget to my mother's death, from the Civil War to dances embodying ancient Jewish texts. I didn't think there was a boundary to what we could dance about until Martha asked me to make this particular piece. Suddenly I felt there might be limits to what art can address, and we were standing at the edge of one of them. That is why I said no.

Martha responded with a quiet passion that is uniquely hers. She told me that the gathering of individuals for the international symposium were dedicated to human rights law and that, even though they all focused on genocide, they needed to be reminded that the thoughts were connected to their bodies. I agreed with her sentiment, but pleaded with her, that if we agreed, she would also need to be our guide. The stories that follow are about this journey; about how we made the piece called *Small Dances about Big Ideas*. It is about how we selected which stories to tell and who would tell them. It is about engaging an audience in the dance itself, being with one another amidst the horrifying historical details.

In spite of the difficulties in dealing with the subject matter, we were inspired by stories of strength, the evolution of change in the law, and how communities resumed life after genocide. In particular, working with the idea of "upstanders" we found a way to have physical impact. An epiphany occurred when we encountered this term "upstander," as opposed to bystander (American Psychological Association, n.d.). It gave us physical language that we could use to bring ourselves back into the present by embodying the actual stance of activists and the stories of their persistence and fortitude.

The Impact

We all learned deeply and comprehensively from making this dance. Research always brings information and contemporary thought into my life and is a constant companion to my work. And there is always the ongoing process of turning ideas into artistic expressions, which, in turn, teaches us new tools for choreography. However, in this case, the subject matter of the Holocaust and the attempts to bring justice to an atrocity that defies our imaginations were uniquely challenging. Adding to this perspective, the necessity to study what had happened after Nuremberg in Bosnia, Rwanda (The Genocide Education Project, n.d.), and even at the moment of this writing, required purpose, zeal, and building a rehearsal environment that allowed for dismal drops in energy, as well as profound moments of caring. In the horrific genocides of Bosnia, Rwanda, and Ukraine, we are reminded of crimes against humanity (The Genocide Education Project, n.d.). The Nuremberg Trials set the stage for all the creation of new laws to address these types of crimes under international law and brought about accountability and punishment under the law (PBS, n.d.). A review by Debra Cash in *The Arts Fuse* describes our dance:

> Dance Exchange's new work would explore how human beings have expanded our ability to articulate the nature of crimes against humanity. It would address the intertribal killing in Rwanda and ethnic cleansing in Bosnia, rape as a newly-recognized war crime, and the nature of admissible evidence ... (Cash, 2005, para. 4)

Several factors aided us in our work. First, of course, was Martha with her words, questions, and guidance as a catalyst for creating. At her suggestion, we read several books and those authors brought us unusual solace, as well as a compulsion to continue. They transformed our rehearsal processes and our characters. It was also the first time I had worked with a sound designer instead of a composer (or my own attempts at synthesizing sounds) and the difference was stunning. Suddenly we had access to voices and sounds; environments that would concretize the experience for the audience and relieve the performers of having to carry all the storytelling. And we had an invested commissioner who was also taking a risk by asking a dance company to open an international conference. Finally, Martha brought another partner into the mix—the organization titled *Facing History & Ourselves*. They aptly note on their website that they use "lessons of history to challenge teachers and their students to stand up to bigotry and hate ... calling on each of us to connect the choices of the past to those we face today" (www.facinghistory.org). This group was already implementing significant work in schools (particularly K-12). However, they were looking for artistic workshops, especially embodied experiences, that would enhance their work that was making a difference for teachers and students and their families.

Both Martha Minow and I are Jewish and feel that our Judaism is a central part of who we are. Our Jewish heritage and commitment to social justice are key elements in our way of thinking and working. We were bequeathed a form of Judaism that makes social action and *tikkun olam*—that is action intended to improve the world—a deep expression of our Jewish selves. Both of us understood the Jewish historical context of Nuremberg and the aftermath of the war and the Holocaust. However, I didn't think that I could add to the vast amount of artistic expression centered around the Holocaust attempting to reckon with its horrors. Sensing my reluctance, Martha implied that the work didn't necessarily have to be about the Holocaust. She asserted that that there were many, many ways into the subject matter. And so, we embarked on our journey to follow the evolution of the law and the practices of reconciliation in communities experiencing genocide since the time of the Nuremburg Trials.

The Research and Creative Synergy

The process for research that informed the creation of this dance encompassed many components that are itemized below. Images, sound, words and books informed all of our work. A synergy developed that consolidated all of these components into the entity that became the dance. When we are heading into a project and as it evolves, it is interesting to note where the hooks are that help us stay with something, even when it gets difficult. There are myriad ways we move from research to the stage through the rehearsal process of mind, body, and story. Sometimes our research is a field trip. We talk to people, we discuss it, and we see historical images. Sometimes the research takes shape in another realm. One particular event was striking in generating a key component to the dance.

At the onset of my research, Martha pointed us in a few directions, which I followed until the subject matter developed its own journey. She guided us to look at the work of Supreme Court Justice Robert Jackson, who in 1945–1946 took a leave of absence from his position on the United States Supreme Court to run the tribunal at Nuremberg. While I was on tour with my company at Chautauqua, NY, I was only a 25-minute drive from Jackson's home and museum known as the Robert Jackson Center in Jamestown, New York (About the Robert H. Jackson Center, n.d.). I visited the site and found so many unusual documents. I love libraries and even the internet for doing research, but museums can provide unique images and objects that transport us to new ways of seeing. There was one such image that caught my attention—a photograph of a room filled with paper.

When looking back at the photo, it looms strong in my mind, perhaps conflating with several of the images, but the impact is significant. In the photo, the paper was all over the place. It was a courtroom, or maybe it wasn't a courtroom. While standing there in the museum gazing at the photograph, the image of mounds of paper burned into my imagination and was a constant propeller during the process of making the dance. At that time, I knew I would use it, but I had no idea how. Finally, one night, just before sleep, I envisioned that this would be the end of the piece. It appeared in the dance with the following stage directions:

The performers enter the stage and are throwing paper everywhere. Simultaneously our narrator is giving the news of the day. Not just any news, but the news being discussed that day in the international criminal court.

Research can keep us going in the creation of a dance, whether struggling because the piece is emotional or struggling because rehearsals aren't working, or whatever else might have been blocking our work. It is a constant companion and, in the best way, nourishes us as we go.

Sound and Words as Inspiration

Martha also suggested that we listen to Judge Jackson's opening remarks about the Nuremberg trial itself. Those opening remarks included, "The wrongs which we seek to condemn and punish have been so calculated, so malignant and so devastating, that civilization cannot tolerate their being ignored, because it cannot survive their being repeated" (The National WWII Museum, 2020, para.4). I sent that idea to Darron West, the sound designer for the piece and that text formed the backbone of one of my favorite moments that I have made. This was my first collaboration with Darron and it was momentous for me. I asked him to pick the words of the speech that he wanted to use. I would have chosen others, and this was an interesting realization for me. It became the first of many with Darron and an example of an extreme form of collaboration that I attempt to live in as much as possible. I know what I would choose, and I can hear it and see it in my mind. I don't know what my collaborators will choose, and I have come to see that this is not a question of right or wrong, better or worse, but rather one of difference. Darron's choice brought to bear a link of Jackson's brilliance to literature in a way I would have eliminated. Darron's choices probably made it possible for more audiences to connect earlier in the work because of that connection (Figure 12.1). Here are the stage directions that emerged:

> 6 men with 6 chairs moving in unison. It is very simple. They turn the chair slowly on one leg. They lower it. They sit slowly. They bend over. They come up. They twist their hands together. They slump. Head way back. They straighten up. They get off the chairs and sink to their haunches. They rise. They stand on the chairs. They snap their torsos tightly in small movements, tipping the chairs perilously as if being electrocuted. Then it is over.

FIGURE 12.1
Martha Wittman, Kevin Malone, Matt Mahaney, Ted Johnson, and Cassie Meador (left to right) in Small Dances About Big Ideas. Photo by Chris Randle

Martha also sent me several books that startled me, gave us a wide range of images to work with, and a group of authors who had also taken arduous journeys looking at genocide. I was surprised, in particular, by the writers Samantha Power (2002), Philip Gourevitch (1999), and Clea Koff (2004). With Power, it was about "upstanding" and finding the verb that held our piece together. With Gourevitch, it was the shared realization that the canonical definition of professionalism often gets in the way of telling the truth. He described having to stop being a journalist because he could not remain neutral and then set about to write a different kind of book. I was emboldened to see my own path differently. And with the work of the young and vulnerable Clea Koff, I was able to feel her incredible passion, curiosity, and compassion on every page. Her writing showed me how extreme detail told in simple prose could give both information and feeling, a synthesis I had been seeking for years.

When I reflect back on making *Small Dances about Big Ideas,* one concept I was beginning to formalize was personally coming to terms with how people within their individual professions confront the definition of professionalism. I particularly noticed when that definition fails them in their work and in their ethics. I have come to see this as a discussion about the Canon. The Canon is not just what gets produced, but also all the decisions that we make that allow that creation or that system to stand despite all the contextual changes in our world. Subsequently, we define those decision-making practices as professional, so that if you begin in any way to fight or rebel against some of those ways of working, you are, by definition, unprofessional. This approach is one way the Canon sustains itself. So, what was very interesting to me was to come across several journalists who were working in the field of genocide, who found themselves within a situation that required them to change professions and writing processes to adequately express what they saw happening. The normal demands or standards within their professions were actually holding them back, silencing them. One of the influential readings for me regarding this was by Philip Gourevitch.

His book, *We Wish to Inform You that Tomorrow We Will be Killed with our Families* (Gourevitch, 1998), is a nonfiction lament. While reading his book, I gleaned insight about my own work. I could see how what I am making is also a creative nonfiction dance. Part of the challenge in making a dance is imparting information while at the same time providing a state of feeling and relationship to the information. So much of our life is set up to get information one way (the attempt at impartial news programs) and to get feeling another way (fictional accounts of historical periods). Gourevitch implicitly suggests another perspective in this book and includes many passages of beauty, anguish, love, horror and statistics. We quote him at the end of the piece as the performers move around the stage with their papers as described below. It is not a direct quote, but, rather, it is altered to enhance sensibility for reading:

> Nobody knows how many people were killed that day. Some say a thousand, and some say fifteen hundred, two thousand, three thousand. Big differences. But body counts aren't the point in a genocide. In genocide the crime is wanting to make a people extinct. The idea is the crime. (Gourevitch,1998, pp. 201–202)

The second influential book for our work, Samantha Power's *A Problem from Hell; America and the Age of Genocide* (2002) provides a brilliant look at character. In particular, her short biography of Raphael Lemkin who coined the term "genocide" gives us insight into heroism, persistence, and physical language that had connection to our work. This was the first time that I saw the word "upstander" coined by Power as opposed to the word bystander. This term is one we came to know and understand because of the work being done today around intervention in sexual assault harassment (Upstander Intervention, n.d.). At the time, I was making this work, this term was new to me and it was startling. In rehearsal, we developed multiple ways of playing with "upstanding" and found to our delight that these movements translated well into tools for workshops and telling the story of processing this subject matter. We needed antidotes for our extreme grief. We also needed to find authentic ways of combating victimization. We were hoping to address the reality of being a victim, but also to find some physicality to literally move in new directions. We joyfully shared our tools and others with our *Facing History & Ourselves* contacts and these tools became a part of their workshops. Below are two tools that we implemented and shared.

In the first, you sit in a chair and then you describe in extraordinary detail how you get to standing. So, it might be something like I move my pelvis forward. I put my weight in the heels. I take my right hand and place it on my knee. I move myself a little bit more forward. I move the left foot back. I take my weight off the chair part way. I begin to straighten my knees. I bring my spine more forward. I come to stand and look outward with my focus. This language was later used to underscore stories from people's lives of standing up for something. The physical description became poetry and an engine to the stories of everyday heroes.

In the second, you find how many ways could you fall down and how many ways could you get up. Eventually, this was the choreographic form for Lemkin himself, and the crashing up and down formed a backbone to the dance.

As our dance began to tour, we found that we could apply these tools in many community settings. I like to say that there are multiple outcomes for the same research, and finding processes that can migrate from the rehearsal hall to participatory experiences for others is one of the most useful approaches for me. It is an antidote to the difficult emotions and stories that a piece about genocide raises for all of us and another way to share the research and to engage others in exploring mind and body.

A third book that we depended on was Clea Koff's *The Bone Woman* (2004). It provided information and a sense of detail that made it possible for us to investigate more with our bodies. Somehow, she led me to fully understand that by confronting the actuality of the situation, and by describing it carefully with specificity and boldness, we could and did discover our courage.

I think we were able to make this link with her writing, because this book described her first job as a forensic anthropologist. It was almost innocent in texture and we got to be with her as she stayed on task, no matter what the task was. In that way, we, too, were inspired to stay on task. Although I had been working for a while with detail as a way to make movement, this book gave me a way forward in embodying detail, without abstraction, and discovering ways to embed the emotion in the movement. Later, by combining text, sound, and music, we gave the audience layers of entry with the idea that people could stay remote or move into the core of ideas at their own discretion and willingness. The combined work of the three authors inspired and sustained us in our creative journey. I am grateful to this day for their efforts.

The final influential book was Martha Minow's beautiful *Between Vengeance and Forgiveness* (1999), which, to some extent, became my guidepost and scaffolding in the creation of the dance. I read it over and over. We may seek an intellectual comprehension of our research, but there is always something more of a spiritual kind of knowing. Martha's attempt to understand the impossible became our hearts and minds, too. And, not surprisingly, we have stayed on the subject matter for years, each participant working on the impact of history in contemporary life and searching for the possibility of forgiveness. We keep trying.

A Surprise in the Creative Process

In the process of research, I spend a great deal of time searching the internet for the sheer depth of discovery. One night, I decided to google Nuremberg and Poetry. This was more of a meditative inquiry than a distinct question because I did not have a question. What emerged from my search was quite surprising. What emerged from the inquiry was a trio of old women from Norse mythology—the Norns—who live under Mount Nuremberg. Their jobs were to give legal advice to the gods, keep the water clean and weave the thread of life each day. I loved this idea. And, so, we began to see what having the presence of three elder women coming from the perspective of that kind of labor would bring to our storytelling and, a host of jobs for them to perform within our piece were everywhere. They gave refuge, they cajoled, they bullied, and they protected. We were so grateful to have them in our lives as we worked. And, of course, we loved the women playing the parts which they imbued with their own lived experiences. The women moved furniture, they hid under the desk of the judge and whispered to the young woman to be strong, they held another older woman who had an unbearable story to tell, they pushed the narrator forward and they talked to the audience.

Engaging the Audience: A Significant Ask from Martha

Almost from the beginning, Martha was hopeful that we would find a way to engage the audience with their own bodies. Although I am familiar with engaging the audience in many formats, and I am actually quite comfortable asking people to participate and not just watch a performance, this subject matter was holding me back. However, Martha persisted and then, finally, we did find a pathway for audience involvement. In performance, we paused the action, asking the audience to respond to a question.

I recalled a dance that I made years earlier in which I got the audience to share stories with me and then turn that into a simple movement phrase which we all did together. Later, in the more formal part of the evening, that movement phrase was used to complete the most compelling image of the dance. I knew how powerful it was then and I wondered if I could use that structure here.

We used this participatory approach part way through the dance. We stopped the stage show, sent the dancers into the audience, and asked people to share a response to this: what is it that we teach our children? When did you first hear the word genocide or holocaust? How do we tell them about war? As you can tell, there were a range of questions circling an idea. This allowed each audience member to go where they needed to, or to just respond to what they had seen so far. The performing company listened and translated what they heard into a movement which everyone in the theater did together. Surprisingly, that movement returned at the end of the dance as a plea and a prayer. We were surprised by the speed with which the memories emerged, and the willingness of most to tell each other. After about 10 minutes, the dancers returned to the stage and then told some of the images that they heard. Importantly, it was fragments, not the whole story. I describe this to myself as "fragments of worth," meaning you don't need the context; you don't need to justify, and you don't need the whole story in order to fill our imagination with the pictures. These fragments were then put into simple gestures by the performer describing the image and, together with the audience, we rehearsed the sequence once, and about 8 or 10 of these gestures were connected. We did the dance to music and then the lights dimmed and the staged performance recommenced (Figure 12.2).

Figure 12.2
Cassie Meador and Lesole Z. Maine in Small Dances About Big Ideas.
Photo by Enoch Chan

Towards the end of the piece, the dancers enter tossing paper everywhere. The narrator is quoting Gourevitch and the question of body counts. Here is the full stage picture, taking us forward and carrying us to the ending:

> Our judge (who we met earlier in another scene) is sitting behind his desk. The performers, their hands now free of their papers, are standing in a diagonal line facing the judge. They begin to walk towards him one at a time while all together doing the dance the audience had made earlier. Each movement becomes evidence in the ongoing story of memory. Each gesture is derived from the memory of a person sitting in the witness chair as the audience, victim, jury, and judge. We are compelled to sense our own complicity to hold the stories of those lost.

Insights

I write this chapter now many years after this piece was performed. I have told only a few stories, but there is one more story left to tell as I reflect on the entire journey from creation to performance.

Martha guided me to look at what the reconciliation efforts have been in countries that have experienced genocide. I was particularly taken with the use of four definitions of truth that the Truth and Reconciliation Commission in South Africa developed (South African History Online, n.d.). There seem to be several formulations of this that I have found over the years. Below are the thoughts that I have settled on with my descriptions.

Factual Truth: What happened
Forensic Truth: What does the body tell you
Narrative Truth: Each person tells their own story in their own manner
Social Truth: What has happened to the community or the group

I have come to see these four ideas about truth as useful in guiding people to reflect. What just happened? How is your body informing you? What story will you tell others about this? What happened to our group? And I have found that when I tell them where this originated, they feel connected to something larger than themselves. I pose these questions because I am very curious as to what people experience, think they experience, have words for what they experience, or even notice what they experience. Reflection becomes tied to our bigger journey together and the role of reconciliation becomes tied to their/our experiences. This questioning likely will come in a post-performance discussion, after a short round of introductions, or even when just sitting in a circle and beginning. This reflection is probably the deepest outcome of making *Small Dances About Big Ideas*. People yearn to belong, to connect, to draw on the wisdom of others, especially when it arises from the ashes.

Coda: A Spell for Forgiveness

I have just finished touring a new work called *Wicked Bodies* about witches and their many jobs. I consider the Norns the beginning of this work, although the pandemic and the policy decisions being made about women's bodies increased the urgency. For this work we wrote many spells. The following is one several of us wrote together after being in rehearsal with Martha Minow.

SMALL DANCES ABOUT BIG IDEAS

Once again she was helping me try to come to terms with the limits of the law: this time about witch trials and how the state legally murders its citizens. I put the words together from my own musing along with those of Leah Cox, Mike Doi-Smith, Will Bond, and Keith Thompson. It makes sense to end this particular journey in this way.

> Sit with me before the jail keep comes.
> Tell me your fears. I am everywhere there's good company.
> I have music in my bag and a shawl to wrap and warm you.
> Is there an amount that you can forgive? Can you name or count all the things you've forgiven? People you know personally, or just barely. Is it many or few, forgiving some but not others, forgiving a part but not the whole? An injustice, a crime, or an act, or are they all the same thing? A reckoning.
>
> Everyone wants to be forgiven.
> Everyone wants to be free of their shame.
> Everyone wants to move unencumbered.
> But perhaps that is not forgiveness.
> I know, because I am forgiveness.
> A caution:
> Make sure you are ready because you won't know yourself when I have finished with you.
> You will not recognize your imagination stripped bare of its suffering.
> You won't comprehend your body now that the weight of history is off your spine.
> You won't be able to perceive the new rhythm of your blood streaming out of a heart as innocent as the day you were born.
> The world is indeed made new.

References

About the Robert H. Jackson Center. (n.d.). https://www.roberthjackson.org/about-us/

American Psychological Association. (n.d.). *Bystander Intervention Tip Sheet.* https://www.apa.org/pi/health-equity/bystander-intervention

Cash, D. (2005, November 15). *Dance Against Atrocity.* The Arts Fuse. https://artsfuse.org/160/dance-against-atrocity-2/

Gourevitch, P. (1999). *We wish to inform you that tomorrow we will be killed with our families.* Picador.

Holocaust Encyclopedia. (n.d.). *Nuremberg trials.* United States Holocaust Memorial Museum. https://encyclopedia.ushmm.org/content/en/article/the-nuremberg-trials

Kibler, T. (2019, October 1). *The Nuremberg Trials and Their Profound Impact on International Law.* https://home.heinonline.org/blog/2019/10/the-nuremberg-trials-and-their-profound-impact-on-international-law/

Koff, C. (2004). *The Bone Woman: A forensic anthropologist's search for truth in the mass graves of Rwanda, Bosnia, Croatia, and Kosovo.* Random House.

Lerman, L. Video excerpt of *Small Dances About Big Ideas* at https://youtu.be/0PKbuTorcGc

Miinow, M. (1998). *Between vengeance and forgiveness: Facing history after genocide and mass violence.* Beacon Press.

Power, S. (2002). *A Problem from hell: America and the age of genocide*, Basic Books.

PBS. (n.d.) *The legacy of Nuremberg.* American Experience. https://www.pbs.org/wgbh/americanexperience/features/nuremberg-legacy/

South African History Online. (n.d.). *Truth and reconciliation commission (TRC)*. https://www.sahistory.org.za/article/truth-and-reconciliation-commission-trc-0

The Genocide Education Project. (n.d.). *Modern era genocides*. *https://genocideeducation.org/resources/modern-era-genocides/*

The National WWII Museum. (2020, November 20). *The grave responsibility of justice: Justice Robert H. Jackson's opening statement at Nuremberg*. https://www.nationalww2museum.org/war/articles/robert-jackson-opening-statement-nuremberg

Upstander Intervention. (n.d.). Stanford University SHARE Title IX Website. https://share.stanford.edu/get-informed/education-and-outreach-programs/upstander-intervention

Part III — Embedding Remembrance

Reflection

The Importance of Witnessing the Unbearable

Nancy R. Goodman, Ph.D.

If the Holocaust is not witnessed it will cease to exist and the Nazi goal to destroy Jewish people and culture will have been successful. Yet, witnessing the unbearable is extremely painful and at times overwhelming. Making oneself ready for witnessing is a courageous and inspirational action involving the soul and the intimacy of profound connection with others. As a psychoanalyst who has written about witnessing the Holocaust, in *The Power of Witnessing: Reflections, Reverberations, and Traces of the Holocaust* (Goodman & Meyers, 2012), I am moved and inspired by the chapters in this section of the book demonstrating the potency of the story, the narrative, and the ability to create forms of witnessing involving theatre and music. When it comes to preparing to witness the catastrophe of the Holocaust, the receiver opens herself or himself to roiling waters never before anticipated bringing closeness to drowning.

I learned about taking testimony and being a witness from Dori Laub who was a child survivor, a psychoanalyst, and the developer in 1979 of the Yale Video Archive of Holocaust Survivors. I was beginning my studies of psychoanalytic psychotherapy at Connecticut Valley Hospital where Dr. Laub directed a residency training for which he asked me to provide supervision. Over four decades of learning from him and writing many of my own papers about witnessing, I discovered that Dori always returned to the astounding events of taking his first testimonies. These events initiated his in-depth study of the human contact made when taking testimony from survivors and all who are traumatized.

As Dori prepared to take the first testimonies from survivors living in New Haven, Connecticut, he admitted that he had no idea what would happen—expecting that each individual would speak about 20 minutes. With the clarity of being witnessed, the survivors started to create their personal narratives that had been dormant and now which went on for hours. Those giving testimony later described that they had no idea what they would say but, as if by a miraculous force, the finding of words broke through numbness and the "being back there" started to evolve. Eventually metaphor, art, music and theatre began forcefully fighting the death trains of the Nazis.

I use the metaphor of a witnessing theatre to convey elements of the witnessing process. As the witness you agree to enter a unique theatre where horrors, beyond imagination, are revealed, and resilience and creativity are felt. The intensities can block one's eyes from seeing or cause momentary deafness to the full orchestral reverberating sound. Of course, the images and stories being revealed arouse helplessness and rage and survivor guilt, as they provide embedding remembrance etched into our psyches forever. These emotions require containment so that the theatre experience where one has come to witness does not explode and disappear as did millions of individuals who were humiliated, treated inhumanly, tortured, worked to death, and murdered. It helps to recognize that others have joined with you as a community in this special place, the theatre of witnessing—and, that no witness need be the perfect witness. Each witness is the right witness to receive a partial knowing of what cannot be fully known, to carry it within, and to bring it to others.

Each of the chapters in this section is based on the performances which have been created by writers, narrators, directors, and musicians. They demonstrate the vitality of a second layer of testimony which is the remarkable creative process that makes truths of the Holocaust available for others. Each chapter is an example of what I call the "living mind" which forever more will accompany the devastation of the "dead places" in the mind made by the madness and irrevocable nothingness of the Nazi genocide. The term nothingness acknowledges how the totality of the annihilation will forever have unclear language—we just keep trying.

It is the power of the arts which ignites the living mind, the living theatre, where symbolic and imaginative scenes can beckon us to witness and carry the realities within us; and, to invite others to join in witnessing. Each of the chapters is an inspirational effort to keep the Holocaust alive for self and other—to find voice. Dr. Bess Rowen's exploration ("They Escape: Paula Vogel's *Indecent*, LGBTQIA+ Issues and Genocide") of how a play within a play confronts the Holocaust without replicating the trauma is a lesson in the importance of layering for witnessing. The reader is brought to the collective trauma of the Holocaust and homophobia through a love story between two women in the 1907 play, *God of Vengeance*, (which was performed in the Warsaw Ghetto) through the 2015 play *Indecent*. This type of connecting of now and then is an essential feature of witnessing when the present and past converge and then passes to new generations. Dr. Gail Humphries' chapter, "A Mosaic of Hope" is superbly relevant to how witnessing takes place as an audience sees and feels the performance. The art form of theatre carries the gravity of Holocaust stories. I worked with Gail to bring a production of *Signs of Life* to the International Psychoanalytic Congress (2013) in Prague at Divadlo Inspirace. The silence and crying from those in the theatre conveyed the absolute strength of theatre production as the emotions of trauma reached the hearts of the audience.

Karin Rosnizeck enlivens capacity to be affected by theatre in her chapter about the five women in a cell in the infamous Pankrác prison in Prague "Nazi Whores, Kapos, and Collaborators: The Women of Pankrác '45." Who is guilty? Who is responsible? Who must be punished? These are the questions raised as each woman's story unfolds. The Czech playwright Martina Kinská takes on the complex topic of collaboration—who is responsible and how much responsible? Women were sexualized and considered guilty by association. It is powerfully disturbing to consider what is collaboration and what each of us would have done to stay alive. In "Hine Ma Tov: A Devised Theatre Project with Holocaust Survivors and Adolescents," Dr. Tim Reagan and Val Issembert describe a project growing out of Witness Theater, an integrated therapeutic program bringing survivors and teenagers together to tell and to listen to the Holocaust story. A multitude of theatre effects are used including narrative, music, and movement to evoke childhood memories. It is a beautiful project bringing together generations to keep the Holocaust alive and to create the path to remembrance.

Having attended the multimedia concert performance at the Kennedy Center, I enjoyed, with exhilaration, Murry Sidlin's and Dr. Karen Berman's descriptions of "Performing Defiant Requiem: The Journey of a Messenger Not a Scholar." The account of making contact with survivor Edgar Krasa resonated with me as, I, too, along with Marilyn Meyers, interviewed Krasa and his wife Hana in 2010 at their home. Murry and Karen bring to life, as witnessing does, the remarkable way that inmates at Terezín were brought together to make beautiful music while annihilation waited at the train track. Witnessing atrocity and brilliance of performance can cross generations to keep the soul alive. In the chapter "The Piano: How We Survived," Manuela Bornstein gives testimony to Dr. Karen Berman who is the secondary witness. The story is powerful as one feels the presence of danger and also of endurance and hope. This chapter illustrates the need for the receiver of the story, "I want to know" and the teller who "wants to make known." Manuela Mendels Bornstein tells her survival story, "The Piano: How We Survived," with details that chill and with the warmth of embracing the second and third generations who want to hear her speak. She is eloquent and determined to continue bringing truth forward. Music, her piano, is a theme she uses for revealing the journey across Europe and to the United States.

Collectively, these chapters convey the power of performance, of voice and music, to bring the human contact needed to keep witnessing of the Holocaust from disappearing. We each join the audience in the theatre of witnessing to make the unknown known over time. In keeping the victims alive in our active listening and representing, we are better psychologically armed to fight the threats of re-occurrences that could bring annihilation of society, culture, and human values.

CHAPTER 13

"They Escape": Paula Vogel's *Indecent*, LGBTQIA+ Issues, and Genocide

Bess Rowen, Ph.D.

> The traumatized, we might say, carry an impossible history within them, or they become themselves the symptom of a history that they cannot entirely possess.
> – Cathy Caruth (1995)

I Can Never Remember the End: Introduction

Toward the end of Paula Vogel's 2015 play *Indecent,* stage manager Lemml stands in a long line in a concentration camp with the rest of the company (Vogel, 2017). He closes his eyes and imagines the two queer, Jewish women from *God of Vengeance* jumping out of line and escaping, mentally sparing them from what he is about to witness and experience. *Indecent* is a play about a play. It tracks Asch's 1907 play *God of Vengeance* (*Got fun nekome*), a hugely influential play about Jewish culture and queerness, from its inception through its performances in the Warsaw ghetto until the current moment (Asch, 2003). *Indecent* is not a play about genocide, but the Holocaust plays a pivotal role in the story of how this play traveled through time, and what it meant to Jewish people trying to celebrate aspects of their culture through horrific circumstances. The play's structure mimics collective traumatic memory, but instead of repeating scenes of horror, the play's refrain is a scene of love that both celebrates the queer, Jewish women in *God of Vengeance* while reminding us that there were queer, Jewish women victims in the Holocaust who are often forgotten.

Indecent begins as Lemml introduces the acting company and then says,

> We have a story we want to tell you. . . .About a play. A play that changed my life. Every night we tell this story—but somehow I can never remember the end. *(He indicates his mind is failing. He turns to the others for help. No one can)* No matter. I can remember how it begins. (p. 10)

Many would rather forget the circumstances of the Holocaust, but there are those that have been erased even when that history is remembered. Through *Indecent*, Vogel has reclaimed the history of queer, Jewish women in the Holocaust through a play structured to show how art can help communities work through collective trauma in ways that replenish the souls of performers and audience members alike. Vogel's approach models the ways in which theatre can serve to highlight social justice issues involving genocide without requiring traumatic reenactments of those events on stage.

Lemml and the troupe exist in and out of time in *Indecent* as they attempt to construct the history of a play featuring an explicit love story between two Jewish women—a sex worker named Manke and her brothel-owner's daughter named Rifkele—as time progresses toward the Holocaust. *Indecent* tracks Sholem Asch's 1907 *God of Vengeance* (*Got fun nekome*), a hugely influential Yiddish-language play about Jewish culture and queerness, from its inception to its performances in the Warsaw ghetto through Asch's disavowal of the play. The troupe plays multiple roles, stepping into the various casts of *God of Vengeance*'s productions, the players in its censorship and court case, and then the people who sought to preserve its legacy as a piece of Polish-

Jewish art during and after the Holocaust. Near the end of *Indecent*, Lemml and the troupe stand in "AN IMPOSSIBLY LONG LINE" in a concentration camp as Lemml "MAKES A WISH" (2015, p. 73). Lemml then says, "*(Softly)* Please don't let this be the ending ..." as "IN HIS MIND, ONLY HE CAN SEE ... RIFKELE AND MANKE BURST OUT OF THE LINE. THEY ESCAPE" (2015, p. 73–74). Lemml's memory has spared the characters of these queer, Jewish women from the realities of the Holocaust while still bringing them back to the time and place of those events. The Nazis exterminated Jewish people and gay people, and certainly queer, Jewish women among them, but those particular narratives have been largely ignored even within the discussions surrounding the Nazi persecution of LGBTQIA+ people.

Remembering, But Not Repeating, the Holocaust

The shadow of the Holocaust looms large over *Indecent*, threatening both the Jewishness and queerness of *God of Vengeance*, and yet Vogel has structured her play in a way that honors the collective trauma of this horrific event without replicating its harmful memories. The play does not repeat the traumatic events surrounding the Holocaust, or even the frustrations that resulted from *God of Vengeance*'s censorship, but instead returns to an explicit love scene between two Jewish women, focusing on the social aspects of celebrating culture and community that can help reinscribe and reclaim the intersection of queer culture and Jewish culture that the Nazis wanted to destroy. Interestingly, the Nazis were less specific about the rules for queer women, instead focusing on queer men. This means that *Indecent* also participates in a reclamation of queer, Jewish women within the narrative of those lost to the Holocaust and then (further) erased by collective culture's resistance to thinking about the LGBTQIA+ victims of that event.

Memory fails Lemml and the troupe when it comes to the darkness of the Holocaust, but the play remembers for them. Yet *Indecent* does not strictly follow Sigmund Freud's concept of "Remembering, Repeating, and Working Through" (1914), which also mirrors the rehearsal process of many pieces of theatre. Instead, *Indecent* incorporates the silences and stops associated with collective trauma. As Dori Laub (1995) notes, "the imperative to tell the story of the Holocaust is inhabited by the impossibility of telling, and therefore, silence about the truth commonly prevails" (p. 64). Laub describes one of the key aspects of the trauma response to the Holocaust as a "collapse of witnessing" (1995, p. 65), which is why it is so crucial that *Indecent* is structured the way it is. Lemml and the troupe fail to remember and repeat the details of the Nazi persecution of Jewish people and LGBTQIA+ people, but they do witness a reality that the Nazis could not erase. Vogel's play shows the power of theatre to represent collective trauma while also enacting a possible path forward: through the embodied representation of positive cultural representations that did indeed live through Nazi rule to stand in front of us today.

In order to understand the impact of Vogel's particular approach to creating a play that deals with queerness and the Holocaust, one must first understand both the content and context of the play at the center of *Indecent*: Asch's *God of Vengeance*, which predates the Nazi rise to power. The next layer of *Indecent*'s complex layering has to do with the ways that the Nazis treated LGBTQIA+ people, particularly women. The final piece of this analysis comes from the sociological and psychological research done on trauma, both individual and collective, that will be used as a tool to understand the dramaturgical handling of the material in the play vis-à-vis the context in the previous two sections. What emerges is a clear picture of a beautifully structured play that deals with seemingly unfathomably large issues such as antisemitism, homophobia, and mass genocide through a story about love— the love between two women and the love of/for the theatre as an artistic medium and tool for storytelling (Figure 13.1).

"THEY ESCAPE": PAULA VOGEL'S INDECENT, LGBTQIA+ ISSUES, AND GENOCIDE

FIGURE 13.1
A scene from Paula Vogel's Indecent Showing Characters Who are Actors Rehearsing the Rain Scene from the Play Within the Play, God of Vengeance.
Photo Credit: Jim Carmody

Washed in the Rain: *God of Vengeance*, Success, and Censorship

God of Vengeance follows a Polish, Jewish brothel-owner named Yekel as he commissions a Torah for his "pure" daughter Rifkele. Handwritten Torahs were (and are) incredibly time-consuming and expensive sacred objects, and by obtaining one as a promised wedding gift for Rifkele's future husband, he both shows off the family's wealth and their dedication to continuing Jewish traditions. Showing wealth and (false) piety are key in attracting a suitor as Yekel (I am using Vogel's spelling, although other translations sometimes list "Yankl" or "Yankel" and "Rivkele" and Sholem Asch's name is also occasionally transliterated as "Sholom.") married one of his sex workers, Sore, but has kept his daughter upstairs, away from the impurities happening in the brothel beneath them. They have financial means, and their best hope of giving Rifkele a good life is, in their minds, to marry her off to a pious young man and get her away from the brothel. But Rifkele has formed a close bond with Manke, one of the sex workers, who often beckons Rifkele outside to talk. As rain falls outside, Manke calls Rifkele down to dance in the downpour with her, and then asks Rifkele if she would let Manke wash her hair in the rain together, kiss her, and pretend that they are getting married. Each of these is met with an emphatic "yes" from Rifkele in a wonderful display of enthusiastic consent. This scene, colloquially called "the rain scene," builds organically and ends with them kissing in the rain before Rifkele decides to run away with Manke. When Yekel realizes that his daughter is missing, he accuses his wife of corrupting her. Rifkele returns and Yekel asks if she is still a pure, Jewish girl, to which she responds, "I don't know" (Asch, 1907, p. 111). This heavily implies that she and Manke have had a sexual encounter, but that Rifkele does not know if such actions between two women "count." The Nazis were also unsure if such actions "counted," which is a topic covered in greater detail shortly. Yet, within the play, this confession is enough for Yekel, and he forces Rifkele down the stairs to join the rest of the sex workers and then gets rid of the Torah, because he says he no longer needs it—meaning that now Rifkele has lost her value as a wife and no longer needs a dowry.

Vogel chooses this scene as her refrain. *Indecent*'s action begins with Asch's wife commenting on how beautiful the scene is. Next the audience hears it read by a group of authors (all of whom are men), then actors rehearse the scene in preparation of the off-Broadway American opening. Next the action moves to a staged reading in the Warsaw ghetto, and finally Vogel gives us a fully staged rain scene, spoken in the original Yiddish without supertitles—the audience knows the scene by now and does not need them—with real rain falling on Rifkele and Manke. Asch's original scene is remarkable for the seriousness with which it treats the love and desire between these two women, and for the explicit way it portrays their

"THEY ESCAPE": PAULA VOGEL'S INDECENT, LGBTQIA+ ISSUES, AND GENOCIDE

relationship. And yet most reactions to the original scene, and play, fell into three categories: people who caught the lesbian scene and were appalled, people who felt general unease but did not (or could not) name the cause of that discomfort, and people who missed the intimate nature of Rifkele and Manke's relationship entirely.

Within the American Jewish community, the play caused concern because it implied that there were Jewish people running brothels and working as sex workers which, of course, there were. It is also worth noting that this was the major backlash against the play, as the previous generations of Jewish immigrants saw these more recent Eastern European Jewish immigrants as a threat to their assimilation into white American culture (Houchin, 2003, pp. 83–84). An English-language production opened on December 20, 1922, at the Provincetown Playhouse in New York City's Greenwich Village and then moved to Broadway's Apollo Theatre in February of 1923. It was there that the play began to garner negative attention (Houchin, 2003; Curtin, 1987).

The events of the play and their critical reaction is the topic that *Indecent* takes up as its central narrative. Vogel's play tells a vaguely chronological story but also includes "blinks in time" and other jump-cuts that move from one critical moment of *God of Vengeance*'s story to the next. There are also fabricated parts of Vogel's narrative, such as the addition of a real lesbian couple playing the original American Manke and Rifkele, highlighting the importance of this Jewish, lesbian representation. Although there is no evidence of this, there are real questions about whether or not anyone would have noticed or cared to record such a relationship between women, which is one hidden history that *Indecent* pulls from *God of Vengeance*. Very few critics, *The Theatre*'s Arthur Hornblow being the main exception, recognized the queer relationship in *God of Vengeance* at all. Hornblow vociferously objected to the play's lesbianism and what, for him, was an explicit tie between that perversion and the distasteful Jewish culture. Arthur Hornblow's son, Arthur

Hornblow, Jr. would go on to produce the next commercially successful lesbian play staged in the United States, *The Captive* (1926), in clear response to his father's condemnation of *God of Vengeance*. In *We Can Always Call Them Bulgarians: The Emergence of Lesbians and Gay Men on the American Stage* (1987), Kaier Curtin chronicles Hornblow's response:

> A more foul and unpleasant spectacle has never been seen in New York ... Mr. Asch's drama deals fundamentally with the vengeful god of Judea ... The Jewish god is a horribly cruel one in this instance. He thwarts the father's purpose by having his pure young daughter fall into the clutches of Lesbians and the audience is treated to a nightgown scene in which the women make overtures to each other which go so far beyond the pale of what is permissible that I can only voice my astonishment at the authorities allowing a thing of this sort to be continued before heterosexual audiences, comprised of individuals young and old who go to the theatre to be entertained and without any conception of what they may be asked to witness. (pp. 31–32)

Hornblow was in the minority here in the sense that he not only noticed, but also named the lesbianism in the play. Although Hornblow was unafraid to identify his discomfort, other reviewers were less sure how to voice their objections to the play's content. In *Censorship of the American Theatre in the Twentieth Century* (2003), John Houchin notes, "Response to the play was generally uneasy. While [Rudolph] Schildkraut was praised, many reviews could not bring themselves to discuss the content of the play. Burns Mantle completely skirted the blatant depiction of lesbianism as did Heywood Broun" (pp. 82–83). And yet, it seems clear that many people truly did not understand what was happening between Rifkele and Manke. Morris Carnovsky, whose first acting job was in the original English-language production of *God of Vengeance*, clearly did not know how to interpret this aspect of the play. In conversation with Curtin, Carnovsky admitted,

> No such thing even occurred to me until some reviewers mentioned it. I would recognize such a thing today, but at the time it seemed to me just a sensitive little scene, very subtly done, in which the prostitute offered to help the daughter, if I remember correctly, run away from home. (1987, p. 32)

Curtin concludes, quite rightly,

> If a young man in the cast of *The God of Vengeance* was unable to recognize the women's relationship for what it was, it is likely that, in 1922, a considerable portion of the audiences, as well as some of the critics, were just as naïve. (1987, p. 32)

Indecent refuses this erasure with the force of the rain scene's repetition and the addition of scenes in which the characters discuss the lesbian content explicitly.

But despite the erasure of the queer women in the play by some, and the outright objection to them by others, it is important to note here that the largest objection to *God of Vengeance* came from the middle-class American Jewish population, who feared the play's translation into English might highlight a seedy underbelly of Jewish culture to gentile Americans. This is what led Rabbi Joseph Silverman from New York City's popular Temple Emanu-El to report the play to the authorities as being immoral and indecent, a scene that Vogel's play depicts and from which it also gets its name. A grand jury then indicted theatre owner Michael Selwyn, the play's producer (Harry Weinberger), and the twelve-person cast—but the production continued, and they were not arrested. The cast reported to court and pled not guilty the next day. In the end, after the play had closed and a court case was officially brought, only Weinberger and lead actor and producer Rudolph Schildkraut were found guilty and fined $200 (Houchin, 2003, pp. 84–85).

The next major event in *God of Vengeance*'s story comes in the form of a *Jewish Telegraph Agency* bulletin from May 27, 1946, which reports:

> Sholem Asch, noted Jewish writer, today announced that he has prohibited the production of his play the 'God of Vengeance' in any language in the United States and in other countries. He explained the ban by stating that 'the situation described in the play is dated and exists no longer.' (n.p.)

Asch, horrified by the realities of systemic genocide of the Jewish people in the Holocaust, no longer thought his play about the Polish Jewish underbelly of society made sense. But while he was thinking about negative Jewish representation that Nazis might find unobjectionable, he failed to see the hopeful queer representation that the play contained. It is this positive aspect of *God of Vengeance* that Vogel uses as her way into the traumatic context that surrounds Asch's play.

The Invisible Pink Triangle: Nazi Persecution of Gay Men and Sometimes Women

In his landmark history of LGBTQIA+ people's treatment during the Holocaust, *The Pink Triangle: The Nazi War Against Homosexuals* (1986), Richard Plant traces the early gay rights movement, often called the "homophile" movement, in Weimar Germany through the Nazi rise to power and the resulting persecution of queer people. Paragraph 175 of the German penal code was added in 1871 explicitly to criminalize sex between men, but it was strengthened by the Nazis after 1935. Neither the original law nor the additions addressed any possible sex between women (Plant, 1986, p. 114). In 1937, high ranking Nazi lawyer Rudolf Klare decided to delineate the particular acts that counted as "felonies" under Nazi rule. They were:

> Simple contemplation of desired object (abstract coitus); Plain touching (which might lead to hyperesthesia, erection, ejaculation, orgasm); Petting, embracing, kissing of the partner with results similar to above; Pressing of the (naked) penis to any part of the partner's body, such as thigh, arm, hand, etc.; Pressing of two bodies against one another with or without friction; Rhythmic thrusts between knees or thighs, or in armpits; Touching of penis by partner's tongues; Placement of penis into partner's mouth; Pederasty or sodomy (placement of penis in anus). (Plant, 1986, p. 113)

Of these nine forbidden behaviors, four can only be committed by individuals with penises. This is not unusual, as many prohibitions on same-sex activities have ignored women because of either confusion about what behaviors to condemn or a general refusal to believe that women would ever choose to be with other women if men were available. Klare realized that the revisions to Paragraph 175 still did not cover acts between women and wanted to add wording that would rectify that, but Himmler was uninterested (Plant, 1986, pp. 114–116). Plant notes that there are some reports of queer women in concentration camps, most of whom were detained for their political views instead of their sexual orientations, but they are few and far between, leaving Plant to conclude, "Most lesbians managed to survive [the Holocaust] unscathed. Fortunately, they fell outside the universe of Himmler's sexual obsessions" (1986, p. 116). Regardless of the numbers of lesbian and bisexual women officially in Nazi records, it is safe to say that there were queer women among the millions of Jewish people in concentration camps, meaning that these women were still victims of the Holocaust and likely faced even harsher challenges with managing that identity within their dire circumstances at the work and death camps.

For my purposes, Klare's list is also important because four of the five remaining banned behaviors (the ones capable of being done by people without penises) are shown in the rain scene in *God of Vengeance*, a scene that is then repeated at least three times during *Indecent*. Manke and Rifkele have dialogue that make clear that they think about each other romantically even when they are not in front of each other, and they certainly touch each other's cheeks and arms in the rain even before they fully embrace (without friction) and kiss. This scene is read in a very early scene in *Indecent*, then shown in rehearsal, then performed in the Warsaw ghetto, then finally realized fully with stage rain falling as an elderly Asch walks away from his home, leaving America after the banning of his play. In addition to using this love scene as punctuation to the more serious events of censorship and genocide that intervene in *God of Vengeance*'s timeline, the inclusion of a scene that so explicitly goes against the Nazi standards of appropriate sexuality and reinscribes queer, Jewish women in the pantheon of Holocaust victims, undoes that erasure while celebrating the queer Jewish lives that existed before, during, and after Nazi rule.

Given the Nazi silence on the subject, it should come as no surprise that there are few recorded Nazi responses to depictions of lesbians, but there is a notable exception. Leontine Sagan's film *Mädchen in Uniform* (1931) depicts a Prussian school where a high school girl, Manuela von Meinhardis, develops an obsessive crush on her English teacher, Fräulein von Bernburg. In a moment of, ostensibly, motherly feeling, Fräulein von Bernburg kisses Manuela on the lips instead of the forehead during a bedtime routine.

"THEY ESCAPE": PAULA VOGEL'S INDECENT, LGBTQIA+ ISSUES, AND GENOCIDE

Manuela's love deepens, but Fräulein von Bernburg says she cannot play favorites. Manuela, despondent about her unrequited love, attempts to throw herself off the top of the staircase, but then is foiled by her friends at the last moment. What happens next is not shown. Despite its explicit portrayal of a teenage girl's love for another woman, the film was well-received. As Valerie Weinstein (2019) notes, "Contrary to popular belief, the Nazi Propaganda Ministry did not ban the film or expunge it from the cultural memory. Instead, primary sources show that it was screened and praised" (p. 144). For the Nazis, the lesbianism and suicidal ideation were connected not only to each other, but to the Prussian ideals that the Nazis sought to counteract. Much like the contemporary "bury your gays" trope that so often finds queer characters introduced in movies and television only to be killed off, the Nazis tolerated depictions of queer people—particularly queer women—if they were killed or condemned at the end of the story. The harsh end to *God of Vengeance* therefore makes the play seem to show both what happens to immoral Jewish people in general, and queer, Jewish women in particular. This is yet another reason that Vogel's choice to repeat a scene of queer women's joy in *Indecent* is such a powerful contradiction to the silence and occasional condemnation that defines the Nazi opinion toward queer women. The theatre allows Rifkele and Manke to perform these forbidden actions in front of an audience not only the one time that the original *God of Vengeance* scripts, but also in a way that connects the repetition of theatre to the strengthening of the scene's message (Figure 13.2). Vogel does not simply repeat the scene intact, but instead enables an audience to watch it grow from the written page through a reading through rehearsal and finally to a fully "produced" version that feels fully realized and real. *Indecent* shows how theatre can physically re-member these queer women through the process of rehearsal and staging, but the increasing production elements also mirror the way that community bonds can help heal collective trauma.

FIGURE 13.2
The final rain scene in Indecent, featuring real rain falling on Manke and Rifkele as an elderly Sholem Asch exits behind them.
Photo Credit: Jim Carmody

Symptoms of History: Remembering, Reclaiming, and Reaching Past Collective Trauma

Repetition has long been associated with traumatic memory, from Freud's important essay, "Remembering, Repeating, and Working Through" through more recent studies from Cathy Caruth (1995, 2013) and Bessel Van Der Kolk (2014). Freud posited that people needed to work through trauma by repeating parts of the scenario in ways that enabled them to work through their responses to it, but Van Der Kolk notes,

> Freud had a term for such traumatic reenactments: "the compulsion to repeat." He and many of his followers believed that reenactments were an unconscious attempt to get control over a painful situation and that they eventually could lead to mastery and resolution. There is no evidence for that theory—repetition leads only to further pain and self-hatred. In fact,

> even reliving the trauma repeatedly in therapy may reinforce preoccupation and fixation. (2014, pp. 31–32)

This false narrative about healing trauma by repeating trauma is precisely why it is so important that Vogel repeats not the trauma in *Indecent*, but the celebration of Rifkele and Manke's love. The characters in the play struggle to remember the events surrounding this scene, but the scene itself is never forgotten or purposefully fragmented. Instead, it becomes stronger and more fully formed, moving from a staged reading to a rehearsal to an English-language version and, ultimately, to a fully staged Yiddish version with real rain. Instead of attempting to gain control or agency over this scene in a Freudian way, Vogel has a community-led focus on the social fabric of queer, Jewish life as an antidote to the unimaginable trauma surrounding the Holocaust.

Indecent is not the first play in which Vogel has experimented with a dramaturgical structure that mimics traumatic memory. In *How I Learned to Drive* (1997), narrator Li'l Bit navigates her experiences of being sexually assaulted by her Uncle Peck mixed in with positive memories of him teaching her how to drive. Ann Pellegrini (1992) notes that the non-chronological movement of scenes, and the jumps in time, mimic the way that memory can work in instances of sexual assault. Pellegrini explains,

> If we conceive of trauma as a break in the mind's experience of time, then the piecemeal quality of Li'l Bit's narration reiterates trauma as its symptom. And yet, this very piecemeal quality also gets at the restlessness of memory and psychic life. In a sense, all memory, and not just traumatic memory, performs a kind of "deferred action" on the self. Li'l Bit's narrative, then, brings us to see not simply the belatedness of trauma, but the revision that just is memory. (pp. 415–416)

Both *How I Learned to Drive* and *Indecent* are memory plays told from the perspective of narrators who are grappling with traumatic events. And yet the difference between these two plays is that *How I Learned to Drive* deals with individual trauma while *Indecent* deals with collective trauma. Lemml, like Li'l Bit, exhibits "deferred action on the self" in the sense that he expresses doubt and hesitation surrounding the parts of his story that involve the Holocaust. But, unlike Li'l Bit, he has a company around him who are there to help create the story. Li'l Bit does have a group of three Greek Chorus Members to help her tell the story, but they all step into scenes she is remembering and do not have the agency to tell stories without her input. *Indecent* also keeps to a chronological progression, but simply skips moments in time in the middle of scenes and in between scenes. The "blinks in time" that occur throughout the play reveal incomplete memories of specific moments, but are never missing enough information to make the audience believe that Lemml is an unreliable narrator. On the contrary, these moments feel somehow more honest—Lemml might recall the emotional truth of these scenes over the specific moment to moment details, but his depth of feeling makes us trust him.

Once again, Lemml is a representative of a larger community here in that the trauma he is remembering is not his alone. The concept of collective trauma, as defined by Kai Erikson (1976), is characterized by:

> a blow to the basic tissues of social life that damages the bonds attaching people together and impairs the prevailing sense of communality. ... "I" continue to exist, though damaged and maybe even permanently changed. "You" continue to exist, though distant and hard to relate to. But "we" no longer exist as a connected pair or as linked cells in a larger communal body. (p. 154)

The rupture of collective trauma is the breakdown of communal ties and collectivity, which is precisely why the rain scene's perpetual return shows a generosity to her characters as well as the audience. At the moments when the community is threatened most with events outside of *God of Vengeance*, the troupe comes together to continue working toward the fully realized rain scene, reminding everyone inside and outside of the action that there were queer, Jewish women before, during, and after the Nazis tried to erase and destroy both of those identity markers. The fact that the characters turn to their community also has some basis in trauma studies. As Van Der Kolk writes, "The autonomic nervous system regulates three fundamental physiological states. ... Whenever we feel threatened, we instinctively turn to the first level, *social engagement*. We call out for help, support, and comfort from the people around us" (2014, p. 82). The fact that it is community that is ultimately used to repair the disruptions to community caused by collective trauma is something found again and again in LGBTQIA+ history. In fact, this was one of the things that the Nazis found threatening about gay men in particular: that they had a separate culture and community. Vogel is once again purposefully using *Indecent* to celebrate the aspects of queer, Jewish culture that the Nazis would have objected to most, but it is still a radical choice to represent these things in a love story between two women, who are not even the first kinds of victims we think of within the less-remembered LGBTQIA+ victims of the Holocaust.

They Escape, We Remember and Renew

In this sense, Manke and Rifkele not only escape the horrors of the camps and gas chambers when Lemml imagines them jumping out of line, but they also escape the erasure of LGBTQIA+ victims of the Holocaust. Vogel specifically uses the structure of her play to reinscribe these forgotten victims into the collective memory as she metaphorically heals the characters' collective trauma by highlighting the social ties produced by Jewishness, queerness, and theatre itself. Each repetition of the rain scene gets stronger and more unified in its realization, almost as if the company was working together to rebuild the intimacy between these two Jewish women that was lost by the disruption of the Holocaust. Freud's concept of "remembering, repeating, and working through" applies more to the theatrical process than the healing of trauma, but in theatre, production teams are working *toward* the final event of a fully staged play instead of working *from* the traumatic event. Instead of following a Freudian framework of trauma, as *How I Learned to Drive* could be said to do, *Indecent*'s rain scene follows what more recent trauma theorists such as Caruth (1995, 2013), Van Der Kolk (2014), and Erikson (1976, 1995) contend about the nature of traumatic memory by having the deepest traumatic events be unspoken and unseen. Vogel does not show her characters experiencing the worst events of the Holocaust, but instead stages the troupe's use of the queer relationship in *God of Vengeance* as a beacon of queer, Jewish community to which social ties they can eventually return. This focus on the power of community memory and action also foregrounds a crucial Jewish idea: that remembering and retelling collective traumas from the past calls to action the social justice activists of the present. Vogel stages the power that art, specifically theatre, has to recreate community and to remember those that history would rather forget. Rifkele and Manke *do* escape—they stand in front of us on stages across the United States—but they were also present throughout the darkest moments of queer, Jewish experience, living inside of the heads of people going through unbelievable individual and collective trauma. Some were silenced by death, others erased because of the blind spot the Nazis had toward queer women, but when Manke and Rifkele dance and kiss in the rain at the end of *Indecent*, their existence cannot be denied.

References

Asch, S. (2003). *The God of Vengeance*. In J. Hodges (Ed) *Forbidden Acts: Pioneering Gay & Lesbian Plays of the Twentieth Century* (pp. 37–81). Applause Theatre & Cinema Books.

Caruth, C. (2013). *Literature in the Ashes of History*. Johns Hopkins University Press.

Caruth, C. (1995). Introduction. In C. Caruth (Ed) *Trauma: Explorations in Memory* (pp. 3–12). Johns Hopkins University Press.

Curtin, K. (1987). *We Can Always Call Them Bulgarians: The Emergence of Lesbians and Gay Men on the American Stage*. Alyson Publications.

Daily News Bulletin, Monday, May 27, 1946. *Jewish Telegraphic Agency 13(22)*. https://www.jta.org/archive/sholem-asch-bans-his-own-play-prohibits-staging-god-of-vengeance-in-any-language.

Erikson, K. (1976). *Everything in Its Path*. Simon and Schuster.

Erikson, K. (1995). Notes on Trauma and Community. In C. Caruth (Ed.) *Trauma: Explorations in Memory* (pp. 183–199). Johns Hopkins University Press.

Freud, S. (1914). Remembering, Repeating and Working-Through: Further Recommendations on the Technique of Psycho-Analysis II. In S. Freud & J. Strachey (Eds.) *The Standard Edition of the Complete Psychological Works of Sigmund Freud* (pp. 145–156). The Hogarth Press.

Houchin, J. (2003). *Censorship of the American Theatre*. Cambridge University Press. https://doi.org/10.1017/cbo9780511486111.

Pellegrini, A. (1992). Staging Sexual Injury: *How I Learned to Drive*. In J. G. Reinelt & J. R. Roach (Eds.) *Critical Theory and Performance: Revised and Enlarged Edition* (pp. 413–431). University of Michigan Press.

Plant, R. (1986). *The Pink Triangle: The Nazi War Against Homosexuals*. Henry Hold and Company Press.

Sagan, L. (Director). (1931). *Mädchen in Uniform* [Film]. Deutsche Film-Gemeinschaft.

Van Der Kolk, B. (2014). *The Body Keeps the Score: Brain, Mind, and Body in the Healing of Trauma.*

Vogel, P. (1997). *How I Learned to Drive.* Dramatists Play Service.

Vogel, P. (2017). *Indecent.* Theatre Communications Group.

Weinstein, V. (2019). The Uniform in the Closet: *Mädchen in Uniform* in Nazi Germany. *Seminar: A Journal of Germanic Studies 55(2)*, 144–165. https://doi.org/10.3138.seminar.55.2.4.

CHAPTER 14

A Mosaic of Hope: Haunting Echoes of the Holocaust on Stage

Gail Humphries, Ph.D.

Embedded Threads, Thoughts, and Memories

Studying the Holocaust has been a dark magnet for me, from my college years of studying German history, to my work as a director staging stories of the Holocaust. A pivotal book for me was historian Peter Gay's *Weimar Culture: The Outsider as Insider* (2001; 1968). It provoked my thinking early on about the fringe existence and the abyss that so many artists live on and over. It also gave me deeper understanding of the biases and hatred that fueled the Nazis. It did not, however, reconcile my emotional understanding and tension when dealing with the Holocaust, the cruelty and antisemitism. I was drawn to the evil balanced by acts of courage, beauty, and honor that the Holocaust manifests, as a dark magnet. As an adult, I am still asking that same fundamental question: how could this be? Theatre is constantly personal for me. I ask myself what I would do if I were to encounter circumstances of extreme hatred, violence, and repression. As an adult, I do know this—the arts afford us the opportunity to tell the stories of the Holocaust, to provide insight, encourage enlightenment and generate action. My art is theatre. As such, I aspire to speak up, to shout out and to carry the gravity of the stories of the Holocaust on to the stage.

In this chapter, I will begin with one of my most recent efforts—staged readings of an originally developed piece titled *Traces in the Wind* (Figure 14.1)—the intertwined stories of three remarkable women survivors—and then reflecting on my early seminal work in Prague with a play titled *Smoke of Home*, written by Jiri Stein and Zdenek Elias while imprisoned at Terezín. Their play was preserved by Kate Elias, wife of Zdenek Elias. *Traces in the Wind* was performed as a staged reading—albeit a tone poem—in various cities throughout the United States and at the Embassy of the Czech Republic in honor of Holocaust remembrance. It was developed over a period of three years, working with theatre students at Stephens College while I was Dean of Creative and Performing Arts in Columbia, Missouri. It is an inherent testimony to the power of the arts and a call to action for the audience. *Smoke of Home* is an allegory, a play that uses the Thirty Years War (1618–1648) as a metaphor for the longing for home when incarcerated. I was introduced to it by fellow Fulbrighter Dr. Lisa Peschel, while on an appointment in Prague. Scenes from the play were originally performed at *Divadlo Komedie* in Prague (2008) and then I subsequently directed the play in Prague, at Terezín and at American University in Washington, DC. Implicit in the content is a compelling question—what happens after the smoke of war is lifted and you are free to return to a home that no longer exists as you knew it?

A MOSAIC OF HOPE: HAUNTING ECHOES OF THE HOLOCAUST ON STAGE

FIGURE 14.1
Traces in the Wind Staged Reading with Actors Clara Bentz, Lauren Hardcastle and Katherine Moore (left to right) from Stephens College.
Photo by Autumn Brown.

Both theatrical works are offered as possibilities for reflection on the capacity of the arts amidst horrific circumstances and the potential to catalyze our contemporary thinking and action against repression. I view both pieces as searing indictments against the cruelty and viciousness of the Holocaust, and an outrage against repression. As I noted in *The Power of Witnessing*, "the theater can provide power to each of us to engender a collective that has the potential to be transformative, to empower and to function as a catalyst for insight and action." (2012)

Traces in the Wind ... A Wistful, Ongoing, and Heartfelt Calling

I am reminded that the root word for courage is *Coeur*—heart in French. Looking at the courageous acts of three women of the Holocaust, I was determined to tell their stories on stage. *Traces in the Wind* originated with my introductions to the writings of Eva Kavanova (1967) and to an interview with her (1995), through fellow Fulbrighter Dr. Lisa Peschel. Eva was an extraordinary woman who had survived the Nazi transit camp of Terezín and went on to study at and teach in Prague at the Academy of Performing Arts. As fate would have it, my Fulbright appointment in Prague was at the same institution where Eva had attended and taught. As an artist, I was compelled by her personal story, the artistic and intellectual life of Terezín, and the infinite human capacity for creativity that Terezín represented. Terezín is located forty-five miles outside of Prague, but, for the artists and intellectuals sent to this Nazi transit camp, it was a lifetime away from the existence they had known.

Authentic voices are compelling. I felt Eva Kavanova's voice resonating to me across time and geography from Terezín to Prague to Washington, DC. I tucked her story away into my psyche and it stayed with me. Years later, I read about two other amazing women who exemplified strength and courage and whose voices compelled me. I was led to their stories, as well as Eva's. Each woman had survived the atrocities of the Holocaust through the arts, but in differing ways. The stories of these women became buried in my soul—Eva Kavanova, Rosalina Glazer, and Charlotte Delbo. Just to think of their names is to give a personal identity to the suffering of the Holocaust. Their stories were of betrayal, humiliation, and unbearable incarceration. Yet, each asserted their spiritual resistance through the arts. With *Traces in the Wind*, I hoped to preserve the chronicles of each of the women while challenging audiences to consider the why, how, and deep commitment to "never again" through the specific lives of these three exceptional women.

Hindsight provides me with a specific gift of gratitude. My gratitude is extended to many: to Dr. Lisa Peschel for opening my eyes as I lived my Fulbright Commission for my time in Prague, the David Milch Foundation for subsequent production support, The Florida Holocaust Museum, the Embassy of the Czech Republic, Dr. Murry Sidlin for his support of the production at Terezín, and the International Psychoanalytic Association for production support and providing a venue for upstanding against hatred, bigotry and antisemitism in Prague and Washington, DC. Finally, I must acknowledge Dr. Felix Kolmer, a survivor who impacted me with his grace, wisdom, and fortitude as I interviewed him in Prague, 2014. Felix touched my heart and soul when I met him at Terezín as a guide for myself and my performers and interviewed him subsequently in Prague (June. 2014). Felix survived three camps and yet his remarkable, penetrating, and impactful voice gave me hope and a desire to continue to tell stories of the Holocaust on stage. This interview inspired me with the genesis of *Traces in the Wind*—using words as weapons to intensely fight for righteousness, to struggle against toxicity, and to encourage all of us to persevere towards the light even amidst the darkest echoes. Is it all *bashert*—meant to be? I now embrace that outlook. *Traces in the Wind* evolved, from my deep desire to preserve the chronicles of each of these women.

The resources for the literary text for *Traces in the Wind* were:

1. *About Terezín Theater A Bit Differently, a personal interview with Eva Kavanova (1995),* translated by Lisa Peschel.
2. Letters to Rosalina Glaser, as presented in *Dancing with the Enemy: My Family's Holocaust Secret (*Glaser, 2013); and
3. *Auschwitz and After* (Delbo, 1997) and *Who Will Carry the Word? (Delbo, 1983)*.

Audience Surveys Reveal Compelling Results

Traces in the Wind was a staged reading with music, one that I often referred to as a tone poem. It evolved at Stephens College while I was Dean of Performing Arts and was shared with audiences ranging from college and high school students to survivors. Findings from the audience surveys of the premiere performance revealed compelling results, as audiences noted their compassion, empathy, and inspiration from the stories of three remarkable women (2017).

Most recently (fall, 2022), students in a course taught by Dr. Barbara Grossman at Tufts University—Imagining the Holocaust on Stage and Screen—revealed the possibilities for connections to these three remarkable women. Students read the text and saw short video clips of the reading. We subsequently had a Zoom conversation and students provided feedback both in discussion and in their journals, noting the potency of the stories.

One student noted in her journal:

> By telling the stories of the few that were able to survive and were brave enough to share, we are ensuring that the millions who did not survive are not forgotten. The few stories that we do have (in the grand scheme of it all because imagine the likes of six million stories) are even more impactful because they try to give us a glimpse into the emotions/thoughts of millions of people who were not able to tell their stories.

Another student noted:

> We will never ever be able to understand the true reality of life in the ghettos and concentration camps, and while we may come close to it in moments, that reality is far from us. Not only have so many stories been lost when a generation of Jews was killed, but the stories we do have are removed from us. These stories are so important, but it is impossible to fully grasp the enormity of the horror experienced by so many during the Holocaust.

Finally, I will share this reverberating thought for me from yet another student:

> I know that I have not lived a tragedy as horrific as the Holocaust, and God forbid I will, but the beauty of this performance is that regardless, the message can be translated into the lives of so many.

Yet, telling the stories of these lives through theatre articulated my thinking about the innate potential of theatre. It results in a shared experience with a validation of the possibilities to provoke thought and generate remembrance through live performance. The final lyric that I wrote with composer Tom Andes for the closing number captures it all …

> Hear our traces, see our faces.
> Art embraces all the races … all.

Smoke of Home … Stepping into the Footprints of Time

My first authentic connection to theatre at Terezín was through *Smoke of Home* (Figure 14.2). It is a morality play, an allegory, and a compelling philosophical treatise on the destruction of war and genocide. It is a story revealed from multiple perspectives during the Thirty Years War, a devasting war in Central Europe. There are two main characters—a philosopher poet (Christian) and a logical and assertive rationalist (Cassellius) as well as an outspoken priest and a bombastic soldier. All four men are imprisoned and, during that imprisonment, debate the meaning of life as they sit amidst destruction of their homeland and devastation in their lives. There is much to consider in this play, but as we near the ending, the priest makes a provocative statement as the men are finally freed from the prison as reminding them that, "the home that they left is in the past, buried in the abyss of time." One can only imagine how many times that thought played compellingly in the playwrights' minds as Zdenek and Jiri sat in the bunks in the Hannover Barracks, at Terezín. Jiri Stein never returned to his homeland. Jiri was transported from Terezín to Auschwitz and then to Dachau in a labor transport. He perished there. Zdenek was repatriated to Prague where he recuperated after a subsequent imprisonment at Auschwitz. Years later when the Communists came to power in Czechoslovakia, Zdenek escaped over the mountains back into Germany rather than live under another totalitarian regime. Eventually he arrived in America and became a journalist with Radio Free Europe.

Figure 14.2
Program cover for Smoke of Home at the Attic Theatre Hamburg Barracks, Terezín. Photo by Lisa Peschel.

Christian and Casselius (perhaps reflecting the diverse perspective of Zdenek and Elias), speak heartily about the love of home. However, Cassellius poignantly reminds the prisoners of the losses they will experience when free:

> Fools. Get ahold of yourselves. Blind! Thoughtless fools! Should I have told you what Walloon actually told me? Should I have told you that three weeks ago General Wrangel lost his brother when they were defeated in Dachau, and that in vengeance he tore through Bavaria like death incarnate sowing all of the horrors of war? That he torched a number of your towns and villages ... There are no stones left standing in your Rine—today your church and parsonage, Father Anselm, are shattered ruins ... And you, Christian, were you to go from Rine up to Stetten, at the crossroads by the three firs, you would see a thread of smoke from the conflagration where Stetten used to stand! That is your smoke of home today! You want to go home? Fools! The home you left behind is in the past, irrevocably buried in the abyss of time! (Humphries, 2012, p. 259)

The play remained unseen during the lifetime of the playwrights but was viewed many times in the 21st century. In an insightful interview conducted by honors student Kera Package at American University after one of my productions, Dorothy Elias, daughter of Zdenek shared a compelling thought about the ramifications of the play:

> Art, especially in the context of Terezín, is not sacred as art and certainly cannot be separated from resistance or survival. For people who had been stripped of all personal power, who had been deprived of every vestige of their former lives, who had lost everything, having a means to express a sense of self would be enormously empowering. (Humphries, 2012, p 260)

My perspective on the potential power of the arts haunts me with this play. Presenting it in Prague was staggering but presenting it in the Attic Théâtre of the Hamburg Barracks at Terezín is inexplicable. On that site, directing the play nearly strangled me. It was hard to breathe through the horror of all that it represented. Yet, the theatre voicing allowed all of us—actors, production team and audience—to somehow breathe. I was torn between such joy at bringing the work to life on site at Terezín, and such sorrow at the tragedy that Terezín represents. When I presented the play subsequently at American University, one of the students spoke in the honors course where we studied Terezín and the play. Her comment is telling.

> What will we do? While we may not leave this semester with the motivation to start a new program or initiative, we will be leaving this class with a sense of responsibility … The responsibility to use our talents, whatever they may be, to share with the world the things we know to be true—whether that be the hope of humanity and self-expression or the pain and hard reality of genocide halfway around the world. (Humphries, 2012, p. 262)

A Haunting Trilogy of Questions

What next? What does it all mean? What must we continue to do through the arts?

When I reflect on the arts, the Nazi camps, the exceptional lives, and stories that I have encountered, it becomes a dreadful funhouse mirror with broken shards of that mirror endlessly piercing my heart and my mind. I still am not sure that I can reckon with the contradictions—the horror, the beauty, the joy, and the sadness. I am torn, as so many of my audiences have been, looking at the worst and best of humankind. However, this I do know. The arts will reach across time with strident chords to challenge us to remember, recall and analyze the creativity of extraordinary humans who grasped the arts as lifelines to provide us with a walk through their footprints in time to touch our souls.

References

Delbo, C. (1983). Who will carry the word? In: Skloot, R. (Ed.), C. Haft Trans.) *The Theatre of the Holocaust, Volume 1*. University of Wisconsin Press.

Delbo, C. (1997). *Auschwitz and after*. (R . Lamont (Trans.). Yale University Press.

Gay, P. (2001) *Weimar culture: The outsider as insider*. W. W. Norton & Company.

Glaser, P. (2013). *Dancing with the Enemy: My Family's Holocaust Secret*. Random House.

Goodman, N. R. & Meyers, M. B. (Eds.). (2012). *The power of witnessing: Reflections, reverberations, and traces of the Holocaust*. Routledge.

Humphries Mardirosian, G. (2012). Giving voice to the silenced through theater. In N. R. Goodman & M. B. Meyers (Eds.). *The power of witnessing: Reflections, reverberations, and traces of the Holocaust*. (pp. 255–265). Routledge.

Kavanova, E. M. (2007) (1967), *About Terezín a Little Bit Differently*. L. Peschel (Trans.), a paper and an interview in 1995.

CHAPTER 15

Nazi Whores, Kapos, and Collaborators: The Women of *Pankrác '45*

Karin Rosnizeck

Pankrác '45—Five Tales of Nazi Collaboration

In *Pankrác '45*, a play by Czech playwright Martina Kinská, translated by Barbara Day, we meet five women sharing one cell in the Prague Pankrác prison awaiting their trial (Kinská, 2016). It's late summer 1945, just weeks after the German defeat. Each of the five women is accused of collaboration with the Nazis who had occupied their Czech homeland for a period of six brutal years. Each of the women has to testify, not knowing what the others will say, but understanding that the gallows are waiting.

Pankrác '45 challenges the term collaboration exploring its complex, ambivalent and controversial nature: What exactly is "collaboration" and when is collaboration necessary and part of a usual co-existence with the occupying forces and, when is it a "crime of treason" against one's home country? What meaning does the word and the act of "collaboration" have in our contemporary political context?

As the world today turns in more authoritarian directions, we are confronted with new—similar and different—choices. If the "illiberals" (a term popularized by foreign affairs journalist and author Fareed Zakaria in 1997) are in charge, how much do we resist? Where do we collaborate? How do people get the food, housing and basics needed to survive brutal circumstances? That was the dilemma in the 1940s; and for many people around the world today, living under the existential threat of an authoritarian regime, this struggle remains. This chapter about the play *Pankrác '45* is dedicated to the forgotten women of the Holocaust.

Women During Wartime Occupation

The *Pankrác '45* women were all part of a Czechoslovakia that had to endure six long years under brutal Nazi occupation. Life was a forced coexistence with the occupant who dictated the rules, leaving the Czechs with little to no options for a self-determined life and, often, impossible choices to survive. Women on the sidelines of wars undertaken by men, trapped in messy circumstances and moral dilemmas, had to deal with the consequences and navigate their lives between their multiple roles as wives, mothers and breadwinners. As the five different stories of collaboration reveal, each of the women makes cruel compromises, becomes complicit and collaborates with the enemy in different ways.

Pankrác '45 presents the cases of two actresses working in a Nazi-owned film industry, a resistance member who slept with her interrogator to save herself and her husband (and later betrayed a co-conspirator), the wife of a Deputy Director of the Protectorate of Bohemia and Moravia who was responsible for thousands of deaths, and a Jewish woman who survived the Holocaust as a concentration camp kapo or "trustee inmate[s] who supervised the prisoners" (Concentration Camp: Kapos, n.d., para. 1). As the five gripping tales unfold, we become witnesses and are constantly challenged in our own moral judgements learning about the different shades of collaboration and variations of moral culpability.

A strong rationale for the presentation of this play was its urgent relevance to our contemporary society and our present struggle as we witness the decline of democracy and the rise of authoritarianism. Often enough, the signs of the times have been compared to the political situation of the newly erected and fragile democracy of the Weimar Republic, soon losing to the propaganda and simple promises of the fascists. We live in a similarly chaotic and transitional world marked by highly polarized political divisions, increasingly autocratic power, a silencing of open political debate and a new terror of political regimes where dissidents are imprisoned or punished and their family members imperiled by acts considered disloyal to the regime. As we watch with open eyes how xenophobic, racist and anti-democratic ideologies are becoming dangerously popular in our so-called free world—how can we resist? And if we don't, are we already collaborating? By dramatizing significant historical moments, theatre alerts us to analogies and differences between past and present, offering a platform to negotiate sociopolitical questions of today. Theatre is at its best when it provides a mirror of our present society inviting us to reflect on the signs of the time and takes the opportunity to interfere with and shape our future. In other words, theatre can be an instrument for democracy in action.

Research Process and Resources

My approach to putting on this play started with a year-long period of research into the large historical context of the play. This history includes the pre-war situation of Czechoslovakia with its unique role of the Sudetenland for Hitler's war strategy in Eastern Europe, and the devastating impact of the Munich conference as the great "Western betrayal" freeing the path for the German annexation of Czechoslovakia. This was soon followed by the Nazi invasion and occupation of the entire country, the oppression of Czech society under Nazi rule, and the turbulent period of liberation, new beginnings and postwar reckoning (Demetz, 2009).

The years of Nazi occupation 1939–1945 starting with the installation of the Protectorate in Bohemia and Moravia and ending with the German capitulation is one of the two distinct time spans in *Pankrác '45,* setting the frame for the protagonists' *past,* their collaborative behavior and reason why they are in prison. The second interval contains the immediate postwar months of national purges, retribution and war crime trials, *the present reality* the protagonists have to deal with as prisoners. The wealth of material compiled by Svanda Theatre in the playbill and in supplementary material for its U.S. guest performance at Georgetown University (2018) was the first go-to-source for myself and the cast. Svanda's supplements (which Expats Theatre also incorporated into our program) explained the particular circumstances and events in Czechoslovakia during the occupation. In addition, the material provided Czech names and locations as well as biographical data on the characters and their situations during and after the war. Regular communication with the playwright Martina Kinská and translator Barbara Day to clarify questions was also part of the preparation process. I relied on a large amount of online sources for research material such as: the United States Holocaust Memorial Museum (https://www.ushmm.org); website and links of the embassy of the Czech Republic (https://www.mzv.cz/washington/); Radio Prague International with its many historical features (made accessible both in audio and text in both English and Czech); as well as the Deutsches Historisches Museum (dhm), specifically its Lebendiges Museum Online (https://www.dhm.de/lemo/). Further, I frequently visited Deutsche Welle Radio (https://www.dw.com) on European affairs and the German online portal "Zukunft braucht Erinnerung" (https://www.zukunft-braucht-erinnerung.de/) dedicated to political education covering mostly European history of the 20th century.

In connection with the subject of war trials and retribution, my major source was Benjamin Frommer's *National Cleansing: Retribution Against Nazi Collaborators in Postwar Czechoslovakia* (2004), a very comprehensive work comparing war crime trials in different countries. Shane Darcy's *Coming to Terms with War Time Collaboration* (2019) and Veronika Bilková's essay on *Post Second World War Trials in Central and Eastern Europe* (2014) were also very insightful.

A large body of film supported my preparation, especially films starring Lída Baarová and Adina Mandlová, two of the five characters in the play. The recent documentary *Doomed Beauty* directed by Helena Třeštíková and Jakub Hejna (2016) based on interviews with Baarová in the final years of her life contained invaluable insights, particularly regarding Baarová's views of her Nazi past. Two notable feature films that covered the assassination of Reinhard Heydrich and its aftermath were *Operation Daybreak* (1975) adapted from the Alan Burgess book *Seven Men at Daybreak* and *Anthropoid* (2016) directed by Sean Ellis.

The Five Women from *Pankrác '45*

Expats Theatre produced *Pankrác '45* (Figure 15.1) in the Fall of 2021 at Atlas Performing Arts Center in Washington, D.C. running October 28—November 21, 2021, co-directed by Karin Rosnizeck and Melissa Robinson with the trailer at https://youtu.be/BN1Cze9gtok. More information, including photos and reviews are available at https://expatstheatre.com/60-2/pankrac-45/ and in additional links listed in the references at the end of this chapter.

ART FOR HEALING AND RENEWAL

FIGURE 15.1
Pankrác '45 Production Photo. From left to right: Lisa Hodsoll as Julie, Sara Barker as Hana, Stacy Whittle as Lída, Karin Rosnizeck as Adina and Aniko Olah as Karola.
Photo credit: Karin Rosnizeck

The play takes us back to the dramatic postwar transition period in late summer/fall 1945 during which Pankrác prison is the arena for war crime reckoning. The liberation euphoria over the German defeat is soon replaced by acts of retribution and revenge. During these turbulent months, the roles of victims and perpetrators are reversed overnight as quickly established People's Courts prosecute suspected traitors and collaborators (Frommer, 2004). Public executions in the Pankrác prison courtyard happened daily.

This crisis-ridden historical moment sets the stage for the prison drama presenting us with the following female offenders of Nazi collaboration crammed into one cell: two famous Czech actresses Lída Barrová, former lover of Propaganda Minister Göbbels, and Adina Mandlová, notorious for her multiple affairs with colleagues and representatives of the theatre film industry; Hana Krupková, surviving member of the Czech resistance, now suspected of betrayal; Julie (or Julča) a concentration camp victim turned Kapo; and a fifth woman who keeps her identity secret until she is revealed as the wife of Karl Herrmann Frank, the number two Nazi in the Protectorate of Bohemia and Moravia and responsible for countless atrocities including the complete annihilation of two Czech villages.

While four of the five characters (Adina, Lída, Karola, and Hana) are based on real life people who have been detained and prosecuted for collaboration, playwright Kinská places all of them into one single cell adding a purely fictional character (Julie) as a concentration camp survivor. Their storylines, developed through confrontational dialogues and competing narratives of the pasts, drive the plot forward. We watch them in their attempts to deal with the threat of trial and execution, trying to negotiate their guilt and justify, belittle or deny their roles as collaborators with the powerful enemy. Under the looming pressure of retributive justice, they struggle for survival a second time, trying to save themselves by bending the truth and turning against each other.

The Czech Film Industry Under Nazi Occupation

As Demetz (2009) points out, the film industry was of great value for the Nazis who used it as a tool to indoctrinate people, spread national socialist politics and keep the fear of the Czech population alive. The occupiers used the brand-new state-of-the art Barrandov Studios located outside of Prague for their propaganda machine, forcing the large Czech film company AB films into bankruptcy, replacing it with the German owned Prague Film AG (Demetz, 2009) and ridding it of all Jewish employees. Between 1941–45, the Prague Film AG was the hub for German films producing over 80 propaganda films. The majority of Czech actors were left to star in shallow comedies for entertainment made "to keep the good mood necessary for war" (Göbbels, 1943, p.3) as the Nazi's leading mass manipulator cynically put it. Needless to say, the occupiers strictly controlled the output of the Czech film industry, demanded absolute loyalty to the Reich and penalized resisting Czech artists and entertainers relentlessly. For the occupants, popular local stars were an effective instrument of power demonstration, and Emanuel Moravec, the Czech Minister of Education and Culture, one of their most loyal collaborators (Radio Prague International, 2022). The character of Adina is very aware of the extent of collaboration in and beyond the film industry and reminds her cell mates that the entire Czech society collaborated with the Nazis: "Where are they going to put everyone? And after them, all the shoemakers the whores, the bakers and the whores. The whores work for the Germans too, you know. You can kiss my ass with that sort of justice" (Kinská, 2015, p. 6). But the spotlight on celebrity culprits is harsh and the opening scene illustrates effectively how the actresses have turned from screen divas to outcast criminals. Like on a catwalk, the women enter in elegant dresses posing for a photoshoot. The camera flash throws their blown-up faces on a large upstage screen turning them to mug shots with name, number and crime of the delinquents. The public shaming of the "Nazi Whores" has begun, their fame has turned to shame. Watching a visiting delegation pass by their window, Lída observes: "they look at us as though we had leprosy, as though we carried the plague … " The glamorous stars have turned to pariahs, wild beasts in a cage, being stared at "as if in a zoo" (Kinská, 2015, p. 5).

Lída—"The Devil's Mistress"

Lída, arguably the most famous Czech screen diva of her time, is perhaps best remembered through her two-year affair with Nazi Minister of Propaganda Josef Göbbels which earned her the name "the Devil's Mistress," also the title of a Czech-Slovak biographical feature film (Renc, 2006). After an early career start in her homeland, Lída came to Berlin—barely twenty—to star in the film *Barcarole* (Lamprecht, 1935) which launched her career with the

German production company UFA and her romance with famous German co-star Gustav Fröhlich (internationally mostly known for his lead in the film *Metropolis*) (Lang, 1927).

She soon caught the attention of propaganda chief Joseph Göbbels, who oversaw the Nazi film industry, and became her lover and most avid supporter. Lída spent over two years in Germany as Göbbel's mistress, socialized with the Nazi elite and even turned down a contract offer from Hollywood in order to continue her infamous affair. A helplessly infatuated Göbbels even planned to divorce his wife Magda and leave Nazi Germany. Their romance ended abruptly in 1938 when Hitler, warned by Magda Göbbels, ordered his propaganda minister to end it. This also ended Lída's UFA film career in Germany as she was pursued by the Gestapo, barred from appearing in films and participating in public life. She returned to Prague where she was shunned and, in 1942, fled to Italy to take up filming. After the war, payback didn't wait: Captured by the Americans she was brought back to her homeland, arrested for collaboration and put into Pankrác Prison.

In the play, Lída obsessively continues to re-enact her movie star life using every moment to reminisce about her lost paradise. She never manages to step out of the spotlight and reflect on her personal responsibility, but instead is (literally) blinded by it. This is wonderfully illustrated by her entrance with blindfolded eyes, playfully flirting with imaginary fans "Boys? Hello—boys ... Where are you? Where are you taking me boys?" (Kinská, p. 3). She never seems to be able or willing to face her present situation. Lída's naive but dangerous Faustian bargain for fame, ignoring the calamities of the Nazis, is especially perturbing:

> Politics is completely beyond me. I'm thick when it comes to that. No one told me what was going on ... I knew nothing about the concentration camps. I thought the Jews were

> transferred to some island somewhere, or being allowed to go to America. (Kinská, 2015, p. 15)

The discrepancy between truth and illusion and Lída's continued denial of her lover's role in the Nazi machinery of terror makes for much of the macabre humor of the dialogues in the prison cell. In scene 6, she twists her narrative *blaming* Göbbels love as the culprit forcing her to stay with him: "He loved me. He loved me so much. He rang me, sent flowers, presents, messages ... I had to" (Kinská, 2015, p. 16). Then she regresses back into her self-aggrandizing narcissism: "Joseph decided he wasn't going to give me up. Not even Hitler could force him. We had a getaway plane waiting. We were at the airport, engines running, my scarf waving ... ." (Kinská 2015, p. 17). Her mindless talk bragging about Fröhlich's and Göbbel's villas in the posh Berlin neighborhood of Lake Wannsee, the very location where the Holocaust was masterminded a few years later, is another mind-blowing example:

> We arranged a beautiful house. Magnificent. Luxurious. The latest appliances.
>
> A villa on the lake. Where only the better classes lived. Wannsee, it was called. Sometimes we went out on the lake in a yacht. You just cannot imagine how it was like ... (Kinská, 2015, p. 9)

Adina—Independent and Controversial

Adina Mandlová is one of the most controversial Czech screen legends. Her "scandal-ridden" film career took off in 1932 when she became the lover of the famed Moravian actor and film director Hugo Haas. Before the Germans invaded, she already had over thirty films under her belt. During the occupation, she continued her work in Czech cinema and had liaisons with several industry representatives, among them the Nazi appointed head of the Prague-based Barrandov film studios Willy Söhnel.

Mandlová was known for her sharp mind, provocative tongue and her promiscuous sex life with many film industry representatives. Her notorious affairs soon became the basis of many rumors. One of them was the widely spread assumption that she had been the lover of powerful Nazi state secretary Karl Hermann Frank. Although this never proved true, this rumor, circulated by the British Radio broadcasts in the Protectorate, not only damaged her life, but was also the basis of her imprisonment as Nazi collaborator. Shunned as "Nazi whore," she barely escaped a lynching by the angry mob. When her cellmates teasingly call her "Frank's lover," Adina screams her anger about the injustice of this accusation into everyone's faces:

> Hello!! I never f***ed Frank ... And my husband didn't kill himself because of him. And I wasn't driven home to his corpse in the early morning, naked in just a fur coat, straight from my lover Frank. A stupid scandal ... the hell with it all. Someone was f***ing the top Nazis but it wasn't me. (Kinská, 2015, p. 13)

In sharp contrast to the life-devastating rumor, was Adina's true story: to silence the rumors she married communist painter Zdeněk Tůma who committed suicide. Her most tragic love, resulting in a miscarriage was with married Jewish fellow actor Vladimir Šmeral. Being Jewish, Šmeral was transported to a Nazi concentration camp which he managed to escape. Adina saved his life by hiding him in a hospital. At the end of the war, Šmeral returned to his wife.

With her untamed temperament, independence of mind and strong opposition to bourgeois values, Adina—less corruptible than Lída—clearly recognizes the hypocrisy of the fast-changing postwar morals of her former colleagues: "if it was me who collaborated, they'll have to sentence half of Barrandov film studio" (Kinská, 2015, p. 6). Adina's biting wit and sarcastic comments ridiculing the distorted morals of their prosecutors often provide the comic relief after high tension moments: When Hana confesses that she slept with her interrogator, Adina boasts: "This could be a new game. Raise your hand if you slept with the Gestapo?" (Kinská, 2015, p. 31).

Hana—Between Nazi Whore and Resistance Fighter

Hana Krupková grew up in Pardubice, where she met Václav Krupká, a lieutenant whom she married as a nineteen-year-old in 1940. Shortly after, the Krupkás joined the resistance and participated in Operation Anthropoid. The secret mission orchestrated by the exiled Czech government was carried out by the paratrooper operation Silver A which relied heavily on the support by the local Czech resistance. Hana Krupková was tasked to facilitate communication among the members, and the Krupká's home provided shelter for paratrooper commander Alfred Bartoš. The operation was the only successful government ordered assassination of a Nazi leader during the war (Heydrich died from his wounds a few days later) and, consequently, German retaliation was a bloodbath and merciless killing spree (Haasis, 2002). Apart from a barbarous hunt down and torture killings of countless alleged suspects and their families, the Nazis massacred the village of Lidice, killed 173 men, deported the mothers and sent the children to the gas chambers. After a large reward was announced for information leading to the culprits, the mission was betrayed by one of their own: Czech army soldier Karel Čurda went to the Gestapo headquarters to reveal names and hiding places of the co-conspirators. The Nazis killed all participants, their supporters and family members and erased the village of Ležáky from the map by burning it down to the ground and killing all 47 inhabitants. The weeks after Heydrich's death is remembered as one of the most brutal periods in Czech history (Svanda Theatre, 2018).

As a result of Čurda's betrayal, Hana and her husband were arrested by the Gestapo. By sleeping with her interrogator Wilhelm Schultze, Hana managed to save herself (and her husband) from death sentences. Instead of being sent to extermination camps, the Krupkás spent the rest of the war in labor concentration camps and prisons. After the war, being the only surviving members of the operation, the couple was suspected of betrayal and accused of collaboration, landing them at Pankrác Prison.

Hana behaves unobtrusively through the first half of the play. Surprised by her arrest, she is confident that "it's all a misunderstanding and that once Vaclav gets back from the concentration camp, everything will be explained" (Kinská, 2015, p. 6). The secret for her survival isn't lifted until very late in the play when she reluctantly reveals what happened in Gestapo headquarters with her German interrogator:

> We had intercourse. I wasn't raped. It simply happened. Then he let me lie on the sofa and interrogated Václav in the next room. He left the door ajar, maybe on purpose. I could hear what Václav was saying. Then I could testify the same ... It was a way of surviving. (Kinská, 2015, p. 31)

While Hana's "way of surviving" can be understood as a sacrifice to save herself and her husband, the second half of what she shares before she finally collapses on the floor shocks her cellmates to the core. By giving out a hint about the hiding place of the co-conspirators, she made herself guilty of betrayal.

Karola, The Nazi Wife

If Adina, Lída, and Hana are the "Nazi Whores," Karola is the "Nazi Wife." Karola Blaschek-Frank's collaboration is arguably closest to moral culpability on war crimes. As the wife of Protectorate's Deputy commander Karl Herrmann Frank, she spent five years on his side with access to the top echelon of the Reich. The couple frequently socialized with the most brutal Nazi of the Protectorate, the so-called "butcher of Prague," Reinhard Heydrich. There is no doubt, Karola was aware of the plan and execution of the "final solution." After Heydrich's assassination, her husband was in charge of the Nazi retaliation which connects Karola very closely to the massacres carried out under her husband's watch. The mass slaughtering of Czech villagers by the Nazis is an unerasable memory of the Czech people and also of Karola's cellmates. Her initial silence in the play upon entering the prison cell poignantly demonstrates her mortal fear of being recognized and punished by the others.

Julie, The Mysterious Kapo

Julie is a fictional multi-dimensional character with a complex past, a composite of a concentration camp inmate, Holocaust survivor and "kapo" who also acts as a liaison with the prison guard. As the playwright shares with us, her fate is "composed of several actual stories" (Svanda Theatre, 2018) and based on a Jewess named Julća mentioned in Lída Baarová's memoirs.

Julie is the most complex, most mysterious and most ambivalent character of the play. Her uniqueness is established right from the beginning: She is already there, stoically waiting "sitting in semi-darkness, as though a part of this strange cellar environment" (Kinská, 2015, p. 3). Julie seems to blend right in, it is almost too easy to ignore her. Her patience is her power and time is on her side. The others respect her authority without asking, obeying her and avoiding her gaze.

Amidst her famous cellmates—two actresses, a resistance fighter and the wife of a high Nazi official—Julie appears almost bland. The contrast is strongly carved out in the entrance scene: Adina, Lída and Hana are paraded in—one after another—unaware of their new reality. Dolled-up, the actresses are posing for the camera, as Hana enters with a suitcase "looks around, searching for someone" (Kinská, 2015, p. 3). The big historical turn at the end of WWII is the reversal of the power dynamics and it is payback time. But for the three new arrivals, the new reality hasn't sunken in yet.

This is Julie's moment and she uses her "exclusive rights" well: photographing the new inmates, she defines them as collaborators, assigning them their new identity, numbers and respective cell corners. Julie unveils the reality and rules of postwar retribution for them while a victorious voice echoes through the prison loudspeakers: They are listening to the speech of freshly returned President Beneš announcing a new beginning of the Czech nation—but they are not included.

Julie is also the one who starts the word association game in the very beginning to keep the women entertained and calm until they are sent to interrogation or have to testify. It is also Julie who—by sneaking in a piece of newspaper, spells out the name of the game for them—it's called the "national purge from Nazis"—and her cellmates "Czech traitors." Announced in the paper is the execution of Josef Pfitzner as the launch of "eight thousand trials to purge the Republic" by the newly erected 'Extraordinary People's court' which "will judge not only Nazi criminals but also Czech traitors" (Kinská, 2015, p. 9).

It is again Julie who will make sure that each of her cellmates gets their hour of justice and truth. One by one, she uses her knowledge advantage to uncover what the women try to hide. Hana, for example, only reveals her darkest secret after Julie keeps pushing further, probing Hana's narrative of the innocent resistance fighter with piercing questions. Julie also coerces Lída to correct her embellished narratives, rid them of hyperbole and semi-truths. Similarly, Julie pressures the silent Nova to reveal herself as Karola Frank.

Having been forced to be a kapo in Auschwitz deepens the understanding of Julie's interior hell. There is hardly a more difficult figure in the Holocaust than the kapo, and Julie's character subsumes the horror of this experience in all its complexity, ambivalence, and repulsiveness. Julie was trapped in the dilemma of what Holocaust scholar Lawrence Langer (1982) calls "choiceless choices" and defines as "crucial decisions ... between one form of abnormal response and another, both imposed by a situation that was in no way of the victim's own choosing" (Langer, 1982, p. 72).

Julie is the only one of the five who refuses to hope and embraces indifference and nihilism instead. Her final monologue followed by her exit into the unknown is an ode to "nothingness," her sentences are a numeration of negations: "It *doesn't* matter who I was. It *doesn't* matter whether my husband was tall and dark-haired. It *doesn't* matter whether I had one child or three ... Anonymity. Nothingness. My memory *doesn't* begin until then [emphasis added]" (Kinská, 2015, p. 33). Julie has *lived* the hell of a concentration camp but she cannot *explain* it. "You simply can't get your mind round it" (Kinská, 2015, p. 33). Denying the signifiers of language the ability to signify is her way of expressing the unspeakable REALITY of the Holocaust, which defies all attempts of comprehension, where language fails. As Bendel (2006) notes, the singularity of the Shoah is reflected in the inability or inadequacy of language to grasp it, it is the unspeakable -*Unsag-bar-keit*- which can only be described "ex negativo." In Diner's (1987, p. 159) words, Auschwitz is no-man's land, a black box, a vacuum devouring and sucking up all attempts of interpretation.

Dramaturgically, the antagonism between Julie and Karola create some of the great tension peaking in their face-off (Figure 15.2). While Julie is the first one in the cell, Karola enters as last one of the five and her silence covers a heavy secret, fatefully related to that of Julie. Karola and Julie are burdened with a knowledge and guilt that make the abyss of the Holocaust palpable. Their dark and mysterious personalities contrast effectively with Adina and Lída's chatter and bickering, making the two gossiping actresses look like tabloid trivia.

FIGURE 15.2
Julie (Lisa Hodsoll) and Karola (Aniko Olah) in 'Pankrác '45.'
Photo by Marvin Bowser

The confrontational moments between Julie and Karola significantly raise the stakes of the play leading up to a final showdown. From the very first moment, Julie attacks and humiliates Karola. When Julie orders the freshly arrived novice to wash the floor, she uses that moment to torment Karola by sharing an insidious joke with the others, unaware of Karola's identity. After Karola is gone, Julie takes off her prison uniform and puts on Karola's dress.

That significant last act can be read in different ways. Is Julie, the Jewish survivor representing the countless Holocaust victims when she puts on the clothes of Karola, the Nazi wife? Or is it an act of appropriation of the dispossessed? After Julie's statement "I don't even have the right to my own story" (Kinska, 2015, p. 33), the physical act of putting on Karola's dress may be a symbolic reclamation of her erased identity or—to go a step further—an appropriation of the perpetrator's identity by its erasure. As someone who has "no right to her own story," Julie can be anyone or no one.

Pankrác '45 as a Challenge for Today's Audience

Pankrác '45 is a highly complex and thought-provoking drama refusing to offer solutions. Instead, Kinská hands the challenge of finding the meaning, the message or the moral of the play over to us and that is where its power lies as a political play relevant for us today: It keeps engaging our minds, promotes critical thinking, asks us to weigh in, to find our position and our arguments to defend it. Through its dramatization of intense existential conflicts and moral dilemmas, the tension and discomfort of sustained ambiguity, the play challenges us, never lets us off the hook. By placing five women threatened by execution into one cell, Kinská creates an immediacy of circumstances and heightened stakes for the characters from the very first page. We are invited to take the role of silent witnesses with the task of moral judgement. Watching their stories unfold, we come to understand the moral dilemmas of the protagonists and problematic concept of "wartime collaboration" with its many shades of grey and blurred lines between resistance, complicity and collaboration. Finally, and ultimately, *Pankrác '45* makes us question the dichotomies of victim-perpetrator, resistance-collaboration and, ultimately, of good and evil.

Pankrác '45 also makes a statement on the frailty of war crime prosecution built on revenge and the dangers of what Frommer (2005) calls "retribution mania" (p. 190). We have seen how famous screen actors like Lída and Adina become easy prey for the angry mob. In the relentless hunt for traitors, their alleged crimes were blown out of proportion.

Pankrác '45 is also a feminist play exposing the double standards and sexist practices in the evaluation of female offenders. As Frommer demonstrates, female collaborators—whether famous or not—served as targets for projected blame and guilt while their male counterparts enjoyed the freedom of the double standard (Frommer, 2005). Closely connected with this double standard is the striking discrepancy between the widely and vaguely defined legal basis for an "offense against national honor" and the brutal revenge acts against these women. Any kind of "social relations with a German man" was punishable as an "offense against national honor" (Frommer, 2005, p. 205.). Whatever the nature of these "social relations," they were all too often and indiscriminately subsumed under the more popular term of "collaboration horizontale," first used by the French (Frommer, 2006) turning the offenders into "Nazi Whores." These expressions not only illustrate the highly inflammatory atmosphere of postwar punishments but also the deeply flawed term of "collaboration" as a basis for war crime justice. As the author of *Dangerous Liaisons* writes, "What other subject area encapsulates sex (the phenomenon of 'horizontal collaboration'), war (the backdrop, 1939–45) and high treason (the ultimate verdict on many collaborators)" (Davies, 2014, p. 10).

Pankrác '45 reminds us of the secret of free will. The contrast between Lída and Adina's stories point to this crucial variable in human behavior in extreme situations. Who decides to resist and who collaborates? Faced with the same choices, but taking opposite paths, the women illustrate the grey areas embedded in this context.

ART FOR HEALING AND RENEWAL

Pankrác '45 in the Context of Present-Day Global Politics

Pankrác '45 is a very timely play that speaks to our current conditions. The signs of the times are screaming for our attention and urgently call us to defend and protect human rights and democratic rights. With today's disturbing ascent of authoritarianism, the resurgence of nationalist tendencies and violent antisemitism, structural and systemic racism, new waves of migration, the erosion of once so solid pillars of democracy, falsification of facts to spread ideological propaganda, demagogical opinion leaders, and a political culture which discourages open debate, our democratic societies are at their most vulnerable point since the 1930s.

Looking at today's dangerous growth of fascist ideology and authoritarianism, we must renew the promise of NEVER AGAIN. To echo Adorno's (1966, p. 2) words, "the single genuine power standing against the principle of Auschwitz is autonomy ... the power of reflection, self-determination, of not cooperating." Anti-ideological, critical thinking is the *conditio sine qua non* to avoid the repetition of the horror of the Holocaust. Rereading Adorno's diagnosis of the "mechanisms" that make way for authoritarian societies make us aware how dangerously close we are to a return of fascist structures and regression into barbarism. The symptoms of aggressive nationalism, xenophobia, the war against free speech and a culture of fear and intimidation are strikingly visible and play into the hands of manipulating rat catchers and dogmatic minds who cannot, and will not, tolerate the polyphony of a pluralist society and the liberating power of free political discourse. The fear of free speech, especially caused by the oppressive practice of censorship and the avoidance of calling things by their names, are the insignias of the danger to come.

> The danger [is] that the horror might recur, that people refuse to let it draw near and indeed even rebuke anyone who merely speaks of it, as though the speaker, if he does not temper

things, were the guilty one, and not the perpetrators. (Adorno, 1966, p. 4)

If we allow any denial of the horrors of the Holocaust, or push realities of globally committed atrocities away from us by criticizing those who make them part of our public discourse, we are complicit and weaken our democracy's resilience against the threats of totalitarian thinking. Much of the discomfort with the current political culture is rooted in this denial, suppression or distortion of a complex reality and point to an urgent need to defend our civil liberties and affect major social change. In this context, *Pankrác '45*, as a compelling piece of live theatre, dramatizing the crucial moments of historical crossroads, has a powerful message for us: beware of the signs of the times. *Pankrác '45* embraces the act of civil courage and celebrates a tolerance of ambiguity. It resists simplified narratives and the mechanisms of the blame game, that shifts guilt onto the scapegoats—mechanisms that are so prominent in our society today.

References

Adorno, T. (1966). *Erziehung nach Auschwitz*. In: Erziehung zur Mündigkeit, Vorträge und Gespräche mit Hellmuth Becker 1959—1969. Edited by G. Kadelbach. Frankfurt a.M., 1970.

Adorno, T. (1966). Education after Auschwitz. https://archive.org/details/education-after-auschwitz-theodore-adorno/mode/2up

Bendel, C. (2006). *Die Shoa und das Problem der Unsagbarkeit*. In: Zukunft Braucht Erinnerung https://www.zukunft-braucht-erinnerung.de/die-shoa-und-das-problem-der-unsagbarkeit/

Bergsmo, (2014). CHEAH Wui Ling and YI Ping (editors), Historical Origins of International Criminal Law: Volume 2, FICHL Publication Series No. 21.

Bilková, V. (2014). *Post Second World War Trials in Central and Eastern Europe.* In Morten Concentration Camps: Kapos (n.d.). Jewish Virtual Library: A Project of AICE.
https://jewishvirtuallibrary.org/kapos

Darcy, S. (2019) *Coming to Terms with Wartime Collaboration: Post-Conflict Processes & Legal Challenges,* 45 Brook. J. Int'l L.
https://brooklynworks.brooklaw.edu/bjil/vol45/iss1/2

Davies, P. (2014). *Dangerous Liaisons—Collaboration and World War Two.* Routledge.

Demetz, P. (2009). "Prague in Danger: The Years of German Occupation, 1939–45: *Memories and History, Terror and Resistance, Theater and Jazz, Film and Poetry, Politics and War.* Farrar, Straus and Giroux.

Diner, D. (1987). *Zwischen Aporie und Apologie. Über die Grenzen der Historisierbarkeit des Nationalsozialismus, Ist der Nationalsozialismus Geschichte?* Zu Historisierung und Historikerstreit, Frankfurt/M, S. 73.

Ellis, S. (Director). (2016) *Anthropoid.* [Film]. LD Entertainment.

Expats Theatre produced an online Docudrama consisting of rehearsal scenes, cast discussions and historical archival footage. This docudrama was presented at the online Atlas "On Air Festival" (https://www.atlasarts.org/on-air/) The docudrama can be watched here:
https://youtu.be/l9n-KbPwrYs

Frommer, B. (2004). *National Cleansing: Retribution against Nazi collaboration in postwar Czechoslovakia.* Cambridge University Press.

Gilbert, L. (Director). (1975) *Operation Daybreak.* [Film]

Göbbels, J. (1942). *Der treue Helfer.* In: Völkischer Beobachter, Vienna, 55/60, 3/1/1942.

Haasis H. G. (2002) *Tod in Prag. Das Attentat auf Reinhard Heydrich.*

Kettner, F. (2008). *Holocaust global—Dan Diner reflektiert die Bedeutungsverschiebungen in der Erinnerung an den Zivilisationsbruch.* In Literaturkritik. de 12/2008

Kinská, M. (2016). *Pankrác '45.* English Translation by Barbara Day (unpublished).

Landšperkova, L. (2016) *Living In a Moral Void* in: DOK.REVUE https://www.dokrevue.com/news/living-in-a-moral-void

Lang, F. (Director). (1927). *Metropolis.* [Film]. UFA.

Langer, L. (1982). *Versions of Survival: The Holocaust and the Human Spirit.* SUNY Press.

Lamprecht, G. (Director). (1935). *Barcarole.* [Film]. UFA.

Pontecorvo, G. (Director). (1960). *Kapo* (1960) [Film]. Criterion Collection.

Radio Prague International (2009). "Die Prague Film AG Kinomatographie unter deutscher Okkupation" https://deutsch.radio.cz/die-prag-film-ag-kinematographie-unter-deutscher-okkupation-8587705.

Radio Prague International. (2010). *Executing Justice—Retributions after WW II.* [Interview with Benjamin Frommer] https://english.radio.cz/executing-justice-retributions-after-wwii-8568703

Renc, P. (Director). (2016) *The Devil's Mistress.* [Film].

Svanda Theatre Playbill (2018). *Four Plays from Prague.* Georgetown University.

Třeštíková, H.& Hejna, J. (Directors) (2016). *Doomed Beauty.* [Documentary film] Aerofilms.

Vocabulary (2022). https://www.vocabulary.com/dictionary/collaboration.

Zakaria, F. (1997). *The rise of illiberal democracy.* In Foreign Affairs; Nov/Dec 1997.

CHAPTER 16

Hine Ma Tov: A Devised Theatre Project with Holocaust Survivors and Adolescents

Valérie Issembert
Tim Reagan, Ph.D.

Beresheet: In the Beginning

In the summer of 2018, Laurie Levy Issembert, an independent theatre producer in Washington, DC, was inspired by an Israeli project produced in Detroit, MI, called Witness Theater (WT). Witness Theater is an intergenerational therapeutic theatre program that brings together Holocaust survivors and adolescents to write, rehearse, and perform stories of the Holocaust using the techniques of drama therapy. Laurie recruited her daughter Valérie to work on the project. Valérie spent over a decade in New York City working as an actor, educator, and director. She currently serves as the Director of Theatre Arts for Alexandria Country Day School in Alexandria, VA. Valérie is also the Artistic Director for BRAVO Productions: Theatre for Young Artists.

Valérie told her mother about a colleague Jessica Asch, and her involvement with the same Witness Theater project in New York. Jessica described Witness Theater (2023) as an opportunity to hear and gather firsthand testimonies of Holocaust survivors in a therapeutic journey of storytelling and story listening resulting in meaningful relationships (personal communication, September 18, 2018). Grazi-Shatzkes, Asch, & Udesky (2021) detail the origins of Witness Theater in Israel in their article *Thank you for telling—Thank you for listening: The Witness Theater Model*. The authors describe a five-phase model about the origins and goals of Witness Theater, which started in Israel more than 10 years ago as a way to link students and survivors. The phases are: (a) group cohesion, (b) testimony sharing, (c) scriptwriting, (d) rehearsal and performance, and (e) closure (Grazi-Shatzkes, et al., 2021, pp. 77–79).

As a volunteer docent at the United States Holocaust Memorial Museum (USHMM) and executive producer of BRAVO Productions: Theatre for Young Artists (2023), Laurie was drawn to the Witness Theater model and its unique place in the evolution of intergenerational storytelling. With the intent to produce a local Witness Theater production, Laurie and Valérie reached out to family friend Tim Reagan, Ph.D., to join the artistic team. Tim is a registered drama therapist/board certified trainer and holds a doctorate in expressive therapies which enabled a safe space for expression and healing. He is also the resident drama therapist at Shady Grove Adventist Healthcare Behavioral Health in Rockville, MD.

Additionally, Valérie engaged her own father Gérard Issembert, a second-generation survivor, to participate as yet another generational voice of those whose lives were profoundly affected by the Holocaust. On May 6, 2019, under the artistic guidance of Valérie and Tim, alongside the four Holocaust survivors, Gérard (2G; second-generation Holocaust survivor), and a group of five teenagers, a production inspired by Witness Theater was presented at The Charles E. Smith Jewish Day School in Rockville, MD, to commemorate Yom HaShoah, Holocaust Remembrance Day.

Yesh Matzav: It's Possible

As a lifelong student of history and a committed Jewish American, Laurie had always felt the weight of the Holocaust, but became more invested in its study after marrying a French Jew, whose family either perished or were greatly damaged as a result of what they suffered. Laurie lives with her husband in Bethesda, MD, less than 10 miles from the United States Holocaust Memorial Museum (USHMM). After volunteering at the museum in visitor services and studying extensively to become a certified guide of both the permanent exhibit and several of the auxiliary exhibits, Laurie dedicated the five years she volunteered there to her husband Gérard's paternal grandfather, Icek Eisenberg, who was deported from the Drancy work camp in France only to be exterminated in Auschwitz. However, to move from this personal connection into a theatrical process, Laurie connected with the organization producing Witness Theater in NY, Self Help Community Services (2023), subsidized by the Jewish Federation. With their guidance and blessings, Laurie set out to realize a Witness Theater inspired production in Washington, DC. Furthermore, determined to see this project to its culmination, Laurie made the decision to underwrite the production herself. Through her volunteer work at the USHMM, she connected with the museum's survivor's administrator to identify people who might be interested in the project. Laurie approached four Holocaust survivors who were comfortable sharing their stories at the museum, and they agreed to participate (Table 16.1). Since many of them were elderly and didn't drive, she arranged for transportation to and from rehearsals. Laurie recruited five middle school students from her production company to participate. They were more than eager to join the cast since several of them were working on their community service component of their Bar or Bat Mitzvah process.

ART FOR HEALING AND RENEWAL

Mishpocheh: The Family

TABLE 16.1

Participants in Witness Theater Washington, DC

Holocaust Survivors	
Ruth Cohen Born: 1930 Mukachevo, Czechoslovakia	"I survived the tragic events of the Holocaust. My father was able to help my sister and me cope with our lives."
Agi Geva Born: 1930 Budapest, Hungary	"I credit my parents with my survival. My mother was always one step ahead of whatever the family faced. My father wisely insisted that I learn a variety of languages that made me a useful prisoner."
Halina Yasharoff Peabody Born: 1932 Krakow, Poland	"I survived with my mother and sister under assumed identities as Catholics."
Rita Lifschitz Rubenstein Born: 1936 Vascauti, Romania	"I tribute my mother for my survival. Always beside me, my mother was my love and protector, blocking out the fear, hunger, and sadness that I felt as a child."
Second Generation	
Yves Gérard Issembert Born: 1947 Paris, France	"I am the son and grandson of survivors and grew up among survivors. Despite their best efforts to shield me, I learned early that there is darkness beyond darkness."
Students	
Jordan 7th grade	"I want to learn more about the Holocaust and ensure that these stories are never forgotten."
Evan 8th grade	"I want to participate in this project with the hopes the memory of the Holocaust will remain alive, ensuring that it never happens again."
Ava 7th grade	"I want to garner first-hand knowledge of the incredible bravery and resiliency of all Jews during the Holocaust, particularly the courageous survivors in this project."
Will 9th grade	"As my generation is the last that will be able to meet Holocaust survivors in person, I want to keep the memories of the Holocaust alive."
Jordyn 7th grade	"I love theater and feel honored and grateful to have the opportunity to participate in this project as part of my Bat Mitzvah project. I look forward to spending time with and learning the stories of the survivors."

Artistic Team	
Valérie Issembert Director	"My identity includes these components: Jew/3G survivor, theatre practitioner, and arts educator. Participating in Witness Theater was an opportunity for me to explore, deepen, and share the most meaningful parts of myself with my family, my students, the remarkable survivors, and my hometown."
Tim Reagan Director	"I am the gentile of the group. Having grown up in a small town in the 1970s with four Christian churches and no synagogue or temple, I had limited knowledge of Judaism, not to mention the Holocaust. I needed to be involved with this project."

Masa: The Journey

Rehearsals began in October 2018, and were held every Thursday from 6:30–8:30 pm until the performance in April 2019. Initial meetings with this intergenerational group of performers were dedicated to building trust, respect, rapport, and cohesion. By January 2019, each survivor shared a first-hand account of their life during the Holocaust in a rehearsal classroom with chairs in a circle, lights off, and a single lit candle to honor the storyteller and their memories. After each story was shared, questions were asked of survivors with thoughts, feelings, and emotions expressed by everyone. This ritual created a framework for participants to process the stories being shared, and for Valérie and Tim to take notes before transforming the data into performance material. Between rehearsals, Valérie and Tim compared notes and drafted a script from the verbal and nonverbal content of the meetings and rehearsals.

This data was synthesized, analyzed, and interpreted. Valérie and Tim wanted to capture and script the realities of survivor stories and student observations during rehearsals in a medium that was compatible for sharing in a script (Saldaña, 2011, p. 15). The goal of documenting this lived, phenomenological experience (Creswell, 2009) was to "communicate the indescribable" (Barone & Eisner, 2006, pp. 96, 101) with a script that displayed and artistically interpreted narratives, stories, and responses into an ethnodrama (Denzin, 2011; Saldaña, 2005). Dramaturgical coding was applied to the themes denoting participant objectives, conflicts, tactics, attitudes, emotions, and subtexts (Saldaña, 2013). In order to understand the meaning of the experience for the participants, Valérie and Tim functioned as participant observers gathering data, which included in-depth observations and detailed descriptions of rehearsals, interactions, interviews, and behaviors of participants. The script evolved into an analysis and interpretation of participant stories and experiences in the rehearsal process (Denzin, 2011; Saldaña, 2005).

Over the course of the six-month rehearsal process, Valérie and Tim met regularly to co-write, artistically interpret the stories, extract imagery, determine appropriate stage conventions, and shape the script. During the process, Valérie and Tim also facilitated rehearsals where staging unfolded organically. As scenes developed, costumes and props were incorporated, much like a typical rehearsal process with a preordained script. By the end of January, the script was complete and had been revised numerous times. However, additions and adjustments continued to occur up until a month before the performance.

Hatzaga: The Production

The production opened with a scene in which the survivors were introduced to the students in overlapping conversation, highlighting many of the commonalities they had with one another, before the consequences of the Holocaust were visited upon the survivors. Shared experiences voiced in the opening scene included playing outside with friends, moments with families, and even going to summer camp. However, the mood shifted after one survivor shared that she also went to "camp" twice, only this camp was called Auschwitz. This tonal shift allowed us to move the piece into a space where the participants were poised to re-tell, re-imagine, and honor stories of survival, including an account by Gérard and how his life was shaped and influenced by the experience of his parents.

After the opening, the company moved into the realm of song. Early in the process, a common theme was discovered: the transformative and transportive power of music and how its ability to give hope saved many throughout the Holocaust. One of our survivor participants wrote a memoir in the USHMM's ongoing publication, *Echoes of Memory* (United States Holocaust Memorial Museum, 2023) in which she describes how hearing opera sung by one of her fellow prisoners in Auschwitz completely elevated her soul and gave her the courage to fight another day (United States Holocaust Museum, 2023). A version of this scene was featured in the production. Additionally, and to impress upon the audience how the power of song worked to unite and uplift, we also created a brief episode of rejoicing in song at the beginning of the script. The whole cast gathered to sing "Hine ma tov" from psalm 133:3 (Tanakh: The Holy Scriptures, 1985), which translates to "how good and pleasant it is for brothers and sisters to sit together."

Ed: Witness

The staging of the stories emerged spontaneously during rehearsals. Actors would improvise a moment from a survivor story and then the ensemble would unpack what pieces of these improvisations felt stage worthy. One of the more fluid moments in the process came about when participants were asked to choreograph a sequence of gestures based on childhood memories. As the actors recalled these familiar or beloved experiences from their childhoods, they created a gestural dance that could be repeated. This resulted in a visual canon of gestural memories which slowly morphed into an ensemble movement piece. Each actor performed their unique physical memory, linking survivor recollections with those of the younger actors. In performance, the ensemble moved downstage in a line towards the audience to share their kinetic sculptures, a visual and communal remembrance of innocence, joy, and discovery. To complete the scene, each company member stepped forward and stated the word: "witness." The word witness is different from the conventional meaning of the word for a "bystander." Instead of allowing for any ambiguity, the audience is invited, through text and staging, to become witnesses themselves. Sajnani (2012) wrote about the concept of witnessing as a relational aesthetic in drama therapy and how witnessing socially effective and affective performances bring audiences into greater proximity to each other and to those performing. This gathering in a communal place, a Theatre, prepares the audience for the journey they are about to witness. Through the staging and storytelling, performers requested that the audience do more than standby and be entertained, but to be accountable, as they were participant-observers, essential to this particular journey of witnesses.

We were determined to prepare and remind the audience why they were in attendance that evening. Therefore, the production was punctuated with cold, hard, and historical facts. After the opening scene, a slideshow produced by the United States Holocaust Memorial Museum (United States Holocaust Memorial Museum, 2023b) was presented. Survivors in this production hailed from the Czech Republic, Poland, Hungary, Romania, and France. The video showed details of when and how these countries fell. It was important to share this history in real time, before diving deeper into the world of storytelling. We also added a convention in performance to honor one person that each survivor had lost to the Holocaust. After survivor specific scenes, each approached one of two podiums on the stage and gestured to an intentionally empty chair that was illuminated in the audience for all to see. The survivors then stated for whom that specific seat was reserved. This convention felt necessary to connect, as well as bookend the diversity of survivor accounts. Subsequently, a student member of the cast would join the survivor at the podium and provide details about the survivor's life and postwar existence.

Edut: Testimony

All of the survivor stories included physical and emotional violence. Perhaps for the sensibilities of our younger performers, during rehearsals when stories were shared, the survivors often left out details of certain brutalities they had endured. In private conversations with the survivors, Tim and Valérie learned that, in fact, they were reluctant to recount the most graphic details of their experiences. For example, one participant was caught in an explosion and lost a thumb. When recounting this experience, the survivor did not speak of the carnage in that particular moment of the memory, but rather moved quickly to explain how she was cared for in the aftermath of the horror. The staging of the play attempted to incorporate the physical nature of such realities without venturing too far into the realm of violence and in some instances, stage combat. In fact, graphic content was predominantly staged in tableau or slow motion, and often used underscoring coupled with survivor narration.

In an attempt to incorporate as many survivors as we could, we worked to honor their individual wishes regarding the sharing of their stories. Ruth, the eldest survivor, was reluctant to join the ensemble as an actor on stage. She had no interest in being in front of a live audience. However, she was eager to participate in the process. In discussions with Ruth about how she might feel comfortable participating, we learned that Ruth was willing to maintain a presence in the production solely in voiceover. It was decided together that while Ruth would never appear physically on stage, she would participate as a voiceover actor and narrate throughout the production. She was as much a part of the ensemble as her fellow actors who appeared on stage (Figure 16.1), and upon reflection, her participation as such was eerily powerful, unique, and important. Her voice carried the stories through difficult moments on stage and in that manner lent a gravity to such instances that would not have been the same with a live actor.

Figure 16.1
Agi's story: Entering Auschwitz to be separated, hosed, and, for some, sent directly to death Photo credit: Kirchner, M., 2019

L'Chaim: To Life

As the script moved beyond the immediate survival of our participants during the war, their postwar stories came to feature heavily in the latter half of our production. Many survivors returned to their homes after the war, only to find those homes had been destroyed, populated with their enemies, or sold to new owners. The homeless, and "homelandless," found themselves in displaced persons (DP) camps, facilities administered by allied authorities and the United Nations Relief and Rehabilitation Administration (UNRRA). Those who were not exterminated were left with nothing. They were free, but their previous lives had mostly been erased. In 1933, the Jewish population in Europe stood around 9.5 million (United States Holocaust Memorial Museum, 2023b). By 1945, two out of three had been killed, and the European Jewish population stood at roughly 3.5 million (United States Holocaust Memorial Museum, 2023b). Of these survivors, over 250,000 landed in displaced person (DP) camps (United States Holocaust Memorial Museum, 2023c).

There are numerous accounts of the ways in which those who survived became, yet again, children of the diaspora—homeless and penniless. Rita's own story, recounted and re-imagined in this production, is one such example. Her mother returned to her home after the war only to find it occupied by soldiers who immediately threw her out. In rehearsal, Rita shared that her mother went to reclaim precious belongings that she had hidden when they were forced to leave. To illuminate this experience of postwar survival in our production, we staged a version of Rita's story. In fact, in a departure from the traditional structure of the Witness Theater (WT) model, this scripted scene was not a direct memory. Rather, it was presented as an entirely re-imagined scenario of what it might have been like for Rita, as a small child, to return to her family home with her mother. In reality, Rita did not accompany her mother on this journey. In the scene, Rita accompanies her mother. Much of the content of the scene and the experience of Rita's mother, Taibl, was historically accurate. However, we wondered if Rita really had returned with her, what that might have looked like. Rita was interested in that exploration, too. What emerged was an artistic interpretation of this imagined homecoming. Taibl did recover her husband's tallit (prayer shawl) and photo albums, which Rita brought to rehearsal to share with the company.

The closing scene of the production was directly linked to the opening. The production started with a group scene in which actors spoke directly and individually to the audience, breaking the fourth wall and inviting them in. In the closing scene, survivors and youth sat together, speaking directly to one another in conversation (Figure 16.2). The closing sought to highlight how the journey of witnessing had formed these individuals into an ensemble, in solidarity and friendship. The ensemble then rose together and reprised their gestural dance. This artistic choice and subsequent repetition of the initial sequence served to recall the collective journey they had taken as student, survivor, and now, audience. In the final moment of the performance, Ruth's voice broke through the underscore, the actors stood in a line along the lip of the stage pointing at the audience, and we heard the ensemble speak in unison—"Witness. Witness. Witness"—once again, with an invitation for them to join the group, to be accountable, and to be a witness (Table 16.2).

FIGURE 16.2
Breaking Bread. Front (left to right): Gérard, Agi, Halina, Rita. Back row (left to right): Ava, Jordan, Jordyn, Evan, Will. Photo credit: Kirchner, M., 2019

TABLE 16.2

Makheshavott Akharonott: Final Thoughts

Holocaust Survivors	
Ruth	"I participated in the production because, I thought it was a worthwhile thing to do. Doing this project with fellow survivors and the youngsters was an experience I did not expect, but was good after all. I felt good about doing the play to help the youngsters understand somewhat more about Shoah and perhaps its consequences."
Agi	"I participated in Witness Theater, as I was curious about something I have not done before. The experience was quite a challenge. It was unexpected in every way. After the performance I felt success and accomplishment. I had a desire to do more and be even more involved."
Halina	"I participated at the urging of my friend, Ruth Cohen, who explained to me what this project was. My experience was a lesson on how I can bear witness about the Holocaust in other ways than by telling my story, which I do frequently."
Rita	"I decided to participate in Witness Theater, because I thought it would be educational. Young people are our future. In our production, the students took on the roles of our lives before, during, and after the War when we started our lives again. I learned a lot from working with these exceptional and respectful students. They had the opportunity to hear our survival stories; all very different. It touched my heart and soul that the students were eager to learn more about us. The directors created a wonderful atmosphere, inspiring and encouraging us along the way. My fellow survivors and I now share another special bond."
Second Generation	
Gérard	"Being a part of this Witness Theater experience was a deeply moving experience for me, on several levels. Born into the remnants of a family torn by the holocaust, I simply inherited their memories and their pain. They survived. And then they lived. And then they gave me life and love. I am in awe of the strength all survivors displayed in reconstructing their lives and in sharing their experiences. Being on stage with three of them, I felt both a great sense of humility and infinite respect. I am honored and profoundly proud that my wife Laurie and my daughter Valérie created this extraordinary event."

Students	
Jordan	"The experience was amazing and important. I formed strong connections with both the survivors as well as the other students and directors in our group. I was always excited to see the survivors at each rehearsal. Our group became like a family. In the end it was an honor to be able to share these stories of survival on stage, as well as play a role in ensuring that we will never forget. I feel privileged to have been able to work with such amazing people, and to be trusted to tell their stories. I felt really proud after our performance. I was proud of our group and how we worked together to share these stories."
Ava	"I participated in Witness Theater, because I knew that someday Holocaust survivors will be gone, and I don't want the Holocaust to disappear with them. This experience had a strong impact on me. In some ways it was heavy, for the stories shared by the survivors were devastating. In other ways, it was light, because of the joy we felt from being with each other. There were many moments we smiled, and many moments we cried. There were moments of song and moments of silence. I feel the contrasts often when I look back, and can never find one word to describe it all. Truly, it was a rollercoaster in all the best ways. I feel stronger and proud for what I have done and what we all have done. We have shown what others went through during the Holocaust and did it in a way that was so powerful."
Will	"I had little experience connecting with Holocaust survivors. I knew Witness Theater would be a great chance to learn more about the Holocaust. The experience was far different from anything that I could have expected. We spent so much of our time together listening to, and attempting to process the stories and experiences of the survivors. While in a traditional theatrical production the story already exists, here that was not the case. In fact, I was so engrossed in the unbelievable stories of the survivors that I saw the theatrical element of the program as secondary to the sharing process. One of my biggest takeaways from this project was that every survivor had a different story to tell. After the performances, I felt proud of the work that had been accomplished. I was humbled by everyone who came up to me and said how moved they were by the production."

Artistic Team	
Valérie	"The experience will remain one of the most important pieces of work I have collaborated on, both personally and professionally. The stakes were high, yet despite the enormous responsibility to deliver exceptional work, the group made me feel creative and capable. Often, I was overwhelmed with emotion. In the face of a subject steeped in 'wrong', the project felt 'right'."
Tim	"There were moments when I was speechless, holding back tears. I was aghast at the brutality these remarkable women faced as children. I was amazed at how they emerged and flourished as strong, perseverant, resilient, loving, patient, and kind and caring human beings. I am honored to have been entrusted to help share these important stories."

Epiylog: Epilogue

The North American Drama Therapy Association (NADTA) promotes the application of drama therapy techniques to create a context in which stories can be told, goals set, problems solved, feelings expressed, and oftentimes catharsis achieved (2023). Witness Theater provides more than a context for storytelling. In our production, we found participants committed to social justice, prepared for taking risks, and passionate about autonomy with the self, other, and group (Amabile and Pillemer, 2012, pp. 8–9). The Witness Theater model embraces these motivators. And, as Beardall (2007) stated, "when people share their own experience or story with another, they give some part of themselves away in order to help someone else; both parties benefit from this" (p. 113). We were all helped in so many seen and unseen ways.

According to Valérie, co-director and co-author of this chapter, her father was born Yves Gérard Eisenberg and was the second of four brothers born in France between 1944–1953. After the war, his family re-established themselves in Paris. Despite growing a successful family business, postwar Paris was still plagued by antisemitism and Jewish sounding names did nothing for their bearers. Four young Jewish boys were certainly not immune to these antisemitic tauntings. In 1962, my grandfather changed the family surname to Issembert, a version of an old French name. If nothing else, it would not be read as Jewish. I believe it helped to offset some of the anti-Jewish hate that my father and uncles would have encountered during the remainder of their childhood. To this day, the only people in the world with that surname are my immediate relatives. We are not numerous, but we are unique.

This chapter is dedicated to the memory of Rita Rubenstein, one of the Holocaust survivors who participated in the Witness Theater Project.

References

Amabile, T. M., & Pillemer, J. (2012). Perspectives on the social psychology of creativity. *The Journal of Creative Behavior, 46*(1), 3–15, doi: 10.1002/jocb.002/jocb.001.

Barone, T. & Eisner, E. (2006). Art-based Educational Research. *Handbook of Complementary Methods in Education Research.* Ed. Green, J., Camilli, G., & Elmore, P. J. NY: Lawrence Erlbaum Associates.

Beardall, N. (2007). *A program evaluation research study on the implementation of the mentors in violence prevention program in a public high school.* (Doctoral dissertation).
http://search.proquest.com.ezproxyles.flo.org/pqdtft/docview/304801317/.

Amabile, T. M., & Pillemer, J. (2012). Perspectives on the social psychology of creativity. *The Journal of Creative Behavior, 46*(1), 3–15, doi: 10.1002/jocb.002/jocb.001.

Bravo Productions (2023). *Theatre for young audiences.*
https://www.facebook.com/www.bravoproductions.org.

Beardall, N. (2007). *A program evaluation research study on the implementation of the mentors in yiolence prevention program in a public high school.* (Doctoral dissertation). http://search.proquest.com.ezproxyles.flo.org/pqdtft/docview/304801317/.

Creswell, J. W. (2009). *Research design: Qualitative, Quantitative, and Mixed Methods Approaches* (3rd ed.). Sage Publications, Inc.

Denzin, N. (2011). The reflexive interview and a performative social science. *Qualitative Research, 1*(23), 23–46.

Grazi-Shatzkes, S., Asch, J., & Udesky, E. (2021). Thank you for telling—thank you for listening: The Witness Theater model. *Drama Therapy Review, 7*, 77–94.
https://doi.org/10.1386/dtr_00062_1.

North American Drama Therapy Association (2023). *What is drama therapy?* https://www.nadta.org/what-is-drama-therapy.

Saldaña, J. (2013). *The coding manual for qualitative researchers.* Sage Publications, Inc.

Saldaña, J. (2012). Theatre finds a way: Questions and some answers about the 2012 survey. *Teaching Theatre, 24*(1), 44–48.

Saldaña, J. (2011). *EthnoTheatre: Research from page to stage.* Left Coast Press.

Saldaña, J. (2005). *Ethnodrama: An anthology of reality Theatre.* AltaMira Press.

Sajnani, N. (2012). The Implicated Witness: Towards a Relational Aesthetic in Dramatherapy. *Dramatherapy, 34*(1), 6–21. https://doi.org/10.1080/02630672.2012.657944

Self Help (2023). *Community Based Programs.*
https://selfhelp.net/community-based-programs/.

Tanakh: The Holy Scriptures. (1985). Jewish Publication Society of America.
https://www.sefaria.org/Psalms.133?ven=Tanakh:_The_Holy_Scriptures,_published_by_JPS&lang=bi

United States Holocaust Memorial Museum (2023a). *Echoes of Memory: Survivor Reflections on Testimonies.* https://www.ushmm.org/remember/holocaust-reflections-testimonies/echoes-of-memory.

United States Holocaust Memorial Museum (2023b). *Holocaust Encyclopedia: What was the Holocaust?* https://encyclopedia.ushmm.org/content/en/article/introduction-to-the-holocaust.

United States Holocaust Memorial Museum (2023c). *Displaced persons.* https://www.ushmm.org/collections/bibliography/displaced-persons.

Witness Theater (2023). *Witness Theatre: Innovative Intergenerational Program.* https://selfhelp.net/witness-theater/.

CHAPTER 17

Performing *Defiant Requiem*: The Journey of a Messenger Not a Scholar

Murry Sidlin
With Karen Berman, Ph.D.

Terezín was a cultural miracle entwined with the norms of insanity, chaos and wholesale murder.—Murry Sidlin

How Verdi's *Requiem* Came to Terezín

The core of my obsession over the ghetto-concentration camp Terezín for the past 20 years lies within the Council of Jewish Elders (Terezín.org, n.d.). This was a group from 1941–1944 that the Nazis instructed to manage the camp, and one of their jobs was to select those who would be deported to various camps in the East. It was up to the Council of Elders to make the moral decisions that undergirded that selection (Terezín.org, n.d.). It was a horrid job. In addition, the Council was required to give the illusion that the Jews were self-governed to the extent that even cultural events were overseen should controversies arise as they did on occasion. While the Council of Elders, including Rabbi Leo Baeck (Plen, n.d.) and Jacob Edelstein (Terezín.org, n.d.), could not improve life at Terezín, they tried desperately with every decision not to make conditions worse.

When the Council of Jewish Elders learned that Rafael Schächter (Karas, 1985) was putting together performances of Giuseppe Verdi's *Requiem*, (Shefer-Vanson, 2015) a renowned 90-minute oratorio of 1874 steeped in the Catholic liturgy, the Elders became quite upset. There were many Orthodox rabbis and congregants who felt that performing the Verdi *Requiem*, or any requiem mass, would be the same as presenting a Catholic service disguised as a concert. When Jews, Jewish culture, and Jewish traditions were under attack and, in fact, when the future of all Jews was threatened, why would a chorus of 150 imprisoned Jews create such controversy?

The Council of Elders was livid, and Schächter was summoned to explain his justification. Although we do not know exactly what happened in that meeting, the logical process would have been for each Council member to state his objections and for Schächter to attempt a response. Schächter's point was a typical and logical clarification by an artist: that the meaning of any great work of art is never limited to its original intent; that Jews can be deeply touched by the beauty of Michelangelo's *Pieta*, Bach's *St. Matthew Passion*, Handel's *Messiah*, any of the great Christian works of art or music.

Furthermore, he was delivering a powerful statement to the Nazis on behalf of the Terezín population, which he knew would not be understood, that beauty was their nutrition. The original Verdi work was begun in memory of Giovanni Rossini, but not completed until the death of Verdi's favorite poet, philosopher, author Alessandro Manzoni. Both Verdi and Manzoni had fought against oppression and for the reunification of Italy. The *Requiem* was not really intended for liturgical purposes. To Verdi it was another opera.

Schächter's interpretation of the lyrics of Verdi's *Requiem* promised judgment by God and punishment upon the Nazis, but would be undetected in Latin: "when the Judge takes His seat, whatever is hidden will be revealed and nothing will remain unavenged" (Verdi's Requiem Text in English, 2013, lines 37–41). Yet in the final phrase of Verdi's *Requiem* "Deliver me, Lord, from eternal death on that awful day. Deliver me" (Verdi's Requiem Text in English, 2013, lines 37–41) was reinterpreted by Schächter as "liberate me," to represent a spiritual reawakening and salvation.

I was made aware of the meeting between Schächter and the Council by my dear friend Edgar Krasa, who was the bunkmate of Rafael (Raphi) Schächter, and shared these events: Edgar told me that he finished his daily work and returned to the hovel that he shared with Raphi to await Raphi's return after which they would walk to rehearsal. Schächter entered the room returning from his confrontation with the Council as Krasa described it to me. Schächter had steam coming from his ears and his neck was bright red. Edgar told me that he was frightened that Schächter was going to have a stroke. Schächter recounted that each Council member had raked him over the coals, demanding that rehearsals be discontinued and performances cancelled. Schächter said he told the Council that he would take their edict to the chorus that evening and they, and he, would make the decision about performing Verdi's music. That evening, Schächter told the chorus what had happened and the order by the Council to discontinue. Schächter, gestured to the door, and said to the chorus members "if any of you do not want to continue, there is the door and I'll understand." The chorus was unanimous and voted to continue rehearsing and preparing for performance. Three members of the chorus who survived reiterated to me the exact story I have indicated. Verdi's *Requiem* in Latin would now be performed courageously with defiance and with the hope that Nazi evil would be punished.

But, here is the surprising last element of that story. Nobody can tell me what went on when Schächter went back to the Council of Elders to announce the defiance of Schächter and his chorus. I have lived with this for several years—the fact that we had no information about what took place in that room or the nature of the final confrontation. This question has inspired me to write a one-act drama entitled *Mass Appeal, 1943* (Mass Appeal 1943, 2017), soon to have a new title change to *The Verdi Verdict,* an attempt to explore what took place in that room between the Council of Elders and Schächter. Let us call it a speculative history.

A Book Beckons Me On My Quest

My work on this subject began when I was on the faculty of the University of Minnesota. I had a terrific job there. I loved the job, but I was offered an excellent position at the Oregon Symphony. I would be working alongside a wonderful conductor and my dearest friend, James DePreist. I took the job and we became the conducting staff of the Oregon Symphony. As I was getting ready to move to Oregon, I was walking down Hennepin Avenue in Minneapolis and I passed a used bookstore. On the street in front of the store was a stack of books on sale piled in a kind of pyramid fashion. I saw a book sticking out half way up the pyramid, and I thought, this looks interesting. That book seemed to be beckoning to me and so I put my hand on it and started to pull it out, slowly, very slowly. I worried that the pyramid would collapse. Without disturbing the pyramid, I successfully pulled the book out. It was titled *Music at Terezín: 1941–1945* by Joža Karas (1985). Karas was a member of the Hartford, Connecticut Symphony Orchestra, and he was not Jewish, and he was not a part of the Holocaust, but he knew a number of Czech musicians who had survived the war. The surviving musicians had provided him with accounts of Terezín, its complexities and brutal starvation, disease and yet thousands of performances and lectures.

First Steps of Discovery

That was the beginning of my journey. I had lost members of my father's family in the Holocaust, and this book spoke to me. The book revealed many names of performing musicians and composers all exposed in short chapters in the book that delved into what is known about these musicians and composers and what they did in Terezín. I opened the book to a random page, to a short chapter on Rafael Schächter (Karas, 1985). I stood on the street corner and read this chapter which said that in Terezín, Schächter had only one smuggled score of Verdi's *Requiem* and was inspired to create a volunteer choir of 150 singers and to teach them to sing Verdi's *Requiem* by rote. I read that statement and I thought to myself, as a conductor, this is nonsense. This monumental concert was accomplished in a forced labor camp without nutrition, without medical attention, without protection from the elements, while inmates lived in terror. Yet, under those conditions, the author said Schächter was able to put together 16 performances of Verdi's *Requiem*. I could not believe this to be true. But if I could prove it were true, there was a significant story here. More importantly, I wondered: why perform Verdi's *Requiem* in a place where everybody is imprisoned for being Jewish. And I needed to expose this story one way or the other: The performances did or did not happen.

Finding Survivors of Terezín

I had now moved to Portland, Oregon. In addition to becoming a conductor on the staff of the Oregon Symphony, I had received a call from a small college outside of Portland, Pacific University. They offered me a chair in the Department of Music if I would lecture once a week and give one concert a semester on campus. I love teaching, so I accepted the offer. When I went to have a get-acquainted lunch with the university president, she said that she had heard that I was entering into serious study of music of the Holocaust era. She introduced me to two professors on the faculty who were very adept at research and both of whom were Holocaust scholars. They taught me how to post on a Holocaust website that I was looking for people who survived Terezín, sang in the choir of the *Requiem* performances, were in the audiences of any musical events of Terezín, or, most importantly, had known Rafael Schächter.

I sat back and waited, and about a week later, I got a very terse response from Israel: "What do you want them for?" That was it. I asked my two professor friends how I should respond. They surmised that the terse response reflected a suspicion that I was in some way looking to make money off of this story. They recommended that I respond with exactly what I was trying to prove: if the story of Schächter and the Elders were true, there might be something monumental, something heroic, about why this conductor chose this particular composition. I wrote back that my only motive was to find the truth, and that I would love to speak to people who knew something about the motives of the conductor and what took place at rehearsals.

A week later, I heard back from an Israeli responder, who turned out to be the niece of the conductor Rafael Schächter, who was living, and still lives, in Jerusalem. She wrote me that her mother was Schächter's sister living in Haifa. I wrote back that "I would love to have more information because I have a feeling that your uncle was a cultural hero and I would like to create his portrait." A few days later, I received an email from the niece saying that her mother remembered that Schächter had a colleague with whom he roomed at Terezín who was also trained as a cook and worked in the (so-called) kitchen. Schächter's sister recalled that the roommate said if he ever got out alive, he had family in the catering business somewhere in the Boston area. She said, unfortunately, that is all she knew. I wrote back thanking her and asked if she knew the name of the roommate. She said his last name was Krasa, which she also said was a common Czech name, and she did not remember the first name, but thought it might begin with an E.

I called the telephone information operator and I said, "I'm looking for the last name, Krasa initial E somewhere in the Boston area." The operator said, "I have an Edgar in Newton, Massachusetts." I said, "Okay, I'll take it." The conversation went something like this. "Hello (deep voice slowly stated)," he said. I remember immediately thinking: right age, right accent. I said "Mr. Krasa, my name is Murry Sidlin and I am a conductor." He said, "Did I win something?" "No," I said, "you didn't win anything. Mr. Krasa, I have one question for you and then, I promise, I'll never bother you again. Does the name Rafael Schächter mean anything to you?" The phone went very quiet, and then he said, "Well, I named my second son after him." I said to him, "If I came to Boston, could I take you to lunch?" He said, "Oh, I did win something, a free lunch."

I knew that if I let it go, this important story was going to disappear. I called him when I got to Boston and told him where my hotel was. He said, "Good. I'll meet you there at 1:00." When he came at 1:00, I said, "Mr. Krasa, it is wonderful to meet you. I have a table booked." He said, "Not tables. Let's get in the car. Lunch is waiting for us at home."

I was a complete stranger and he took me into his home where I spent six hours. While we were going over the whole story, he picked up the phone and he called Eva Rocek, a Holocaust survivor who sang in Schächter's chorus and who lived outside of Chicago. Then, I was able to connect with another surviving member of the choir, Marianka Zadikow-May of Pine Bush, New York who died only recently at age 99. I also discovered another major character in this story who was Zdenka Fantlova (Fantlova, 2023), a Czech actor and writer, and she passed away at 100 just two weeks before I began writing this chapter. These were my teachers. They told me this amazing story that, in Terezín, a conductor taught a choir Verdi's *Requiem* by rote and gave 16 performances in the camp. In fact, Verdi's *Requiem* was performed for the Red Cross (Defiant Requiem—Verdi at Terezín, n.d.); when they arrived in Terezín as a ploy by the Nazis to deceive the world into believing this was a "Jewish paradise," given by the Führer to the Jews as a model village or spa town (The History Press, n.d.).

However, the *Requiem* was used to defy secretly the Nazis with the Latin words that evil would be punished. Schächter said to the chorus, "we will sing to the Nazis what we cannot say" (Gray, 2013, para. 27). At the same time, it was a very hopeful, spiritual work that reminded the Jews of their humanity. Schächter knew that this was one of the great masterworks in the choral repertoire and managed to put together a volunteer choir of 150 people. I learned that, after the first performance, two-thirds of the choir were deported, and, so, with deportations came importations and new singers recruited by Schächter who started over again twice, ultimately with three different choirs.

Fred Terna, a survivor who attended Verdi's *Requiem* at Terezín three times, said "our main weapon against the Nazis was art and intellectual activity" (Brodeur, 2022, para. 24). "It was harmony." I responded "Yes, Verdi was a great composer." "No, not that kind of harmony" he said. "150 people on stage. One person guides the voices, the mood, the expression, the light and dark, and we in the audience sensed every nuance." Fred was saying it was not a matter of superficial harmony. It was the act of being harmonious and telling the audience through Verdi's music, it was still possible, in spite of the profound degrees of chaos and insanity. Terezín survivor and chorus member in Terezín Vera Schiff said "the words and music took us out of our misery, out of the drabness and the hunger and the fear … " (Reich, 2017, para. 10).

Learning from the Survivors About Music as Hope

In addition, I learned there were approximately 20 composers who were creating new music in Terezín. It is hopeful when people create new music, the opposite of giving up and accepting defeat. Now, there is music that goes over the barbed wire and connects with the music that was present throughout Europe at that time, and there is music that was being created as an eyewitness. The kind of music that was created there had character, longing, and a broken heart. It was music of the messenger, hopeful music of fate. Now that we have this music, we must perform it or we will be murdering these composers a second time.

Making music was spiritual resistance for the prisoners. Viktor Ullmann (Karas, 1985) was one of the most important composers in the camp. He would have been a remarkably famous composer had he lived. It turned out that he, Viktor Ullmann, was the self-appointed music critic of the camp. The Terezín musicians all faced evaluation of their music and music-making because a high standard had to be upheld as a sign of respect for the audience.

Krasa, who died in 2017, illuminated this for me, along with the six other people with whom I spoke who were survivors of Terezín. Survivor and chorus member Marianka Zadikow-May told me that they could not whisper in rehearsal for fear of inviting the wrath of Schächter (Figure 17.1). As a conductor myself, I think I understood; that was the only way they could make progress and achieve the level of music-making and the level of power, drama and beauty that he required. The chorus members were not professional in any way. Most of them could not read music, and it would not have helped if they did, because Schächter had the only score. Schächter also had to conduct from memory because he had to give his only score to the pianist, Gideon Klein (Music and the Holocaust: Gideon Klein, n.d.)

FIGURE 17. 1
Rafael Schächter and Inmates Performing Verdi's Requiem at Terezín in 1944.
Photo from Defiant Requiem Foundation Website Courtesy of The Terezín Foundation

I asked one of the survivors, who was a pianist in the Terezín camp, Edith Kraus Steiner, about the quality of the musical performances. She said "you would have been proud of this choir in any urban setting." Then, she told me more that struck me as remarkable. She told me she played daily and people came into the room where she was playing or practicing, and they would sit; sometimes it was three people, sometimes it was 10 people, sometimes it was 30 people. They were hungry and they were sick, and she played and she could see the difference that the music was making. While playing this music for her fellow prisoners, she said she remembered why she became a musician. It was not about the business of music, just about the music. She said the prisoners were so deeply inside the music that they had all returned to Verdi's desk. She said she had always been a musician—but in Terezín, she rediscovered music.

I was obsessed with what she said about being so deeply inside the music that she had returned to Verdi's desk. And I thought, have I ever returned to the absolute source of any work of art, to the moment of its creation, to the big bang of any musical creation. Edith then said to me, "keep looking, keep probing and, above all, be humble, and surely, the composer will invite you to his or her desk."

Creating *Defiant Requiem* to Uplift

People asked Viktor Ullmann: How can you compose in a place where 200 people die each day? Ullmann replied, according to Zdenka Fantlova, that, "it was very simple because, for him, composing music is like struggling for life. It was uplifting. It was strength. It was energy. It was part of the history of the Holocaust." Fantlova went on to say, "I have a suspicion that most people see the Holocaust as only gas chambers and the number of six million that died. What I was seeing was this kind of strength and survival which you cannot compare to anything else" (Composers of the Holocaust, n.d. & Karas, 1985). That is exactly why I, and my colleagues, through *Defiant Requiem*, explore these composers who were there and the music they created. For many throughout the world, even the musical world, this music is entirely unknown.

Composer Viktor Ullmann stated: "Many may ask: Why new music? Aren't there already enough old masterpieces to delight music lovers? But a secret law forces productive people to create" (Ludwig, 2022, p. 199). If you are an artist, if you are a creator, there is a secret law that forces productive people to create new music, inspire and transform audiences. This is my manifesto given to me by Ullmann, my explanation of how terrified prisoners could produce such beauty. Schächter wrote his last two piano sonatas for Edith Kraus Steiner, and Edith premiered them in Terezín. When pianist Alice Herz-Sommer (Stoessinger, 2012) was asked why make music in a place like this, she answered "music prevented hatred." There were a number of people trying to use the one piano there. I wondered how they worked out rehearsals.

All I had learned compelled me to begin to create a full concert and narrative presentation representing Verdi's *Requiem* as presented by the volunteer choir at Terezín. My hero Schächter had died in 1945 on a death march, having been deported to Auschwitz and three other camps. He died one month before liberation.

As I was reviewing the compositions by the Terezín composers, one interesting piece touched me by Karel Berman (Karas, 1985) who survived the war. Not only was Karel a great composer, but also a wonderful pianist, excellent conductor, and a magnificent bass singer. When they sang the Verdi *Requiem*, he was the bass soloist. After he survived the war, he changed the name of the second movement of this composition to *Auschwitz Corpse Factory*.

I learned early on that most people did not know about the events of spiritual resistance through the arts that took place at Terezín and a multitude of other such prisons that gave hope and some element of harmony to the prisoners. It was because of this book that I had stumbled upon with the revelations of such rich and significant artistic community that I became obsessed with finding out more. Bottom line, here is what I learned. Terezín was a cultural miracle entwined with the norms of insanity, chaos and wholesale murder. I was inspired to uncover what other people knew about Terezín.

Three incidents I will share made me realize how little known the rich musical heritage of Terezín was at the time. The first incident occurred when I was in Prague and I had a very close friend who was there at the time guest conducting the Czech Philharmonic. We were having lunch one day and we were joined at lunch by the marvelous pianist and conductor Daniel Barenboim (Duchen, 2022) who was going to appear with my friend in concert. We discussed Terezín and I gave him a five-minute overview of my exploration of the music from Terezín. Barenboim asked how it was that he did not know about this. He had lived in Argentina among Germans and in Jerusalem, and he had lived among a lot of survivors and he considered himself well-versed on the issues of the Holocaust.

The second incident: I was assembling a board of directors for my Defiant Requiem Foundation (Defiant Requiem Foundation, n.d.) and one of the people I was interested in having on our board was a man named Christian Kennedy, who at that time was a Special Envoy for Holocaust Issues at the State Department (U.S. Department of State Archives, 2007). I asked him when he first learned about the fact that Terezín had this deep and rich musical history, and he said he learned about it the day I came into his office and told him.

The third incident: I was living in Portland, Oregon and I was at a friend's birthday party and I was sitting next to Rabbi Emanuel Rose (Oregon Jewish Museum and Center for Holocaust Education, n.d.). I said to him that I had just come back from doing research at the Holocaust Memorial Museum in Washington, D.C. I had gone through the museum shop on the way out and saw many new books and new recordings and all sorts of memorabilia pertaining to the Holocaust that I had not seen before. Rabbi Rose said this new information was all coming from the grandchildren who were becoming the spokespeople for the history and stories of their own families. Then he said, when there were events of an apocalyptic nature such as the Holocaust, the facts come out right away, but it is the truth that takes a long time, and it appears that we are finally ready for the truth.

Performing *Defiant Requiem*

In 2002, we premiered *Defiant Requiem* at the Portland Expo Center with the Oregon Symphony. This became what I refer to as the concert-drama with actor narration, full orchestra, 150 singers, film of the Terezín camp that also included testimony from survivors. We gave our first performance of *Defiant Requiem* in Portland, Oregon in April 2002. In 2006 we were invited by the Terezín Memorial and Prague Spring to present our first of three performances in Terezín. Altogether we have presented *Defiant Requiem* 53 times around the world.

We performed in Terezín again in 2009 invited by the Czech government to be the concluding work at the conference on terrorism attended by 47 countries. Heading the American delegation of that conference was Ambassador Stuart E. Eizenstat (U.S. Department of State, 2021). Following the performance, the Ambassador came over to me, in part prompted by the enthusiasm of his wife Fran, and insisted that we bring *Defiant Requiem* to Washington and perform at the Kennedy Center. I said to him, thank you Ambassador, that is very kind of you and that would be extraordinary. He said, you will be hearing from me and I said, thank you so much and I thought I would never hear from him again. People mean well and they get very excited, but rarely do they follow through. Two days later, after returning to the States and now situated at the Aspen Music Festival where I would teach and perform for the rest of the Summer, the first message on my email was from Ambassador Eizenstat suggesting dates for us to meet in his office and begin planning for the Kennedy Center performance.

(If you're wondering about the title of our performance *Defiant Requiem*, along the way it occurred to me that the performances of Verdi's *Requiem* will represent a character that transcends the religiosity and speaks directly to the strength and determination of the Terezín performers and audiences. I decided for them that their best defense was defiance.)

I am very blessed to have been introduced to Ambassador Eizenstat and to have been able to create something of which he is proud. We decided that it would be best to have a board of directors and a formal structure for the Defiant Requiem Foundation. Ambassador Eizenstat's involvement added enormous distinction to our mission and attracted members who felt similarly. He is still the chair of the board of the Defiant Requiem Foundation (Board of Directors, n.d.) created in 2008.

I am not a scholar. I am not representing myself as a scholar. I rely on scholars to see if there is some way that we can present materials effectively in a concert setting that scholars have discovered. This is an important fact for me. I recall when my production director and I were in Jerusalem in 2015, visiting with the people who were running the Israel Festival as I prepared to conduct *Defiant Requiem*. We had a meal at a rustic Italian restaurant, conversing about the concert. Our food arrived and this guy at the table next to us, who had a yarmulke on and was working at his computer, did something very unusual. He turned his chair and joined our table, and said, "I've been listening. What's all this about?" He seemed pleasant enough, so I gave him an explanation and I took about 10 minutes or so talking about *Defiant Requiem*, while our food was getting cold. He said to me, "Are you a scholar?" And I said, "No, I consider myself well read, but I am not a scholar." And he said, "Ah, so you're not a scholar, you're a messenger. We have a lot of messengers here in Israel. Good luck to you, and remember, you're a messenger." This was the first time I thought of my role in that capacity.

Edgar Krasa and Marianka Zadikow-May attended the sold-out performance of *Defiant Requiem* at the John F. Kennedy Center for the Performing Arts in Washington, D.C. in 2010 (Figure 17.2). Ambassador Eizenstat lined up every Congressional leader on both sides of the aisle as sponsors of the Kennedy Center performance. Eizenstat said "I've never experienced something so powerful and so meaningful" (Starosta, 2010, para. 15). In 2015, at Boston Symphony Hall, the performance of *Defiant Requiem* was dedicated to Edgar Krasa and his wife. His wife had died just two weeks before the concert. Krasa, who had sung in all 16 performances of *Defiant Requiem* in Terezín, was in the audience as his two sons, Daniel and Rafael, and his grandson Alexander sang in the choir.

Figure 17.2
Murry Sidlin Conducting a Defiant Requiem Performance.
Photo from Defiant Requiem Foundation Website

At the end of the performances of *Defiant Requiem*, there is a train whistle and an excerpt from the Jewish Mourner's Kaddish is played by a solo violin as each member of the orchestra and choir leave the stage one by one in silence to symbolize what is on screen—the deportation of the Jews at Terezín. I ask the audience instead of applause to observe a moment of silence. The same year, 2015, the *San Diego Tribune* reviewer said "We shall never forget that silence" (Chute, 2015). "Never again will I hear Verdi's *Requiem* without thinking of this performance and what happened in Terezín" (Reich, 2017, para. 16) observed critic Howard Reich of the *Chicago Tribune*.

An Account of the Performance

Solene Le Van, a classical soprano and violinist, wrote a review of the Costa Mesa, California Segerstrom Center performance that described *Defiant Requiem:*

> Sidlin reminded this reviewer of Leonard Bernstein ... with a larger-than-life showmanship ... as he exerted his entire body and beads of sweat rolled down his face. He leapt upon his podium during the *Dies Irae,* eliciting a savage pummeling of the timpanis that sent a visceral *frisson* down the spines of every audience member ... The *Dies Irae* followed the deeply affecting words of one of the survivors and well-articulated readings by the actors standing at each side of the chorus ... Nathan Stark sang *Mors Stupendit,* the bass aria that affirms that all creation and death itself will answer incrediously to the pronouncements of a divine judge ... When mezzo-soprano Ann McMahon Quintero performed the *Liber Scriptus,* the robust lower range balanced quivering high notes that registered as ire-full outbursts. Some audience members fall back in their seats inadvertently ... A mournful clarinet introduced *Quid Sum Miser* for soprano, mezzo and tenor ... A piece of overpowering majesty, it nevertheless contains a weighty atmosphere that reminds one of how insignificant the speaker is before the Lord ... The soprano's golden tone drew the auditor in [with] expressive outburst coloring the words "ante diem rationis:" (*"before the day of reckoning"*) ... In tenor Edgaras Montvidas we sensed the radiance accompanying the sinner's hope for mercy ... Before the *Offertorio,* the screen above the orchestra showed the video testimony of another

survivor, who attested to the personal qualities of conductor Schächter ... [In] the *Sanctus* ... we heard the joy described throughout the movement as the strings sprung their bows of the string in Verdi's brilliant use of *spiccato* technique ... The audience was plunged into sorrow again as a propaganda film lit up the black screen. One of the shots read, in German, "the Fuhrer Gives a City to the Jews." ... A Hebrew melody sounded ... as the screen showed a reel of trains leaving to death camps. The chorus slowly abandoned the stage. The text below the video imparted the following numbers: 140,000 imprisoned at Terezín in 4 years, 33,430 dead within the ghetto walls, and 88,000 sent to death camps (15,000 children). Then white text flashed upon black: We can sing to them what we cannot say to them. (LeVan, 2019, para. 3–12)

The Impact of Defiant Requiem

Leonard Slatkin, conductor and former music director of the National Symphony Orchestra in Washington, D.C. said that *Defiant Requiem* "is an event not to be missed by anyone who is willing to have his or her life changed forever" (Annual Report, 2022).

Responses from Performers

One choral member Karen Ward speaks of being part of *Defiant Requiem* in Asheville, North Carolina, calling it "the most moving and glorious experience of my life" (Tributes, n.d., para. 24). Another choral member, Barbara

Kingsbury, said "This was an extraordinary event which impacted me deeply" (Tributes, n.d., para. 30).

Responses from Audience Members

Audiences have been transfixed by the power of the multimedia production, replete with elaborate film footage from the camp, narration, actor portrayal of Schächter and survivors present. As I look out, my audience members are in tears. Audience member Ramon Franco wrote, "to all who made the *Defiant Requiem* a symbol of the suffering, the overcoming, and the triumph of the spirit ... These efforts will stand the test of history as one of mankind's highest accomplishments" (Tributes, n.d., para. 6). Sara Bloom, an audience member, wrote "Maestro Sidlin is a giant of our generation—of several generations—to have created this monument, a contribution to humanity that is beyond measure" (Tributes, n.d., para. 19). Audience member Amy McLaughlin-Hatch wrote "Murry—Thank you for sharing the story of Theresienstadt and Rafael Schächter. Your work is an inspiration for all of us involved in Holocaust education" (Tributes, n.d., para. 10). A reviewer wrote: "The concert demonstrated once more that in the darkest conditions, it is music and art that light the brightest lights" (Mike Dunphy, Tablet Magazine).

The Mission

The Defiant Requiem Foundation's mission is to use our educational materials to teach tolerance and inspire students to challenge antisemitism and genocide. The Foundation performances of *Defiant Requiem* and the concert film and stories, along with educational materials developed for middle and high school children, serve this purpose. Readers can find resources at defiantrequiem.org. When we perform *Defiant Requiem* in person around the world, we have as many as 2,400 people in the audience. When we show our feature-length documentary film about Terezín and Schächter, created in 2012 which premiered at Yad Vashem in Jerusalem (Shultz, 2012), it always reaches hundreds of people. The film has been on PBS in the United States several times for approximately a million people (Defiant Requiem—The Documentary, n.d.) each time. The film has been seen on BBC in England and both France's and Brazil's national television. It has also been seen on the Jewish Channel in Budapest, and five or six times on television in Israel. It has been shown at various film festivals and special screenings in schools and in churches, and synagogues. That is my way of disseminating information; we go to audiences and we create for audiences, and that is our mission and I am a messenger.

We have discovered a lot of the music of these composers from Terezín. We do not have all of it, but we have a great deal. Now that we have this music, it is up to us to explore and to perform it, because if we have it and do not perform it, it is almost as if we were to murder these victims of the Holocaust a second time. These people, dedicated to beauty, to genius, to strength, to meeting nightly to learn one of the greatest and most demanding compositions in service to mankind, achieved a miracle. This is the best of mankind.

As our mission statement of the Defiant Requiem Foundation affirms:

> By honoring the defiance and bravery of the prisoners in the Theresienstat Concentration Camp (Terezín) during World War II, performances by The Defiant Requiem Foundation show the role that music and art play in confronting contemporary challenges, including increased Holocaust ignorance, Holocaust denial, and antisemitism. In refusing to forfeit their humanity, the Terezín prisoners taught a universal lesson about the power of music and art to foster hope and inspira-

tion even in the face of monumental suffering, disease, and the constant presence of death. (Honoring the Terezín Legacy, n.d., para. 3–4)

It is our responsibility to perform this music and that is what I, as the conductor, and all of those who collaborate with me, have done with *Defiant Requiem*. With *Defiant Requiem*, we return to the moment of the concert's achievement in Terezín, to Schächter's desk.

References

Annual Report. (2022). Defiant Requiem Foundation.
    https://online.flippingbook.com/view/489212601/2/
Board of Directors (n.d.). Defiant Requiem Foundation.
    https://www.defiantrequiem.org/about/board-of-directors/
Brodeur, M. A. (2022). *Defiant Requiem mines musical hope from the horrors of the Holocaust*. The Washington Post.
    https://www.washingtonpost.com/music/2022/04/15/holocaust-defiant-requiem-turns-20-at-strathmore/
Broughton, S. (2021, April 28). *Terezín Ghetto: How the persecuted Jewish community created music within Theresienstadt*. Classical Music: BBC Music Magazine.
    https://www.classical-music.com/features/articles/Terezín-ghetto-how-the-persecuted-jewish-community-created-music-within-theresienstadt/
Chute, J. (2015, May 11). The San Diego Tribune.
Classical Notes. (n.d.). Guiseppe Verdi: Messa Da Requiem.
    http://classicalnotes.net/classics2/verdirequiem.html
Composers of the Holocaust (n.d.). https://www.leonarda.com/notes/note342.html

Defiant Requiem Foundation (n.d.). https://www.defiantrequiem.org.

Defiant Requiem—The Documentary. (n.d.). Defiant Requiem Foundation. https://www.defiantrequiem.org/film/description/

Defiant Requiem—Verdi at Terezín. (n.d.). Defiant Requiem Foundation. https://www.defiantrequiem.org/concert-performances/defiant-requiem/description/

Duchen, J. (2022, February 22). *Who is Daniel Barenboim: Everything you need to know about the legendary pianist and conductor.* Classical Music: BBC Music Magazine. https://www.classical-music.com/features/artists/who-is-daniel-barenboim/

Fantlova, Z. (2023). *The tin ring: My memoir of love and survival in the Holocaust.* McNidder and Grace.

Finney, B. (2016, June 20). *Irony: Truth's disguise.* Los Angeles Review of Books. https://lareviewofbooks.org/article/irony-truths-disguise/

Gray, D. D. (2013, June 25). *We will sing to the Nazis what we cannot say.* The Times of Israel. https://www.defiantrequiem.org/concert-performances/defiant-requiem/acclaim/we-will-sing-to-the-nazis-what-we-cannot-say/

Honoring the Terezín Legacy. (n.d.). Origins & Mission. The Defiant Requiem Foundation. https://www.defiantrequiem.org/about/mission-statement/

Karas, J. (1985). *Music In Terezín 1941–1945.* Beaufort Books Publishers.

Le Van, S. (2019). *Segerstrom center presents The Defiant Requiem Review: Verdi and the artistic heroes of the Terezín concentration camp.* https://www.picturethispost.com/segerstrom-center-presents-the-defiant-requiem-review-verdi-and-the-artistic-heroes-of-the-Terezín-concentration-camp/

Ludwig, M. (2022). *Our will to live: The Terezín music critiques of Viktor Ullmann.* Steidl.

Mass Appeal (2017, June 15). Czech Center New York.
   https://new-york.czechcentres.cz/en/program/mass-appeal
Music and the Holocaust: Edith Kraus (n.d.).
   https://holocaustmusic.ort.org/places/theresienstadt/edith-kraus/
Music and the Holocaust: Gideon Klein (n.d.).
   https://holocaustmusic.ort.org/places/theresienstadt/klein-gideon/
Music and the Holocaust: Carlo Taube. (n.d.). ORT: Impact Through Education.
   https://holocaustmusic.ort.org/places/theresienstadt/taube-carlo/
Obituary: Edith Kraus (2013, November 9). Independent.
   https://m.independent.ie/entertainment/music/obituary-edith-kraus/29741048.html
Oregon Jewish Museum and Center for Holocaust Education (n.d.). Rabbi Emanuel Rose 1932–2020.
   https://www.ojmche.org/oral-history-people/rabbi-emanuel-rose/
Plen, M. (n.d.). *Leo Baeck: Theologian who emphasized the ethical center of Judaism.* My Jewish Learning.
   https://www.myjewishlearning.com/article/leo-baeck/
Reich, H. (2017, March 17). *Defiant Requiem in Chicago: A revival of Verdi sung in concentration camp.* Chicago Tribune.
   https://www.defiantrequiem.org/concert-performances/defiant-requiem/acclaim/httpwww-chicagotribune-comentertainmentmusicreich/
Reich, H. (2017, March 24). *Defiant requiem conjures tragedy, triumph of music in Holocaust.* Chicago Tribune.
   https://www.chicagotribune.com/entertainment/music/howard-reich/ct-defiant-requiem-review-ent-0325-20170324-column.html
Shefer-Vanson, D. (2015, June 22). *A night to remember.* The Jerusalem Post.
   https://www.jpost.com/blogs/from-dorotheas-desktop/a-night-to-remember-406755

Shultz, D. (Director) (2012). *Defiant requiem*. [Documentary Film]. Partisan Pictures.

Sidlin, M. (2020). *Conduct becoming*. Politics & Prose.

Starosta, G. (2010, October 5). *When Verdi's Requiem took on new meaning*. Roll Call.
https://rollcall.com/2010/10/05/when-verdis-requiem-took-on-new-meaning/

Stoessinger, C. (2012). *Lessons from the life of Alice Herz-Sommer the world's oldest living Holocaust survivor: A century of wisdom*. Random House

Terezín.org. (n.d.) *The Jewish leadership*.
https://bTerezín.org.il/wp-ontent/uploads/2017/09/The-Jewish-Leadership.pdf

The History Press. (n.d.). *Theresienstadt: Paradise camp*.
https://www.thehistorypress.co.uk/articles/theresienstadt-paradise-camp/

Tributes. (n.d.). The Defiant Requiem Foundation.
https://www.defiantrequiem.org/about/tributes/

Ullmann, V. (n.d.). *Review of recital of Karel Berman in Terezin*.

U.S. Department of State (2021, December 27). Biography of Stuart Eizenstat.
https://www.state.gov/biographies/stuart-eizenstat/

U.S. Department of State Archives. (2007, May1). Biography of J. Christian Kennedy.
https://2001-2009.state.gov/r/pa/ei/biog/75229.htm

Verdi's Requiem Text in English. (2013, August 28). Classical Music: BBC Music Magazine.
https://www.classical-music.com/features/articles/verdi-requiem-text/

Zimmerman, D. (2016, October 20). 240+ performers under 1 baton for Verdi's Requiem. Illinois State University.
https://news.illinoisstate.edu/2016/10/240-performers-under-1-baton-for-verdis-requiem/

CHAPTER 18

The Piano: How We Survived

Manuela Mendels Bornstein
A First Person Narrative as Told to Karen Berman, Ph.D.

Part I: Music at Home in Paris

People here in this country don't know about what happened to the Jews in France. I have a story to tell and I am obligated to tell it. When I speak, especially to adults, they are always very moved. I tell my survival story as often as I am asked to do it.

Introduction

My name is Manuela Mendels Bornstein. I was born in Paris in August 1933, but my parents were not French. My mother, Ellen Hess, was German and my father, Frits Mendels, was Dutch, and my mother became Dutch by marriage. So I was actually born Dutch. My parents were married in 1930 in the synagogue in Hamburg, Germany, but my father had already lived and worked in France, so they settled in Paris in August 1930. My parents lived in France for their entire married life, were very loyal to France, but never became French.

My mother was a pianist and her mother was a pianist. My great grandmother Jenny Cronheim Hess in Hamburg was also a singer, so there was music in the family for many generations. My grandmother Sophie Hess taught piano to my mother. When my mother was a baby, her cradle was placed under the piano, and she heard music. So it is no surprise that she herself became a pianist.

I was given several lessons by my mother in Paris. There was a piece by Robert Schumann, "The Happy Farmer," that was the first piece I learned. With the occupation of Paris, my piano lessons stopped.

A Family of Musicians

At first, my mother did not have a piano, but somehow in 1940, or a little before, when France was already at war, she somehow obtained a piano. It was a spinet, a Gaveau, a very good brand of piano. A particularity of this piano was that the soundboard was a mirror, which was unusual. It was a beautiful piano. We were already at war and a piano is not a cheap item. It was a lovely piano, shiny, dark, mahogany, I think. My mother played many pieces that we enjoyed. In particular, we enjoyed a sonata for piano by Mozart that we called in French "Mozart Page Neuf" (Mozart Page Number Nine), because that particular sonata was on page nine of the piano book. We loved to hear it and, even today, it is a favorite.

I remember that we lived in an apartment one flight up in a nice suburb of Paris, nothing fancy, to the Southeast of Paris, Saint-Mandé, metro station Saint-Mandé Tourelle. My sister Jacqueline was two years younger. My father would come home for lunch. When he came home, he would whistle the first bars of Mendelssonn's "The Unfinished Symphony" when he entered the courtyard so we knew he was on his way up the stairs. He was a very good whistler until the end of his life. I cannot whistle.

Just so you understand, five kilometers and five stops on the metro from where we lived was the Jewish Quarter near the Bastille that is now very picturesque and has become quite the thing. In Saint-Mandé where we lived, there was a zoo close by that was forbidden to Jews during the occupation. There was a post office, a city hall, a church and schools, and a butcher and all kinds of shops. My mother taught me at home at first so that my sister and I could start school at the same time. We weren't in the same class because I was two years older, but my mother taught me to read so that I would be learning what other kids were learning.

When war was declared September 3, 1939, the French were told to report for military service (United States Holocaust Memorial Museum, n.d.). Germans invaded Paris on June 14, 1940 (History.com, n.d.).

My grandmother's younger brother, my Great Uncle Erwin Hess in Hamburg, had a good life. In addition to the two grand pianos he played in his house, he also composed music. He had a business and he was well-off. He worked in the morning and went home in the afternoon to make music with his friends. He had four children, all musicians, and there was music at home all the time. At the beginning of World War II, Germany was experiencing antisemitism and Jewish parents and children were in great danger. There was an organization in England that invited Jewish children in Germany and Austria to go by train to England for safety, called "Kindertransport." Their parents arranged for the four children (the twins Ursala and Gisela, Jürgen, and the eldest Marion) to leave Hamburg and go by train to London, England. At first, their mother wanted them to go to Holland where she had a brother who had invited them. But their mother said "no they should go to England where it is safer." This was a good thing because, of course, Holland was also later occupied and unsafe for Jews. In November 1938 during "The Night of Broken Glass," Kristallnacht (Friedländer, 2009), my Great Uncle Erwin was arrested and sent to Sachsenhausen in Oranienburg, Germany, near Berlin, one of the first concentration camps built by the Nazis (Evans, 2005, p. 85). That was on my mother's side of the family. On my father's side, my father's brother Bernard Mendels and his wife Annie in Holland had two children, blonde like their father, Thea and Eda, who were sent away to be protected by a family in a village.

In France, Paris was occupied in June 1940 and there were gradual measures against the Jews. One at a time. Very, very gradual. That was their way of doing things. There is an expression for that way of doing things, a Latin expression I learned only recently (though I had six years of Latin). It is *festina lente*: "to make haste slowly" or "proceed deliberately."

So gradually measures began a little bit at a time, and first the registration around September 1940. So we thought, "Oh, it is only that. OK, we can do that." Nazis took rolls from synagogues. On pain of imprisonment, Jews had to register at City Hall by having their ID cards stamped in big red letters "JUIF" in French ("JEWISH" in English). Everyone was saying "if we do what they ask, they will leave us alone."

Next, my father had to give up his radio. The Jews were ordered to give up their radios because Jews were accused of broadcasting false views and false descriptions of the progress of the Germans, when, in fact, they were broadcasting the truth. My father bought a cheap radio to give them, but secretly kept his good one.

My father's business involved the import and export of fancy foods and my father traveled by train to sell samples, and then he brought back samples from various countries in Europe. And then, of course, there were roundups all the time. But, you know, my father went to his office. He sometimes went by car to the company, sometimes by metro, sometimes by bicycle. He was never arrested; it was a miracle of survival. And then a very nasty thing happened that Jews were no longer allowed to work in their professions. For instance, just as an example, a university professor was no longer allowed to teach. Jewish doctors were no longer allowed to treat non-Jews. Jewish lawyers, and you know there were quite a few Jewish professionals, were not allowed to practice law or to defend non-Jews. It was a very, very gradual humiliation.

Then my father was ordered to have his business Aryanized. He was the owner, but he had a partner. He had to sell his business to his partner for very little money. He was no longer allowed to work. Can you imagine? There were very many Jews affected. Many Jews were in the "schmatta" (in Yiddish, clothing in English) business selling furs and clothing. They could no longer have that income, so that was very bad. And then we were restricted. We couldn't go to concerts, museums. I wasn't allowed to take swimming lessons, and there was a sign at the front entrance to the park, "Restricted: No Blacks, Dogs, or Jews." We used to go there on our bicycles. It was close by. And we were to remain within our immediate surroundings and there was a curfew: we could not go out after 6 p.m.

The other insult was when we had to go to City Hall in the Spring of 1942 to obtain a piece of yellow material with the Jewish star printed on it. To add insult to injury, we had to pay and give up ration tickets. So everyone got two stars that way. We were supposed to sew it on the outside of our outside garment. My mother disobeyed and she attached it with a safety pin because we had more clothes; we didn't wear the same thing every day.

Going Into Hiding

Then we went into hiding and that is another story by itself. There was no music then. But, it is a story of miracles.

My sister and I were no longer Dutch. We had become French. The law had allowed children born of foreign parents to have French nationality. But our French nationality was removed from us when Paris became occupied. My sister and I had to wear our yellow stars. My teacher was quite brave and asked the class to be good to me because we were in danger. But the nights of the 16th and the 17th of July in 1942, the French police had a quota to round up a certain number of Jews, and children and parents were separated and most were sent to Auschwitz. 13,000 Jews, including 3,000 children, were rounded up (Friedländer, 2009, p. 325). They were driven in busses to the indoor bicycle arena Vel d' Hiv used for races. They were kept there for several weeks without water or food and then taken in trucks to a camp in Drancy in Eastern France. From there, they were sent to Auschwitz and most never came back (Friedlander, 2009, p. 325). The concierge downstairs and our neighbors all knew we were Jewish and no one denounced us. Somehow, the French Police did not come for us; that is a miracle.

Two weeks later at the very end of July 1942, after the roundup when so many Jews were rounded up and sent to concentration camps—and we were lucky that we had not been found—my parents decided we had to leave even though forbidden. France had been divided and there was a demarcation line you were not allowed to cross. Before we left, my father and a neighbor carried my mother's lovely piano across the courtyard to this neighbor's apartment for safekeeping. The neighbors had a little boy named Jackie who was not allowed to touch the piano for fear it would be discovered.

We were not told by our parents that we were fleeing. We thought we were going on vacation. We were excited, it was July and we were going on vacation. We did not ask any questions; we were very naïve. We didn't know that we were in grave danger.

Part II: Escaping From Paris

Two teenage boys Michel Paris and Pierre Deneux who worked for the Resistance brought us backpacks. My parents filled the backpacks. My parents packed my doll, which had eyes that opened and closed, in a separate suitcase hoping it would be delivered later. They told us our bicycles would be delivered later and, as I said, my sister and I thought we were going on vacation. We went to Michel Paris' home in Paris, a Catholic family, where we had dinner. The father of the family burned our yellow stars. On this hot evening in July, he lit the furnace in the basement and burned our stars. The very devout mother gave us Catholic medals, and encouraged us to convert to Catholicism thinking it would help us to stay safe. Converting would not have saved us because we had Jewish grandparents.

The two boys bought us train tickets. My father knew if they rounded up Jews on the train, we would never come back. We were sitting on the train and my parents were very nervous. There was a delay, so my father got off the train. They were rounding up Jews on the other side of the platform. If the roundup had been on our side of the platform, that would have been the end of us. But the train left and that was the end of a very frightful episode for my parents—I call it a miracle. When we changed trains, I fell and hit my head on the concrete and I still remember it. We then spent two nights in a hotel on the northern part of the demarcation line.

We then walked for two kilometers towards the border to meet sons of a barber and farmer who met us with their bicycles, my sister and I riding, and my parents running behind. They took us across the demarcation line at night avoiding the German Border Patrol. One of our teenage smugglers ("passeurs" in French) went ahead to make sure it was safe. It was a miracle that no patrol came at that time and there were no patrol dogs.

On July 31, we crossed the demarcation line in the center of France to the side of the Vichy regime that was unoccupied, and did so without being caught. Now in the "free zone," we were greeted by the French Army who gave us a bed for the night.

The French soldiers then took us to a hotel in Riberac. However, there we were arrested by the Vichy Police for having crossed the line illegally without a permit after we entered the free zone. My parents were interrogated and we were taken to Périgueux to the Chief of Police. But, the Chief of Police only fined us, and then told us to go into hiding. We stayed in a hotel for a couple of weeks. While we were in the hotel waiting for a place to go, I remember I was given nine peaches in the hotel as a gift for my ninth birthday on August 16. My parents saw a sign for two rooms in a house to rent in the small village of Le Got. We asked the Chief of Police if this was acceptable and he said "yes." He told us to "disappear"—he was a good man.

The Good People Who Helped Us

Our Catholic friends sheltered us during our escape. When we arrived in Le Got, the mayor of Le Got referred us to a farmer who gave my father the job of farmer, so my father could provide food for our family. Le Got was very small—a train station, a store, a post office, and that's all. The mayor was very brave, more than brave, a courageous man, to get my father a job. The community knew who we were, yet they protected us.

The story needs to be known. Everyone knows about the horrors, but people don't know what the good people did. Even the priest came to see us and said "I'll hide you in my church tower if the Krauts come." The mayor made false ID cards for my parents with the last name "Pascaud" using the cards of two people who had died. The mayor pasted my parents' pictures on the cards. These cards are in pristine condition in the United States Holocaust Memorial Museum in Washington, D.C. (Birn, 2013). Resistance workers helped us. The teenage boys and their Catholic parents helped us. The mayor Paul Delpech, who helped us was listed posthumously in Yad Vashem in Jerusalem—The Righteous Among the Nations (yadvashem-france.org, n.d.). These are the good people.

These people were putting their lives in danger to help us. They would have been severely punished if caught—tortured or killed. My parents provided emotional support. Most children were separated from their parents. My cousin's parents never came back. My parents were strong and hid their terror from us. We were young, we didn't know the danger. I was nine when we left home and 11 when we came back home. For my sister and me, it was a big adventure.

Our New Life

I don't remember being told to say I was not Jewish. What I remember is that my father told us "don't use your last name" which is Mendels. He said use "Frederic" as your last name. So my father said "if people ask you your last name, say 'Frederic.'" And you know, it is really surprising, but my sister and I didn't question it.

We went to school in the free zone and we made friends with children our age. We walked to school with some friends, my sister and her friend. I had my friend. We had friends between the two of us. She was with the younger kids at school with a female teacher. I was with the older kids with a male teacher, who was probably working for the Resistance. He must have known that we were Jewish. We came from Paris and we were dressed properly, especially in the beginning. Then we outgrew our clothes, but then my mother would sew and knit. After a while our shoes were too small, so we wore wooden shoes like the other kids. One day, we received our bicycles, probably sent by our upstairs neighbor in Paris, Mme. Deneux.

The farmers grew grapes and chestnuts. My father would peel the chestnuts and he would boil them, then peel the inner skin and his fingers would be pink from skinning the chestnuts. My mother did what she could with the chestnuts, cook them and make bread or cakes. In the village, we ate pork, even though we were Jewish; we ate what we could. Life was very restricted. There was milk. There were geese. The fathers would kill the geese after they would fatten the geese and they would render the skin, and the fat from the skin was delicious. They would grill, and we would eat the fat. They also grew tobacco in that part of France, and probably still do. My father would dry it, the big leaves, and then chop them and roll them with paper into cigarettes. I don't know how he got the paper.

My father spoke four languages. His first language was Dutch, which is close to German—not exactly the same. His mother was German by birth. I don't know if she spoke Yiddish. She may have spoken Yiddish, she kept kosher. He spoke Dutch, German, French, and English, fluently. I think it helped him survive. My mother spoke German, as she was German born. She spoke German, English and French, but she had more of an accent in French than my father. I never really noticed my father's accent except one time when he recorded something and I heard his accent on the recording. The Dutch accent to me is very recognizable and difficult to lose. It is very different from the German accent. It is a very guttural language, much more so than German. My parents were very likeable and their knowledge of languages helped us.

Being in Hiding

Then life became very restricted. Hitler was angered when the Americans landed in French North Africa and decided to punish France. After November 1942, there was no more free zone and there were concentration camps in France (Civs.gouv.fr, n.d). Yet we continued to survive.

It was a terrible time for my parents. My parents always toasted each other, "Until next Sunday" ("a dimanche prochain" in French). It makes me cry, thinking of my parents hoping to be alive another week, until next Sunday. So we were living from day to day, from week to week, in terror in France. It was a very poor part of France. Now it is a very touristy, a very rich area. But back then, they were poor people, farmers.

My mother told me about a suicide pill if we were ever arrested. My mother said she had pills and we would all die without pain. But we just forgot about it, my sister Jacqueline and I. When we went back to the village in 1997, which is a number of years ago already, our friends of that time reminded us that we had told them about the pill. So the village knew that we were Jewish. My sister and I forgot about the pills our mother mentioned—we children were naïve. We were young enough that we didn't know.

One day, while we were at school, the Gestapo appeared at our house to arrest a young man who lived downstairs suspected of working for the Resistance, but they never climbed the stairs where they would have found my parents listening to the illegal radio station from London on the shortwave radio—another miracle.

The village could have denounced us, but they protected us. Nobody denounced us, except there was one horrible incident that I am hesitant to tell, especially to children. It is such an ugly insult. We were walking in the street and two little girls our age were nearby and one of the little girls said "Aren't you ashamed to play with these girls, Jacqueline and Manuela. They are Jewish and don't you know that Jews are as dirty as pigs in a pigsty?" It is a horrible insult, so I don't tell it to children because I don't want them to feel that. So how did that little girl hear that? She heard it from her parents, I don't know. She must have heard it somewhere. But nobody else said anything or did anything to us: they protected us.

Nights in the Forest

My father would hide in an underground hiding place for many days where one couldn't stand, but only crouch. He would sometimes spend the night in the forest with other young men working for the Resistance (the Resistance was very active in that area) because they were going to be recruited to the obligatory work in Germany. Germany needed a lot of young men since Germany had already lost a lot of soldiers, so they were recruiting young men in occupied countries. The young men were in danger, and my father, as far as

I know, was the only Jew, and they would hide one or two nights in the woods. My mother would hang a sheet or pillowcase in the window, something in the window signaling to him that it was safe to come home. One time, he spent three nights in the forest and his beard had grown in white and my father had very black hair, and yet his beard was white.

My mother became pregnant in November 1942 and had a baby boy, born August 7, 1943, while we were in hiding. My parents planned to have a midwife at home, but her condition was very precarious. The baby was a breach birth and my parents took the risk of travelling to a doctor in another county. She lost a lot of blood and she almost died. In honor of President Franklin D. Roosevelt, who was my parents' only hope, my parents named the baby Franklin. If it had been a girl, she would have been named Marianne, which is the emblem of France.

As all of France was now occupied, there were sudden warnings of roundups. The whole family would have to hide in the woods where others hid with Resistance workers. One time, we and my baby brother had to hide in the woods. He was 10 years younger than me, exactly 10 years within a few days. I don't know what time of year we had to hide with him in his baby carriage in the woods, and he didn't cry. The five of us and other villagers hid in the woods, and my baby brother Franklin did not cry! If he had cried, I don't know. It was another miracle. And then it was safe to come home to the house.

Before D-Day, the Resistance had blown up railroad tracks and bridges to prevent the Germans from taking their prisoners East. After D-Day, June 6, 1944 (BBC.com, 2019), German troops were retreating and went by the house, which was on the main road, where we were hiding, and my mother said, "Don't look out the window as they may still have weapons." On August 25, 1944, Paris was liberated, but the war was not over.

THE PIANO: HOW WE SURVIVED

Part III: The Return Home

29 months after we fled Paris, we began to made our way back home. It is a story of miracles, and the biggest miracle is that there were four of us going into hiding and there were five coming home. My father made his way back to Paris first, as soon as the railroad tracks were repaired. He went back home, by himself, in September 1944. As soon as the concentration camps were liberated there were many refugees, and they were moved into vacant apartments. Would our apartment have been requisitioned to other refugees? The rental apartment we had left had been occupied by the German troops. My father went to claim the apartment, and somehow it was vacant. There was damage and the furniture was damaged and dispersed. My father was able to gather the furniture, including my mother's piano which was still at the neighbor's apartment. My father returned to Le Got on the 10th of October to bring us home to Paris. To my mother's great joy, on November 16, 1944, when we arrived back home after a harrowing trip, the piano was there! We were away from July 1942 to November 1944, almost two and a half years. I was 11 years old, my sister was nine, and my brother was one. My mother had to have the piano tuned. She gave me piano lessons, and then I had lessons also from a piano teacher.

Little by little life had started to be normal. But my father's business was nonexistent. There was no money. My mother made jam and cakes that my father sold door to door. My mother sold some good jewelry she had hidden and pawned it for cash. Mme. Chastel, the owner of a private school ("*l'école privée*" in French) Le Cours Racine, had worked for the French Resistance and gave us, my sister and me, free tuition for several years.

I was able to get piano and violin lessons. For the violin lessons, the teacher was a very nice man. He gave me free violin lessons and he also found an old violin which he gave to me. It was a little too big and I was not too tall and violins come in different sizes depending on the child's size. But I grew and soon it was the right size for me.

I was able to play both piano and violin. Then, I don't know why, I guess my violin teacher thought I was gifted, and he recommended that I have Harmony and Composition classes. I played all the way through high school, but then it was too much and I couldn't do both. So I let the piano playing stop and now I can't play the piano at all.

My sister had cello lessons and my little brother, when he was old enough, had piano lessons also. My father listened patiently and paid the bills. When my father was a teenager, I think he played the ukulele or the banjo, but he was not particularly musical. However, since my mother was a pianist, I was a violinist, and my sister was a cellist, we had a musical trio at home. My mother again played for us "Mozart Page Neuf" of her piano book.

I also played a lot of music with other young people. There was an organization in France, Jeunesses Musicales de France, the Musical Youth of France (I don't know if it still exists). I joined it and so I met other musical young people. I did a lot of playing. My sister did more because she was preparing for the conservatory, and for a while she even did high school by correspondence. But then she became too nervous and abandoned a musical career, but she continued to play cello as a semi-professional for her entire life.

We had no toys, just our precious dolls. I still have my doll to this day, and now that my sister passed away in 2019, I have my sister's doll also (Figure 18.1). We didn't have paper for school work and we had no fabric materials for sewing, but we never went hungry. But you know we bounced back. My parents lived a successful long life. But they wouldn't talk about the war. My sister wrote a book about it called *A Dimanche Prochain: A Memoir of Survival in World War II France* (Birn, 2013). My father wrote a three-page essay, "Odyssey of a Jewish Family in France," (Birn, 2013) given as an interview of my father by a friend, and is included in my sister's book.

FIGURE 18.1
2022 photo in Manuela's home of her and her sister's precious dolls that have been with her since she fled her home in France during the Holocaust.
Photo by Paul Guy Accettura

My sister wrote in her book that she "fell in love with the cello" (Birn, 2013, p. 169). I played in a community orchestra later in Atlanta but I had to stop recently—my age, my shoulder, my arms, and my fingers don't work very well anymore.

I was 11 when we came back home and we learned gradually what happened to our relatives. I know my parents went to a building where they were posting the names of survivors or victims, and I know one day we came back from school for lunch and my sister and I were arguing. We used to argue. We were close, but we were also like other girls. So my mother said "Don't fight with each other. We just got a telegram that your uncle, your aunt and Oma (Dutch for "grandmother on my father's side") died in concentration camps." So I was 12 or 13 maybe, when I learned what had happened. Little by little, we learned that my father's parents and cousins had perished in Auschwitz. I had no grandparents, no uncles or aunts, and only a few cousins left. My father's sister Therese (Thea) died in Sobibor concentration camp. We were very sad our extended family had passed away. We found out we didn't have any family anymore. All died. We found out little by little. At one point I had nightmares.

My mother's mother, Sophie Hess, my Omi, ("maternal grandmother" in German), died by suicide in November 1941. My grandmother was in Hamburg and was forced to leave her lovely apartment and move to a decrepit house in the Jewish community. She was able to take her piano with her and musicians came to play with her. When the other musicians did not show up, it was because they were ordered to report and were shipped to a concentration camp. My father had encouraged Sophie to leave, but she refused to join us in Paris. She wrote to my mother that, if she was ordered to report, she would not. My mother then received a farewell letter. When my mother was notified about the suicide, she played Chopin's "Funeral March" on the piano to express her sorrow. My mother was an only child. My sister, much later on, played the cello when our brother died.

I knew I had two cousins, Thea and Eda, who were hidden in the same village as their parents and they survived while their parents died in Auschwitz. I didn't know them. I was too young. I know my mother's mother came to visit us. There is a picture in my sister's book (Birn, 2013, p. 75). The Dutch family, they came to visit one time, but there was a war you know. So I really didn't know my family. Anyway, at first Thea and Eda did not want to leave the host family in Holland that protected them, a very courageous family. But the two cousins' mother had left instructions that if the parents were to die during the war, Thea and Eda were to go to her uncle and aunt in California, which they did. Many families had such instructions.

Crossing the Atlantic

I, too, had to memorize the name and address of these same two people in California. My Uncle Bernard was married to my Aunt Annie. Annie's sister Clara, a pediatrician, was married to Josef Gans, an attorney. Their children were Ida and Yetty (Henrietta) Gans. Ida was a musician who played viola and piano her whole life and married a conductor, Edgar Braun. The instructions I got were to memorize the name and address of this family Gans, and for a long time I remembered it. And I had to memorize Erna Hess (she was my mother's first cousin) and her address. They lived in Brooklyn and it was a street address with many numbers. So I had to memorize these two families' addresses in case my parents died during the war, and for many years I had them in my memory. But I never had to use these addresses right away because my parents had survived.

When I was 27, I was still living at home in France and it was time for me to be on my own. My sister was living in New York with her new husband. When I left France in 1960, I left with my violin, of course. I remember when I went across the Atlantic on a Dutch ship. It was a seven-day boat trip (it now only takes five days) and there was an orchestra on board conducted by a man named Mendels which was, of course, my maiden name. I talked to him and played with the orchestra on the ship. We crossed the Atlantic from Rotterdam to Newark. On the ship, I met all these musicians that were Americans and that was all a lot of fun, that was the most exciting.

After crossing the Atlantic I lived in New York for one year, at first with my sister and her husband, and we went to many concerts. In 1960–1961, there was lots of free music in New York City in churches and elsewhere. It was wonderful. I loved the music in New York. I even had occasions there to play in orchestras.

Then I crossed the country. My father's brother, Bernard Mendels, had two children, my cousins Thea and Eda, now in California. Their parents had died the same day in Auschwitz, but the two cousins who were hidden in the same village were not turned in to the Germans.

So I had saved my money to go visit my two cousins in California. I went by bus—I think it was $99 for 99 days, or something like that. My younger cousin Eda met me by car in Denver and we visited national parks, the Grand Canyon, Bryce Canyon and Zion. I made the ride to San Francisco with my violin, and again I had the gift to make music. I met the man who would become my husband in San Francisco. His name was Murray Simon Bornstein. He was just right. I met him in 1961 when I was 28 and he was 32. We had the same interests, morals, same religion. He was a linguist and had lived in Europe. We were not spring chickens. By that time, I knew what I wanted. I had to make a quick decision because he had a job waiting for him in Hawaii and I had told my parents I was coming home. I decided to get married. I married at my cousin's house and then we later went back to Paris and had a Jewish wedding.

Then we returned to New York. My husband was from New York and my sister lived in New York. Then we went back to San Francisco, at the end of 1961 into January 1962 and flew to Hawaii.

It was supposed to be a six month stay in Hawaii in 1962. My husband sublet his apartment in San Francisco. It ended up being a year in Hawaii, and then we moved back to San Francisco. My husband had three recorders with us in Hawaii and he taught me to play, so my husband and I made music on the recorders.

THE PIANO: HOW WE SURVIVED

In January 1963, we moved back to San Francisco and I got pregnant in February 1963 with my first son, Jack, who was born on November 2, 1963. My son was three weeks old when President Kennedy was assassinated. When my son was three years old, he started piano lessons. The piano teacher, Mrs. Kopriva, used the Yamaha method to teach young children to play piano. She had little tablets with black magnets and the tablets were printed with the staffs and that was how he learned to read music. My son couldn't read books yet, but he could read music. He did very well, but when he got a little older he decided not to pursue piano and became a percussionist, which he is to this day.

My second son Niel was 20 months younger and he also took piano lessons for a while and later played in his high school and college bands. He did not pursue it later. His daughter took cello lessons, but didn't continue. At first, she wanted to perform, but not to practice. She now has my sister's cello which she plays.

The Descendants are Musicians

All of the descendants are musicians. The family of my Great Uncle Erwin Hess in England who left Germany as children on the Kindertransport continued to pursue music. The children were the twins, Ursula (Uschi) a cellist and Gisela (Gisi) and their older sister Marion and older brother Jürgen (John). Marion was a pianist. Her daughter got a Ph.D. in music playing the flute and is a professional flutist. Ursula's husband had an attic that contained rare cellos which he showed me. Gisela (Gisi) married and they had a daughter and son. The daughter Tanya is a violinist and the son Steven Smith is a violinist and the owner of a rare violin shop in London. His wife is Korean and is also a violinist and pianist. When I visited Steven a few years ago, he was the manager of the store and showed us the valuable instruments in the safe. He came out with two of the rarest of the violins. In one hand he was holding a Stradivarius and the other hand a Guarneri and, to my delight, he played one.

One of the twin cousins, Gisela (Gisi), died of Covid in March 2020 which was awful because no one could be with her. Her twin Ursula (Uschi) had died several years before.

My son, Jack, who plays drums, is 59 and just went to a reunion of his marching band, "Spirit of Atlanta."

My mother played the piano all of her life. When my sister got married in New York and I got married, my parents had two daughters in the United States. So my parents left France to join me and my family in San Francisco, also bringing my brother who was 18 at the time. My mother still had that lovely piano. She was told that the Gaveau piano would not travel. So with a heavy heart she sold it. When she arrived in San Francisco, she bought another piano, a Hallet Davis, and she played it, but she did not like it very much. She gave it to me and she bought a Yamaha piano which she liked very much.

Later my mother and father decided they did not want to stay in San Francisco because my husband was an engineer and was traveling. My sister married a diplomat and they were also traveling, and my brother was now a professor who was traveling as well. So they went back to France, not to Paris, but to Cannes. She did take her Yamaha piano back to France and that piano did travel across the Atlantic.

I kept taking violin lessons; I had various professors. My husband, when the job in San Francisco was ended, was transferred to the head office in New York. We couldn't live in the city with two young children, so we bought a house in Princeton Junction, New Jersey. I found other musicians. My husband took the train to Manhattan. I played music with a pianist and a violinist and cellist. We played in the synagogue, at retirement homes, and I played a lot. You know playing with others is very exciting.

In 1976, my husband's civil engineering company offered him a transfer to Atlanta, Georgia. We started in California, then Hawaii, then New York and then Atlanta. In Atlanta, I joined the Atlanta Community Symphony Orchestra (ACSO). They took a break because of the pandemic, but they are playing again now. I played with them for many years. We rehearsed every Tuesday night. I had a friend in the orchestra and we carpooled and shared a music stand. We gave free concerts and that was very good. My friend, unfortunately, is very hard of hearing and cannot play and we are both the same age. My hearing is still good, but my shoulder, wrist and now my fingers, are not good, so I stopped playing.

My two married sons are in Atlanta. I have lived to know my four grandchildren, all in college. I am the matriarch of my family. To keep healthy, I don't eat fast food and I go on walks, exercise, and do yoga. I just went to see the Metropolitan Opera's *La Boheme* livestreamed at the movie theater. I cried and cried.

Postscript

The war did change my way of looking at the world. These days I read about antisemitism, active in Europe, in France, England and Holland and here in America. The answer is education. The only thing I can do is keep talking. When I see antisemitism today, I talk so that people will know what can happen (Figure 18.2). We need to help other people.

ART FOR HEALING AND RENEWAL

FIGURE 18.2
Manuela speaking to Georgia high school students in 2022 about her experiences during the Holocaust in France, with Rabbi Prass of the Atlanta, Georgia Breman Museum. Photo by Paul Guy Accettura

You can tell siblings, your parents, and your children that you heard from a child survivor. Some don't believe in the Holocaust. It did happen and a few of us are still around.

I would have asked my parents to tell me more about their story. Listen to your grandparents, ask questions, they won't be here forever, write it down.

Listen to me and tell the story of the horrors and don't let it happen again. There were good people who risked their lives for us so I could enjoy freedom, and my walks, and my family, and, of course, music.

References

BBC.com (2019, June 6) *D-Day: What happened during the landings of 1944?* https://www.bbc.com/news/world-48513108.

Birn, J. (2013). *A dimanche prochain: A memoir of survival in World War II France.* United States: Author.

Civs.gouv.fr (n.d) *The demarcation line.* French Ministry of Defence. http://www.civs.gouv.fr/images/pdf/documents_utiles/documents_dhistoire/the_demarcation_line.pdf

Evans, R. J. (2005). *The third Reich in power.* Penguin Books.

Friedländer, S. (2009). *Nazi Germany and the Jews: 1933–1945.* Harper Perennial.

History.com. (n.d.). *Germany invades Paris.* https://www.history.com/this-day-in-history/germans-enter-paris.

United States Holocaust Memorial Museum (n.d.). *Britain and France declare war.* https://www.ushmm.org/learn/timeline-of-events/1939-1941/britain-and-france-declare-war.

yadvashem-france.org (n.d.)

APPENDIX 1

Holocaust Theater: Representation or Misrepresentation

(This is a transcript of a speech given by Arnold Mittelman, President/National Jewish Theater Foundation, Founding Director NJTF Holocaust Theater International Initiative at the University of Miami Miller Center for Contemporary Judaic Studies to Association of Holocaust Organizations on 1/10/12.)

I wish to thank Bill Shulman, President of the Association of Holocaust Organizations, and member of the National Jewish Theater Foundation/Holocaust Theater Archive Advisory Board, for inviting me to make this presentation to you, his constituents, at the United States Holocaust Memorial Museum.

Facts are not the enemy of art, and art is not the enemy of facts. However, humankind often sees everything subjectively, even as we aspire to see the world objectively. Everything we see, touch, and feel is subject to individual interpretation. The late great Italian author Luigi Pirandello's plays often examine how it is impossible to look at something truly objectively, since we are always looking at things subjectively through our own experience and understanding. And to a great extent, that is the power of theater: it has the ability to be seen individually and understood personally, defying all our collective attempts to view it objectively.

The aesthetic experience of the theatrical audience is to relate, not just to the live performance onstage, but to the reality and sense of each other's presence. And therefore, although we are seeing the same performance together, we are never actually seeing the same collective performance because we all see the world differently. No wonder one person's sense that a play is an accurate representation can be thought by another person to be a total misrepresentation. Such is Theater.

Theater comes in many forms: from solo performances to avant-garde; to pageant plays and historic drama; farce, tragedy; musicals; reviews; multimedia. The combinations and possibilities are endless, and have maintained themselves and evolved throughout thousands of years. And many historic subjects have been treated theatrically, and some have become a part of the "classic repertory," such as much of the work of Shakespeare and many of the ancient Greek plays.

Into this world of historical theater enters a profoundly important subject: the single greatest atrocity of the twentieth century, which has in its aftermath been named the Holocaust. And the fundamental question for me is this: how does any artist interpret or portray a systematic series of crimes that are almost unimaginable and represent these events without wholesale misrepresentation?

One thing is certain: that conscientious theater artists have attempted, over time, to wrestle with this problem and use their power to truly represent the actual reality without misusing this power to misrepresent. However, it is impossible for theater artists to become aware of the stories and individual scenarios that took place and give voice and insight to that reality without some degree of theatrical license.

The other great dilemma that we all face is that the primary reporters of the Holocaust, the eyewitness survivors, have now reached an age where inevitably in the near future, their voices will not be heard except through recordings, manuscripts, and their portrayals within the framework of movies and theater.

Theater has the unique power of telling these stories and individualizing the personas and their biographies, which is the exact opposite of what the Nazis attempted to do by depersonalizing, through numbers and mass deaths, the victims of the Holocaust. Therefore, every play that is created, that has integrity, honesty, quality, and truth, proves that the attempt to annihilate individuality did not succeed. When those kinds of plays and their issues are performed publicly, in front of what Arthur Miller calls "the blood brotherhood of perfect strangers" (i.e. the audience), the phenomenon of individual awareness often accompanied by the dramatic power of catharsis, creates an indelible impression on any sensitive human, ideally in the moment of watching, or upon reflection. Amazingly, through the power of theater it often invokes not just sadness but often inspiration for all our lives while revising our previous impressions and understanding. The remarkable fact that those theater moments then live in our memory for the rest of time is a unique human phenomenon that often guides our future behavior.

Over time, there have been great attempts to document survivor testimonies, led primarily by the USC Shoah Foundation Institute, now under the leadership of its Executive Director Dr. Stephen Smith and its Managing Director Kim Simon. However, in these interviews, the survivor functions often as an artist, in that, even though they are attempting to recall, they are still capable of distilling, rearranging, accentuating, and, in many cases reliving, the horrors that they either witnessed or lived through. These testimonies are in many ways their own act of theater—an often solo story told to an interviewer or a camera to be held sacred for all time as a record. Occasionally, these testimonies have been challenged for their validity, and been found to be truly artistic in that the speaker or survivor has amalgamated many stories that they have been told by others, into their own personal life scenario. I do not believe that there is ever intent on the part of these people, any more than I believe there is intent on the part of well-intentioned playwrights, to misrepresent, but only to more vividly present what actually occurred. The difference between those survivor testimonies and the work of the theater artist is that the playwright has a responsibility to interpret and guide an audience to a deeper understanding of the subject; to shed, not just the light of history, or recollection, but to provide an opportunity for us to understand not just what occurred, but oftentimes why it occurred; how and why it could possibly occur again; and, of course, what lessons must be learned from its occurrence.

A case study of many of the issues and themes I have mentioned occurs in a new American play by Jeff Cohen, entitled *The Soap Myth*, which I am about to direct and produce in New York City. This play, set in New York and written for four actors playing multiple roles, has as its central figure, the character of Milton Saltzman, who is inspired by Holocaust survivor Morris Spitzer, whose crusade about soap was profiled in an article in *Moment Magazine* in 2000, written by Josh Rolnick.

The Soap Myth is a dark tale that asks us to examine how we define, understand and reflect upon human history. The play chronicles the struggle of a determined old man's fight to be heard. Milton Saltzman, a seemingly underappreciated Holocaust survivor, is pitted against his own people and the inability of Holocaust historians to accept what he believes to be an incontrovertible truth.

Saltzman approaches journalist Annie Blumberg to assist him in revealing to the academic community, and the world, that the rumors of Nazis making soap from their Jewish victims is undeniably true. He recounts attending a funeral in his hometown, where a casket was filled with soap created from human remains. Although the Nazis were originally convicted of these vile and ruthless acts at the Nuremberg Trials, Holocaust historians later determined that the theory lacked sufficient documented evidence, and thus, without adequate proof, the story was erased from the history books.

Milton Saltzman finds the denial of nearly unfathomable atrocities unacceptable, and proceeds to hound Holocaust scholars and pursue every possible avenue to have the decision to omit these stories overturned. He therefore appeals to Annie Blumberg for assistance, as museum representatives refuse to grant the old man satisfaction. The historians in the play question how far the credibility of an eyewitness account should extend; and Blumberg feels caught between two equally passionate but opposing forces.

Beautifully and heartbreakingly narrated by the profoundly conflicted Blumberg, we watch as she interviews: Saltzman, the survivor; Daniel Silver and Esther Feinman, the scholars; and Brenda Goodsen, the manipulative Holocaust denier, all based on actual people. In the end, Blumberg concludes that discovering or solidifying irrefutable facts is not the important thing; the important thing is to grieve the loss of firsthand accounts of these momentous events with the painful progression of time. Rather than question or fixate on the validity of "subjective" evidence that had once been perceived as sufficient fact, one must take the time to appreciate the survivors that remain, and be grateful for their wisdom, patience and willingness to speak, so as to educate and guide future generations. As Blumberg phrases it in the play's final lines, "The real story was not what it takes for a man like Milton to survive the Holocaust. The real story was what it takes for such a man to survive surviving."

The development of The Soap Myth toward its production has been aided by input from Holocaust Theater Archive Advisory Board Member, the renowned historian Michael Berenbaum, who was quoted, with permission, in the play: "Noted scholar Michael Berenbaum agrees that it is possible that successful experiments in making soap from human fat may have occurred, but he contends that the mass manufacture of soap from human remains was a myth, because it was not economically feasible." The play has also been read and approved by Dr. David Marwell, Director of the Museum of Jewish Heritage: A Living Memorial to the Holocaust in New York City. For myself as an artist, the journey in developing this play has made me feel much like young Annie, more determined than ever to use my talents to draw attention to future generations that Milton and millions once lived.

Another example of a major contemporary author attempting to successfully meet the challenge of the interaction of survivor and the next generation is found in the French author Enzo Cormann's play *Storms Still*, which I am developing for production in New York City in its English-language premiere. The National Jewish Theater Foundation/Holocaust Theater Catalog commissioned the translation.

Enzo Cormann's *Storms Still* is a cerebrally charged piece of theater dedicated to the examination of what it means to suffer a life all-consumed by survivor's guilt. The play opens on an "old isolated farm," where Theodore Steiner, a former actor, has spent twenty-five years as a recluse. He is a man clearly haunted by the ghosts of his past, indulging in painting as a form of escapism and creative catharsis. However, his self-imposed solitude comes to an abrupt halt one tempestuous night, when acclaimed director Nathan Goldring shows up on his doorstep. He demands that the aged actor come out of hiding and star in a Berlin-based production of Shakespeare's *King Lear*. Steiner's initial reaction is one of almost irrational outrage and fury, as he roars at Goldring and chases him out into the stormy darkness.

Storms Still chronicles the ongoing psychological battle between and within these two men. Goldring pries into Steiner's past and persists in trying to entice the retired performer back to the stage. It is revealed at the start that Goldring's monomaniacal pursuit of Steiner as his leading man is derivative of the fact that he saw the actor perform *Macbeth* as a young boy in Vienna, and has wanted to work with him ever since. In the meantime, although evasive at first, Steiner gradually revisits the reasons that drove him to seek sanctuary in the seclusion of nature, and he ultimately reveals the reasons why he inexplicably disappeared after a performance of *Macbeth*, before the run of the production was completed, and was never seen by his adoring public ever again.

The play's progression is divided into thirteen chapters, each set at a different hour within a two-day time period and designated by apposite *King Lear* quotes. The weather depicted outside the small cottage corresponds to the events taking place within, whether it be a calm discourse between a pair of artists, or a raging storm of emotions unleashed by two tortured and conflicted men. Their constant clashing culminates with the revelation that Steiner is a survivor of Theresienstadt concentration camp. He participated in the plays produced in Terezín, including performing a rendition of Edgar in *King Lear*. And in 1944, he knowingly saved his own life over the opportunity to save his pianist father or opera singer mother from certain death. Steiner's life is spared solely based on his acting talents and the subjectivity of one Nazi officer, who offered him the choice of scratching any one name off a list of prisoners bound for Auschwitz. Steiner has forevermore been tormented by the memory of the victims he knew and lost to the horrors of Auschwitz, and the knowledge that he could have sacrificed himself in order to save one of his parents.

Binary oppositions form the foundations of *Storms Still*. We see an old man at odds with a young man, an actor and a director, performer and observer, respectively. Climatic conditions frequently switch back and forth between day and night, light and dark, sunny and stormy. Furthermore, the play oscillates between passionate prose and lyrical Shakespeare quotations; when neither character can find the words themselves to express the profundity of emotions they experience, they resort to quoting the Bard without a moment's hesitation.

The subject matter encompassed by *Storms Still* is a torrential downpour of contentious topics, ranging from issues concerning nationalism and emigration, spirituality and religious identity, intergenerational mobility and conflict, societal morality, and personal responsibility. At the play's conclusion, some sort of reconciliation is found between these polar opposite men, although there is no definitive resolution. One senses a profound tension and uncertainty still lingering in the hearts and minds of both characters. Steiner's most frequently used phrase throughout the play is "when all is said and done." In the end, he asks Goldring what he will expect of the aging actor "when all is said and done," to which Goldring replies, "I don't know."

"I don't know" is a condition I often feel when contemplating the subject of Holocaust related theater. "I don't know" is also often the condition all artists feel just before he or she takes the leap of faith toward creation. I first heard of *Storms Still* in a brilliant paper by Juan Mayorga titled, "The Theatrical Representation of the Holocaust," which was delivered as a lecture in the conference, The Holocaust and Its Significance for Our Generation, held in Madrid in September 2007. This paper by Dr. Mayorga, who is also a Spanish playwright, appears in its totality on the Holocaust Theater Catalog website. However, I would like to quote its final two paragraphs:

> "As in all historical theatre, but with more responsibility than ever, the theatre of the Holocaust will look for its form beginning with a moral question rather than from an aesthetic impulse. It will look for a form of presentation that will take care of the ultimate impossibility of the presentation. That Holocaust theatre will not aspire to compete with the witness. It has another mission. Its mission is to build an experience of loss; not to symbolically settle the debt but to remind that the debt will never be settled; not to speak for the victim, but to make the victims' silence reverberate. The theatre, art of the human voice, can make us hear the silence. The theatre, art of the body, can make visible its absence. The Theatre, art of the memory, can make us feel the forgetting.
>
> But if a theatre about Auschwitz is necessary and urgent, as much if not more is needed a theatre against Auschwitz; a theatre that battles authoritarianism and submissiveness; a theatre that will be the mask that will unmask a counter-current of the propaganda and half-truths; a theatre that will make its spectators more critical and more compassionate, more vigilant and braver against the domination of man over man;

a theatre against Auschwitz would also be a negative, paradoxical, profoundly Jewish way of representing the Holocaust. The theatre against Auschwitz would be a defeat of Hitler and a way to mourn."

For the characters in the two plays I have mentioned, memories, recollections, guilt and hauntings have created actions on their part that make them, in many ways, victims of their own memories. In both of the referenced plays, the playwrights have taken it upon themselves to, with the highest level of respect, portray the damage done by the atrocities witnessed and present in the lives of their main characters. By doing so, and with their artistic talent, they are enabling us to see the circumstances of these men's lives, but to also allow us to bear witness through the younger generation characters' reactions, how one person's horrible circumstances might allow the future generation to not only remember, but to also act responsibly, on their behalf. These plays are but two of thousands of entries that will ultimately be part of the National Jewish Theater Foundation/Holocaust Theater Catalog, whose bibliography development is being supervised by the prominent Holocaust Theater historian and member of the Holocaust Theater Archive Advisory Board, Dr. Alvin Goldfarb.

As the playwright Colin Greer reminded me recently, public life was once an entirely daytime affair. Night was dark and dangerous. You rushed home before it came in. With the advent of gas and electric street lighting, social life could occur at night. As dark arrived the lights went on and so scary shadows could become friends and neighbors. He then eloquently stated the following:

"The theater too illuminates the dark. It is at its richest at night because it creates a social space for discovery and inspiration at the time of darkness where the good and bad angels of our selves have, for millennia, roiled around. Theater, like street lights, can light the twilight, restrain the darkest spirits, and yes, enlightens the midnight of the soul where a passionate myopia infects the better angels of our nature."

So, where do we go from here? How do we make certain that the power of artistic creation will always triumph over the powers of destruction? How do we meet the challenge of tomorrow while maintaining the artistic standards that will inspire future generations to understand this atrocity and create, in its memory, with their own unique voices? In part, we must define, ever vigilantly, what Holocaust Theater represents, and what it must never misrepresent. We must enlist professionals from many disciplines to reinforce this goal. And, finally, we must challenge ourselves to open our minds and provide to all of our audiences the great gift of theater as a unique tool in Holocaust education and awareness.

APPENDIX 2

Study Guide created for *The Voices of Terezín Project*

at American University, supervised by Gail Humphries

Arrival of Jews at the Theresienstadt Ghetto

This Study Guide was developed in 2010–2011
by students and alumni of American University for the
VOICES OF TEREZÍN Project at American University
Directed and supervised by Dr. Gail Humphries Mardirosian
Designers: Undergraduates
Ouida Maedel
Victoria Mattiuzzo
Ezree Mualem
and
Inga Bunsch Sieminski
in partial fulfillment of her graduate degree
In Art Management/Arts Education

Terezín Background

Introduction

Since the early 1600s, the area of the modern day Czech Republic had been part of the Austro-Hungarian Empire ruled by the royal House of Hapsburg. Following the collapse of the Empire after World War I, the independent republic of Czechoslovakia was created in 1918. While Germany struggled with the aftermaths of the Treaty of Versailles, Czechoslovakia experienced, for the first time in its history, political autonomy.

The new country incorporated regions of Bohemia, Moravia, Silesia, Slovakia and the Carpathian Ruthenia. It provided rather extensive rights to its German, Hungarian, Polish and Ruthenian minorities, but did not afford actual territorial and political authority to them. This created tension among the minorities.

Adolf Hitler took advantage of this weakness and gained the largely German-speaking Sudetenland in the Czech lands through the 1938 Munich Agreement. When Hitler broke the Agreement and marched into the remaining Czech lands, he ended the 20 year existence of the Czech Republic by naming the area a "Protectorate." As a result, Jewish populations began to fall prey to the same harsh treatment as in the Reich.

The Terezín Ghetto

In the late 18th century, Emperor Josef II of the Hapsburg Empire decided to build a walled city and fortress at the nexus of the Labe and Ohre rivers in order to maintain control of the waterways and deter invasions. Located roughly 40 miles northwest of modern-day Prague, the Nazis considered Terezín to be an ideal location for a concentration camp, which was established under SS commander Reinhard Heydrich in November of 1941.

After evicting all civilians and renaming the fortress "Theresienstadt Ghetto", the Nazis proceeded to turn Terezín into a work and transit camp for Jews and Jewish sympathizers. Even though Terezín was branded as a camp for "privileged" Jews–former civil servants and employees of the Third Reich, intellectuals, Jews married to Aryans, half-Jews, war veterans, and the elderly–conditions were still dire. At its most crowded, 50,000 prisoners lived in Terezín, which was originally meant to house no more than 6,000 people. Camp inmates were placed on a starvation diet of cabbage and potatoes, and were forced to work extraordinarily long days. While some inmates were condemned to hard labor, others documented the German war effort with intricate and elaborate written reports. The smallest mistakes, even a simple typographical error, were punishable by death. Due to the crowded, unhygienic, and harsh conditions, pandemics of fatal illnesses were common.

ART FOR HEALING AND RENEWAL

In August of 1943, a transport of 1260 Polish children arrived in Terezín from the liquidated Bialystok ghetto. In miserable condition, they were held in isolation and nursed back to health by Terezín inmates, only to eventually be deported to Auschwitz-Birkenau together with 53 of their caretakers.

Despite this reality, Terezín became a dynamic center for artistic innovation and performance. Through concentrating the members of the Jewish *intellegencia* in one camp, the SS inadvertently created the circumstances for a wealth of cultural activities to take place. A multitude of actors, playwrights, dancers, musicians, visual artists, composers, writers, and scholars were imprisoned at Terezín. Committed to find meaning in their confinement, to develop creative ways to resist the Nazi regime, and to fulfill a "great hunger for culture in a place where there was not even enough bread to eat"[1], the artists at Terezín literally created works of art in order to survive. After long days of work and weak from hunger, Terezín's artist-inmates, both professionals and amateurs, rehearsed and performed.

While these activities were initially forbidden, the Nazis eventually used these artistic activities for their own ends. For example, in 1944, the Nazis hosted the International Red Cross at Terezín in a desperate attempt to quiet rumors from the international community about atrocities occurring in the camps. During the Red Cross visit, Terezín's artists were forced to mount theatrical performances and make a propagandist "documentary", portraying life at Terezín as luxurious and care-free. The Red Cross inspectors were taken in by this deception.

Ultimately, however, this deception could not hold off the inevitable. The Third Reich was losing the war, and with the armistice in late April to early May of 1945, the SS fled Terezín and the International Red Cross stepped in

---

1 Platz, Naomi. "What You Need to Know about Terezín to Enrich Your Understanding of This Play." http://www.lexhamarts.org/theater/200906/BackgroundInfo.htm

with the assistance of Czech volunteers.² Due to an ongoing deadly typhus epidemic, all of Terezín's inhabitants were placed under strict quarantine and could not leave the camp immediately. However, by June, the camp was closed and all of the people who survived in Terezín had been repatriated to Germany or Austria.

Terezín's Artistic Legacy

Among the contributions of Terezín's prisoners are some of the most notable and moving artistic works of the 20th century, many of which became lost after the Holocaust and are slowly being rediscovered. Even Terezín's children became part of this movement through writing poetry and drawing pictures. During its operation as a work camp, more than 12,000 children under the age of 15 passed through Terezín. While 90% of these children died during the Holocaust[3], they leave their art behind.

Signs of Life celebrates and honors the artists of Terezín and the legacy of the art made at the concentration camp. For the Terezín inmates art was a strategy for survival, and we carry these implications with us into confronting contemporary conflicts and genocides, and into reflecting on how we all live each day of our lives, individually and collectively.

---

2 "Terezín/ Theresienstadt." Holocaust Education and Archive Research Team. http://www.holocaustresearchproject.org/othercamps/Terezín.html
3 Volkanova, Hana, ed. *I Never Saw Another Butterfly: Children's Drawings and Poems from Terezín Concentration Camp 1942–1944*. Pantheon Books: New York, 1993.

ART FOR HEALING AND RENEWAL

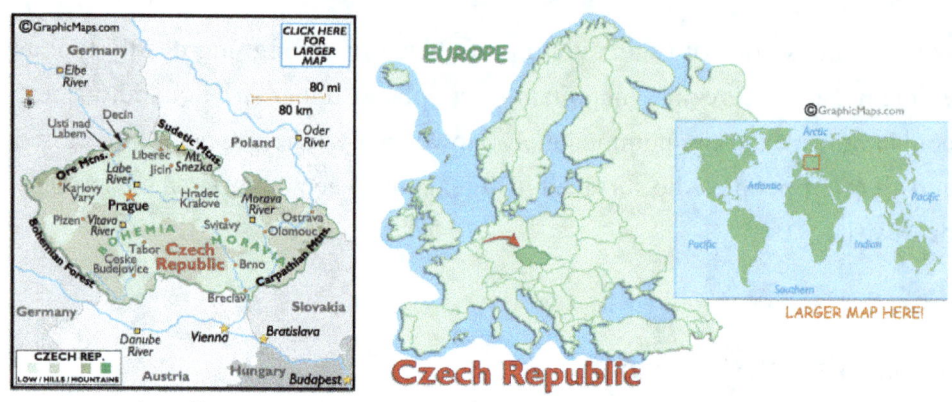

http://www.worldatlas.com/webimage/countrys/europe/cz.htm

Chronology[4]

1938	October	**Germany occupies the Sudetenland**
1939	March	Germany occupies Bohemia and Moravia; both become the "Reich Protectorate."
	June	A decree defines "Jews," based on the Nuremberg racial laws. New regulations are enacted for the registration and liquidation of property and assets owned by Jews in the Protectorate.
	July	Jewish students are excluded from German-language public schools and high schools in the Protectorate. Jewish students in Czech-language schools are restricted.
	August	Jews in provincial areas of the Protectorate are ordered to leave their homes and resettle in Prague within one year.
	September	**Germany invades Poland**
1940	January	A decree mandates the "elimination of Jews from the Protectorate economy," resulting in the "Aryanization" or liquidation of "Jewish enterprises."
	February	The Protectorate Administration in Prague excludes Jews from attending theater performances and movies.
	April	**Germany occupies Denmark, invades Norway**
		The Gestapo imposes a curfew between 8 p.m. and 6 a.m. on Jews in the Protectorate.
	May	**Germany invades Western Europe**
		The Netherlands surrenders to Germany
		Belgium surrenders to Germany
		Prague police prohibit Jews from using public parks and gardens in the city.
	June	**France surrenders to Germany**
	October	The Prague municipal administration decrees that Jews will not receive ration cards for clothing.

---

4 Adapted from Dutlinger, Anne D., and Moravian College. Payne Gallery. *Art, Music, and Education as Strategies for Survival: Theresienstadt, 1941–45*. 1st ed. New York: Herodias. 2001.

1941	January	The Protectorate Department of Agriculture refuses to issue Jews ration cards for apples. By 1942, these restrictions expand to include prohibitions on receiving rations of sugar, vegetables, fruits, meat, fish, poultry, dairy products, soap, and tobacco products.
	June	**Germany invades the Soviet Union**
	September	Jews are prohibited from using public libraries and lending libraries in the Protectorate. Later in the year, this decree is expanded to include museums, exhibitions, galleries, and archives.
		All Jews above the age of six in the Reich, including the Protectorate, are ordered to wear a six-pointed yellow Star of David, with the word "Jude" ("Jew") in black calligraphy.
	October	Reinhard Heydrich, Adolf Eichmann, and six other members of the Nazi occupation staff meet in Prague to discuss the "solution of the Jewish problem" for the Protectorate. They decide to convert Terezín into a ghetto for Jewish deportees en route to the East.
	November	The first transport with 342 Jewish men from Prague arrives in Terezín as a construction labor detail, AK1 (Aufbaukommando).
		The first large transports of Jews from Prague, including the elderly, arrive in Terezín. Women and children are housed separately from men in the Dresden barracks.
1942	January	The first transport to the East departs Terezín for the Riga ghetto.
	February	All original non-Jewish inhabitants of Theresienstadt are ordered to move out of the town.
		Prague police headquarters prohibits Jews from using laundries and cleaners.
	April	Transports of Jewish men, women, and children to the East (Poland) continue. Those fit for labor are sent to labor camps; those considered unfit are killed.
	May	Reinhard Heydrich, Protector of Bohemia and Moravia, is ambushed near Prague by Czech partisans. He dies from his injuries.
	June	In reprisal for Heydrich's assassination, 199 male residents over the age of 15 in the village of Lidice are shot. Commandant Seidl has 30 men deported from Terezín to Lidice, where they are ordered to dig a mass grave. All buildings are destroyed with explosives.
		Transports of Jews from Berlin and Vienna arrive in Terezín.
	July	The children's homes L410 for Czech girls ages eight to sixteen and L417 for Czech boys ages ten to fifteen are opened in Terezín.

	August	Construction begins on a three-kilometer rail spur connecting the Bauschowitz station with the Terezín ghetto, which will eventually eliminate the forced march for the Jewish deportees.
	September	A crematorium with four ovens is built to deal with the dead too numerous to bury according to Jewish tradition.
		During this month, 3,941 inmates die from inadequate shelter, hygiene, and food.
		All Jewish schools are closed in the Protectorate. The Protectorate Department of Education prohibits private lessons for Jewish children by paid and unpaid teachers.
		Mischlinge (part-Jews) of the first degree (non-practicing half-Jews with two Jewish grandparents not married to Jews) are barred from German and Czech language educational institutions, although they are still allowed in vocational, agricultural, and art schools with special permission issued by the Department of Education.
	October	The first transport is sent from Terezín to Auschwitz-Birkenau. During the next two years, a total of 25 transports with more than 44,000 prisoners are deported. Most of them are killed.
1943	April	The first Jewish transports from the Netherlands arrive in Terezín.
	August	A transport of 1,260 children arrives from the liquidated Bialystok ghetto. They are held in isolation until being deported to Auschwitz-Birkenau together with 53 Terezín inmates who were assisting them.
	October	The first transport of Danish Jews arrives in Terezín.
	December	On RSHA orders (Central Office of Reich Security), "beautification" of the Terezín ghetto begins for international visitors.
1944	June	An International Red Cross delegation composed of two Danish officials and one Swiss representative, inspect the ghetto for six hours. The prisoners were instructed on how to "perform" a happy life and convey positive ghetto conditions.
	July	Several Jewish artists are arrested and jailed in the "Small Fortress" prison for distributing "atrocity propaganda" through their realistic artwork. After brutal interrogations and torture, they are deported to Auschwitz. Only two of them survive.
	August	A camera crew from a Prague newsreel company is ordered to shoot a propaganda film about Terezín, *Theresienstadt: A Documentary of the Jewish Settlement Territory*.

	November	In the wake of a losing war, Germans begin to dismantle gas chambers and crematoria in Auschwitz-Birkenau. Surviving prisoners are transferred to concentration camps in the Reich and the Terezín ghetto.
1945	January	Transports of several thousand German and Czech Jews from mixed marriages and part Jews (Mischlinge) arrive in Terezín.
	February	A transport of 1,200 Jews is released from Terezín on a transport to Switzerland.
		The construction of a gas chamber begins in Terezín.
	March	Adolf Eichman orders a new "beautification" of the ghetto for another inspection by the International Red Cross in April.
	April	Swedish Red Cross buses remove 423 Danish prisoners from Terezín for transfer to Sweden.
		About 15,000 prisoners from eastern concentration camps arrive in Terezín. A typhus epidemic begins.
	May	The International Red Cross assumes control of the Terezín ghetto and the Small Fortress prison.
		SS men leave Terezín.
		Soviet army tanks arrive and take control of Terezín. Approximately 30,000 prisoners are liberated, including those from evacuation transports.
	August	Repatriation of former prisoners from Terezín takes place.

Terminology[5]

Allies: The nations—the United States, Britain, France, and the Soviet Union—that joined together in the war against Germany and its partners—Italy, Japan, Bulgaria, Hungary, Romania, and Slovakia—known as the Axis.

Antisemitism: Hatred of Jews; the term "antisemitism" was popularized in 1879 by the German journalist Wilhelm Marr.

Aryan: The Nazis applied the term to themselves as descendants of an ancient Indo-European people, claiming their "Aryan race" superior to all other racial groups. For the Nazis, the typical "Aryan" was blond, blue-eyed, and tall.

Auschwitz-Birkenau: The largest of the Nazi extermination camps in Poland, in which at least 1.1 million Jews were killed, mostly through gassing. Thousands of Roma and Sinti (Gypsies), Poles, Soviet prisoners, homosexuals, Jehovah's Witnesses were also gassed at the camp.

Axis: The nations who opposed the Allies.

Concentration Camp: A facility in which political prisoners, prisoners of war, or other perceived enemies are confined. The first concentration camp set up by the Nazis was Dachau in 1933. By the end of World War II there were thousands of camps. Many prisoners were killed or died of starvation or disease.

Death Marches: Forced marches of concentration camp prisoners towards Germany. Death marches occurred toward the end of the war, as camps were evacuated ahead of the advancing Allied troops.

Deportation: Removing people from their homes. Jews were transferred to ghettos or camps, usually in train cattle cars without windows, food, water, or toilets. Many people died during deportation.

---

5 Adapted from the Teacher's Guide *Meeting Hate with Humanity: Life During the Holocaust*. Museum of Jewish Heritage, New York.

Displaced Person Camp: A camp set up after World War II for survivors from concentration camps and others whose homes were destroyed. Thousands of people remained in camps for several years until they could immigrate to the new State of Israel, the United States, or other Western countries.

"Final Solution of the Jewish Question": The Nazi code name for their plan to eliminate all European Jews. The plan was coordinated in January 1942, at a Nazi conference near Lake Wannsee outside of Berlin.

Gas Chambers: Specially constructed bath houses in the six Nazi extermination camps in Poland. Victims were crowded into the rooms and died from deadly Zyklon B gas streaming out of the shower heads.

Genocide: A word first used in 1944 to describe an official governmental policy of killing an entire people.

Gestapo: Short for the German *Geheime Staatspolizei* (secret state police). This police force was known for its brutal methods and became the main instrument of Hitler's anti-Jewish policies.

Ghetto: The term probably originates from a 1516 walled-in area in Venice, Italy (Geto Nuovo), where Jews were forced to live. Eventually the term was used for all closed-in quarters where Jews lived separately from other populations.

During World War II, the Nazis created Jewish ghettos throughout Europe to facilitate the separation and deportation of Jews to the camps.

Hebrew: The ancient language of the Jewish people, used for prayer and study. It is now the official language of the State of Israel.

Hitler, Adolf: (1889–1945) Nazi party leader and German chancellor, who placed antisemitism at the center of Nazi politics. He committed suicide in his Berlin underground bunker, as Allied troops were approaching the city.

Holocaust: A word of Greek origin meaning complete destruction, especially by fire. It is used to describe the murder of European Jewry. The Hebrew word for Holocaust is *Shoah*, meaning catastrophe, destruction, or disaster.

Liberators: Soldiers and staff of the Allied Armed Forces who reached the various concentration camps toward the end of World War II in 1945. They cared for the prisoners until they could return home or went to Displaced Persons camps.

Nazi: A member of the National Socialist German Workers' Party that took political control of Germany under Adolf Hitler in 1933.

Nuremberg Laws: Two laws issued in 1935 to exclude from German life people whom the Nazis considered alien. The first law removed German citizenship from "non-Aryans", and the second law prohibited them from marrying Germans.

The term "non-Aryan" was applied to Jews and all non-Germanic peoples, including Roma and Sinti (Gypsies), and African-Germans.

Partisan: A member of an organized fighting group that attacks the enemy within occupied territory. During World War II, partisans fought Nazi occupying forces by harassing and killing Nazis and sabotaging their war efforts.

Propaganda: Materials created and disseminated to influence public opinion or to spread false information.

Rabbi: A Jewish religious leader trained in Jewish law. The term comes from the Hebrew word for "my teacher."

Roma and Sinti: A nomadic ethnic group that originated in India and has lived in Western Europe since the 15th century. They are referred to as "Gypsies", a name given to them by Europeans, who mistakenly believed they came from Egypt.

Shabbat: The Jewish Sabbath, which begins on Friday evening and ends on Saturday night. It is a day of spiritual rest and reflection.

SS: Specially chosen Nazi troops, assigned to the brutal tasks of implementing the "Final Solution." The term stands for the German "Schutzstaffel," which means "protection unit."

Theresienstadt: A ghetto established in 1941 in the Czech town of Terezín. The Nazis planned it as a model settlement, to create propaganda for the world about how well they treated the Jews. Many well-known Jews were sent to Theresienstadt, including artists and writers,

Despite the horrible living conditions and the constant fear of deportation, inmates struggled to maintain an active cultural life.

Most of the ghetto's prisoners were eventually deported to Auschwitz.

THE VOICES OF TEREZÍN PROJECT

Quotes

From: *We Are Children Just the Same*

Vedem—"In the Lead"—the Secret Magazine by the Boys of Terezín[6]

The Jewish Council of Elders ("Aeltestenrat") was set up to give the appearance of the ghetto's self-administration by the Jews. Functioning under strict daily SS orders, the Council was responsible for all internal affairs, including the welfare of the children and youth.

The Elders made great efforts to keep the intellectual vitality of the ghetto community alive. While cultural and artistic expression was tolerated by the Nazi within the "Freizeitgestaltung" (leisure time activities), education had to be pursued secretly.

On arrival in the ghetto, families were separated and men, women, and children housed in different barracks. Much care was taken to mitigate the fate of the children. Boys lived in building L 417, the former town school, in ten separate rooms called "homes." Tutors selected by the Elders secretly taught the older children and provided intellectual stimulation through discussions, readings, and cultural activities.

The secret magazine *Vedem* ("In the Lead") was published in "Home no. 1."

---

6 Krízková, Marie Ruth, et al. We Are Children Just the Same : Vedem, the Secret Magazine by the Boys of Terezín. Philadelphia: Jewish Publication Society, 1995.

ART FOR HEALING AND RENEWAL

From *Vedem*:

Interview of two surviving teenage boys from Home no.1

> Kurt: "It may seem incredible, but the magazine was all our own idea ... Every Friday night we would sit around the table, or find room on the bunks, whatever, and then anyone who had written something during the week would read his contribution."
>
> Zdenek: "The magazine was never actually published in the true sense of the word. We simply read it aloud every Friday night."
>
> Marie: "Why did you call your magazine *Vedem*—'In the Lead?'"
>
> Zdenek: "Home Number One was always first. Home Number One will always be so!"

***

"Old ones go
And young ones go.
Healthy ones go,
And sick ones go,
Not knowing if they will survive."
("Untitled" by Zdeněk Weinberger")

***

THE VOICES OF TEREZÍN PROJECT

Hanus Hachenburg, age 14

> "What am I?
> Who are my people,
> Wandering child that I am?
> Are ghetto walls my homeland?
> Or is it a ripening land
> Going somewhere, small, beauteous?
> Is Bohemia my homeland, or the world?"

As a 14-year old boy, Hanus Hachenburg was deported from Terezín to Auschwitz-Birkenau, along with his mother. According to verbal reports by former fellow prisoners, he continued to write poems for a while. There is no further written information.

***

> "And my last thought before falling asleep is: What will tomorrow bring?"
>
> ("Two Recollections" by Rudolf Laub)

***

> "... Look bravely forward, swallow all your sorrow,
> Even though its bitterness might make us choke.
> Do not be broken in this tattered labyrinth,
> A dream will always end when we awake."
>
> ("Avowal" by Zdeněk Ornest)

***

"But anyone who worked with the children of Terezín knew full well that sometimes there was a strange light in the eyes of a child, a look full of so many 'whys,' to which no caretaker knew the answer. He knew that the children woke up at night, staring into the empty darkness, and he sometimes heard their quiet sobs, and knew there was no cure."

(Zeek Shek's deposition)

***

"I envy you a little warmth, my friends,
When, numb with cold, I crawl out of my bed,
When nothing else but coldness could I feel
Still wrapt in all the lovely dreams I had,
No wish have I to wash under the cold tap
Slowly I drown, not in my shame, but filth.
Oh, lovely warmth, oh warmth so dearly purchased,
I want to warm myself in your kind lap.
And when at last, with heavy heart, I wake,
And know that I am starving, I would weep
For all the hope that I must now abandon.
I only want to sleep and sleep and sleep."

("Just a Little Warmth" by Zdeněk Ornest)

***

"... Mrs. Bachnerová got the corridor beautifully clean (poor woman, she had to use cold water), so don't hesitate to strew pieces of paper or dirty bandages about. It won't look so monotonous ... "
  ("Motto: Destroy Whatever You Can—A Terezín Proverb?"
                                                    by Leo Demner)

From: *I Never Saw Another Butterfly*[7]

The Girls' Home was in building L 410. While most of them perished, their story is told through the many drawings and poems.

Their teacher was Friedl Dicker-Brandeis. She was a Viennese artist who was deported to Terezín in 1942. She provided secret art lessons as a way to help children deal with their emotions in the ghetto.

Before she was taken away to Auschwitz, she gave one of the tutors in the barracks two suitcases filled with 4,500 drawings. The drawings survived. Friedl did not.

  "Everything leans, like tottering, hunched old women ...
  This evening I walked along the street of death."
                          ("The Closed Town" Anonymous)

                                ***

---

7 Volavková, Hana, U.S. Holocaust Memorial Museum., and Statni zidovske muzeum (Czech Republic). *I Never Saw Another Butterfly : Children's Drawings and Poems from Terezín Concentration Camp, 1942–1944*. Expanded 2nd ed. New York: Schocken Books, 1993.

"We got used to it that from time to time, one thousand unhappy souls would come here and that, from time to time, another thousand unhappy souls would go away … "

(Petr Fischl age 15, perished in Auschwitz 1944)

***

"Death, after all, claims everyone,
You find it everywhere.
It catches up with even those
Who wear their noses in the air.
The whole, wide world is ruled
With a certain justice, so
That helps perhaps to sweeten
The poor man's pain and woe."

("It All Depends On How You Look At It" by Miroslav Kosek;
perished in Auschwitz at age 12)

***

"And the cannons don't scream and the guns don't bark
And you don't see blood here.
Nothing, only silent hunger.
Children steal the bread here and ask and ask
    and ask
And all would wish to sleep, keep silent, and just go to sleep again … "

("Terezín" by Mif 1944)

***

THE VOICES OF TEREZÍN PROJECT

"I was once a little child ...
But now I am no more a child
For I have learned to hate."
    ("Terezín" by Hanuš Hachenburg; died in Auschwitz at age 14)

***

"All that is left is a few lines scribbled on the wall of the barracks ... "
    ("Lights Out" from the diary of Helga Weissová; survived)

***

"Food is such a luxury here ...
... "I'd like to stay here, a small patient,
Waiting the doctor's daily round,
Until, after a long, long time, I'd be well again.
Then I'd like to live and go back home again."
    ("Pain Strikes Sparks on Me, The Pain of Terezín"
    by Anonymous)

***

"Your forehead was as heavy as the heavens before it rains."
    ("Concert in the Old School Garret" by Anonymous)

***

"... For seven weeks I've lived here,
Penned up inside this ghetto.
But I have found what I love here.
The dandelions call to me
And the white chestnut branches in the court.
Only I never saw another butterfly.
That butterfly was the last one.
Butterflies don't live in here,
   in the ghetto."

("The Butterfly" by Pavel Friedman, 4.6. 1942;
perished in Auschwitz 1944 at age 13)

From: The Terezín Diary of Gonda Redlich[8]

Gonda Redlich, whose hidden diary was discovered in 1967, arrived in 1941 with credentials as a 25 year old educator of the Zionist youth movement Maccabi Hatzair. He was chosen by the Jewish Council of Elders in Terezín to be responsible for the Youth Welfare Department and the 15,000 children in the ghetto.

Eventually, his wife also arrived on a transport. After the birth of their son, Dan, in March 1944, Gonda Redlich began a second diary dedicated to him.

Later that year, Gonda, his wife, and Dan were deported to Auschwitz, where they perished in the gas chambers.

---

8 Redlikh, Egon, and Saul S. Friedman. *The Terezín Diary of Gonda Redlich*. Lexington, Ky.: University Press of Kentucky, 1992.

Of the 15,000 children, 100 children survived the war. Of the total population of 140,000 just 17,000 were alive at the liberation by the Red Army on May 8, 1945.

From the diary:

January 10, 1942 ... An order of the day: nine men were hanged. The reason for the order: they insulted German honor.

February 14, 1942 ... The lines of people are like deaf mutes during the time when coffins are taken out of the barracks. It really is one of the strongest impressions in Terezín.

February 22, 1942 ... Yesterday there was a children's play. The children are great actors and I liked their songs.

March 17, 1942 ... What do you tell a child that steals coal? The child sees everyone stealing and loses all sense of morality.

August 20, 1942 ... Very hot. Yesterday, they stripped the clothes from women that came from Germany and checked them naked. Maybe they wanted to find gold or silver. They thoroughly check the transport which will leave the ghetto, until few retained anything but the clothes on their backs.

June 17, 1943 ... If you go to the place where food is distributed, you will always witness the same scene. People ask for soup, which is only warm water.

October 6, 1944 [last entry in the diary for Dan] ... What is going to happen? Tomorrow, we travel, my son. We will travel on a transport like thousands before us. As usual, we did not register for the transport. They put us in without a reason. But never mind, my son, it is nothing. All of our family already left in the last weeks. Your uncle went, your aunt, and also your beloved grandmother ... We hope to see her there ... . They send small children, and their prams are left here. Separated families. On one transport a father goes. On another, a son. And on a third, the mother ...

Tomorrow we go, too, my son. Hopefully, the time of our redemption is near.

THE VOICES OF TEREZÍN PROJECT

From: My Lucky Star
By Zdenka Fantlova[9]

Zdenka Fantlova was brought up in a Jewish family in prewar Czechoslovakia. She was nineteen when she and her family were sent to Theresienstadt. Fantlova's entire family perished in the Holocaust.

At the end of the war, after a grueling 300 mile death march, she was rescued by an unknown British Army officer in the Bergen-Belsen camp and sent to Sweden for recuperation under the care of the International Red Cross. She now lives in London.

She begins her book by trying to reconcile her memories of "home" with what she finds during a return visit after World War II.

> "Home? Why, naturally. Home is forever. The firm ground beneath our feet, certainty and order, now and forever. The whole family together. There is no other way of life. Or is there?"

> "Time itself seems unreal. Do we merely flutter along like leaves blown at random? Do we feel at home only when we have firm ground underfoot and a loved one by our side?"

> "She feels like someone waking from a dream, confused about who she is, needing to wait a little for the scattered pieces of her life to settle in their right places."

---

9 Fantlová, Zdenka. *My Lucky Star*. 1st ed. New York ; London: Herodias, 2001.

"How did it all happen? Where were we before we came here? Where did it all start?"

***

During her elementary school years, Fantlova's father bought a leather-bound blank book and wrote bits of wisdom in it. She asked her school teacher to add to it.

"Never envy, never slander, never despair,
wish well to all, work hard, and hope."

"Just keep calm. Remember, calmness is strength."

"Life hastens on, and we are scarce aware
how, pace by pace, we too are hastening . . .
those dear ones who loved us—these alone
always, and gratefully, we shall recall."

"Never say something's too hard to learn. Tell yourself that if a circus elephant can learn to walk on bottles, you can train yourself to do anything. If you really want to, that is."

"Never try to have too much of anything in life ... just see that you have what you need and a little more. That's good enough. When you die, all you will take with you is what you've given to other people."

"You'll meet all sorts during your life. Form your own judgment about them—not by how they earn their money but by what they spend it on."

"Look around you, observe, learn, and educate yourself. We are put here to develop and perfect ourselves as much as we can, not to climb social ladders. They don't lead anywhere. Remember, if a dwarf climbs even to the highest mountaintop, he is still a dwarf."

***

Shortly before Fantlova's family was deported to the Terezín ghetto, a new family moved into her neighborhood in Prague, including Arnost, "a striking young man."

"One glance and lightning stuck—love at first sight and quite inevitable. From that day on we met as often as we could."

"Love would overcome all obstacles."

"The outside world vanished. All we had was love, wild, eager, intoxicating, endless … If only that night could have gone on forever. We pledged to each other our eternal love and imagined our future together, after the war, as soon as peace came. The next day we rode home, still in a dream."

"Life began to seem absurd, yet the thought that he was sleeping only a short distance away, thinking about me as I was about him, warmed my heart."

ART FOR HEALING AND RENEWAL

***

Late one night in the fall of 1941, the door bell rang. A friend of her father's warned them of the upcoming transports to the east and offered to hide some of their belongings in his house. In January 1942, several Jewish families, including hers and Arnost's, were ordered to report for deportation to Terezín.

> "The barracks seemed to vanish along with the Germans, Terezín, and the world itself. Here, together, one soul, one body alone in the universe."

> "There was no time for tears and personal woes. A collective tragedy had descended on us all, like some natural disaster that forces people together. All that remained was hope and the determination to survive."

***

> "Many people had a deep yearning to express themselves artistically; both in words and music, and the rest welcomed the results with gratitude as a compensation for their confinement. Every cultural event buoyed up their hopes and morale and reinforced their faith in human values."

> "Everyone gave their best, whatever their ability. There were no names in neon lights, no fame, no fortune—only the satisfaction of a job well done and the appreciation of a grateful audience. To this end professionals and amateurs worked hand in hand, free of envy and self-importance."

"The Czech Theatre in the ghetto was no mere entertainment, or social distraction, but a living torch that showed people the way ahead and lent them spiritual strength and hope. For many, cultural experience became more important than a ration of bread."

***

A 25 year old writer, composer, actor, clown, Karel Svenk, had written a political satire for the inmates. The closing song was adopted by performers and spectators as the Terezín "anthem":

"Where there's a will there's always a way
So hand in hand we start,
Whatever the trials of the day
There's laughter in our heart."

"To find scapegoat for all the misrule and shortages they have caused, they pick on one group of people who can be blamed for everything."

***

After the war, in Sweden:

"Everyone we met was kind and full of compassion, even though they could hardly conceive of what conditions we had come from and what we had endured."

***

Fantlova decided not to find out where and how her father had died. She wanted to remember him the way she had last seen him being led off by the Gestapo, tipping his hat and saying:

"Just keep calm. Remember, calmness is strength."

Resources for Teachers

Related Websites

American University's Department of Performing Arts
http://www.american.edu/cas/performing-arts/

The American University Voices of Terezín Project (Spring 2010)
http://www.american.edu/cas/Terezín/index.cfm

The United States Holocaust Memorial Museum
http://www.ushmm.org/

Holocaust Literature: Voices of the Victims
http://fcit.usf.edu/HOLOCAUST/ARTS/litVicti.htm

Terezín, the Czech Republic
http://www.czechtourism.com/eng/uk/docs/what-to-see/towns-cities/all/Terezín/

ART FOR HEALING AND RENEWAL

Selections from the Voices of Terezín Project at

American University Reference List

Terezín and The Arts

Austin, Patricia. "Fireflies in the Dark: The Story of Friedl Dicker-Brandeis and the Children of Terezín." *Book Links* 12.5 (2003): 37.

Bor, Josef. *The Terezín Requiem*. New York: Avon Books, 1978.

Burian, Jarka. *Modern Czech Theatre: Reflector and Conscience of a Nation.* Iowa City: University of Iowa Press, 2000.

Burnett, Michael. "Creation Amid Death." *The Times Educational Supplement.* 4109 (1995): SS17.

Cantu, Amy. "Last Dance." *Library Journal* 128.8 (2003): 165.

Chapman, Clare, Rachel Levy, and Igal Avidan. "Dateline." *The Jerusalem Report* (2003): 44.

Cohen, George. "The Diary of Petr Ginz, 1941–1942." *The Booklist* 103.15 (2007): 20.

Cook, William. "Escape Artists." *New Statesman* 133.4685 (2004): 40–43.

Courtenay, Tom, et al. *The Last Butterfly*. Shanachie, United States, 2005.

Daly, Peter M. *Building History: The Shoah in Art, Memory, and Myth*. New York: P. Lang, 2001.

Dormitzer, Else. *Theresienstädter Bilder (Images of Teresienstadt)*. Hilversum: De Boekenvriend, 1945.

Dutlinger, Anne D., and Moravian College. Payne Gallery. *Art, Music, and Education as Strategies for Survival: Theresienstadt, 1941–45*. 1st ed. New York: Herodias, 2001.

Elias, Zdenek, and Jiri Stein. "Smoke of Home." Unpublished work.

Estvanik, Nicole. "Unpacking History." *American Theatre* 24.1 (2007): 28.
Fantlová, Zdenka. *My Lucky Star*. 1st ed. New York ; London: Herodias, 2001.
Felsmann, Barbara Prümm Karl. *Kurt Gerron–Gefeiert Und Gejagt, 1897–1944: Das Schicksal Eines Deutschen Unterhaltungskünstlers: Berlin, Amsterdam, Theresienstadt, Auschwitz. (Kurt Gerron–Celebrated and Persecuted, 1897–1944: Destiny of a German Entertainer: Amsterdam, Theresienstadt, Auschwitz)*. Beiträge Zu Theater, Film Und Fernsehen Aus Dem Institut Für Theaterwissenschaft Der Freien Universität Berlin. 1. Aufl. ed. Berlin: Hentrich, 1992.
Fergus, M. Bordewich. "Song of Defiance." *Reader's Digest* 162.972 (2003): 142.
Frye, Elizabeth C. "Elsa Bernstein's Life as Drama: Memories of Theresienstadt—Introduction and Translation." v, 87 leaves; 29 cm. Dissertation: Thesis (M.A. in Germanic Studies)–University of Illinois at Chicago, 2007.
Glazer, Hilda R. "Children and Play in the Holocaust: Friedl Dicker-Brandeis–Heroic Child Therapist." *Journal of Humanistic Counseling, Education & Development* 37.4 (1999): 194.
Green, Gerald. *The Artists of Terezín*. New York: Hawthorn Books, 1978.
Greenfield, Philip. "Waxman: Song of Terezín; Zeisl: Requiem Ebraico." *American Record Guide* 62.4 (1999): 216.
Hirsch, Edward. "Two Suitcases of Children's Drawings from Terezín, 1942–1944 (Poem)." *American Poetry Review*. Vol. 31. American Poetry Review, 2002. 9.
Hoenig, Leonard J., Tomas Spenser, and Anita Tarsi. "Reminiscence Dr Karel Fleischmann: The Story of an Artist and Physician in Ghetto Terezín." *International Journal of Dermatology* 43.2 (2004): 129–35.
Honigberg, Steven, et al. *Darkness & Light*. Albany Records, Albany, NY, 2002.
Isherwood, Charles. "Theater Review; Children Do Battle with a Greedy Hurdy-Gurdy Man." *New York Times* (2006): 1.

Karízková, Marie Ruth, et al. *We Are Children Just the Same: Vedem, the Secret Magazine by the Boys of Terezín*. Philadelphia: Jewish Publication Society, 1995.

Kalin, Tom. "New York: "Seeing through 'Paradise'"." *Artforum* 30.2 (1991): 124.

Karas, Jo za. *Music in Terezín 1941–1945*. 1st ed. New York: Beaufort Books, 1985.

Kavanova, Eva M. *About Terezín Theater a Little Bit Differently*. Unpublished manuscript, 1967.

Kift, Roy. "Comedy in the Holocaust: The Theresienstadt Cabaret." *New Theatre Quarterly* 12.48 (1996): 299.

Kimmel, Daniel M. "Voices of the Children." *Variety* 37.1 (1997): 63.

Kimmelman, Michael. "Art View; Visions of Truth, Smuggled out of Hell." *New York Times* (1991): 27.

Kramer, Aaron. "Creative Defiance in a Death-Camp." *The Journal of Humanistic Psychology* 38.1 (1998): 12.

Kurt, Moses. "Ullmann: Quartet 3; Piano Sonatas 5,6,7." *American Record Guide* 66.3 (2003): 154.

___. "Krasa: Brundibar; Overture for Small Orchestra; Laitman: I Never Saw Another Butterfly." *American Record Guide* 70.3 (2007): 118.

Lawrence, L. Langer. "The Art of Atrocity." *Tikkun* 17.4 (2002): 67.

Lessner, Joanne Sydney. "Anne Sofie Von Otter and Christian Gerhaher: "Terezín/Theresienstadt"." *Opera News* 73.1 (2008): 52.

Long, Joanna Rudge. "The Cat with the Yellow Star: Coming of Age in Terezín." *The Horn Book Magazine* 82.4 (2006): 468.

Lorencova, Anna. "Eva Kavanova." Interview notes Nov. 7, 1994.

Makarova, Elena, Sergei Makarov, and Victor Kuperman. *University over the Abyss: The story behind 520 lecturers and 2,430 lectures in KZ Theresienstadt 1942–1944*. Jerusalem: Verba Publishers Ltd, 2004.

Makarova, Elena Dicker Friedl, and Regina Seidman Miller. *Friedl Dicker-Brandeis, Vienna 1898-Auschwitz 1944: The Artist Who Inspired the Children's Drawings of Terezín.* 1st ed. Los Angeles, CA: Tallfellow/Every Picture Press, in association with the Simon Wiesenthal Center/Museum of Tolerance, 2001.

Migdal, Ulrike. *Und Die Musik Spielt Dazu: Chansons Und Satiren Aus Dem Kz Theresienstadt. (And the Music Plays, Too: Chansons and Satires from the Theresienstadt Ghetto).* Serie Piper. Originalausg. ed. München: Piper, 1986.

Moore, R. "Terezín–Theresienstadt." *American Record Guide* 71.4 (2008): 252–53.

Moore, Robert A. "Never Broken." *American Record Guide* 69.1 (2006): 279.

Mott, Michael. "Two Poems." *Sewanee Review* 110.4 (2002): 548.

Opfermann, Charlotte. *The Art of Darkness: Marat/Sade and Adolf Eichmann: The Truth About The "Paradise Ghetto" And the Cultural Programs Known as Freizeitgestaltung at the Nazi Concentration Camp Theresienstadt with Special Focus on Music and Theater Programs Performed 1942–1945: Facts and Fiction during and since World War II with many Drawings, Created between 1942 and 1945 by My Fellow Prisoners.* Houston, TX: University Trace Press, Houston, 2002.

Pearce, Joe. "Brundibar at Theresienstadt: A People's Struggle to Maintain a Level of Musical Culture in the Face of Imminent Peril." *The Opera Quarterly* 10.4 (1994): 39.

Pechova, Oliva. *Kunst in Theresienstadt 1941–1945: Sammelband Zur Ausstellung (Art in Theresienstadt 1941–1945: Exhibition Catalogue).* Terezín: Pamatnik, 1972.

Peschel, Lisa. " 'There Everyone Knew How to Play Comedy:' Is There a Place for Pleasure in the Archive of the Holocaust?" (2005): 17.

___. "The Law of What Can Be Said: The Archive and Theatrical Performances in the Terezín Ghetto." 2006. 21.

———. "Nonsurvivor Testimony: Terezín Ghetto Theatre in the Archive and the Second Czech Cabaret." *Theatre Survey* 48.1 (2007): 143.

———. "Smoke of Home: Introduction." Unpublished manuscript, 2007.

———. "Theatre in Terezín, 1945–2006." Educational and Cultural Center of the Jewish Museum, 2007. 22.

Peschel, Lisa, et al. "Theatrical Texts from Terezín". Precis for book.

Peschel, Lisa, and Alan Sikes. "Staging Terezín: A Performance-Based Research Project." *Baylor Journal of Theatre and Performance* 2.1 (2005).

———. "Risking Representation: Performing the Terezín Ghetto in the Czech Republic." *Theatre Topics* 18.2 (2008).

Petrásová, Markéta Parik Arno. *Terezín in the Drawings of the Prisoners, 1941–1945*. [Prague]: State Jewish Museum in Prague, 1983.

Porges, Felix, Viteslav Horpatzky, and Pavel Weisskopf. *Second Czech Cabaret*. Unpublished manuscript, 1944 (?).

Pozar, Diane C. "Social Studies—We Are Children Just the Same: Vedem, the Secret Magazine by the Boys of Terezín Edited by Maria Rut Krizkova, Kurt Jiri Kotouc and Zdenek Ornest." *The Book Report* 15.1 (1996): 59.

Rochman, Hazel. "The Cat with the Yellow Star: Coming of Age in Terezín." *The Booklist* 102.19/20 (2006): 100.

Meyer, Sarah. "Tommy's Tale Comes of Age." *The Jerusalem Report* (2002): 24.

Schwarz, Paul, and Leo Lowit. *Witness in the Anteroom to Hell: The Theresienstadt Drawings of Paul Schwarz & Leo Lowit*. South Yarra, Vic.: Jewish Museum of Australia, 1990.

Schweitzer, Vivien. "Songs of Tragedy, Triumph and Hope 'Terezín/Theresienstadt'." *New York Times* (2008): 27.

Schwertfeger, Ruth. *The Women of Theresienstadt: Voices from a Concentration Camp*. New York: Berg, 1989.

Sherman, Courtney Jade. "A Performance Analysis of Ellwood Derr's I Never Saw Another Butterfly." D.M.A. Arizona State University, 2008.

Sprehe, J. Timothy. "Defiant Requiem: Verdi at Terezín." *Society* 44.1 (2006): 89–93.

Stapen, Nancy. "Reviews: Seeing Through 'Paradise'." *ARTnews* 90.9 (1991): 152.

Terry, Hong. "Where the Bad Things Are." *Moment* 29.2 (2004): 25.

Tuma, Mirko. "Memories of Theresienstadt." *Performing Arts Journal* 1 (1976): 12–18.

Volavková, Hana, U.S. Holocaust Memorial Museum., and Statni zidovske muzeum (Czech Republic). *I Never Saw Another Butterfly: Children's Drawings and Poems from Terezín Concentration Camp, 1942–1944*. Expanded 2nd ed. New York: Schocken Books, 1993.

Wadler, Aleeza Nemirovsky. "Strings in the Shadows: A Portrait of Three Violinists at the Terezín Concentration Camp." D.M.A. Boston University, 2003.

Weissová, Helga. *Zeichne, Was Du Siehst: Zeichnungen Eines Kindes Aus Theresienstadt/Terezín = Maluj, Co Vidís, Kresby Jednoho Dítete Z Terezína = Draw What You See, a Child's Drawings from Theresienstadt*. Göttingen: Wallstein, 1998.

Weissová, Helga, and Niedersächsischer Verein zur Förderung von Theresienstadt/Terezín. *Das Künstlerische Schaffen (Artistic Creation)*. Göttingen: Wallstein, 2002.

Willoughby, Susan. *Art, Music, and Writings from the Holocaust*. The Holocaust; Variation: Holocaust (Chicago, Ill.). Chicago, Ill.: Heinemann Library, 2003.

Wlaschek, Rudolf M. *Kunst und Kultur in Theresienstadt : Eine Dokumentation in Bildern (Art and Culture in Theresienstadt: A Pictorial Documentation)*. Gerlingen: Bleicher, 2001.

Zatzman, Belarie. "Fifty-One Suitcases: Traces of Hana Brady and the Terezín Children." *Canadian Theatre Review*.133 (2008): 29–37.

Holocaust Representation and Instruction

Arendt, Hannah. *The Human Condition*. [Chicago]: University of Chicago Press, 1958.

Auron, Yair. *The Pain of Knowledge: Holocaust and Genocide Issues in Education*. New Brunswick, N.J.: Transaction Publishers, 2005.

Berlin, Elliot, et al. *Paper Clips*. Hart Sharp Video, New York, 2006.

Bruner, Jerome S. *Acts of Meaning*. The Jerusalem-Harvard Lectures. Cambridge, Mass.: Harvard University Press, 1990.

___. *The Culture of Education*. Cambridge, Mass.: Harvard University Press, 1996.

Burton, Bollag. "Learning to Teach the Holocaust for the First Time." *The Chronicle of Higher Education* 45.21 (1999): B2.

Caille, Sugarman-Banaszak. "Stepping into the Past: Using Images to Travel through Time." *Teaching History*.130 (2008): 24.

Chu, Jeff. "10 Questions for Elie Wiesel." *Time*: Time Inc., 2006. 8–8. Vol. 167.

Church, Michael. "Dancing beneath the Gallows." *The Times Educational Supplement*.4031 (1993): SS9.

Council of Europe. *Teaching About the Holocaust and the History of Genocide in the 21st Century: 90th European Teachers' Seminar, Donaueschingen, Germany, 6–10 November 2000 : Report*. Strasbourg Cedex: Council of Europe, 2003.

Davies, Ian. *Teaching the Holocaust: Educational Dimensions, Principles and Practice*. London: Continuum, 2000.

DeCoste, F. C., and Bernard Schwartz. *The Holocaust's Ghost: Writings on Art, Politics, Law, and Education*. Edmonton, Alta., Canada: University of Alberta Press, 2000.

Donnelley, Mary Beth. "Educating Students About the Holocaust: A Survey of Teaching Practices." *Social Education* 70.1 (2006): 51.

Drew, Margaret A. *Facing History and Ourselves: Holocaust and Human Behavior : Annotated Bibliography*. New York: Walker, 1988.

Duboys, Tibbi. *Paths to Teaching the Holocaust*. Rotterdam; New York: Sense Publishers, 2008.

Edward, J. Katz. "Bearing Witness: Teaching About the Holocaust / the Spirit That Moves Us, Vol. 3: Using Literature, Art, and Music to Teach About the Holocaust at the Secondary and College Level." *Journal of Adolescent & Adult Literacy* 46.6 (2003): 533.

Fallace, Thomas D. *The Emergence of Holocaust Education in American Schools*. Secondary Education in a Changing World. 1st ed. New York: Palgrave Macmillan, 2008.

Florczyk, Katie. *Holocaust Studies: Art, Literature, and Media*. Ill: Central CommunityHigh School, 2008.

Gardner, Howard. *Frames of Mind: The Theory of Multiple Intelligences*. 10th anniversary ed. New York, NY: BasicBooks, 1993.

___. *Intelligence Reframed: Multiple Intelligences for the 21st Century*. New York, NY: Basic Books, 1999.

Geras, Norman. *The Contract of Mutual Indifference: Political Philosophy after the Holocaust*. Pbk. ed. London; New York: Verso, 1999.

Glenn, David. "Verbatim." *Chronicle of Higher Education* 51.24 (2005): A14–A14.

Haggith, Toby Newman Joanna. *Holocaust and the Moving Image: Representations in Film and Television since 1933*. London: New York, 2005.

Hamerow, Theodore S. *Why We Watched: Europe, America, and the Holocaust* New York : W.W. Norton & Co., c2008.

Hamot, Gregory E., David H. Lindquist, and Thomas Misco, J. "Breaking Historical Silence through Cross-Cultural Collaboration: Latvian Curriculum Writers and United States Holocaust Memorial Museum Fellows." *Educational Studies* 42.2 (2007): 155.

Hawkes, Terence. *Metaphor*. London: Methuen, 1972.

Hornstein, Shelley, and Florence Jacobowitz. *Image and Remembrance: Representation and the Holocaust*. Bloomington, IN: Indiana University Press, 2003.

Iorio, Dominick A., Richard Libowitz, and Marcia Sachs Littell. *The Holocaust: Lessons for the Third Generation*. Studies in the Shoah ; V. 18. Lanham, Md: University Press of America, 1997.

Keller, Bess, Kathleen Kennedy Manzo, and Vaishali Honawar. "Genocide Claiming a Larger Place in Middle and High School Lessons. (Cover Story)." *Education Week* 27.9 (2007): 1–15.

Kohn, Murray J., and David Patterson. *Is the Holocaust Vanishing? A Survivor's Reflections on the Academic Waning of Memory and Jewish Identity in the Post-Auschwitz Era*. Lanham, MD: Hamilton Books, 2005.

Kwiet, Konrad, and Jürgen Matthäus. *Contemporary Responses to the Holocaust*. Praeger Series on Jewish and Israeli Studies. Westport, Conn.: Praeger, 2004.

LaCapra., Dominick. *Representing the Holocaust: History, Theory, Trauma*. Ithaca: Cornell University Press, c1994.

Lang, Berel. *Holocaust Representation: Art within the Limits of History and Ethics*. Baltimore, Md. ; London: Johns Hopkins University Press, 2000.

Lindquist, David H. "Guidelines for Teaching the Holocaust: Avoiding Common Pedagogical Errors." *The Social Studies* 97.5 (2006): 215.

___. "Five Perspectives for Teaching the Holocaust." *American Secondary Education* 36.3 (2008): 4–14.

Lucy, Russell. "Recalling Rwanda." *The Times Educational Supplement*.4566 (2004): T6.

Millen, Rochelle L. *New Perspectives on the Holocaust: A Guide for Teachers and Scholars*. New York: New York University Press, 1996.

National Catholic Center for Holocaust Education. *Holocaust Education: Approaches That Work*. Greensburg, Pa.: Seton Hill College National Catholic Center for Holocaust Education, 1997.

Paula, Mountford. "Working as a Team to Teach the Holocaust Well: A Language-Centred Approach." *Teaching History*.104 (2001): 28.

Perl, Sondra. *On Austrian Soil: Teaching Those I Was Taught to Hate*. Albany: State University of New York Press, 2005.

Rokem, Freddie. *Performing History: Theatrical Representations of the Past in Contemporary Theatre*. Iowa City [Iowa]: University of Iowa Press, 2000.

Rubin, Janet. *Voices: Plays for Studying the Holocaust*. Lanham, Md.: Scarecrow Press, 1999.

Samuel, Totten. "What Will Students Remember? Closing a Lesson on the Holocaust." *Social Education* 66.7 (2002): 436.

Samuels, Robert. *Teaching the Rhetoric of Resistance: The Popular Holocaust and Social Change in a Post-9/11 World*. 1st ed. New York: Palgrave Macmillan, 2007.

Schafft, Gretchen E. *From Racism to Genocide: Anthropology in the Third Reich*. Chicago: University Press of Illinois, 2004.

Schumacher, Claude. *Staging the Holocaust: The Shoah in Drama and Performance*. Cambridge Studies in Modern Theatre; New York: Cambridge University Press, 1998.

Schweber, Simone. *Making Sense of the Holocaust: Lessons from Classroom Practice*. New York: Teachers College Press, 2004.

Shimoni, Gideon, and International Center for University Teaching of Jewish Civilization. *The Holocaust in University Teaching*. 1st ed. Oxford England ; New York: Pergamon Press, 1991.

Simone, Schweber. ""Holocaust Fatigue" In Teaching Today." *Social Education* 70.1 (2006): 44.

Smith, Helmut Walser. *The Holocaust and Other Genocides: History, Representation, Ethics.* 1st ed. Nashville Tenn.: Vanderbilt University Press, 2002.

Supple, Carrie. *From Prejudice to Genocide: Learning About the Holocaust.* Stoke-on-Trent: Trentham, 1993.

Totten, Samuel. *Holocaust Education: Issues and Approaches.* Boston: Allyn and Bacon, 2002.

Totten, Samuel, Paul R. Bartrop, and Steven L. Jacobs. *Teaching About the Holocaust: Essays by College and University Teachers.* Westport, Conn.: Praeger, 2004.

U.S. Holocaust Memorial Museum. *A Resource Book for Educators: Teaching About the Holocaust.* Washington, D.C. (100 Raoul Wallenberg Place, SW 20024-2150): United States Holocaust Memorial Museum, 1995.

United States Holocaust Memorial Museum. *Resistance.* Washington, DC (100 Raoul Wallenberg Place, SW, Washington 20024): U.S. Holocaust Memorial Museum, 1993.

___. *Remember the Children : Daniel's Story: Teacher Guide.* Washington, D.C. (100 Raoul Wallenberg Pl., SW, Washington 20024-2126): U.S. Holocaust Memorial Museum, 1999.

___. *Teaching About the Holocaust: A Resource Book for Educators.* Washington, D.C. (Washington, D.C., 100 Raoul Wallenberg Place, SW 20024-2126): United States Holocaust Memorial Museum, 2001.

Waterston, Alisse, and Kukaj Antigona. "Reflections on Teaching Social Violence in an Age of Genocide and a Time of War." *American Anthropologist* 109.3 (2007): 509.

Wink, Karen A. "A Lesson from the Holocaust: From Bystander to Advocate in the Classroom." *English Journal* 96.1 (2006): 84.

"Art springs from truthful and extreme experience perhaps even more than it does from talent and it has the capacity to be stronger than death."

Vaclav Havel

5 October 1936–18 December 2011; Czech playwright, essayist, poet, dissident and politician; Nobel Peace Prize nominee; the ninth and last president of Czechoslovakia (1989–1992) and the first President of the Czech Republic (1993–2003). He wrote more than 20 plays and numerous non-fiction works, translated internationally.

Editors

KAREN BERMAN, PH.D., is Dean Emerita, College of Fellows of the American Theatre; Past President, Association for Theatre in Higher Education; Past Chair and Artistic Director, Department of Theatre and Dance, Georgia College. Dr. Karen Berman's extensive experience encompasses the direction of over 150 theatre productions from the Smithsonian to off-Broadway, administration at both universities and non-profit theatre organizations, and teaching and curriculum development in theatre  for social change, theatre directing and acting. Prior to becoming Theatre and Dance Chair at Georgia College (GC), she taught at Georgetown University in Washington, DC. Karen has been awarded the Georgia Governor's Award for the Arts, the Hillel Heroes Award, four NEA grants, and numerous awards for her film *Giving Voice: A Black Lives Matter Musical* including: Best Feature Film at the Canadian Diversity Film Festival; Best Social Justice Film at the Silk Road Film Awards Cannes; and Best Social Justice Feature at the Cannes World Film Festival. Her publications include the chapter "Transformative Education Processes: Difficult Dialogues and Global Citizenry" in the book *Arts Integration in Education: Teachers and Teaching Artists as Agents of Change,* the chapter "Translations and Transgressions: Twenty-First Century Questions Regarding Zayas" in the book *Remaking the Comedia: Spanish Classical Theater in Adaptation*, and "Transformative Cross-Cultural Dialogue in Prague: Americans Creating Czech History Plays" in the *Theatre

Symposium journal, as well as numerous other journal articles. Karen has presented papers, conducted workshops, led plenary sessions, made keynote addresses, and led panel discussions at numerous conferences, including ATHE, American Association of Colleges and Universities (AAC&U), American Society for Theatre Research (ASTR), Association for Hispanic Classical Theatre, and Association of Holocaust Organizations, among many others. She directed and co-wrote four original plays about Czech heroes that GC students performed in Prague and at an international theatre festival in the Czech Republic. Karen co-founded and continues to serve as Artistic Director of Washington Women in Theatre and she has directed numerous plays with Holocaust and Jewish themes. She was a thought leader for the *Lives Eliminated Dreams Illuminated* multi-media exhibit on the Holocaust and was academic liaison for the inaugural NJTF Holocaust Remembrance Readings.

GAIL HUMPHRIES, PH.D., is Dean Emerita, College of Fellows of the American Theatre; Likhachev/Yeltsin Cultural Fellow, St. Petersburg, Russia; Fulbright Senior Scholar, Prague, CZ; Dean Emerita, Stephens College; Professor Emerita, American University. Dr. Gail Humphries' broad experience encompasses academic administration, curricula and program development, fundraising, and the direction of over 180 productions, including drama, musical theatre, children's theatre, the classics, and new works. She has taught master classes in theatre and arts administration, as well as directed in countries including Greece, Russia, Slovakia, Sweden, the United Kingdom, and the Czech Republic. She has served on multiple boards for non-profit arts organizations. Gail has been awarded several outstanding teaching, faculty and directing awards, and has published articles in multiple professional journals. She is the co-editor and contributing author to the book titled *Arts Integration in Education: Theory, Research and Practice* (Intellect Books Ltd. 2016; 2018). She has contributed chapters to two books published by Routledge: *The Power of Witnessing: Reflections, Reverberations and Traces of the Holocaust* (2012) and *The Courage to Fight Violence Against Women* (2018). She has developed curricula and new degrees in arts administration and arts education for various colleges and universities. Finally, her presentations have included nearly 100 panel discussions, workshops and keynote addresses at various conferences ranging from the Association for Theatre in Higher Education, the Association for Arts Administration Educators, to the International Psychoanalytical Association and the Women's Bar Association of Maryland. Gail is currently a thought leader for the *Lives Eliminated, Dreams Illuminated* multi-media exhibit on the Holocaust, an academic liaison for the Holocaust Remembrance Readings, a reviewer for Fellowships through the Association of Arts Administration Educators, and an adjunct professor in Arts Leadership and thesis advising at Rider University.

Volume I Contributors

PAUL ACCETTURA, J.D., is the co-author of four plays about Czech heroes each of which was performed by students of Georgia College in the Czech Republic. The four plays (*The Vision of Čapek, The Mystery of Mucha, The Flights of Jan Wiener*, and *The Women of Havel and Kafka*) were performed at the European Regions International Theatre Festival in Hradec Králové (now called the REGIONS International Theatre Festival Hradec Králové) as well as several venues in Prague. He also co-adapted Russell Baker's memoir *Growing Up* that was performed at Wordstage Theatre in Arlington, Virginia. For 32 years he was an attorney in the Office of Chief Counsel, Internal

Revenue Service in Washington, DC. He was a Senior Technician Reviewer who specialized in regulations and litigation regarding exempt organization issues, including churches, schools, and other charities as well as political action committees and section 501(c)(4) social welfare organizations. He received his B.A. from George Washington University and his J.D. from the Washington College of Law at American University. He currently resides in Milledgeville, Georgia.

Manuela Mendels Bornstein was born in Paris, France in 1933. Following the German occupation of France, her family began to feel the effects of anti-Jewish measures throughout France. When the roundup of Jews began in 1942, she with her younger sister and her parents fled into Vichy France with the help of the French Resistance. The family hid in a very small village in Southern France where they remained until the end of World War II. While the family was in hiding, her brother was born in 1943, and after the war the family returned to the Paris suburbs. She immigrated to the United States from France in 1960 where she married and had two children, eventually settling in Atlanta, Georgia. She spent many years playing the violin as part of the Atlanta Community Symphony Orchestra. She is active throughout the Southeastern United States sharing her experiences as a survivor with school children under the auspices of the Weinberg Center for Holocaust Education of the William Breman Jewish Heritage Museum in Atlanta.

Miřenka Čechová, Ph.D. is a Czech director, choreographer, performer and scholar. She is co-founder and house director of two internationally acclaimed theater companies: Spitfire Company and Tantehorse. She began her career as a classical ballet dancer at the Dance Conservatory in Prague. After earning two Masters degrees in theatre and nonverbal theatre, she was awarded a Ph.D. in physical theatre direction from the Academy of Performing

Arts in Prague, where she has served as a professor of authorial theatre since 2012. She received a Fulbright scholarship to teach and research in the United States. She has combined her two disciplines of theatre and dance to create her own physical and dance theatre style. As a performer she has established a strong international reputation, particularly for her solo works, in which she serves as both playwright and director. She received a Herald Angel Award at the Edinburgh Fringe Festival, Best of Performance Award from the Prague Fringe, Best of Fringe in Amsterdam, and the Best Overseas Production of the National Arts Festival in South Africa. As a director, she has contributed to more than 25 productions.

DAVID A. CRESPY, PH.D., founded the University of Missouri's Writing for Performance program, serves as its Co-Director, and is the founding Artistic Director of MU's Missouri Playwrights Workshop. A recipient of the Gold Medallion from the Kennedy Center American College Theatre Festival (KCACTF), he received the Fulbright to Spain and Greece in 2022–23 to write plays about the Spanish origins of the Jewish Communities of Thessaloniki and Veria, of which he is descendant, titled *Mi Corazón Español Vive Ahora En Grecia: Six Plays of Sephardic Greece*. His current book is *Dreamwrighting: Dreamwork for Dramatic Writing for Stage & Screen* (Brill, 2024).

VIRGINIA CRISTE, J.D., is an attorney practicing family law in Palm Springs, California. She received her B.A. from Mount Holyoke College and her J.D. from George Washington University. She has a National Board of Trial Advocacy certificate and has held an AV rating with Martindale Hubbell for many years. After the Berlin wall fell, and during Havel's first year as Chief of State of the then country of Czechoslovakia, Virginia went to Terezín to try to learn about her grandparents who spent their final years there. At that time, there were only a small exhibit and a depository of artifacts that she was allowed to view alone in the company of a museum official. Spending a day with the remnants of hand-drawn posters announcing show performances, cabaret tickets, albums of dorm life, and so much more, was hard to forget. A stop at a London theatre on her return to the United States helped form the thought, if *Les Misérables* and *Miss Saigon* could be musicals, why not Terezín? After all, inhabitants of Terezín kept music and theatre as a vital part of their lives in captivity. In such a manner, the musical theatre production of *Signs of Life* was born. She brought together the composer, lyricist, and book writer, who had never worked together before.

SARA HERRNSTADT CROSBY, M.S.W., CSW-PIP received her B.F.A. in Theatre from Stephens College and enjoyed a varied acting career based out of New York City. Her roles brought her to Off-Broadway, television and film, as well as regional theatres. In 1986, she received an M.S.W. from Loyola of Chicago's Graduate School of Social Work and has worked as a psychotherapist since receiving her degree. She has given numerous workshops around the country on women's issues, prejudice and discrimination, and suicide prevention, among others. In 2001 she co-founded the award-winning Dakota Academy of Performing Arts (DAPA). She is the lead facilitator and a director for DAPA at the Pavilion Plays for Living Theatre Company, where high school acting students give voice to and teach empathetic understanding of important human issues through live theatre. She recently returned to the stage in several productions for Augustana University and Monstrous Little Theatre Company. She recently published her first book, *The Deep Dive*, a collection of poetry, and she is writing a second book for loved ones of people with addiction. She is the 2013 Champion for Children Award winner for South Dakota Voices for Children and was awarded the 2020 Sioux Falls Stage Award of Excellence for her longstanding excellence and dedication to local performing arts.

EDITORS AND CONTRIBUTORS

CAROLYN DORFMAN, a choreographer and founding artistic director of Carolyn Dorfman Dance (CDD) is known as a creator of evocative dances that reflect her concerns about the human condition. Hailed as a consummate storyteller, she is a child of Holocaust survivors who has also created a celebrated body of work that honors her Jewish legacy, its trials and triumphs, its treasured uniqueness and, most importantly, its universal connections. Touring nationally and internationally, her 10-member, multi-ethnic company appears at major theatres, festivals, universities and non-traditional performance venues. She is a former assistant professor of Dance at Centenary College in New Jersey, is a master teacher, mentor, and guest artist, choreographer, and lecturer at major universities, pre-professional and professional training programs across the United States and abroad. Since founding CDD in 1982, she has garnered significant artistic and civic awards for her contributions as an artist, leader, industry partner, educator, and humanist. Multiple tours, to Poland and Bosnia and Herzegovina, were supported by The Trust for Mutual Understanding, United States Arts International and the United States State Department, all valuing CDD's art and programming that explores what Dorfman describes as: "The world as it is … and the world as it can be."

NANCY R. GOODMAN, PH.D., is a training and supervisory analyst with the Contemporary Freudian Society (CFS) and the International Psychoanalytic Association (IPA). She is on the permanent faculty of the CFS and has served as Institute Director of the CFS Washington, DC program. She writes on female development, analytic listening, and Holocaust trauma. Her most recent publications include: *The Courage to Fight Violence Against Women: Psychoanalytic and Multidisciplinary Perspectives* (co-edited with Paula L. Ellman) published by Routledge Press, 2019; *Finding Unconscious Fantasy in Narrative, Trauma, and Body Pain: A Clinical Guide* (co-edited with Paula L. Ellman) published by Routledge Press, 2017; and *The Power of Witnessing: Reflections, Reverbera-*

tions, and Traces of the Holocaust: Trauma, Psychoanalysis, and the Living Mind (co-edited with Marilyn B. Myers) published by Routledge Press, 2012. She has a psychoanalytic practice in Bethesda, Maryland.

RUTH GORDON received her B.Ed. from the University of Florida and her M.Ed. from the University of Maryland. In 2004 she founded and has served as director of Holocaust Impact Theater in Dade County, Florida. Since 2004 she and her husband Ira have continued to operate the Holocaust Impact Theater that is their way of giving back to the community, while inspiring students to utilize this creative platform which allows students to teach and celebrate the importance of tolerance, acceptance, and diversity. She received "The My Life, My Choice" award from Channel 10 in Miami for her work with Holocaust Impact Theater. She is passionate about studying and teaching the Holocaust. She is a Holocaust Documentation Education Certified Instructor. Her father Irving J. Whitman was a World War II veteran who helped liberate Buchenwald and, in 2010, he was awarded France's Congressional Medal of Honor for helping liberate France from Hitler's regime. In 2016, after 35 years as a teacher, she retired from Dade County Schools. She is an adjunct professor at Florida International University. She is the author of *Inside Out, Outside In*, a children's book teaching diversity.

MIRA HIRSCH earned her B.A. in Theatre from the University of Denver. She is a theatre director, educator and actor who recently returned to the classroom as a secondary school theatre teacher at the Atlanta International School. She recently served as Director of Education at Atlanta's Theatrical Outfit. She was the founder and Artistic Director of Jewish Theatre of the South for the whole of that company's thirteen-year history. She is a Past-President of the Alliance for Jewish Theatre and a former advisory board member of the Metropolitan Atlanta Arts Fund. She is co-author (with Arnold Mittelman and Janet Rubin) of the Routledge Press book *Enacting History:*

A Practical Guide to Teaching the Holocaust Through Theater. She is a freelance theatre director in Atlanta, Georgia with numerous directing credits, including at Theatrical Outfit, Atlanta Lyric Theatre, The Center for Puppetry Arts, Synchronicity Theatre and Stage Door Players. She is director/facilitator of Project Tolerance, a teen social issue theatre project creating and presenting original theatre pieces about the Holocaust and contemporary prejudice, discrimination, and bullying. Additionally, she serves as an educational consultant with the National Jewish Theater Foundation's Holocaust Theater International Initiative.

VALÉRIE ISSEMBERT is a Washington, DC based educator, director, actor, and playwright. She is the Director of Theatre Arts for Alexandria Country Day School and the Artistic Director for BRAVO Productions: Theatre for Young Artists. Valérie holds a B.S. in Theater from Skidmore College and an M.A. in Educational Theater from New York University. As an artist and educator, Valérie has directed and created numerous pieces of original and scripted work with students ranging in age from five to 18 years old. Valérie is a proud member of the Actor's Equity Association, a dual citizen of France and America, and the grandchild of Holocaust survivors.

LIZ LERMAN is a choreographer, writer, educator, and speaker, and the recipient of honors including a 2023 Guggenheim Fellowship, 2002 MacArthur "Genius Grant" and a 2017 Jacob's Pillow Dance award. Key to her artistry is opening her process to various publics, resulting in research and outcomes that are multi-disciplinary, participatory, urgent, and funny. Current projects include building the *Atlas of Creative Tools*, an online resource, her touring production of *Wicked Bodies*, and the retrospective at Yerba Buena Center for the Arts titled *Reflection & Action*. She founded the Dance Exchange in 1976 and led it until 2011. She is the author of several books including *Teaching Dance to Senior Adults*, *Hiking the Horizontal*, and most recently, co-authoring

Critique is Creative with John Borstel, which addresses the Critical Response Process: a communication system for giving and receiving feedback that she invented decades ago. She is currently Institute Professor at the Herberger Institute for Design and the Arts at Arizona State University. A former fellow of the Robert W. Deutsch Foundation, she is currently a senior fellow at the Yerba Buena Center for the Arts and a fellow at the Center for the Study of Race and Democracy at Arizona State University.

MOTTI LERNER is an award-winning Israeli playwright and most of his plays deal with political themes. Among plays produced in Israel are: *Kastner, Pangs of the Messiah, Paula,* and *Pollard* in the Cameri Theatre in Tel Aviv; *Exile in Jerusalem, Passing the Love of Women, Doing His Will,* and *The Abandoned Melody* in Habima National Theatre; *Autumn* in the Beit Lessin Theatre in Tel Aviv; *Hard Love* in Haifa Theatre; *The Hastening of the End* in the Khan Theatre in Jerusalem; and *The Admission* in Jaffa Theater. His productions abroad include: *Kastner, Autumn, The Murder of Isaac* in Heilbronn Theater, Germany; *Exile in Jerusalem* in Stuttgart, Berlin, and Vienna; *Hard Love* in New York, Rome, and Berlin; *The Murder of Isaac* in Centerstage, Baltimore; *Passing the Love of Women* in Theatre J, Washington, DC; *Pangs of the Messiah* in Theatre J, Silk Road Rising, Chicago, and Theater of Ideas, New York; *Benedictus* in Golden Thread Theater, San Francisco; *Paulus* in Silk Road Rising; *The Admission* in Theatre J; and *After the War* in Mosaic Theater, Washington, DC. He is a recipient of the best play award (1985), the Israeli Motion Picture Academy Award for the Best TV Drama (1995 and 2004), the Prime Minister's of Israel Award (1994), and the Landau Prize for Performing Arts (2014).

JOAN LIMAN, M.D., MPH, has a B.A. in Psychology from the State University of New York at Buffalo where she was elected to Phi Beta Kappa. She is an honors graduate of New York Medical College where she earned a master's degree in Public Health in addition to her medical diploma. She served as

Associate Dean for Student Affairs at New Jersey Medical School before relocating to New York City to become the deputy to the medical director of Metropolitan Hospital Center. She invested in several off-Broadway theatre productions before partnering with Virginia Criste to produce *Signs of Life*. She wrote about overcoming serious medical challenges in her musical memoir *A LimanAde Life*, and has three plays and numerous music videos to her credit. She is the board liaison for Yiddishkayt Initiative, a docent at The Museum of Jewish Heritage—A Living Memorial to the Holocaust, a former board member of Theater Resources Unlimited (TRU), and a past president of the board of directors of Amas Musical Theatre. Favorite role to date: "Nonny" to her two grandchildren, Ryan and Marissa.

ARNOLD MITTELMAN is a producer, director, educator and author with a nationally recognized career of artistic and educational achievement. He has created almost 300 diverse productions of plays, musicals and special events in all art forms. He helped found and/or lead five major not-for-profit theatres including the acclaimed New York Free Theater, The Whole Theater Company and the Coconut Grove Playhouse. Employing innovative development strategies, he has launched numerous world premieres and commercial theatrical productions for Broadway, Off-Broadway, national tours and the West End. His distinguished teaching, educational and innovative training programs have accompanied his body of work. In 2007 he created and was named President and Producing Artistic Director of the National Jewish Theater Foundation, Inc./National Jewish Theater (NJTF/NJT) which celebrates the cultural significance of Jewish history, themes and creativity including significant Jewish playwrights, composers, lyricists, authors and performers. He, guided by a prestigious Board of NJTF/NJT Advisors, developed the first comprehensive production and research-oriented Holocaust-Related Theater Catalog (HTC).

EDITORS AND CONTRIBUTORS

WENDY MULLEN, D.M.A., is a Professor of Music and Vocal/Music Theatre Coordinator at Tennessee Technological University. An accomplished soprano and violist, she has performed both nationally and internationally and serves as a master class clinician and adjudicator throughout the Southeastern United States. Her research interests include the music of Viktor Ullmann and the World War II concentration camp of Terezín. She is an active member of the National Association of Teachers of Singing (NATS) and has held several leadership positions at both the state and national level. Prior to her appointment at Tennessee Technological University, she served as Vocal Coordinator, Interim Chair, and Provost Fellow at Georgia College in Milledgeville, Georgia. She was the Founding Director of the School of Music at Tennessee Technological University. She received her Doctorate of Music in Vocal Performance at Arizona State University and her Masters and Bachelors of Music degrees from The University of Tennessee, Knoxville.

SHOSHANA OLIDORT, PH.D., is a writer, critic, and translator. Her work has appeared or is forthcoming in *Asymptote*, the *Columbia Journal*, *The Cortland Review*, *In geveb: A Journal of Yiddish Studies*, the *Los Angeles Review of Books*, *LitHub*, the *Paris Review Daily*, *Prooftexts: a Journal of Jewish Literary History*, and *Public Books*, among other publications. She holds a Ph.D. in comparative literature from Stanford University and is web editor for the Poetry Foundation.

TIM REAGAN, PH.D., RDT, APTT, is a registered drama therapist and accredited Playback Theatre trainer. He holds a doctorate in expressive therapies, master's degree in performing arts management, and bachelor's degree in drama. Tim is the resident drama therapist at Adventist HealthCare Shady Grove Medical Center – Mental Health. His research focuses on Playback Theatre with youth. As a director and teaching artist, Tim has worked on both devised and applied theatre projects with young children to senior adults with and without disabilities in professional, community, educational, and therapeutic settings for more than 30 years.

Karin Rosnizeck is the founder and Artistic Director of Expats Theatre which aims to bring works by international contemporary playwrights to Washington, DC and to engage audiences in current global socio-political debates with a focus on female perspectives. For Expats Theatre, she has directed several productions: *Surfacing*, a play about trapped, isolated and marginalized people in society; *Einstein's Wife*, a story about the gifted woman (Mileva Marić) in the shadow of a brilliant man (Albert Einstein) and the challenges of a female scientist in early 20th century Europe; *Pankrac '45*, a play about five women accused of collaboration shortly after the end of World War II; and *Christmas Eve*, a gripping thriller about a female philosophy professor accused of having planned a bomb attack on Christmas Eve. Before coming to the United States in 2007, she worked in transatlantic relations and intercultural dialogue at the United States Consulate in Munich and at the Institute for Cultural Exchange in Stuttgart, Germany. She is a graduate of the Honors Conservatory at the Theater Lab and holds a Masters degree in American/English and French Literature from the University of Stuttgart, Germany. She has lived and taught in Paris, France and has been living in Washington, DC for 14 years.

Bess Rowen, Ph.D., is a theatre theorist, historian, and practitioner. Her work focuses on what she terms "affective stage directions," which are stage directions written in ways that engage the physical and emotional responses of future theatre makers. Her first book, *The Lines Between the Lines: How Stage Directions Affect Embodiment*, was published by University of Michigan Press in October 2021. Her next project stems from her work with the Transfeminisms working group at the American Society for Theatre Research, where she and her collaborators take up important issues of trans and nonbinary representation in theatre and performance. While pursuing her doctorate at City University of New York, she was the recipient of the Andrew W. Mellon Fellowship in Public Humanities as well as a Graduate Center Dissertation Fellowship. She is a member of the Actors' Equity Association. She also serves as the Performance Review Editor of *The Eugene O'Neill Review* and the Conference Planner for the American Theatre & Drama Society. Recent articles can be found in *Modern Drama*, *Theatre Topics*, the *Journal of Dramatic Theory and Criticism*, and *Theatre Journal*, among others. Her avid interests include stage directions, gender and sexuality theory, women playwrights, Irish theatre, and theatrical riots.

LAURENCE SHERR, D.M.A., is a composer of Holocaust remembrance music, researcher and lecturer on Holocaust music topics, producer of remembrance events, and Holocaust music educator. He has presented these activities in the Czech Republic, Germany, Poland, England, Norway, San Marino, Israel, Australia, New Zealand, and across North America. He is the son of a survivor. His Music of Resistance and Survival Project features his *Sonata for Cello and Piano—Mir zaynen do!*, a composition that integrates Holocaust songs from the partisans, ghettos, and camps with newly composed material. Music of Resistance and Survival events have been produced in Australasia, Europe, Israel, and the United States. Dissemination of his work includes lectures and performances at international conferences and a workshop on teaching music and the Holocaust at Yad Vashem in Jerusalem. He developed the course Music and the Holocaust. Through all his work, his purpose is to foster greater understanding, mutual respect, and tolerance. He is Composer-in-Residence and Professor of Music at Kennesaw State University in Kennesaw, Georgia. He has been awarded numerous prizes, grants, and fellowships. Performances of his work have been given in France, Austria, Holland, Switzerland, Finland, Turkey, China, Japan, Canada, and Mexico, and CDs released by labels in Europe and the United States include his compositions.

EDITORS AND CONTRIBUTORS

MURRY SIDLIN, a conductor with a unique gift for engaging audiences, continues a diverse and distinctive musical career. He is the president and creative director of The Defiant Requiem Foundation, an organization that sponsors live concert performances of *Defiant Requiem: Verdi at Terezín* and *Hours of Freedom: The Story of the Terezín Composer*; as well as other projects including the documentary film, *Defiant Requiem*; a new docudrama called *Mass Appeal, 1943*, which was premiered in June 2017; and The Rafael Schächter Institute for Arts and Humanities at Terezín Camp. He began his professional career at the Baltimore Symphony as Assistant Conductor, served as Resident Conductor of the National Symphony Orchestra of Washington, DC, was Music Director of the New Haven Symphony and Music Director of the Long Beach Symphony in California.

JOSHUA SOBOL is a dramatist, author and director. He has written 80 plays and three novels. His plays, translated into many languages, have been performed in 25 countries and have won prestigious Israeli and international awards. He recently directed a Chinese production of his play *Ghetto* in Beijing in Mandarin Chinese. In the 1996 production of *Alma* he developed, together with the Austrian director Paulus Manker, the groundbreaking dramatic form of the Poly-Drama. His plays have won the "David's Harp Award" for best play of the year in Israel five times. His play *Ghetto* has won numerous awards throughout the world including: The Theater Heute German Critic's Choice for Best Foreign Play; the Jefferson Award for Best Play in Chicago; the Mainichi Art Prize for Best Play, the Yumiuri Shimbun Grand Prize for Best Play of the Year, and the Yoshiko Yuasa Prize for Best Play of the Year, all in Japan; and the Evening Standard Award and the London Critics award for Best Play of the Year in England. He won the Rosenblum Award for the Contribution to Israeli Theatre and the Israeli Theatre Award for A Life's Achievement.

LORI WEINTROB, PH.D., is Professor of History and founding director of the Wagner College Holocaust Center, Staten Island, New York. She teaches about the Holocaust in Film, Theater and the Arts. Lori has connected Holocaust survivors with thousands of youths of all faiths. Using their testimonies, she co-wrote the original play *Rise Up: Young Holocaust Heroes* with Theresa McCarthy and Martin Moran. She is co-curator of the permanent exhibit at the Wagner College Holocaust Center focusing on rescue, resistance and women. She has received awards for interfaith activism. She is co-editor of *Beyond Bystanders: Educational Leadership for a Humane Culture in a Globalizing Reality* (2017) and *Heroines of the Holocaust: Reframing Courage and Resistance in Genocide* (Routledge, 2024). Lori received her B.A. from Princeton University and her M.A. and Ph.D. from the University of California, Los Angeles (UCLA).

www.ingramcontent.com/pod-product-compliance
Lightning Source LLC
LaVergne TN
LVHW021331080526
838202LV00003B/139